DEVON AND CORNWALL RECORD SOCIETY
New Series, Vol. 24

T0373189

DEVON & CORNWALL RECORD SOCIETY

New Series, Vol. 24

THE ACCOUNTS OF THE FABRIC

OF

EXETER CATHEDRAL, 1279–1353

PART 1: 1279–1326

Edited and translated with an Introduction by

AUDREY M. ERSKINE

Printed for the Society by
THE DEVONSHIRE PRESS LTD.
TORQUAY
ENGLAND

1981

ISBN 0 901853 24 0

CONTENTS

ABBREVIATIONS

Colvin	H. M. Colvin (ed.), *Building Accounts of King Henry III* (1971).
D. & C. Exeter	(Muniments of the) Dean and Chapter of Exeter Cathedral.
MLW	*Revised Medieval Latin Wordlist*, prepared by R. E. Latham (1965).
Oliver	G. Oliver, *Lives of the Bishops of Exeter and a History of the Cathedral* (Exeter, 1861).
Reg. Bronescombe	*The Register of Walter Bronescombe, 1257–80, and Peter Quivil, 1280–91, Bishops of Exeter*, ed. F. C. Hingeston-Randolph (1889).
Reg. Grandisson	*The Register of John Grandisson, Bishop of Exeter, 1327–69*, ed. F. C. Hingeston-Randolph, 3 vols (1894–9).
St John Hope	The MS notebooks of Sir William St John Hope (1916), Add. MSS 6, Borthwick Institute of Historical Research, York.
TDA	*Transactions of the Devonshire Association.*

INTRODUCTION

The cathedral church of St Peter of Exeter is the successor of a Saxon minster, which became the seat of a bishop when the then existing dioceses of Crediton and Cornwall, comprising between them the whole geographical area of Devon and Cornwall, were united into the single diocese of Exeter in 1050. Leofric, the first bishop of Exeter, intended his cathedral to be served by regular canons organized under the rule of St Chrodegang, but by the beginning of the twelfth century the canons had adopted a secular way of life, without a common refectory or dormitory, living in their own houses around the churchyard, so that no conventual buildings were needed.[1] There is no information about the form of the cathedral church at that time, but according to chronicle evidence a new large Norman church was begun in 1112, whose high altar was dedicated in 1133,[2] though the whole building may well have taken all the rest of the twelfth century to complete. There is no written evidence of its progress, only physical examination of such of its fabric as now survives can suggest how long it took to be finished or the outlines of its plan. Nor is there much firm evidence about additions or alterations in the first part of the thirteenth century. The only documentary hint of new building is the grant by Bishop William Briwere of part of his garden as the site for a chapter-house in 1225, which was just at the time when the establishment of the new office of dean meant that the constitution of the chapter was undergoing a reorganization which would make such a permanent meeting-place necessary.[3] Beyond this there is nothing to be gleaned from records; the earliest period of the history of the fabric of Exeter cathedral cannot be said to be well documented.

The last quarter of the thirteenth century was in all likelihood the period of the beginning of the extension and transformation of the existing Norman church into the form of the Gothic cathedral much as it survives today. It was during the episcopate of Bishop Walter Bronescombe (1258–80) that an eastern extension was projected and well advanced, by the addition of a new square-ended Lady chapel (bearing quite a close resemblance to the new fashion in Lady chapels set by Salisbury cathedral, consecrated in 1258), with flanking chapels and a new ambulatory. From this beginning a grand new project developed, nothing less than a complete transformation of the interior and vault on the basis of the existing Norman exterior walls, first the presbytery, then the choir and finally the nave, while retaining the pair of great Norman towers, though

[1]On the early history of English secular cathedrals, including Exeter, see Kathleen Edwards, *The English Secular Cathedrals in the Middle Ages* (2nd ed., 1967), *passim*.

[2]F. Rose-Troup, *The Consecration of the Norman Minster at Exeter in 1133* (Exeter, n.d.), pp. 3–4.

[3]Audrey M. Erskine, 'Bishop Briwere and the Organization of the Chapter of Exeter Cathedral', *TDA*, cviii (1976), pp. 159–71.

changing them into transepts by demolishing their lower inner walls.[1]
This great rebuilding seems to have been virtually finished by about
1360, except for the completion of the external western image wall, and
this is substantially the fabric of the building as it now stands. But of course
no great church, continually in use through the centuries until the
present day, can ever be said to be wholly finished. Additions, repairs and
alterations, though most of them on a minor scale, have continually
been undertaken, with programmes of restoration from time to time, the
most thorough-going of all of which was that directed by Sir Gilbert Scott
in 1870–7. And one major recent loss was the destruction of one complete
side-chapel and supporting exterior buttresses by a high-explosive bomb in
1942. But in spite of changes, the essential character of the cathedral is
still that of the fourteenth century.

Documentation of the history of this building is to be found in the
accounts of the fabric fund of the dean and chapter which have survived.
It is true that such records do not set out to provide a history of the fabric,
they are not compiled for the information of posterity; it is only by
indications of the kinds and amounts of materials obtained, the amount
of work paid for, and the occasional explicit reference, that any idea can
be formed about what was going on at any given time. And they cover
much more than the church itself—work in the quarries, work on subsidiary buildings and masons' lodgings around the main site, even the
gates of the close and walls and water supply. But they are invaluable
evidence of week-by-week activity through many years. They remain to
us in considerable quantity through the medieval period (even though
in broken series and often in a very bad state of preservation) in comparison with similar records of their type relating to great churches
elsewhere, and are of particular interest because they relate to a fabric
by far the major part of which still stands. The years for which these
accounts survive among the archives of the dean and chapter of Exeter
are as follows (ref. D. & C. Exeter 2600–2704/11): a summary account,
1279–87; then yearly rolls running from Michaelmas to Michaelmas,
though often incomplete within the year, for 1299–1300, 1301–4, 1306–7,
1308–11, 1312–13, 1316–22, (with additional altar accounts 1316–17 and
1318–22), 1323–6, 1328–9, 1330–2, 1333–4, 1340–2, 1346–7, 1348–53,
1371–3, 1374–8, 1381–4, 1386–8, 1389–94, 1395–8, 1399–1404, 1405–6,
1407–10, 1411–14, 1415–16, 1418–21, 1422–5, 1427–8, 1429–32, 1433–5,
1436–8, 1441–3, 1444–5, 1446–8, 1449–57, 1459–60, 1461–2, 1464–5, 1466–
7, 1479–80, 1486–7, 1493–4, 1505–6, 1507–8, 1513–14, and four undated
fragments.

This considerable group of records is not only of value for the light
it throws on the building sequence of the cathedral. If it were, the isolated
excerpts documenting the progress of construction, furnishing or alteration
which have so frequently been quoted in histories of the cathedral
might perhaps suffice for many students. However, the receipts sections
show how the fund was financed; and the great numbers of payments
entered week by week and year by year, repetitious and trivial though
many of them may appear, gain cumulative significance by their very

[1]For a concise general account of the sequence of building, see Vyvyan Hope and
L. J. Lloyd, *Exeter Cathedral, a Short History* (1973), pp. 11–26.

repetition. They show the preoccupations of the accountant and the master mason, and supply the only means, in spite of their deficiencies in complete continuity and legibility, of constructing a full picture of what was entailed, down to the repair of buckets, in the building and maintenance of a great medieval church. They enable comparison to be made with other buildings not so well documented, and also, in spite of gaps, provide a remarkably full account of the labour force, for a notable element throughout is provided by the weekly wages lists of named tradesmen and craftsmen as well as the numbers of unnamed labourers, carters, carpenters and others employed, with their rates of pay.

Unfortunately the very quantity of these records is too great for publication of the whole series to be feasible. The present edition covers only the earlier group of the account rolls, those of them which more or less coincide with the main building period. Since there is a most regrettable loss of the records for the last sixteen years of Bishop John Grandisson's episcopate, the natural break occurs after 1353. Moreover, the problem of printing costs is so great that it has been found necessary to issue even this section of the accounts in two parts:—

Part 1 contains the first isolated and incomplete roll covering the years 1279–87, written at one time after 1287, and comprising entries for the last year of the episcopate of Bishop Bronescombe and the first seven years of the episcopate of Bishop Peter Quinil[1] (1280–91). The main series of yearly accounts then begins, the first to survive (reckoning in years beginning at Michaelmas) is for 1299–1300. There are four more which fall within the episcopate of Bishop Bitton (1292–1307), those for the years 1301–4 and 1306–7. The rest are the survivals of the accounts kept during the episcopate of Bishop Walter Stapeldon (1308–26) and are for the years 1308–11, 1312–13, 1316–22 and 1323–6. In addition within this period there are particular accounts for making a new high altar, for the period June 1316—Michaelmas 1317, and for 1318–22. There are no accounts surviving for the years 1326–8, and this break coincides with the end of Stapeldon's episcopate and the beginning of that of Bishop John Grandisson. It also marks a stage in the work, since the new high altar was consecrated in 1328.

Part 2 will contain the surviving accounts from the period of Grandisson's episcopate, that is those for the years 1328–9, 1330–2, 1333–4, 1340–2, 1346–7 and 1348–53. Since this part has the shorter text, no attempt is made here to relate the documents to the progress of the building, to discuss its financing in detail, or to consider the work force. All this will be reserved for Part 2, which will also contain a plan of the cathedral, a glossary and the index.

No apology is made for describing the accounts in terms of their relevance to episcopates. This does not of course in any way imply any suggestion that the bishop was personally responsible for the design of the work. This idea has by now been discussed at wearisome length and has long since been abandoned. However, as well as the close relationship which existed between bishop and chapter in secular cathedrals, fund-raising in the diocese had of necessity to be on the bishop's initiative, and

[1]The spelling of this name presents difficulties. Quinil/Quivil are indistinguishable in most contemporary scripts, but as the form Quinel is also to be found, it seems to resolve the n/u confusion, so Quinil is adhered to throughout.

it is also clear that the personal generosity of successive bishops was by far
the most important element in the financing of major projects. The dean
and chapter had their own endowments and organized financial system
and did what they could; from the late-thirteenth century onwards they
contributed half their salaries annually towards new building. But they
had no other direct means of augmenting the building fund, and were
duly grateful to the bishop as patron. For instance, in 1300 they set up a
lavish annual celebration of the anniversary of Bishop Quinil's death
because by his gifts he personally had almost completely subsidized their
new building.[1] Bishops, on their part, took their duties as patrons for
granted. Bishop Grandisson solicited assistance from the Pope soon after he
had dedicated the new high altar in December 1328, because the church
to which he had come was only about half finished, and *post pecuniosum
modum habens penuriosum sponsum*.[2] His predecessor Walter Stapeldon had
been a most munificent benefactor of the building, both personally and as
diocesan, whereas he, though very short of financial resources at the very
beginning of his episcopate, obviously assumed it was his responsibility to
raise funds immediately.

BACKGROUND TO THE ACCOUNTS

By the late-thirteenth century, the chapter of Exeter cathedral consisted
of twenty-four canons, of whom four were dignitaries: that is a dean, who
was its head, and a precentor, treasurer and chancellor; and four were
archdeacons. Of the dignitaries, the treasurer was responsible for the plate,
vestments and other treasure of the church, but not for the fabric of the
building itself. The canons received yearly salaries, called prebends, of
£4 each, and the dignitaries were each separately endowed with estates
the income from which increased the amount of their prebends. Besides
this comparatively small yearly salary, the canons also received daily and
weekly distributions of food and money if they were in residence, and
payments for their attendance at chantry and obit celebrations in the
cathedral. There was also a staff of minor clergy, the most important of
whom was the body of twenty-four vicars choral.[3]

It was the normal practice in all English secular cathedrals, to which
Exeter was no exception, to organize their finances by the maintenance of
two separate and distinct funds: a common fund into which almost all
their revenues were received, and from which salaries and allowances of all
kinds and general expenses were paid; and a fabric fund devoted to the
physical upkeep and when necessary new building of the church itself.
There are no explicit descriptions of how the fabric fund was organized,
but from a 'custom' (probably compiled in the early-thirteenth century)
and the detailed statutes regulating the whole cathedral organization
promulgated by Bishop Bronescombe in the third quarter of the thirteenth
century, a clear idea can be gained of the workings of the common fund.
A central exchequer (*scaccarium*) was under the control of two stewards
(*senescalli scaccarii*) who were both canons, who received into the exchequer

[1] D. & C. Exeter 2124.
[2] *Reg. Grandisson*, p. 97.
[3] Nicholas Orme, *The Minor Clergy of Exeter Cathedral 1300–1548* (1980), p. xiii.

the receipts from all sources of the chapter's revenue except for those of the fabric, and so in consequence were deeply involved in the complicated business of the administration of its estates. They paid out each year all salaries and special allowances, kept 'ordinary' and 'extraordinary' accounts of cathedral and estate expenses, and supervised a variety of subsidiary accounts necessary for the general administration of this central fund.[1]

Unfortunately few actual accounts relevant to the common fund survive before the mid-fourteenth century. There is a solitary stewards' account for 1296, and thereafter a broken series from 1304. The subsidiary accounts are similarly lacking, for the only series which does survive is a record of the performance of obits and anniversary masses through the year and the distribution of payments accruing from these, together with the distribution of the Whitsuntide and other offerings and the contents of the alms-boxes in the cathedral; this series runs continuously for a long period from 1305 onwards.

Therefore any suggestions which can be made about the organization of the fabric fund cannot be based on much information about the practical workings of the common fund, though a few details can be gleaned. It is worth remarking that the first fragmentary composite roll of fabric receipts and expenditure, which records receipts from 1280–7, and expenses only for 1279–81 and 1285–7, is in fact the first account of any sort surviving among the capitular archives.

THE FABRIC FUND

Opus and *fabrica* may be assumed to be synonymous terms in their application to the fabric work of a medieval church, so references to either of them are relevant in a search for the origins and administration of a fabric fund. A warden of the fabric (*custos operis*) is first mentioned in 1204,[2] but in view of the amount of organization which the building work of the Norman church must have required, it is very probably an office with its beginnings in the twelfth century. It seems that the settled custom in Exeter was to have had only one warden, not two as was the practice elsewhere, for with the solitary exception of the account for 1299–1300, only one warden at one time held office during the fourteenth century. In this exceptional year, the heading of the account states that Robert of Ashburton (*de Aspertone*) and Roger the mason are jointly wardens of the New Work. This association of the master-mason is unique; it led Professor Hamilton Thompson to suggest that the master mason regularly kept a counter-roll as a check upon the warden,[3] but there is no evidence to support this contention, except perhaps that the endorsement gives the name of Robert alone. Indeed it is very likely that the master mason did find it necessary to keep his own accounts, not only of the acquisition of materials, but particularly of the intricate details of the very various weekly payments of wages to tradesmen and labourers. And Roger was an established master; he is recorded in 1297 as living in his own house, which

[1]Audrey M. Erskine, 'Medieval Financial Records of the Cathedral Church of Exeter', *Journal of the Society of Archivists*, ii (1962), pp. 258–62.
[2]D. & C. Exeter 1129.
[3]A. Hamilton Thompson, *The Cathedral Churches of England* (1925), pp. 132–5.

was provided as part of his emoluments by the dean and chapter,[1] so
already he had had at least some years of experience in Exeter of organizing
the Work. But none the less, there is no other explicit evidence that he
accounted for it. After 1300 Robert of Ashburton, who was one of the
vicars choral,[2] held the office of warden of the Work until 1315.[3] He was
succeeded by John of Sherford (*de Shyreforde*), who may also possibly have
been a vicar, though he is not recorded as such, who is the only other
warden recorded during the period under review.

The foundation of a fabric fund, by the endowment of a regular income,
is very probably to be found in 1204, in the grant in alms of the church of
St Erth in Cornwall made by Bishop Henry Marshal to the cathedral
church *ad eius reparacionem*.[4] The gift was to be in the first place of only two
marks yearly, while one Harvey remained vicar of St Erth, but after his
death the whole of the profits of the church were to be devoted to the
cathedral fabric, except for the maintenance of a chaplain there, and the
payment was to be made annually directly into the hands of the warden of
the Work, which is a clear enough indication of the maintenance of a
separate fund. The profits from St Erth must have remained an element
in the sources of revenue for the fabric from then on, but very little else is
recorded as having been apportioned to it during the next three-quarters
of a century. Even during Bishop Bronescombe's episcopate, when one
would suppose that the fund would require augmentation, his statutes
only mention the profits of a share of the cathedral alms-boxes, and fines
for non-performance of obit celebrations, as being assigned to it. In the
earliest receipts which have survived, for 1280–7, in the composite and
incomplete account which has lost its heading, there is evidence of only a
meagre regular revenue: the content of two alms-boxes, the red chest and
the one at the foot of the statue of 'old' St Peter, a few shillings-worth of
rents from property in Exeter, and offerings on the feast of St Peter-*ad-
vincula* and Whitsuntide. The whole account is difficult to interpret as a
financial document, for there is no attempt to set receipts against expenditure, and while receipts for these few years rarely total more than £2
annually, expenditure in the five years for which we have totals (1279,
1280, 1284, 1285 and 1286–7) is usually about £6 annually and once is as
much as £11. It is difficult to view this document as an account in any
true sense, it seems more to be a general memorandum of some of the
receipts and payments made during these nine years, and as it is so
incomplete it is useless to try to draw any definite conclusions from it
about the workings of the fund.

If then our information about the workings of the fabric fund are so
obscure even for a period when we have some sort of a record of it, it is
even more so in the next two decades, until in 1299 we have the first of the
surviving annual accounts. This is stated in its heading to be the account
of the wardens of the *novum opus*, and the evidence of the endorsement
'year nine' on the account for 1306–7 would indicate that it is the second

[1] D. & C. Exeter 2123.
[2] Orme, pp. 3, 14.
[3] D. & C. Exeter 3764 fo. 16r.; the first appearance of John Sherford as warden is in
Michaelmas 1315, following directly after Robert of Ashburton in the same office in the
previous term.
[4] D. & C. Exeter 1129.

of a new series. How then can the *novum opus* be defined, and can this heading mean that it was only begun in 1298? This is unlikely, from the evidence of the stage the new building had reached to be found in the accounts themselves of the first years of the fourteenth century, but we have only fragmentary evidence about the implications of the meaning of the term.

The headings of the 1280–7 expenses entries are 'for the fabric' (*ad fabricam*). However, by 1296 a different word is introduced, for the stewards of the exchequer record a payment to dom R., warden of the old fabric (*custodis veteris fabrice*) of £4 13s 4d.[1] There is therefore a hint to be found here that a distinction was being made between the finances of the old fabric and the new fabric. It would appear that a special fund for a new fabric, a *novum opus*, was largely endowed by Bishop Peter Quinil. In 1300, eight years after his death, the dean and chapter expressed their gratitude for all his benefactions to the cathedral by endowing it with churches and *quoad novam eius fabricam ampliando et pro magni sui parte sumptu proprio consummando* both during his lifetime and by his will (*tam inter vivos quam in ultima voluntate*), by establishing a celebration of his anniversary obit from their common fund, with special commemoration of him as *primum et precipuum* among the dead on various feasts of the Blessed Virgin.[2] An entry in 1305 among the obit accounts where the payments were entered for the celebration of this anniversary calls him *primus fundator novi operis*;[3] and the fifteenth-century tradition for the date of this foundation is 1288.[4] If this is acceptable as at least a likely date for the foundation of the fund for the new Work, it does not of course follow that nothing would have been in progress between 1280 and 1288, only that a distinction would thereafter have been made between the *vetus* and the *nova fabrica* in accounting.

It is possible that the obit celebration was not set up until February 1299/1300 because such a tribute was not appropriate, to the extent of justifying the verb *consummando*, until a legacy received from Quinil after his death had been used up. Therefore it is perhaps possible to conjecture that the new series of accounts begun in 1298 was a new system of accounting begun because the fund for the new fabric was on a new basis; regular annual payments were given to it by Bishop Bitton, and the dean and chapter contributed half their salaries. Though this is only a guess, there is evidence that a separate account was kept for the old fabric in the first ten years of the fourteenth century. This dual accounting system is not without precedent, for the same sort of division was made at St Paul's cathedral, though in a more elaborate manner.[5] In Exeter the same warden administered the funds of both fabrics, as is indicated in the book recording the distribution of funeral and obit payments surviving from 1305 onwards, which was also used for noting the distribution of the contents of alms-boxes and Whitsuntide offerings and part of the canons' contribution to the fabric. From Michaelmas 1305 Robert of Ashburton

[1] D. & C. Exeter 2777, account of the stewards of the exchequer 1296–7.
[2] D. & C. Exeter 2124; the text is printed in Oliver, p. 51.
[3] D. & C. Exeter 3673 fo. 62r., book of obit payments.
[4] D. & C. Exeter 3630C p. 7: *Anno domini m°cc° octogesimo viii° fundata est hec nova ecclesia a venerabili patre Petro huius ecclesie episcopo in honore beati Petri principis apostolorum.* The dates cited in this chronicle are not in general very accurate, particularly when recording events in the twelfth and thirteenth centuries.
[5] Edwards, pp. 231–2.

regularly received quarterly payments of either £4 or £4 5s from the church of St Erth for the *vetus fabrica*, while being paid the share of the canons' prebends, varying sums in alms from the red chest, and a few testamentary bequests, all for the *nova fabrica*. This system continued until 1310, but in Midsummer term of that year a memorandum under the heading of 'the old fabric and the new fabric' notes payments to Robert in the separate categories but adds *et ordinatum est per decanum et capitulum quod de cetero sit una fabrica*.[1] This is borne out by the existing accounts, for all of those whose headings survive up to that date describe Robert as warden of the new Work, whereas the heading of the account beginning at Michaelmas 1310 describes him as warden of the new Work and the old church, and thereafter he is described simply as *custos operis*. Obviously he had been warden of the new Work and old church throughout, but keeping the two accounts separately. The profits from St Erth begin to appear in his later receipts, as do other small items which had previously been assigned to the old fabric. This unified system of accounting was continued by his successor John of Sherford, and even though the term 'new Work' crops up occasionally between 1310 and 1326 it is not applied to the accounting system but only to an occasional donation, to which it would still be appropriate.

THE FORM OF THE ACCOUNTS 1299–1326

Physical form   The accounts are kept yearly in continuous roll form, on several membranes of parchment in most cases, sewn head to tail, of varying lengths but of fairly regular width of about eight to ten inches. The receipts section is usually entered onto a shorter membrane sewn to the following long membrane upon which the expenses section begins, and as a result a number of the accounts have lost their receipts section completely by the detachment of this membrane. The condition of almost all of the rolls is far from perfect and some of them are very fragmentary indeed. Unfortunately they were subjected to very unsatisfactory repair at some unknown period, probably in the mid-nineteenth century. They are backed and patched with low-quality paper which has by now itself crumbled and decayed, or covered on both front and dorse with tissue which has become opaque with time and which now obscures the text, and even prevents ultra-violet light from being much help in deciphering it. Numerous words and passages are in addition almost or completely illegible owing to the application of galls in the past to revive them. Oliver complained about this staining in his extracts published in 1861, so it must have been applied before he first examined the rolls in 1824;[2] it has appreciably darkened with the passage of time, for some entries which Sir William St John Hope found at least partially legible when he examined them in his turn are now completely unreadable. In view of their condition, it has been thought more useful to preface each account in the text with a separate description of its state rather than to attempt a detailed description of the deficiencies of the whole group here.

The scripts   There is no reference to be found to a clerk of the fabric to assist the warden of the Work, so the obvious assumption is that the

[1] D. & C. Exeter 3673 fo. 99r.
[2] See p. xvii.

warden wrote out his own accounts. The first six rolls, 1299–1309, are all in the same hand, written in a neat and regular though highly abbreviated manner (hand A). The rolls from 1309–13 are in a slightly different script on a smaller scale though with almost indistinguishable letter forms and manner of lay-out, which may well be by a different clerk, but could be the original writer working on a different scale (hand A1). From 1317 until the end of this series a quite different script (hand B) is in use, somewhat less neat and legible and with slightly different conventions in setting out totals. But the altar roll covering the period June 1316 to Michaelmas 1317 is of interest, as here there is the note of receipts at the head of the roll in hand B, weeks 1 to 41 in hand A1, then an abrupt change to hand B which enters up the rest of the account. Since the change of office from one warden of the Work to the other took place at Michaelmas 1315, and the changes of script do not match this change, it can be suggested that even if hand A can be assigned to Robert of Ashburton and hand B to John of Sherford, the accounts from 1309 to 1317 were not written up by either warden personally but by a different clerk.

Endorsements No system of filing can be deduced from the endorsements, as there is no significant notation; only note .b. on the roll for the year 1310–11 and D on the roll for 1312–13; the immediately preceding, intervening and following accounts are not extant so there is not enough continuity from which to draw any conclusions.

Arrangement The system in use throughout is that of a simple charge and discharge account, with the receipts for a year and arrears carried forward from the previous year itemized and totalled, followed by expenses entered by the week for the four terms of the year: Michaelmas, Christmas, Easter and Midsummer. Entries are itemized and totalled weekly throughout each term, and these weekly totals added up to give the total expenditure for each term. In the final week of each term (which are not of equal numbers of weeks because of course Easter is a moveable feast) are a group of regular entries, including the salaries of the warden himself and of the master mason, and the expenses of stabling, shoeing and general care of the cart-horses and pack-horses for the term. After the end of the weekly accounts and term total for Midsummer there are usually to be found itemized entries of bulk purchases of stone, iron, lead, glass, tiles, and sometimes tin and colours, made during the year, and a general reckoning of similar bulk purchase of hay and oats. Inserted too at this point in the general account in a few cases are itemized accounts for special work performed and the cost of materials for it; the most interesting is that for the felling and preparation of timber for the bishop's throne, but there is also an account for building a wall by Broadgate and for houses in Kalendarhay.[1] When John of Sherford became responsible for the accounting he seems to have found that the reckoning for oats for fodder for the horses gave him trouble, and he presents his account in terms of the weekly ration per horse, which somewhat alters the form of the totals of oats at the end of the year; but this is the only substantial difference between the methods of the two accountants. The total expenditure of the whole year in all the accounts, is set against the receipts with a note of deficit or payments outstanding, but it is remarkable that none of the rolls,

[1] See pp. 71, 153.

though apparently prepared in a most orthodox manner to show the situation of the accountant, have any indications upon them that they have been subjected to audit. The only exceptions to this completely self-contained system are the short series of special accounts for materials and work on the high altar; in these either the sum to be expended is received directly from the hands of the stewards of the exchequer, or it is accounted for in the expenses of the general account of the fabric for the relevant year.

HISTORY OF THE EDITION

The fabric accounts have been regarded as an important source of information about the cathedral from the mid-eighteenth century onwards. Before this, descriptions of the building were largely based on that included in *A Catalog of the Bishops of Exeter, with the description of the Antiquitie and first foundation of the Cathedralle Church of the same* by John Vowell alias Hooker, City Chamberlain of Exeter, which was first published in 1584. It was Dr Charles Lyttelton, dean of Exeter from 1748 to 1762, and thereafter bishop of Carlisle, who was the first person to publish extracts from the fabric rolls, and, to judge by the endorsements of date now to be seen on them in his handwriting, the first to attempt to put them into sequence. He was a fellow of the Society of Antiquaries of London (he was to become its president in 1765)[1] and delivered a paper to the Society in 1754 on the subject of the building sequence of the cathedral, mainly disputing a number of points made in Hooker's account. This paper, under the title of *Some remarks on the original foundation and construction of the present fabric of Exeter Cathedral*, was printed as a preliminary to John Carter's great folio survey of the cathedral published by the Society of Antiquaries in 1797. His quotations from the accounts, and also from a good many more of the capitular archives, are well chosen; this short study contains many shrewd observations, and provides a foundation of great value to later writers.

It was doubtless from Dean Lyttelton's paper that John Britton a few decades later gleaned the knowledge that fabric accounts survived in Exeter, and as he was writing up the history and antiquities of a whole series of English cathedrals, he turned his attention to Exeter in 1823 and was determined to explore them. He encountered some difficulty, as he recounts with indignation in the preface to his *History and Antiquities of the Cathedral Church of Exeter*, published in 1826. He somewhat unreasonably accuses the cathedral authorities of 'insolence of office' and 'proud contumelies of haughtiness and arrogance' because the reply to his request to examine the archives was delayed for five weeks, even though it was in fact a civil offer to search them for him. In the event, the Revd George Oliver and Mr Pitman Jones, the most prominent among the antiquarians of Exeter at that time, under the supervision of their friend Ralph Barnes, the chapter clerk, made extracts for him. Their notes are still extant,[2] and

[1] Joan Evans, *A History of the Society of Antiquaries* (1956), p. 131.
[2] D. & C. Exeter 4619: 'A summary of the Receipts and Disbursements of the Custos Operis Ecclesiae Sancti Petri Exoniae made August and September 1824 by the Revd George Oliver and Mr Pitman Jones in my presence. R. Barnes, Chapter Clerk, 29 Sept. 1824'.

though rather sparse give useful indications of the condition of the documents. The use made of these notes by Britton is shown in chapter IV of his work, which makes more citations of the rolls than Lyttelton had done but often their context and implications are misunderstood.

The experience of working over the rolls in 1824 must have greatly aroused Dr Oliver's interest in them. His *Lives of the Bishops of Exeter and a History of the Cathedral* appeared in 1861, and he included a full description of the nature and content of the fabric accounts in one chapter of his book; more important, however, were the extracts from most of the rolls up to 1438 and a full transcript of the roll for 1299–1300 which he printed as an appendix. It is his extracts which have until the present time served as the most easily accessible means of reference to the fabric accounts, and they have been most extensively quoted.

No further attempt to return to the originals can be traced until Sir William St John Hope visited Exeter in the winter of 1916–17. He spent several weeks making extracts of all the entries which appeared to him directly relevant to the building of the fabric.[1] The notes of so distinguished a historian of medieval building were of course greatly superior in accuracy to Dr Oliver's more random extracts, and when Prebendary Herbert Bishop and Miss Edith Prideaux projected a new full history of the building of the cathedral they were able by the good offices of Professor Hamilton Thompson to borrow the Hope notebooks from Lady Hope, Sir William having died in 1919. All the numerous quotations in *The Building of the Cathedral Church of St Peter in Exeter*, published in 1922, are drawn from the Hope transcripts. Many of their interpretations were due to advice of Professor Hamilton Thompson, who himself proposed a full edition of the accounts from the Hope transcripts, but he did not realize how very summary they were until after he had already raised the question of their possible publication with the Royal Historical Society. When he saw that they were such short notes, he knew that a new complete transcript would have to be made, and in consequence two of his research students, Miss Muriel Curtis (now Mrs Clegg) and later Mr D. H. Findlay undertook the task. Miss Curtis worked from 1930 onwards on this project, taking her transcript up to 1353, and Mr Findlay proceeded with the later ones. Miss Curtis was not able to get even the whole of her work into typescript, much of it remains in her own very clear pencil script, but Mr Findlay was able to complete his work and presented it as a doctoral thesis to the University of Leeds in 1939.[2]

It is upon Miss Curtis's unextended transcripts of the original Latin that this edition is based, and the debt owed to her by the present editor is obvious; without her labours the production of an edition in translation would have been a vastly longer task than it has proved. She has always been extremely generous with her work, and loaned her transcripts to numerous experts and other students of medieval building, finally

---

[1] I have had the good fortune to have had access to the first two of the Hope notebooks while preparing this edition. These are the only ones that appear to have survived, and were brought to my notice by the kindness of Dr David Smith, Director of the Borthwick Institute of Historical Research, where they have been deposited among the papers of the late Professor Hamilton Thompson (Add. MSS 6). They have proved helpful in elucidating some readings of passages which have become illegible since the notes were made.

[2] A Xerox copy of Dr Findlay's transcript has been deposited in Exeter Cathedral Library for reference purposes.

depositing them in Exeter Cathedral Library so that they could be consulted by readers there instead of the often fragile originals, and giving full permission for them to be used as a basis for publication. One of the most valuable and tedious of the tasks of editing has been almost wholly hers, that of abstracting the names of tradesmen and their pay and setting them into weekly and termly tables; the much lesser task, though equally tedious, has been that of checking these tables and preparing them for publication, though of course any errors are the editor's sole responsibility. Unfortunately some parts of her transcripts must have become lost in their travels from one student to another before they were deposited in the library, so some of the basic transcription of the text has had to be done again by the editor, who has, of course, checked all the transcripts with the originals. A number of the present readings differ from hers, partly because she did not have the assistance of ultra-violet light, partly because the effort of providing a translation has thrown light on the actual spelling and form of a number of doubtful words.

EDITORIAL PRACTICE

The translated Latin text is in roman type. Quotations of the original Latin are given in italic in round brackets; wherever there is doubt of the correctness of the extension of the Latin the word is left suspended in the form in which it appears, the suspension marked as an apostrophe, because inflexions and sometimes the word form itself are very uncertain. Vernacular words, either English or French, are given in original form in quotation marks, but it is difficult to be consistent here, as such words are sometimes given Latin endings. Lacunae, where parts or the whole of words or figures, or whole phrases or passages, are illegible or lacking, are indicated by three points . . . and editorial additions are supplied in square brackets. The use of square brackets is also extended to one other convention: cancellations of substance are included in the text at the place they appear but enclosed in square brackets. This is contrary to recently recommended practice,[1] but the reason for doing so is the incomplete nature of the record; if an item is cancelled because it is entered in the wrong place, whether it be the wrong term or wrong year, it may never appear at all in the right place, and so if all cancellations were relegated to footnotes a good deal of important information could very easily be overlooked when removed from its context. Only minor corrections have been mentioned in footnotes.

Figures Figures are translated from roman into arabic numerals throughout. *Libri, solidi, denarii, oboli* and *quadrantes* have been rendered in £ s d. Pounds weight have been abbreviated to lbs, hundred-weights to cwt. Small errors sometimes occur in the accountant's addition or multiplication, which have not been individually pointed out by the editor. However, it must be remembered in connection with items bought by the hundred or thousand that apparent errors may be explained by the fact that the 'long hundred' of 120 may sometimes be in use.

Names Place-names have been translated into their modern form, original forms are quoted in italic in round brackets on at least the first

[1] R. F. Hunnisett, *Editing Records for Publication* (1977), pp. 39–45.

occasion of their occurrence, thereafter only significant variants are quoted. Unidentifiable place-names are given in their original form in quotation marks. In the matter of personal names, fore-names are translated into their modern forms, surnames are retained in their original forms. A modification of this is the treatment of names in the tables of wages, which is explained in the note prefacing these tables. The title *dominus* universally accorded as a courtesy title to clerics who have no claim to the title of Master is an awkward one to render satisfactorily, and here is given as 'dom' throughout.

Calendaring No legible entry has been wittingly omitted. Calendaring in terms of omissions has largely been limited to leaving out some unneccessary lead-in prepositions, though some of these have been retained: for instance, the regular use of 'In' followed by the number of labourers, carters etc. and their pay indicates *stipendiis* omitted by the accountant himself and so it is retained. Only the long and repetitious items accounting for the quantity of oats expended for fodder which occur in some of the later rolls have been omitted, and [see above] substituted, referring back to the original full entry. The most important aspect of the calendaring is the extraction from the weekly payments entries of the lists of named tradesmen and the amount they have each been paid. This is in every case indicated by 'In wages*.', the asterisk showing the omission. These lists have been arranged in tables according to the year, term and week of their occurrence, following the main text. It must therefore be remembered that the weekly totals in the main text do not represent the sum of the items in that week, but whenever a week contains a wages list the cost of wages must be included from the tables.

Rearrangement of the layout of the entries has also been necessary. Marginalia of relevance, such as the week number, the note of feast days kept as holidays and so not worked, the changes from summer to winter and winter to summer hours, have been taken into the beginning of each weekly entry. Irrelevant marginal notes, mere repetitions of a word of a text entry to call attention to a particular item, have been omitted; so have the occasional end-of-roll instructions to continue on to the dorse, such as *respice in deorsum*, which are unnecessary as the membrane numbers are given.

Numeration The rolls are numbered in the text according to their call-numbers. In this part of the volume they are D. & C. Exeter 2600–2624. 2600/1 and 2606/7 are so numbered because two separate membranes, first discovered separately, have been reunited. 2612A was first misdated and numbered 2625 in error, so this latter number has been cancelled and the roll re-numbered into its correct position. Throughout this introduction all references have been made by date, as the easiest direct means of referring to the text.

NOTE ON TRANSLATION

There can be little justification for the publication of full transcriptions of a series of late-thirteenth and fourteenth century accounts such as these in the original Latin, since they are largely highly repetitive in content, written in a compressed and abbreviated form so that inflexions are

frequently in doubt, and even the exact form of many words, particularly
verbs, cannot be accurately determined, with the result that they cannot
with certainty be fully extended. The words of L. F. Salzman, without
whose remarkable work on medieval building no such translation as this
could be attempted,[1] cannot be improved upon in discussing such highly
technical records: 'The clerks who wrote these documents were not only,
like all men, liable to make slips of the pen, but often were putting on
parchment purely local technical terms of which they could at best give a
phonetic rendering when they did not complicate matters by attempting
to Latinize them', and what is more they were compiling accounts for
contemporaries who knew what they meant. Certainly any attempt at
translation cannot help being an interpretation, but for that matter an
extended transcription is equally so, and the requirements of translation
have sometimes resulted in an improvement in accuracy of the transcription because of the need to search for the meaning of ambiguously written
words. It is hoped that the translation is acceptable, the aim has been to
keep it as clear, simple and consistent, and as near to the Latin as possible,
though of course some inconsistencies have crept in, for which apology is
offered. Great effort has been made to allow the reader to make his own
corrections and interpretations: it has been the aim to quote the Latin for
every term translated where it first appears, and thereafter if the context
would seem to modify the meaning; and whenever a transcription or
translation is in doubt or a whole phrase seems to be of particular
significance, the Latin is quoted fully.

Some abbreviations are so truncated that they result in particular
ambiguity, among which the most common are:

clav': which may mean boss or key-stone; key; nail; weight.

ser': which may mean saw, sawyer or, extended to a verb, sawn; or
lock.

plaustr': which may mean plastering, a plasterer; or wagon.

gross': which may mean large; or a measure of quantity.

hernes': which may mean the tracery of a window; or cart-harness.

Again, some verbs may be translated in more than one way, of which *car'*
is the most common, which might be extended to either *cariata* or *carianda*,
though the meaning rather than the grammar of an entry is not much
affected by it; on the other hand, *locatus* may mean hired; placed, in the
sense of situated; or unloaded.

The meaning of some words cannot be clarified because they are
without context. The dictionary meaning of *lodic'*, for instance, is a sheet or
blanket, but its meaning in relation to use by masons is obscure. One
frequently recurring term is 'burl', to which no certain meaning has been
assigned; it is stuff bought by weight usually in connection with carts or
harness, and though it would seem to be connected in form with

---

[1] L. F. Salzman, *Building in England down to 1540* (1952). This great mine of information
about medieval building terms and practice, together with H. M. Colvin's edition of
Building Accounts of King Henry III (1971) which has facing pages of text and translation,
have been my main guides in translating, and I am greatly indebted to both these works.
In spite of the examining of a good deal of comparable material, and searching in many
glossaries and dictionaries, Mr R. E. Latham's *Revised Medieval Latin Word List* has proved
indispensable throughout, and has suggested the meanings, even at one or two removes, of
almost all the Latin words encountered in these accounts.

burellus, coarse woollen material, its application is never specific enough to show its use and consequently its meaning remains uncertain.

Some special conventions in translation have been observed which should be explained:

opus: besides the usual meaning of this word as 'work', it is of course also used in the sense of the whole work of building, and labourers *in opere* are those working on site, at the church. To distinguish this special application of the word it is capitalized throughout, as Work.

bateria: this occurs almost every week and has been translated as 'sharpening' but 'battering' would give a better idea of the meaning, though perhaps unduly misleading in context. Tools had to be 'beaten' regularly to restore them to a working edge; this is distinguished from 'steeling', the smith's work of re-steeling cutting edges, which is usually applied in the text to axes only.

ad tascam: at task, is a term applied to piece-work of all kinds, even to sawing wood by the foot, not only to large or specially skilled pieces of work at a cost fixed by prior agreement.

de proprio ferro: is translated as 'from our own iron', as the phrase implies that the items so described were made from the stock of iron in hand, so the cost of the material is not included in the cost of the item.

garcio: translated as 'boy', but it is not thereby intended to imply either great youth or the status of apprentice, as in other less specialized records of this period the term can mean merely 'servant'.

This list could be prolonged to much greater length, but it is hoped that the frequent quotation of the original Latin provides sufficient explanation of tentative translations in other cases.

ACKNOWLEDGEMENTS

My greatest debt is owed to Mrs Muriel Clegg, as I have already indicated, to whom I offer my gratitude while exonerating her from responsibility for any of the deficiencies of this publication. I am indebted to the Dean and Chapter of Exeter Cathedral for permission to publish their records, and for a grant towards the cost of publication. I am very grateful to the Chairman, Professor Frank Barlow, and the members of the Council of the Devon and Cornwall Record Society for their encouragement to proceed with this edition over a number of years and for the great effort which has been made, in this time of financial stringency, to raise sufficient funds. I must thank many people for help along the way of a protracted piece of work, of whom I will mention particularly Dr C. A. Ralegh Radford, and above all Professor Joyce Youings, who has, as general editor and by way of friendship, given me continual advice and assistance, and has also spent so much time and trouble ungrudgingly on my behalf to bring this work to publication. The Record Society joins its gratitude with mine to the British Academy, the Pilgrim Trust and the University of Exeter, without whose very substantial grants there would have been no possibility of producing this edition.

Exeter, December 1980.   AUDREY M. ERSKINE

EXETER CATHEDRAL FABRIC ACCOUNTS
1279–1326

2600/1   1279–1287

Fragmentary account for the covering years, not a yearly account in regular form. 2 membranes, head to tail, previously separated but now restitched, both of which are badly damaged and fragile, partially repaired over the whole surface; m.1 lacks its head (with loss of receipts for 1279); the bottom of m.2 is mutilated, so that there is a gap between this and the reverse to m.1, resulting in the loss of the record of expenditure for the years 1281–4, and the expenditure for 1287 is also missing at the end of the roll.
Printed: Extracts in Oliver, p.379.

(m.1)   [RECEIPTS]

Item from Whitsuntide offerings in 1280 to the red chest (*de oblationibus Pentecost' a.d. m⁰cc⁰lxxx ad rubeam archam*) . . . . . . in broken silver. Item 17s from rent for the fabric (*de redditu ad fabricam*). Item 5s from offerings (*de oblationibus*) on the feast of St Peter-*ad-vincula* [1 August]. . . . for 3 tombs (*pro iij tumb'*). Item 4s 3¾d from the red chest (*de rubea archa*).
Total 44[?]s 2¾d.

Item from Whitsuntide offerings in 1281 13s 4¼d. In broken silver . . . . . . 2d on the feast of St Peter-*ad-vincula* from offerings . . . Item 10d for 3 tombs. 17s from town rent (*de redditu ville*).   Total 34s 7¼d.

In the year 1282 12s 8¾d from Whitsuntide offerings. And 3s ½d on the feast of St Peter-*ad-vincula*. 15d for 3 tombs. Item 17s from town rent. 4s 2d from the red chest.   Total 38s 2¼d.

In the year 1283 12s 5¾d from Whitsuntide offerings with broken silver. Item 2s 8d from offerings on the feast of St Peter-*ad-vincula*. 17s from town rents. 5d for one tomb. 4s for one stone sold (*pro j petra vendita*).
Total 36s 6¾d.

In the year 1284 11s 3½d from Whitsuntide offerings. Item 2s 4d on the feast of St Peter-*ad-vincula* from offerings. . . . from town rent. 5d for one tomb. 4s for one stone sold. 3s 8d from the red [chest].
Total 38s 8½d.

In the year 1285 9s 11½d from Whitsuntide offerings. 2s 3d from offerings on the feast of St Peter-*ad-vincula*. 17s . . . from town [rent]. 3s 8¾d from the red chest. And 10d for 2 tombs.   Total 33s 9¼d.

In the year 1286 11s 1d from Whitsuntide offerings. 3s 1d on the feast of St Peter-*ad-vincula*. 10s from town rents . . . And 10d for 2 tombs. And 10s 4¼d from the foot of old St Peter (*de pede sancti Petri veteris*). 2s 1¼d from the red chest.   Total 37s 5¼d.

In the year 1287 from Whitsuntide offerings 12s. 3s ½d on the feast of St Peter-*ad-vincula*. 10s from town rent.   Total 25s ½d.

1

[EXPENSES]

[IN 1279/80] EXPENSES FOR THE FABRIC [MICHAELMAS TO EASTER]

Saturday before the feast of St Michael [23 September] 1279   For laths
(*pro latis*) ...   ... Item for one cord bought (*pro j cordula empta*) 4½d. And
for laths 9d. And 200 [seams] of sand (*pro ij*ᶜ ... *de arena*) 3s. One sieve
(*in j crebr'*) 1d. For 8 ... for covering (*ad cooperiendum*) 16s.

Total 25s 6?½d.

Morrow of St Michael [30 September]   For 3 windows for the chapel of
St James by order of the steward (*pro iij fenestris ad capellam beati Jacobi ex
precepto senescalli*) 8s 9d. Ironwork (*ferramentis*) ... And to roofers (*cooper-
ator'*)[1] 4s 5d. And a carpenter (*carp'*)[1] 2s 1½d. To Punfr'[2] (*Punfr'*) 5d. For
repairing 4 locks 5 ... (*In iiij seruris reparandis v ...*)

Total 18s 3¾d.

Glass (*Vitrum*)   Glass bought (*In vitro empto*) 16s.

Total shown (*patet*).

Saturday before the feast of St Denis [7 October]   To roofers 4s 5d. To
a carpenter 2s 1d.

Saturday following (*Sabbato sequente*)   To a carpenter 2s 1¼d. To Punfr' 6d.
Timber bought and made at task (*In meremio empto et ad tassas facto*) 3s 4d.

Total 16s 10¾d.

Saturday after the feast of St Luke [21 October]   To roofers 3s 8d. To a
carpenter 21d. To Punfr' 5d. For laths 4½d.   Total 6s 2½d.

Feast of SS Simon and Jude [28 October]   To roofers 4s 5d. To a carpenter 2s 1½d. For ... 5½d. Roof spars (*sparr'*) 10½d. For 3 trusses (*Pro iij
trussis*) 3¾d. ....   Total 9s 3¼d.

Feast of St Martin [11 November]   Item a roofer roofing with timber
(*coopertor' cooperient' merem'*) 9d. 5 trusses of straw (*trussis fur'*) 7½d. To
Punfr' ...   Total 20½d.

Saturday following   To a carpenter 2s 1¼d. To a roofer 13¼d. Punfr'
6d. ....   Total 4s ...

Saturday before the feast of St Nicholas [2 December]   To a mason
(*cementar'*) 2s 8d. To a roofer 11d. Punfr' 5d.   Total 4s 6d.

Saturday after the Epiphany [13 January]   To a smith for 2 stone-
axes (*Fabro pro ij secur' ad lap'*) 8d. For steel (*pro acero*) 1½d. And for 6000 ...
To paviors (*Paviator'*) 3s 2½d. Punfr' 6d.   Total 16s 6d.

Saturday following   To paviors 3s 2½d. Punfr' 6d. To a smith for a bell-
clapper (*Fabro pro batello ad campanum ...*) 12d.   Total 4s 8½d.

Saturday after the feast of the Conversion of St Paul [27 January]   To
paviors 2s 8d. To Punfr' 4d. 2000 lath-nails (*clavibus ad latas*) 15s. For
purifying lead-ashes (*ciner' plumbi purific'*) 22d. For charcoal (*Pro carbon'*)
12d. For carrying earth (*Pro terra carianda*) 1½d. For carrying water for
washing the ashes (*aqua portanda ad lavand' cin'*) ... 1d.

Total 21s ⅛d.

After the purifying to the paviors (*post purificationem ad paviator'*) 3s 2d.
Punfr' 5d.   Total 3s 7d.

Saturday following   To paviors 3s 2½d. Punfr' 6d.

Total 3s 8½d.

Saturday before the feast of St Peter's Chair [17 February] To paviors 3s 2½d. One barrow bought (*j civera empta*) 1¼d. Punfr' 6d. Total 3s 9¾d.

Saturday following To paviors 3s 2¾d. Total shown.

Saturday before the feast of St Gregory [9 March] To paviors 3s 2½d. And to roofers 2s 6d. For placing one window opposite the alt[ar of St Kathe]rine (*In positione j fenestre contra alt . . . . . . rine*) 14d. To a smith for ironwork (*Fabro pro ferramentis*) 13d. Punfr' 5d. Total 8s 4½d.

Saturday following To paviors 4s 2½d. To a carpenter 2s 1¼d. For a certain window on the south side . . . (*Pro quadam fenestra in australi parte . . .*) . . . To a smith for ironwork 8½d. For one labourer (*Pro j operario*) 10¼d. Punfr' 6d. Total 12s 10½d.

Saturday after the Annunciation of the Blessed Mary [30 March] To paviors 4s. . . . For 550 laths (*latis*) 2s ¾d. To a glazier for placing one window . . . . . . Edmund (*Vitrario pro locatione j fenestre*[3] *. . . . . . Edmund'*) . . . 4s 6d. To a smith for ironwork and mending saws (*Fabro pro ferramentis et seris emendend'*) 12d. Punfr' 6d. Total 22s 3¼d.

And 51 quarters of lime bought 27s 6d. Total is shown.

Sum Total £11 2s . . .

(m.2) [IN 1280/1] EXPENSES FOR THE FABRIC [FROM MIDSUMMER TO EASTER]

The Candlestick: expenses incurred for the Easter candlestick from the feast of St John Baptist [24 June] 1280 For horse-hire to Barnstaple for the tools of Richard de Malmesbyr' the painter (*In locatione j equi apud Barnestaple pro utensilibus Ricardi de Malmesbyr' pictoris*) 12d.
First Saturday after that feast [29 June] To the same Richard 2s 1d.
Second Saturday after the octave of that feast [6 July] To the same Richard 2s 1d. And to a smith for repairing the tools of the same Richard (*Fabro ad reparand' utensilia eiusdem Ricardi*) 1½d.
Saturday following To the same Richard 2s 1¼d.
Saturday following To the same Richard 2s 1¼d. And 6 labourers for 2 days for carrying timber from Kalendarhay[4] (*Kalend'*) to the work-house (*usque ad domum operis*) 20d.
Saturday following To the same Richard 2s 1¼d. And to a carpenter 2s 1¾d. Total 15s 4½d.

Saturday following the feast of St James [27 July] To Master R. 2s 1¼d. To a carpenter 2½d. To a smith 3d. . . . Total 6s 1¾d.

Saturday the feast of St Laurence [10 August] To Master R. 2s 1¼d. And 2 carpenters 3s 8½d. For carrying timber (*pro meremio cariando*) 12d. To a sawyer for a whole week 2s. To a smith 4d. Punfr' 3d.
Saturday following To the same Richard 2s 1d. To the same Master R. 1s 1d. To 2 carpenters 2s. To 2 sawyers 2s. Punfr' 4d. Total 16s 10¾d.
Feast of St Bartholomew [24 August] To Master R. 2s 1¼d. To a sawyer 2s 6d. To a carpenter 3s 10d.

Saturday following . . . a horse to Buckland Monachorum for the tools of Michael the carpenter (. . . *j equi apud Boclonde Monachorum pro utensilibus Michaelis carpentarii*) 12d. To Master Michael 2s 2½d. To a sawyer 2s 6d.
Total 16s 2¼d.

Vigil of the feast of the Nativity of the Blessed Mary [7 September] To Master R. . . . . . . 2½d. To a sawyer 2s 6d.
Vigil of Michaelmas [28 September] To Master R. and Michael 4s 2d. To carpenters 2s 1¼d. Punfr' 6d.
Saturday following To Master R. and Michael 4s 2½d. To a carpenter 2s 1¼d. To a sawyer for one day . . . . . . For carrying timber . . .
Total 13s 11d.

Saturday after the feast of St Denis [12 October] To Master R. and Michael 4s 2½d. And to 2 carpenters . . . 8½d.
Saturday following To Master R. and Michael 4s 2d. To a carpenter 12¾d.
Total 13s 1¾d.

Saturday before the feast of SS Simon and Jude [26 October] To Master R. and Michael [4s] 2½d. To a sawyer 5½d. . . .
Morrow of All Saints [2 November] . . . . . . To a carpenter 2s 2¼d.
Saturday following To Master R. and Michael 4s 2½d. To a carpenter 2s 1d.
Saturday following To Master R. and Michael 4s 2½d. To a carpenter . . .
Total . . . 8d.

Feast of St Clement [23 November] To Master R. and Michael 4s 2½d. . . .
Saturday following To Master R. and Michael 4s 2d. To a carpenter 21d. To a turner (*turnator*') . . .
Total 16s 3½d.

Morrow of St Nicholas [7 December] To Master R. and Michael 4s 2d. To a carpenter 2s 1d. To a turner 19d.
Saturday following To Master R. and Michael 4s 2d. To a turner 19d.
Total 13s 7½d.

Feast of St Thomas the apostle [21 December] To Master R. and Michael 4s 2½d. To a carpenter 21d. To a turner . . .
Total 7s 6d.

Vigil of Christmas [24 December] To Master R. and Michael . . . To a carpenter 8½. . . .
Total . . . 11½d.

[Three] Saturdays following To Master R. and Michael . . . [each week].
Saturday after the feast of the Purification of the Blessed Mary [8 February] To Master R. and Michael . . . . . . Master R. and Michael 4s 2½d.
Feast of St Peter's Chair [22 February] To Master R. and Michael 4s 2½d. To a carpenter . . .
[Two] Saturdays following To Master R. and Michael 4s 2½d [each week].
Total 14 . . . d.

Saturday after the feast of St Gregory [15 March] To Master R. and Michael 4s 2½d. To a carpenter . . .
[Three] Saturdays following To Master R. and Michael 4s 2½d. . . . [each week].
Total 16s 9d.

Vigil of Easter 1281   To Master R. and Michael 4s [2½d].

Sum of the totals £11 8s 9½?d.

[There is here a break in continuity because of the loss of the end of the membrane].

(m.1d) [IN 1284/5 EXPENSES] FOR THE FABRIC

Concerning the tower beyond the exchequer (*circa turrim ultra scaccarium*) 1284/5.

Saturday after Ash Wednesday [10 February]   To 2 carpenters 4s 2½d. To 2 carpenters 2s 8d. To a certain labourer (*cuidam operario per ebdomada*) 8½d a week.   Total 7s 6d.

Saturday following   To 2 carpenters 4s 2½d. To 2 carpenters 3s 2½d. To 2 sawyers 2s 9½d. To a certain labourer for 2 days 3d.

Total 10s 4½d.

Saturday following   To 2 carpenters 4s 2d. To 2 carpenters 2s 8d. To a certain labourer 7½d.   Total 7s 5½d.

Saturday following   To 2 carpenters 4s 2½d. To 2 carpenters 3s 2½d. And to 2 sawyers 2s 8½d. For a cooper (*In circulator'*) 1½d.

Total 10s 3d.

Fifth Saturday   To 2 carpenters 4s 2½d. And to 2 carpenters 3s 2½d.

Total 7s 5d.

Sixth Saturday   To 2 carpenters 4s 2d.   Total is shown.

Vigil of Easter [24 March]   To 2 carpenters 4s 2d. To a certain carpenter (*cuidam carpentario*) 21¼d.   Total 5s 11¼d.

First Saturday after the octave of Easter   To 2 carpenters 4s 2¼d. In 3 masons for 3 days 18d. And 2 quarters of lime (*quarteris de calce*) 9d.

Total 8s 5½d.

Saturday following   To 2 carpenters 4s 2½d. And to 2 masons for 2½ days 9½d. And to 2 labourers for a week 18d.   Total 6s 6d.

Saturday following   2 carpenters 4s 2½d.   Total is shown.

Saturday following   To 2 carpenters 4s 2d. For carriage of timber from Norton (*pro cariagio meremii de Norton'*) 8d.

Total 4s 10d.

Saturday following   To 3 carpenters 6s 3¾d.   Total is shown.

Saturday following   . . . carpenters 8s 8½d. To a smith for the ironwork of 2 windows in the west face (*Fabro pro ferramentis ij fenestrarum in fronte occidentali*) 6s. For founding . . . (*ad fund* . . .)   Total 10s 5½d.

Saturday following   . . . 6s 8d. 2400 nails 4s, at 2d a hundred (*pro quolibet c ijd*).   Total 10s 8d.

Saturday following   . . . to a plumber for covering the same (*plumbatori ad eandem cooperiend'*) 14s 7d. For sand for the use of the plumber (*arena ad opus plumbatoris*) 6d. For nails . . .   Total 17s 1d.

Saturday following ... ... and the work of a weather-vane on the same tower (*operi ventilogii super eandem turrim*) 10d. And to a smith for an iron rod for the weather-vane (*j virga ferrea ad ventilogium*) 21d.

Total 2s 7d.

Sum of the totals £6

IN 1285 EXPENSES FOR THE FABRIC

Saturday before Michaelmas [22 September] To 2 carpenters working ... in the chapel of the Blessed Mary Magdalene (*ij carpentariis operant' ... in capella beate Marie Magdalene*) 4s 2d. To one turner 18d.

Total 5s 8d.

Saturday following To 2 carpenters 4s 2d. And to one turner 18d. And for one key to the door of the choir (*pro j clave ad hostium chori*) 1d. For repair ... (*Pro reparacione ...*) 3s 9d. Total 9s 6d.

On the Saturday following ... carpenters 4s 2½d. Total is shown.

Saturday following ... For making a larger window in the said tower and removing the altar of the same (... *fenestr' largior' faciend' in turri predicti et ad altare eiusdem removend'*) 6s 4d. And to the glazier ... for making the window (*Item vitrear' ... fenestr' faciend'*) 3s 9d. To a smith for ironwork of the same (*Fabro pro ferramentis eiusdem*) 13d. And for ... 1½d.

Total 11s 3½d.

Saturday following To a certain carpenter 2s 1d. For ironwork for the trellis (*In ferramentis ad* 'treyliz') 5d. For a lock (*pro serura*) for the same 4d. And to a plasterer (*dealbatori*) 8d. Total 3s 6d.

Saturday following Item for a glass window in St John's tower[5] (*pro j fenestra vitrea in turri sancti Iohannis*) 5s. And to a smith for ironwork for the same 12d. 8 lbs of tin (*viij li. stagni*) 13d. And for ironwork of a certain ambry in the vestry of the chapel of the Blessed Mary at-the-head (*Item pro ferramentis cuiusdam almario in vestario beate Marie ad capud*) 16d. And for a lock for the same 10d. And for canvas bought for lining the same ambry (*Item in canevac' empt' ad idem almarium lineandum*) 6d. For tacks and red leather and for the labour for the same (*In taccis et coreo rubeo et ino pere ad idem*) 4¾d. Total 10s 2¾d.

[Saturday] after the feast of All Saints [3 November] To 2 carpenters working on the door which leads from the choir to the treasury (*ij carpentariis operantibus circa hostium quod ducit versus thesaurum a choro*) 4s 2d ... To a turner 18d. Total 5s 8d.

On the Saturday following To 2 carpenters 4s 2d for the same. And to 2 carpenters for the same for the other week (*per aliam ebdomadam*) 4s 2d. To a smith for one bell-clapper (*Fabro pro j batello ad campanum*) 6d. And for 3 glass windows at St Erth (*Item pro iij fenestris vitreis apud Launedono*) 6s. And on the Saturday following To 2 carpenters 4s 2d.

Total 19s.

On the Saturday following To a smith for ironwork for the same door (*Fabro pro ferramentis ad predictum hostium*) 2s 6d. For a lock (*serura*) for the same 4d. Total 2s 10d.

And for making windows in St Paul's tower⁶ at task (*Item pro fenestr'
faciend' in turri sancti Pauli ad tascam*) 19s 2½d. To a glazier for making glass
windows (*pro fenestras vitreas faciend'*) for the same 6s. To a smith for ironwork 2s. To a certain mason for removing the altar of St Paul and plastering the window (*Cuidam cementario ad altare sancti Pauli removend' et fenestr'
plaustrand'*) 12d. And to one plasterer for plastering the same tower (*Item
j dealbatori ad eandem turrim dealbandum*) 3s. 4 quarters of lime bought 20d.
And to 6 labourers for 3 days for throwing down the wall in the arch of
St Paul's tower (*Item vj operariis per iij dies ad prosternendum murum in archa
sancti Pauli*) 2s 3d.   Total 35s 1½d.

Sum of the totals 107s ¼d.

(m.2d)⁷ [IN 1286/7] EXPENSES FOR THE FABRIC

Saturday before the feast of St Peter's Chair [16 February] For expenses
concerning the closing of the organs (*In expensis circa organa claudenda*) for
locks for the doors, carpentry for the work and the smith's iron (*in hostiis
serura carpentaria in opera et ferro fabri*) 4s. For one clapper (*batello*) 12d.
And to Roger the bellfounder and his son about the bell which is called
Walter and making other bell-wheels (*Item Rogero campanario et filio eius
circa campanum que vocatur Walterus et circa alias campanarum rotas faciend'*) 2s.
And to the same Roger and his son for the same for another week 2s. And
to a smith for repairing one clapper with iron and his labour (*Item fabri
pro j batello reparando in ferro et oper'*) 18½d. For boards and nails for the same
wheels (*In bordis et clavis ad easdem rotas*) 8d.   Total 11s 2½d.

For throwing down the wall under the arch of St John's tower⁷ (*In muro
prosternendo sub archa de turri sancti Iohannis*) 2s 3d. To a labourer for opening
out the large window in St John's tower (*Item operario ad magnam fenestram
in turrim sancti Iohannis apperiend'*) 12d. And to one carpenter making the
same window at task (*Item j carp' ad tassam faciendo eiusdem fenestr'*) 2s 1d.
And to a certain carpenter for the same for another week 2s 1d. And to
a certain other carpenter for the same week 20d. And for a glass window
(*fenestra vitrea*) for the same 11s. And for a half cwt of tin (*pro di.c stagni*)
4s 2d. For tallow (*Pro sepo*) 1d. To a smith for ironwork for the same 6s.
                                                            Total 30s 4d.

First Saturday after the octave of Easter About the vestry (*circa vestiarum*)
to 2 carpenters for the week 4s 2½d. And to 2 labourers for the week 15d.
To masons making 2 doorways from stone at task (*Item cementariis ij
hostia facientibus de petra ad tascam*) 8s.   Total 13s 8½d.

[Four] Saturdays following To 2 carpenters 4s 2d [each week].
Saturday following To 2 carpenters 4s 2d. And to one turner for 2 days
6½d.   Total 21s 4½d.

Saturday after the feast of Trinity [10 August] To 2 carpenters 4s 2d.
And to one turner for a week 19½d. 1000 tiles bought for the vestry (*tegula
in vestario emptis*) 17s 3d. For their carriage 2d. 300 tiles for the same 3s 7d.
And to a certain mason making steps towards the treasury (*cuidam cementario facient' gradus versus thesaurum*) 2s 1d. And to his boy (*garcioni eius*) 7½d.
                                                            Total 29s 6d.

[Saturday] ... ... in the vestry 4s 4d. And for ironwork of the bell called Clermatyn (*pro ferramento campane que vocatur Clermatyn*) 2d. For repair ... of bells (*In reparacione ... campanarum*) 12d. And to a smith for a clapper for the bell called Peter (*pro batello Petri*) 13d. And to Roger the bellfounder and his son for hanging 2 bells (*Item Rogero campanario et filio eius ad pendend' ij campanas*) namely S ... erel and Chaunterel 2s. To a smith for iron and his work on the ironwork of the same 5s.

Total 13s 8d.

Sum of the totals 119s 6½d [altered from £6 8½d].

[Cancelled: Receipts for throwing down the tower by one tally (*Recepta ad prostracionem turris per j talliam*) 70s].

---

1   These words are frequently so closely abbreviated through this roll that it has been necessary to judge from the sums of money paid whether they are to be read as singular or plural.

2   It is assumed that this is a personal name.

3   W. St John Hope (in notes made in 1915) recorded as his reading *contra? altari* [*sancti*] *Edmundi* but there is now no sign of the words *contra altari* in this badly damaged passage.

4   The area near the west front of the cathedral where the vicars choral lived was known as Kalendarhay.

5   The South tower was called St John's tower from the dedication of the altar there.

6   The North tower was called St Paul's tower from the dedication of the altar there.

7   On the right-hand side of the beginning of m.2d *Candelabr' Pasch'* is written in large script, apparently as an endorsement, since the entries about the Easter Candlestick are at the beginning of m.2 above.

Editor's note: This roll of miscellaneous receipts and payments over a period of 9 years cannot have been the total amounts either received or spent during that time. Apart from there being no record of gifts from the bishop, nothing is shown in the receipts from the church of St Erth, the gift of which in 1204 by Bishop Henry Marshal was the foundation of a fabric fund (D. & C. Exeter MS 1129); however, the cost of windows for St Erth is shown above in 1280 as a charge on this fabric account. The *taxatio* of the vicarage of St Erth in 1269 states that 10s was to be assigned yearly to the warden of the Work of Exeter Cathedral (*Reg. Bronescombe*, p.171).

2602   1299, 29 September—1300, 29 September

2 membranes, head to tail, complete except for small holes and cracks in m.1, but completely covered, both front and dorse, with slightly obscuring paper tissue.

Endorsed: *Compotus domini Roberti de Asperton de novo opere ecclesie beati Petri Exon' de anno m⁰ccc⁰.* As the account for the year 1306–7 is endorsed 'year nine', this roll would appear to be the second yearly account of the New Work, the first of which has not survived.

Printed: Oliver, full but inaccurate transcript in Latin, pp. 392–407.

(m. 1) THE ACCOUNT OF DOM ROBERT DE ASPERTON AND MASTER ROGER THE MASON WARDENS OF THE NEW WORK OF THE CHURCH OF THE BLESSED PETER OF EXETER FROM THE FEAST OF ST MICHAEL 1299 TO THE FEAST OF THE SAME MICHAEL 1300 THROUGH ONE WHOLE YEAR.

Arrears (*arreragia*) The same [Robert and Roger] render account of 46s 10½d of the last account (*de arreragiis ultimi compoti*).

Total 46s 10½d.

RECEIPTS

The same render account of £35 18s 8d of ballard coin (*ballard'*)[1] ... from dom Thomas de H[ar]petru chaplain of the lord bishop without tally (*de domino Thoma de H . . . petru capellano domini episcopi sine tallia*). And of £12 of ballard coin received from the steward of the exchequer (*de senescallo scaccarii*) of the church of the blessed Peter without tally. And of £6 of ballard coin received from dom Robert de Veteri Terra from the goods (*de bonis*) of Master Roger Be . . . without tally. And of 66s 8d from the church of St Sancreed (*Sancredi*) in Cornwall by the hands of William de Mileburne clerk by one tally. And of 6s 8d from dom Richard de Hacche without tally. And of 2s from the testament of the vicar of Hennock (*de testamento vicarii de Hanok'*). And of 2s from the testament of William de Plympton'. And of 3d from the testament of Alice de Toriton'.

Total £57 14s 9d.

Sum total of all the receipts with arrears from the preceding account £60 19½d.

[EXPENSES]

THE COST OF THE NEW WORK FOR MICHAELMAS TERM

First Saturday (*Sabbato primo*) They reckon in wages (*in stipendiis*)*. Sharpening (*in bateria*) 5½d. In wages of 4 labourers (*operariorum*) 3s 4d and of 2 labourers 18d. 100 loads of stone bought from Barley (*centum summis petrarum de Berlegh'*[2] *emptis*) 3s 6d. Half a pound of wax bought (*dimidio libre cere empt'*) 6d. 13 lbs of pitch bought (*xiij libris picis empt'*) 12d. One barge-load of stones carried from Branscombe (*in una bargeata petrarum de Brankescombe cariata*) 6s. In wages of 4 carters (*carectariorum*) 3s 6d. 5½ quarters of oats bought (*in v quarteriis dimidio avene emptis*) 6s 6¾d, price 16½d a quarter (*prec' quarterii xvj. d ob*). Total 67s 8¼d.

Second Saturday In wages*. Sharpening 4¾d. In wages of 4 labourers 3s 4d. And 3 labourers 2s 3d. 100 loads of stones bought from Barley 3s 6d. 100 seams of sand (*in c summis arene*) 2s. In wages of 4 carters 3s 6d. 15 lbs of tallow bought for the carts (*sep' empt' ad carectas*) 1s 1½d. 5½ quarters 6 bushels of oats bought 7s 6¾d, price 16d a quarter for 5 quarters and 2¾d for 2 bushels (*busellis*). Total 68s 10d.

Third Saturday In wages*. Sharpening 5¾d. In wages of 6 labourers 5s. And 3 labourers 2s 3d. One boat-load of stones bought from Caen (*in j naviata petrarum de Kain empta*) 16s. For their carriage (*in eis cariendis*) 26s 8d. A barge-load of stones carried from Branscombe 6s. 100 stones bought from Barley 3s 6d. In wages of 4 carters 3s 6d. 13 wheel-plates made (*clippis factis*) 5d. 6 quarters of oats 8s, price 16d a quarter. Total 117s 9¾d.

Fourth Saturday   In wages*. Sharpening 7¾d. In wages of 6 labourers 5s. And 3 labourers 2s 3d. 100 stones bought from Barley 3s 6d. 100 seams of sand 2s. In wages of 4 carters 3s 6d. 9 quarters of great oats (*grosse avene*) bought 14s 3d, 18d a quarter. 10 quarters of small oats (*minute avene*) bought 11s 8d, price 14d a quarter.   Total £4 15s 3¾d.

Fifth Saturday   In wages*. Sharpening 3½d. In wages of 7 labourers 5s 10d. 100 loads of stones from Barley 3s 6d. In wages of one man loading carts with timber with cartage for 4 days (*In stipend' j. hominis chargiand' carecta meremii cum cartaria per iiij dietim*) 7d. 2 cart-loads of timber carried from Chudleigh (*carectar' meremii de Chuddelegh' cariatis*) 3s. 2 carts of stones carried from 'la Sege' (*carect' petrarum de la Sege³ cariatis*) 12d. In wages of one carpenter repairing the carts (*emendent' carect'*) for 5 days 17½d, 3½d a day. For 12 clamps, 53 dowels, 3 bands for blocks, 26 wheel-plates and 18 clouts with nails made from our own iron (*In xij gropis liij doulis iij bendis ad truncos xxvj clipp' et xviij clut' cum clavis de proprio ferro factis*) 4s. In 4 carters 3s 6d.   Total 68s 8d.

Sixth Saturday   In hire (*conductione*)*. Sharpening 7d. In wages of 7 labourers 4s 11½d, 8½d each. 100 loads of stones from Barley 3s 6d. 100 seams of sand 2s. In wages of 4 carters 3s 6d. 16 quarters of oats bought 19s 8d, of which the price of each of 12 quarters is 15d, and each of the others 14d.   Total 79s 1½d.

Seventh Saturday   In wages*. Sharpening 8½d. In wages of 3 labourers 2s 6d. And 6 labourers 4s 6d, 9d each. 100 loads of stones from Barley 3s 6d. 50 seams of sand 12d. For hooping and repairing tubs and buckets (*in tinis et bokets ligandis et emend'*) 1d. In carriage of one cart-load of stones from Topsham (*una carectata petrarum de Toppisham carianda*) 18d. One cart-load of timber (*meremii*) carried from Chudleigh 18d. In wages of 4 carters 3s 6d.   Total 59s 7½d.

Eighth Saturday   In wages*. Sharpening 4¾d. For scouring out the lantern in the churchyard at task (*In lanterna cemitarii scuranda ad tascam*) 4s. In wages of 3 labourers 2s 6d. And 6 labourers 4s 6d. 2 marble stones bought for the altar (*petris marmoreis ad altare emptis*) 13s. 100 seams of sand 2s. 100 board-nails (*clav' ad bordas*) bought 6d. 100 lath-nails (*clavis ad lathas*) bought 1¼d. For fitting a cart-axle (*In j carecta axianda*) 2d. In wages of 4 carters 3s 6d.   Total 65s 6d.

Ninth Saturday   In wages*. Sharpening 7¼d. And 3 labourers 2s 6d. And 3 labourers 2s 3d. And 4 carters 3s 6d.   Total 56s 3¾d.

Tenth Saturday   In wages*. Sharpening 3½d. In wages of 3 labourers 2s 6d. And 3 labourers 2s 3d. And 4 carters 3s 6d. 10 quarters of small (*minute*) oats bought 11s 8d, price 14d a quarter.
                Total 48s 5½d.

Eleventh Saturday   In wages*. Sharpening 6¾d. In wages of 3 labourers 2s 6d. And 3 labourers 2s 3d. 100 seams of sand 2s. In wages of 4 carters 3s 6d. For fitting 2 cart-axles 4d. An axle bought (*in j axa empta*) 2d. For white-tawing a leather hide (*in j coreo dealbando*) 8d. In wages of a smith for new iron-work of the new carts made from our own iron (*In stipendio fabri pro novis ferramentis carectarum novarum factis de proprio ferro*) 8s. For repairing the carts for 3 days 9d. 4 quarters of small oats bought 5s 4d, price 16d a quarter.   Total 48s 11¾d.

Twelfth Saturday   In wages*. Sharpening 5½d. In wages of 3 labourers 2s 6d. And 3 labourers 2s 3d. 50 loads of stones from Barley 21d. 50 seams of sand 12d. 56 lbs of pitch 3s 6d. Wages of 4 carters 3s 6d. For fitting 2 cart-axles 4d. For fixing 6 wheel-plates (*clippis assedendis*) 1d. 12 pairs of gloves (*paris cirothecarum*) bought 6s. One barge-load of stones carried from Salcombe (*In j bargeata petrarum de Saltcombe careata*) 6s. 60 quarters of oats bought 65s, price 13d a quarter.   Total £6 4s 4½d.

Thirteenth Saturday   In wages*. Sharpening 2d. In wages of 3 labourers 15d. And one labourer 4½d. And 4 carters 3s 6d. For hire of a stable at Newton (*stabulum apud Niweton*[4] *locato*) for one term 6d. Farriery of the horses for the same term with our own iron (*In equis marschallandis per eundem terminum cum propriis ferris*) 19d. 1500 horse-nails (*clavis equorum*) made from our own iron 15d. One quarter of oats bought 15d. Wages of Master Roger the mason 30s and of Robert de Asperton 12s 6d.

                                                        Total 55s ½d.

Fourteenth Saturday   In wages of 4 carters 3s 6d. For 'burl' bought to strengthen and repair the harness (*In burla empta ad hernesium perimplenda et emendenda*) 4d. Grease (*pinguendine*) bought 6d. In wages of one man for repairing panels (*panell'*) 3d. One thin whip-cord (*minute cordis ad wippas*) bought 4d. One chain for a cart-axle (*vinculo ad axem carecte*) bought ½d.

                                                        Total 4s 11½d.

Sum total of the whole expenses of Michaelmas term £47 10s 8¼d.

(m.2) And thus they are owed £12 10s 11¼d in small ballard coin and in the same doubled they are owed £6 5s 5¾d.

RECEIPTS FOR CHRISTMAS EASTER AND MIDSUMMER TERMS

Arrears and other receipts

The same [wardens] render account of £6 5s 5¾d from arrears of Michaelmas term in doubled ballard coin (*ballardis dupplicatis*) as is shown above. And £20 of doubled ballard coin received from dom Thomas de Harpetre chaplain of the lord bishop by one tally. And of £12 in doubled ballard coin received from the stewards of the exchequer from the prebend of the canons (*de prebenda canonicorum*) from Easter term without tally. And of 6s 8d in double ballard coin by the testament of Richard de Feres. And of £54 sterling received from dom Thomas de Herpetre by one tally. And of £12 sterling received from the stewards of the exchequer from the canons' prebend in Midsummer term without tally. And of £10 received from the testament of Roger le Rous with tally. And of £6 7s 4d sterling from the dignity of the dean of Exeter (*de dignitate decani Exon'*) for the whole year. And of 60s from the dignity of the precentor for the whole year. And of 20s sterling from the testament of Henry de la Barbilonde. And of 6s 8d from the testament of Thomas de Sancto Martino.

Total of the whole receipt with arrears from the first term
£125 6d 1¾d.

COST OF CHRISTMAS TERM

First Saturday of the second term   They reckon in wages of 4 carters 3s 6d.   Total 3s 6d.

Second Saturday   In wages*. And on carpenter 10d. And 2 labourers 20d. And 4 carters 3s 6d. For fixing one cart-axle 2d.

Total 16s 9½d.

Third Saturday   In wages*. And one carpenter 20d. And 2 labourers 20d. And one labourer for 4 days 6d. And 4 carters 3s 6d. For fixing one cart-axle 2d.   Total 26s 3¾d.

Fourth Saturday   In wages*. Sharpening 7d. In wages of one carpenter 20d. And 4 labourers 3s 4d. And 4 carters 3s 6d.   Total 23s 1d.

Fifth Saturday   In wages*. And one carpenter 20d. And 4 labourers 3s 4d. And 4 carters 3s 6d. 2 sieves (*cribris*) bought 2½d.

Total 31s 3d.

Sixth Saturday   In wages*. Sharpening 3¾d. In wages of one carpenter 20d. In one roofer with his boy (*cum garcione suo*) for 4 days 20d. For 100 laths (*lathis*) 3½d. 400 lath-nails 6d. 2 gutters (*canellis*) 3d. In wages of 4 labourers 3s 4d. And 4 labourers 3s. And 4 carters 3s 6d. For fixing a cart-axle 2d. 15 clouts with nails (*clutis cum clavis*) made from our own iron 18½d. Expenses of dom Robert and Master Roger going to the mine (*versus minam*)[5] 4s. 33 quarters of oats bought 49s 6d, price 18d a quarter.

Total £4 6s 11½d.

Seventh Saturday   In wages*. And one carpenter 20d. Sharpening 5½d. 4 labourers 3s 4d. And 4 labourers 3s. An iron hammer, 6 wedges, one pick, 6 wheel-plates and 9 cart-clouts (*in malleo ferri vj weggis j ligone vj clippis et ix clutis*) and nails made from our own iron 5s 6d. Steel (*acere*) bought 15d. In wages of 4 carters 3s 6d. 100 seams of sea [?] sand (*sablonis*) bought 2s.   Total 50s.

Eighth Saturday   In wages*. Sharpening 3½d. In one carpenter 16¾d. And 4 labourers 3s 4d. And 4 labourers 3s. For one cart carrying timber from Chudleigh for 3 days 3s 2d. In wages of 4 carters 3s 6d. 18 quarters of lime (*calcis*) carried 3s.   Total 44s 8¾d.

Ninth Saturday   In wages*. Sharpening 2d. In wages of one carpenter 20d and the other carpenter 18½d. And 4 carpenters 3s 6d, 10½d each. And 4 labourers 3s 4d and 5 labourers 3s 9d. 7 lbs of tallow bought for the carts 2s 1d. 5½ quarters of lime carried 11d. 100 seams of sand bought 2s.

Total 42s 7½d.

Tenth Saturday   In wages*. Sharpening 4d. In 4 labourers 3s 4d. And 5 labourers 3s 9d. And one carpenter 20d and the other carpenter 18½d. And 4 carters 3s 6d. 7 quarters of lime carried 14d. Wages of one roofer and his boy for one day 5d.   Total 42s 9½d.

Eleventh Saturday   In wages*. Sharpening 2d. In 4 labourers 3s 4d and 5 labourers 3s 9d. And 4 carters 3s 6d. 1000 horse-nails made from our own iron 12d. 9½ quarters of lime carried 19d.   Total 46s 8d.

Twelfth Saturday   In wages*. Sharpening 4d. And 4 labourers 3s 4d and 5 labourers 3s 9d. And 4 carters 3s 6d. 30 quarters of lime carried 5s. 18 quarters of oats bought 24s, price 16d a quarter.

Total £4 4s 7d.

Thirteenth Saturday   In wages*. Sharpening 2¼d. In 4 labourers 3s 4d and 5 labourers 3s 9d. 15 quarters of lime carried 2s 6d. 2 ropes for the use of the church (*cordis ad opus ecclesie*) 3s 5d. Stone from Caen with carriage (*In petra de Kain cum cariagio*) 60s. In wages of 4 carters 3s 6d. One barge-load of stones carried 6s.   Total £6 4s 8½d.

Fourteenth Saturday   In wages*. Sharpening 2¼d. And 4 labourers 3s 4d and 5 labourers 3s 9d. And 4 carters 3s 6d. 10 quarters of lime carried 20d. 100 seams of sand 2s. For hire of a stable at Newton for this term 6d. Farriery for the horses for the whole term 9d. For shoeing the same (*In ferrario eorumdem*) with our own iron 2s 2d. For fixing a cart-axle 2d. In wages of a smith repairing equipment at Barley quarry when required (*In stipendio fabri emendatis utensilia quaerere de Berleghe per vices*) 2s 6d. Candles for the carts (*candelis ad carectas*) 2s. In wages of Master Roger the mason for this term 30s and of dom Robert de Asperton 12s 6d. 8 quarters of oats bought 12s, price 18d a quarter. And 20 quarters of oats bought 26s 8d, price 16d a quarter.   Total £7 12s 6½d.

Total of all the totals of the cost of Christmas term £39 16s 6½d.

(m.1d) COST OF EASTER TERM

First Saturday   500 horse-nails made from our own iron 6d. For grease 4½d. For fat (*uncto*) 4s 2d. And 3 lb b . . . 3d. For repairing harness 2½d. For hooping and repairing tubs (*trinis*) and buckets (*boket'*) 3½d. In wages of 4 carters 3s 6d. 3 quarters of oats bought 4s 4½d, price 17½d a quarter.
Total 13s 8d.

Second Saturday   In wages*. Sharpening 3d. And 2 sawyers (*secatorum*) 2s 3d. And 4 labourers 3s 4d. And 5 labourers 3s 9d. And 4 carters 3s 6d. For repairing a barge 10d. 20 quarters of lime carried 3s 4d.
Total 59s 9d.

Third Saturday   In wages*. Sharpening 4½d. And 2 sawyers 2s 3d. And 4 labourers 3s 4d. And 5 labourers 3s 9d. And 4 carters 3s 6d. 20 quarters of lime carried 3s 4d. 100 seams of sea sand (*sabulonis*) bought 2s.
Total 58s 9d.

Fourth Saturday   In wages*. Sharpening 1d. And 2 sawyers 22½d. And 4 labourers 2s 10d. And 5 labourers 3s 1½d. And 4 carters 3s 6d. 13½ quarters of lime carried 2s 3d. 100 seams of sand (*arene*) 2s.
Total 53s 7d.

Fifth Saturday   In wages*. Sharpening 4½d. And 2 sawyers 2s 3d. And 4 labourers 3s 4d. And 5 labourers 3s 9d. And 4 carters 3s 6d. For making 9 wheel-plates 4½d. For fixing a cart-axle 2d. In wages for making and repairing hooks (*gumfeis*) at Barley quarry 15d. 10 quarters of lime carried 20d. 100 seams of sand 2s. For white-tawing a horse-hide (*in coreo equi dealbando*) 8d.   Total 65s 4d.

Sixth Saturday   In wages*. Sharpening 2d. And 2 sawyers 2s 3d. And 4 labourers 3s 4d. And 5 labourers 3s 9d. And 4 carters 3s 6d. For 9½ quarters of lime carried 19d. 1½ lb of wax bought for cement (*cere ad cementum empta*) 9d.   Total 58s 6d.

Seventh Saturday   In wages*. Sharpening 4½d. And 2 sawyers 2s 3d. And 4 labourers 3s 4d. And 5 labourers 3s 9d. And 4 carters 3s 6d. For 9 empty casks (*doleis vacuis*) bought 6s 1d. 17 quarters of lime carried 2s 10d. For repairing hooks and hammers (*gumfis et martellis*) at Barley quarry 2s 6d.   Total £4 2s 9½d.

Eighth Saturday   In wages of 4 carters 3s 6d. 250 horse-shoes bought at Lopen (*apud Lopene*)⁶ 15s. 2500 nails bought for the same 3s 1½d. One pair of iron cart-bands (*ligam' ferri ad carect'*) bought there 6s 7d. 1000 large board-nails (*grossis clavis ad bordas*) bought there 2s 1d. 1000 lath-nails 10d. For one man's expenses in going to Lopen to buy the said iron (*In expensis j hominis euntis apud Lopene ad dictos ferros emptos*) 12d. One great rope (*magna corda*) bought 13s. 20 quarters of oats bought 16s 8d, price 10d a quarter.   Total 51s 9½d.

Ninth Saturday   In wages*. Sharpening 3½d. And 2 sawyers 2s 3d. And 4 labourers 3s 4d. And 2 labourers 18d. And 4 carters 3s 6d. 100 seams of sand 2s. 4 quarters of oats bought 2s 6d.   Total 48s 3½d.

Tenth Saturday   In wages*. Sharpening 3d. And 2 sawyers 2s 3d. And 4 labourers 3s 4d. And 2 labourers 18d. And 4 carters 3s 6d. For 12 empty casks bought 8s 6d. 2 cart-saddles (*sellis ad carectas*) bought 4d. 9 lbs of lard (*uncti porcorum*) 6d. 16½ quarters of lime carried 2s 9d. 100 seams of sea sand (*sablonis*) 2s. 6½ quarters of oats bought 5s 5d, price 10d a quarter.
                                                       Total 62s 4d.

Eleventh Saturday   In wages*. Sharpening 3½d. And 2 sawyers 2s 3d. And 4 labourers 3s 4d. And 2 labourers 18d. And 4 carters 3s 6d. For the stable hired at Newton 6d. Farriery for the horses for the whole term 9d. For horse-shoes (*ferr' equorum*) made from our own iron for the whole term 22d. One barge-load of stones from Salcombe 6s. For hire of a boat to carry stones (*In j batello ad cariandum petras*) from Salcombe 8s. 15½ quarters of lime carried 2s 7d. 12 pairs of traces (*trahic'*) bought 5s. Wages of Master Roger for the whole term 30s. And of dom Robert the vicar (*vicarii*) 12s 6d.   Total 108s 2½d.

Sum total of the whole cost of the Easter term £33 13s.

COST OF MIDSUMMER TERM

First Saturday   In wages*. Sharpening 3½d. And 2 sawyers 2s 3d. And 4 labourers 3s 4d. And 2 labourers 18d. And 4 carters 3s 6d. For fixing a cart-axle 2d. Whip-cord (*vippe cordis*) 5d. 100 seams of sand 2s. 20 quarters of oats bought 13s 4d, price 8d a quarter.   Total 61s 11½d.

Second Saturday   In wages*. Sharpening 3d. And 2 sawyers 2s 3d. And 4 labourers 3s 4d. And 2 labourers 18d. And 4 carters 3s 6d. 17 quarters of lime carried 2s 10d. One barge-load of stones carried from Salcombe 6s. 12 quarters of oats bought 10s, price 10d a quarter.

                                                       Total 63s 10d.

(m.2d) Third Saturday   In wages*. Sharpening 4½d. And 2 sawyers 2s 3d. And 4 labourers 3s 4d. And 2 labourers 18d. And 4 carters 3s 6d. 26 alders bought 18s 1d. In wages of one carpenter for felling the same alders (*prosternentis eadem alneta*) 13d. One barge-load of stones carried from Salcombe 6s. 17 quarters of lime carried 2s 10d. One auncel, cart-clouts and wheel-plates (*In j ancora clutis et clippis*) made from our own iron and repaired 2s 3d. For repairing a tie (*ligonis*) and hook (*gumfis*) at Barley quarry 5d. Total 69s 9½d.

Fourth Saturday   In wages*. For sharpening 2½d. And 2 sawyers 2s 3d. And 4 labourers 3s 4d. And 2 labourers 18d. And 4 carters 3s 6d. 8 quarters of lime carried 16d. One barge-load of stones carried 6s.

Total 56s 11½d.

Fifth Saturday   In wages*. Sharpening 3¾d. And 2 sawyers 2s 3d. And 4 labourers 3s 4d. And 2 labourers 18d. And 4 carters 3s 6d. For carrying the said alders away from the wood (*In dictis alnetis portandis de bosco*) 18d. 19 quarters of lime carried 3s 2d. 100 seams of sand 2s.

Total 60s ¾d.

Sixth Saturday   In wages*. Sharpening 9¾d. And 2 sawyers 2s 3d. And 4 labourers 3s 4d. And 2 labourers 18d. And 4 carters 3s 6d. 21 lbs of tallow bought for the carts 20d. Total 57s 6¾d.

Seventh Saturday   In wages*. Sharpening and steeling of tools (*In bateria et utensilia aceranda*) 11d. And 2 sawyers 2s 3d. And 4 labourers 3s 4d. And 2 labourers 18d. And 4 carters 3s 6d. One barge-load of stones carried from Salcombe 6s. 6 quarters of oats bought 5s, price 10d a quarter.

Total 65s 6d.

Eighth Saturday   In wages*. Sharpening 3d. And 2 sawyers 2s 3d. And 4 labourers 3s 4d. And 2 labourers 18d. And 4 carters 3s 6d. One barge-load of stones carried from Salcombe 6s. Total 59s 9d.

Ninth Saturday   In wages*. Sharpening 3d. And 2 sawyers 2s 3d. And 4 labourers 3s 4d. And 2 labourers 18d. And 4 carters 3s 6d. 2 barge-loads of stones carried from Salcombe 12s. For repairing one auncell (*ancora*) 10d. One beam (*bemo*) bought 8d. 4 quarters of oats 4s. 16 quarters of oats 13s 4d, price 10d a quarter. 10 quarters of lime carried 20d.

Total £4 2s 11d.

Tenth Saturday   In wages*. Sharpening 3d. And 4 labourers 3s 4d. And 2 labourers 18d. And 4 carters 3s 6d. 28 wheel-plates made from our own iron 14d. 9 quarters of oats 9s 9d. Total 53s 3d.

Eleventh Saturday   In wages*. Sharpening 3d. And 2 sawyers 2s 3d. And 4 labourers 3s 4d. And 2 labourers 18d. And 4 carters 3s 6d. 10 quarters of lime carried 20d. 5 quarters of oats bought 4s 8¼d, price 11¼d a quarter. Total 50s 11¼d.

Twelfth Saturday   In wages*. Sharpening 5d. And 2 sawyers 2s 3d. And 4 labourers 3s 4d. And 2 labourers 18d. And 4 carters 3s 6d. For curing one horse-hide (*In coreo unius equi coriando*) 10d. 2 wheels bought for a cart 5s 7d. 10 quarters of oats bought 9s 2d, price 11d a quarter.

Total 53s 4d.

Thirteenth Saturday, preceding Michaelmas. In wages*. Sharpening 2½d. And 4 labourers 3s 4d. And 2 labourers 18d. And 4 carters 3s 6d. For hire of the stable at Newton for the whole term 9d. Farriery of the horses for the term 9d. For shoeing them with our own iron for the term 23d. In wages of Master Roger the mason for the term 30s and of dom Robert de Asperton 12s 6d. 3 quarters of oats 2s 9d, price 11d a quarter.

Total £4 12s 11½d.

Cost of hay (*Custus feni*) For 15 stacks of hay bought at various prices (*In xv mullonibus feni diverso precio emptis*) 59s 1d. For carriage of the same hay in 119 trusses (*In carriagio eiusdem feni videlicet in cxix trussis*) 13s 7½d. For making one large stack (*uno magno mullone*) 13½d. Thatching straw (*stramine ad cooperturam*) bought for covering it 4d. 2 loads of twists (*summis plicarum*) bought for the same 4½d. For covering the same 7d. 3 stacks of hay bought at Newton 13s. And there remains (*Et remanet ibidem*).

Total £4 8s 1½d.

Purchase of iron (*Empcio ferri*) 2000 [pieces] of iron bought for storage (*In ij millenis ferri emptis ad warnesturam*) 46s 8d. For their carriage by sea from Dartmouth to Topsham (*In cariagio eiusdem per mare ab*[7] *Dertmewe apud*[8] *Topsham*) 16d. Total 48s.

Payment for Caen stones (*Solutio pro petris de Kain*) In payment made to Henry Mauger merchant of Caen for stones previously bought from him in the time of Peter the lord bishop (*In solucionis facta Henrico Mauger mercatori de Kain pro petris ab eo nuper emptis tempore domini Petri episcopi*) 40s. And this by order of the dean and chapter (*precepto decani et capituli*).

Total 40s.

Sum of all the totals of the whole expenses of Midsummer term
£50 5s 11¼d.

Total of the totals of the whole cost of Christmas Easter
and Midsummer terms because the first term is reckoned
above £122 15s 5¾d.

And there is owing 50s 8d. And 38s from the dignity of the chancellor and 64s from the dignity of the treasurer from the present year. And so there is owing clear (*de claro*) £7 12s 8d.

Total of the totals of the whole cost of the new Work
this year £170 6s 2d.

* List of wages of named craftsmen is not included here, see pp. 175-7.
1 *ballard* is equivalent to 'pollard', base coin in circulation at this time.
2 Barley quarry was situated on the western outskirts of Exeter, on the north side of the road from Dunsford Hill to Pocombe bridge.
3 'La Sege', in Topsham parish, was the nearest landing point for access by land to Exeter, on the east bank of the river Exe, just south of Countess Wear. (See Andrew Jackson, 'Medieval Exeter, the Exe and the Earldom of Devon', TDA, 104, 1972, p. 64 ff.).
4 Newton St Cyres.
5 *minam* not identified.
6 A yearly fair at Lopen in Somerset specialized in iron and goods manufactured from iron.
7 MS *ad*
8 *apud* is used consistently through these accounts in the sense of 'to' and not 'at'.

Editor's note: Though this is the first surviving account of the general series, it is untypical in that it has two receipts sections. It illustrates the practical difficulties of drawing up accounts in a year in which the coinage was being reformed. By 1299 money had seriously depreciated in value due to the large numbers of base coins known as pollards and crockards which had been introduced. By the Statute of Stepney of March 1299 it was proclaimed that these coins were to pass current as pence up to Christmas 1299, but from then on they were only to pass at half their value. Therefore there are receipts in this roll for Michaelmas term only, then after Christmas a second section for the rest of the financial year dealing in doubled ballards and sterling. (See C. G. Crump and A. Hughes, 'The English Currency under Edward I', *Economic Journal*, 5, 1895, p. 61 ff.).

2603 1301, 1 October–1302, 30 September

3 membranes, head to tail, partially cracked and stained: m.1. has badly flaking surface; m.2 is completely covered on both sides with slightly obscuring paper tissue; m.3 has holes and is backed with paper.
Endorsed: *Summa summarum totius custus per annum* ... [amount illegible] *Et debet xxxix li. viijs. ix d.*
Printed: Oliver, extract, pp. 379–80.

(m.1) THE ACCOUNT OF DOM ROBERT DE ASPERTON CONCERNING THE NEW WORK (*DE NOVO OPERE*) OF THE CHURCH OF THE BLESSED PETER OF EXETER BEGINNING FROM SUNDAY AFTER THE FEAST OF ST MICHAEL 1301 ENDING ON SUNDAY AFTER THE FEAST OF ST MICHAEL 1302.

RECEIPTS

He renders ... of 30 ... (... *reddit ... de xxx* ...) And of £54 18s 7d received from dom Thomas de Harp*etre* chaplain by one tally from the previous year (*receptis de domine Th ... de Harp ... capellano per j talliam de anno preterito*). And of £110 received from the same Thomas by one tally. And of £48 received from the canons' prebend (*recepta de prebend' canonicorum*). And of 60s from the dignity of the precentor from the previous year (*de dignitate precentoris de anno preterito*). And of 37s from the dignity of the chancellor from the previous year (*de dignitate cancellarii de anno preterito*). And of 64s from the dignity of the treasurer from the same year (*de dignitate thesaurarii de eodem anno*). And of 100s from the testament of Master Adam le Blound. And of 40 ... from the testament of Master John de Dratton. And of ... ½d from Richard de Hacche from the testament of Master Hamund Perleben. And of 6s 8d from Master Walter de Bodmine for .... And for £ ... 11s 4d from dom Philip de Schillingford from the goods of dom John ... of Exeter ... And ... 12d from Master Walter de Esse from a certain testament. And of ... 1d from Master John de Vpauene. And of 2d from Master Roger le Mason. And of 12d from the testament of Thomas de Allfington. And of £6 7s 4d from the dignity of the dean for this year (*de dignitate decani de isto anno*).

Sum total of all the receipts with arrears of the preceding account £281 14s 3d.

EXPENSES

(m.2) MICHAELMAS TERM

First Saturday In wages*. Sharpening 6d. And 7 labourers 5s 3d, to each 9d. And 2 carters 21d. 23 ... 24 dowels and 11 clouts made from our own iron (*In xiij ... ppis xxiij doulis xj clutis de proprio ferro faciendis*) ... d. And 3 labourers 2s 6d. For making 8 iron bars for the windows (*viij barris ferri ad fenestras*) from our own iron 13d. 100 stones from Barley 2s 7¼d. 2 barge-loads of stone carried 12s. 3 quarters of oats 2s ... 11d a quarter.
Total 75s 8¼d.

Second Saturday   In wages*. Sharpening 4d. And 3 labourers 2s 6d.
And 4 labourers 3s. And 2 carters 21d. 100 lbs of tin bought (*In c.li stagni
emptis*) 14s 7d, price 1¾d a lb. 3 cart-loads of stones carried from 'la Sege'
18d. For making 12 cramps (*crampon'*) from our own iron 4½d. One cart-
load of stones carried from Hamdon (*Hamedone*)[1] 4s 6d. 6 quarters of oats
5s 9½d, at 11½d a quarter and ½d more in total (*et ob. ultra in toto*).

Total £4 20d.

Third Saturday   In wages*. Sharpening 3d. 4 cart-loads of stones carried
from Topsham (*Toppesham*) 2s. 100 loads of stones from Barley (*Berle*)
2s 7¼d. 1000 great nails (*magn' clav'*) made from our own iron 15d. In
wages of 4 labourers 2s 6d. And 4 labourers 3s. And 2 carters 21d. 21
quarters of oats 20s.   Total £4 8s ¼d.

Fourth Saturday   In wages*. Sharpening 2d. And 3 labourers 2s 6d. And
4 labourers 3s. And 2 sawyers (*secator'*) 15d. And 2 carters 21d. 14 lbs of
pitch (*picis*) bought 12d. Carriage of a barge-load (*bargia*) of stones 6s.
A barge-cable bought (*In j cabelo ad barg' empto*) 6s. For making 4 stone
bosses for the vault, at task (*In iij clavis petr' ad voltam faciendam ad tascam*)
14s. 100 loads of stones from Barley 2s 7¼d. Cask for provender . . . together with the purchase of one tub and one bucket (*In j doleo ad prebend'*
. . . una cum empcione j tine et j boketi) 11d.   Total £4 4s 3¾d.

Fifth Saturday   In wages*. Sharpening 1½d. And in 3 labourers 2s 3d.
And 4 labourers 2s 8d. And 2 carters 21d. One barge-load of stones carried from Salcombe 6s. 100 loads of stones from Barley (*Berl'*) 2s 7¼d.
For a certain plot at Barley purchased from Robert Le Hayward as well
as carriage of stones this year (*In quadam placea apud Berl' empta de Roberto
le Hayward tam cariag' petrarum hoc anno*) 5s. 3 cartloads of stones carried
from 'la Sege' 18d. For carving 2 bosses for the vault at task (*In ij clavis
taillandis ad volturam ad tascam*) 7s. 54 lbs of iron for making cramps (*crampon'*) and nails at task 17d.   Total 64s 1¼d.

Sixth Saturday   In wages*. Sharpening 3¼d. In 4 labourers 3s. And 4
labourers 2s 8d. And 2 carters 21d. 2 barge-loads of stones carried 12s.
250 lbs of iron for making hooks and door-bands (*ad gumfas et vertivellas
faciendas*) 2s 3d. 300 stones from Silverton for the vault (*ad volturam*) 12s.
2 quarters of oats 3s.   Total 75s 3½d.

Seventh Saturday   In wages*. Sharpening 3d. 2 sawyers for 3 days 7½d.
And 4 labourers 3s. And 3 labourers 2s 8d. And 2 carters 21d. 54 lbs of
iron for making cramps and other things necessary for the work (*crampon'
et alia necessaria operis faciendis*) 19d.   Total 48s 2½d.

Eighth Saturday   In wages*. Sharpening 2½d. In 4 labourers 3s. And 4
labourers 2s 8d. And 2 carters 21d. 100 loads of stones from Barley 2s 7¼d.
78 lbs of iron for making things necessary for the work (*necessaria operis*)
2s 2d. 21 quarters of oats bought 22s 9d, 9d a quarter.

Total 71s 9¾d.

Ninth Saturday   In wages*. Sharpening 2½d. In 4 labourers 3s. And 4
labourers 2s 8d. And 2 carters 21d. 2 brass rollers bought for the vault
(*In ij trokeles eneis ad volturam emptis*) 14d. 100 loads of stones from Barley,
2s 7¼d. One barge-load of stones carried 6s. 27 lbs of iron for making requirements (*ad necessarie*) 11d. For carving one boss for the vault (*In j
clav' ad volturam tailland'*) 3s 6d.   Total 58s 5¾d.

Tenth Saturday   In wages*. Sharpening 1½d. 4 labourers 3s. And 4 labourers 2s 8d. In 2 carters 21d. 3 stones of grease (*iij petr' sepi*) for the carts 3s. 5 lbs of tin for solder (*stagni ad solduram*) 8¾d. One barge-load of stones carried 6s. For making 4 clouts with nails (*clut' cum clav'*) 4d.

Total 54s 3¼d.

Eleventh Saturday   In wages*. Sharpening 2d. 4 labourers 3s. And 4 labourers 2s 8d. And 2 carters 21d. For carrying three great stones from Hamdon 12s. 100 stones from Barley 2s 7¼d. One half lb of wax for cement (*cere ad cement'*) 3d. 3 barge-loads of stone carried 18s. 5 quarters of oats 5s.

Total 67s 9¼d.

Twelfth Saturday   In wages*. Sharpening 1½d. In 4 labourers 3s. And 4 labourers 2s 8d. And 2 carters 21d. For carving one boss for the vault 3s 6d. For making 17 cramps from our own iron 7d. 200 stones from Barley 5s 2½d. One pig-skin bought for panels (*In j coreo porcino empto ad panell'*) 9d. One quarter of grease (*pingued'*) 2½d. One barge-load of stones carried 6s. For the stable at Newton (*Neweton*) hired for this term 6d. For horse-shoes (*ferrura equorum*) made from our own iron 18d. Farriery for the horses for the whole term, 9d. In wages of Master Roger the mason for this term 30s and of Robert de Asperton 12s 6d. 10 quarters of lime bought 4s 2d, price 5d a quarter. 4 quarters of oats 3s.

Total £4 15s 7d.

Cost of lead etc (*Custus plumbi etc*) 3½ fothers of lead bought at St Botulph's fair[2] (*In iij foth' di. plumbi ad nundinas sancti Botulfi emptis*) £9 6s 8d, at 53s 4d a fother. Carrying the same by sea 12s 10d. 100 fotmels of lead bought from the bishop's warden (*In c fotmellis plumbi de cuistode episcopi emptis*) £10 4s. 140 quarters of . . . from the same, without carriage 35s, at 3d a quarter. In hire of 6 men for washing the ashes of the lead for 2 days (*In conductione vj hominum lavant' cineres plumbi per ij dies*) 2s 6d, to each man 2½d a day. For smelting 39 fotmels of lead from the said ashes at task (*In xxxix fotmellis plumbi de dictis cineribus fundendis ad tascam*) 9s 2¼d. 3 quarters of coal bought for the same purpose (*In iij quarteriis carbonis ad idem emptis*) 22d. In wages of one roofer with two servants roofing over the aisles of the New Work and over the exchequer (*In stipendiis j coopertoris cum ij garcion' cooperient' super alas novi operis et super scaccarium*) for 3 weeks, 15s. For 6 empty casks bought 6s.   Total £23 13s ¼d.

Sum total of the first term £56 10s 10¼d.

CHRISTMAS TERM

First Saturday   The same reckons in wages of 2 carters 21d.

Total 21d.

Second Saturday   In wages of 2 carters 21d. For putting an axle on a cart (*In j carecta axanda*) 2d.   Total 23d.

Third Saturday   In wages*. Sharpening 1½d. And in wages of 2 labourers 18d. And 1 labourer 8d. And 2 carters 21d. 15 casks 15d. 6 quarters of oats 6s 6d.   Total 37s 9½d.

Fourth Saturday   In wages*. Sharpening 3½d. In wages of 2 labourers 18d. And of one labourer 8d. And 2 carters 21d. 13 empty casks bought 13s. 2 quarters of oats bought 2s 6d.   Total 45s 1¾d.

Fifth Saturday   In wages*. Sharpening 3d. In wages of 3 labourers
2s 3d. And of 2 labourers 16d. And 2 carters 21d. One cart-saddle (*sella
ad carectam*) bought 3d. For repairing the roads to the quarry (*in viis
versus quereram emendendis*) 6d. For repairing Clyst bridge (*In ponte de Clyst
emendendo*) 6d. For repairing the iron tools at Barley quarry (*In ferramentis
quarar' de Berlegh' emendendis*) 10d.   Total 32s 4¼d.

(m.3) Sixth Saturday   In wages*. Sharpening 3d. In wages of 3 labourers
2s 3d. And of 2 labourers 16d. And 2 carters 21d. For carving (*tailland'*) a
boss 3s 6d. 3 barge-loads of stones carried 18s. 22 trusses of straw (*trussetis
simarum*) bought 3s 8d. 3 iron pulleys bought (*In iij poleyis ferri emptis*)
2s 10½d. 11 quarters of oats bought 11s 11d.   Total 74s 11¾d.

Seventh Saturday   In wages*. Sharpening 2½d. And of 3 labourers 2s 3d.
And 2 labourers 16d. And 2 carters 21d. For mending tools at Barley
quarry (*In utensilia quarar' de Berlegh' emendenda*) 11½d. One cart-saddle
with a pad? bought (*sella cum panello empta*) 4d. For making 5 wheel-
clouts (*clutis*) and 22 wheel-plates (*clippis*) 6d. 1300 nails made from our
own iron 14d. 8 loads of stakes (*summis pelorum*) bought 10½d. 3 quarters of
oats bought 3s 3d.   Total 36s 11¼d.

Eighth Saturday   In wages*. Sharpening 5d. In wages of 3 labourers
2s 3d. And 2 labourers 16d. And 2 carters 21d. One barge-load of stones
carried 6s. 5 quarters of lime bought 20d. 3 quarters of oats bought
2s 9d.   Total 45s 4¾d.

Ninth Saturday   In wages*. Sharpening 3d. In wages of 3 labourers 22½d.
And of 4 labourers 2s 4d. And 2 carters 21d. One cart-saddle (*sella*)
bought 3d. For carving 2 bosses 7s. 100 loads of stones carried from
Barley 2s 7¼d. 3 quarters of oats 3s 6d.   Total 46s 6¾d.

Tenth Saturday   In wages*. Sharpening 3d. In 3 labourers 2s 3d. And 4
labourers 2s 8d. And 2 carters 21d. For 7 cart-clouts (*clutis ad carect'*) and
tempering steel for the use of the masons (*in acero temperando ad opus
cementar'*) 19d. 3000 lead-nails (*clavorum ad plumbum*) 9s 1d. 100 loads of
stones from Barley 2s 7¼d.   Total 53s 5¼d.

Eleventh Saturday   In wages*. Sharpening 2¼d. In wages of 3 labourers
2s 3d. And of 4 labourers 2s 8d. And 2 carters 21d. 8 quarters of lime
bought 2s 8d. 1000 roofing-nails (*clavorum ad cooperturam*) 2s 2d. For making
1000 horse-nails (*clavorum ad equos*) 10d. One cart-saddle with all its fittings
(*cum toto attiro*) bought 12½d. For carving 2 bosses 7s. 10 quarters of oats
8s 10½d.   Total 64s 2¾d.

Twelfth Saturday   In wages*. Sharpening 3½d. And for wages of 3
labourers 2s 6d. And of 4 labourers 3s. And 2 carters 21d. 2 barge-loads
of stones carried from Barley 2s 7½d. 5½ quarters of lime bought 22d. For
carving 2 bosses 7s. 6 trusses of hay bought 3s 5d.   Total 62s 6¾d.

Thirteenth Saturday   In wages*. Sharpening 4½d. In wages of 4 labourers
2s 6d. And of 4 labourers 3s. And 2 carters 21d. For carrying 4 bosses from
Hamdon 8s 8d. For making and gilding 3 banners (*In iij vexillis faciendis et
deaurandis*) 9s 8d. For making 3 iron lances (*lanceis ferri*) for the same from
our own iron 5d. 100 stones carried from Barley 2s 7½d. 2 barge-loads of
stones carried 12s. 6 quarters of lime bought 2s. 7 casks bought 5s 3d.

                                                 Total £4 7s 1¾d.

Fourteenth Saturday   In wages*. Sharpening 4½d. In wages of 4 labourers 3s 4d. And 4 labourers 3s. And 2 carters 21d. For 27 wheel-plates (*clippis*) made from our own iron 9d. 17 quarters of lime bought 5s 8d, at 4d a quarter. 100 loads of stones from Barley 2s 7½d. One barge-load of stones carried from Salcombe 6s. 2 quarters of oats 22d.

Total 70s 8¾d.

Fifteenth Saturday   In wages*. Sharpening 5d. In hire (*In conductione*) of 4 labourers 3s 4d. And 6 labourers 4s 6d. And 2 carters 21d. For 15 quarters of lime 5s. For 100 loads of stones carried from Barley 2s 7¼d. One barge-load of stones carried from Salcombe 6s. 2 cart-wheels (*rotis ad carect'*) bought and carried from Taunton 5s 6d. Bands for them and other equipment for the same wheels made from our own iron (*In ligamini-bus ad easdem cum alio attiro ad easdem rotas de proprio ferro facto*) 5s 6d. 'Whippecord' bought 4½d.   Total £4 3s ¾d.

Sixteenth Saturday   In wages*. Sharpening 3½d. And 4 labourers 3s 4d. And 6 labourers 4s 6d. And 2 carters 21d. 22 quarters of lime bought 7s 4d. 50 loads of stones carried from Barley 15½d. 100 seams of sand (*arene*) 2s. For carrying one barge-load of stones by sea 6s. For putting an axle on a cart 2d. 14 quarters of oats 14s.   Total £4 11s.

Seventeenth Saturday   In wages*. Sharpening 4d. And 4 labourers 3s 4d. And 6 labourers 4s 6d. And 2 carters 21d. For hire of the stable at Newton for this term 6d. Farriery for the horses for the whole term 9d. For horse-shoes (*ferramentis equorum*) for the whole term with our own iron 22d. One cart-axle bought 3d. 100 stones from Barley 2s 7¼d. 200 stones carried 12s. 2 ox-skins (*coreis bovinis*) bought for the carts 7d. 2500 nails for lead bought 3s 4d. 17 boards bought from Tiverton (*In xvij bordis de Tyverton emptis*) 8d. Timber bought for scaffolds (*scarefor'*) 6d. For making 1000 horse-nails 10d. For putting a new axle on a cart 2d. For making 8 cart-clouts (*clutis*) 6d. For wages of Master R. the mason for this term 30s. And of Robert de Asperton 12s 6d. 14 quarters of lime 4s 8d.

Total £6 12s 11¼d.

Sum total of the expenses of the second term £48 7s 11½d.

EASTER TERM

First Saturday   In wages*. And of 2 carters 21d. 6 lbs of 'burl' bought for harness (*In vj lib. burl' ad hernes emptis*) 4d. One potel of grease bought (*j potello pinguedinis empto*) 3d. For repair of harness (*hernes'*) 6½d. 5 axles bought 11½d. 6 empty casks bought 6s. 6 quarters of oats bought 6s.

Total 15s 10d.

Second Saturday: 2 feasts in the week   In wages*. Sharpening 5d. And 5 labourers 3s 6d. And 6 labourers 3s 9d. And 2 carters 21d. 200 seams of sand 4s. 5 . . . bought 13d. 2 barge-loads of stones carried 12s. For repair of the iron tools (*ferramenta*) at Barley quarry 11d. For putting an axle on a cart 2d.   Total 72s 8¼d.

Third Saturday   In wages*. Sharpening 4½d. and 4 labourers 3s 4d. And 7 labourers 5s 3d. And 2 carters 21d. 200 loads of stones carried from Barley 5s 2½d. 2 barge-loads of stones carried 12s. For making 3 buckets ('*boket*') 6d. For binding one bucket and other vessels (*et aliis vasis*) 3d. For repair of iron tools at Barley quarry 9d. 11 quarters of oats 11s.

Total £4 10s 9d.

Fourth Saturday   In wages*. Sharpening 4½d. And 4 labourers 3s 4d. And 7 labourers 5s 7d. And 2 carters 21d. For carving (*taill'*) 4 bosses 14s. For carrying the same from Hamdon 8s 8d. 300 loads of stones from Barley 7s 9d. For repair . . . at Barley quarry 9d. 29 quarters of lime bought 3s. 3 quarters of oats 3s.   Total £4 15s 6¾d.

Fifth Saturday   In wages*. Sharpening 4½d. . . . 4 labourers 3s 4d. And 6 labourers 5s 3d. And 2 carters 21d. For 350 loads of stones . . . 20 quarters of lime 6s 6d. 8 quarters of lime 2s 10d. 50 seams of sand 12 . . . . . . barge bought 8s 1d. 6 quarters of oats 6s.   Total 75s 9¾d.

(m.2d) Sixth Saturday   In wages*. Sharpening 3½d. And 4 labourers 3s 4d. And 7 labourers 5s 3d. And 2 carters 21d. For making 42 great spikes for the chapel of St John and St Gabriel (*In xlii magnis spikis ad capellam sancti Iohannis et sancti Gabrielis*) from our own iron 4s 4½d. 100 stones from Barley 2s 7½d. One barge-load of stones carried by sea 6s. 8 quarters of lime bought 2s 7½d. For repairing tools (*utensilia*) at the quarry 6d.   Total 61s 6¾d.

Seventh Saturday   In wages*. Sharpening 4½d. And for 4 labourers 3s 4d. And 7 labourers 5s 3d. And 2 carters 21d. 300 stones from Barley 10s 5d. For carrying 2 barge-loads of stone by sea 12s. For making (*ca . . .*) and clouts (*clutis*) 5¼d. For repair of tools (*utensilia*) at the quarry 10½d. 12 quarters of lime bought 4s 6d, price 4½d a quarter. 6½ quarters of lime bought 2s 2d, price 4d a quarter.   Total 76s 10½d.

Eighth Saturday   In wages of 2 carters 21d. 11 quarters of lime bought 3s 8d. 95 horse-shoes bought at Lopen fair (*In iiij^{xx}xv ferris equorum ad nundinas de Lopene emptis*) 6s 6½d. And 100 horse-shoes bought 6s. 1000 horse-nails bought 18d. One barge-load of stones carried 6s. 4 quarters of lime bought 16d. 6 quarters of lime bought 2s 3d. In expenses of Master Roger the mason with one horse going to Lopen and returning (*In expensis magistri Rogeri cementarii cum j equo eundo apud Lopene et redeundo*) 18¼d. 19 quarters of oats bought 19s.   Total 49s 6¾d.

Ninth Saturday   In wages*. Sharpening 3d. And 4 labourers 3s 4d. And 3 labourers 2s 3d. And 2 carters 21d. For hire of the stable at Newton 6d. Horse-shoes for this term from our own iron 16d. Farriery for the horses for this term 9d. For putting an axle on a cart 2d. For wages of Master Roger the mason for this term 30s. And of Robert of Asperton 12s 6d.

Total £4 2s 8d.

Sum total of all the expenses of the third term £31 15¾d.

MIDSUMMER TERM

First Saturday   In wages*. Sharpening 2d. 4 labourers 3s 4d. And 3 labourers 2s 3d. And 2 carters 21d. 4 quarters of lime bought 18d. 4 quarters of lime 16d. 14 quarters of oats bought 14s.

Total 61s 2½d.

Second Saturday   In wages*. Sharpening 2d. 4 labourers 3s 4d. And 6 labourers 4s 6d. And 2 carters 21d. 150 seams of sand 3s. For carrying one barge-load of stones 6s. 10 trusses of hay (*feni*) bought 8s 4d. For their carriage 7½d. 3 trusses of hay bought at Newton 2s. 3 quarters of oats bought 2s 10½d. Total 66s 5d.

Third Saturday   In wages*. And for 3 labourers 2s 6d. And for 4 labourers 3s. And 2 carters 21d. Sharpening 1½d. 200 seams of sand 4s. 4½ quarters of oats 4s 10½d. Total 37s 1d.

Fourth Saturday   In wages*. Sharpening 1½d. In 2 labourers 18d. And one labourer 10d. And 2 carters 21d. 7½ quarters of oats 7s 6d.

Total 27s 4½d.

Fifth Saturday   In wages*. Sharpening 1½d. And 2 labourers 18d. And one labourer 10d. And 2 carters 21d. 4 wheel-clouts for the carts made from our own iron 4d. One auncell (*ancora*) bought 5s. One barge-load of stones carried 6s. 8 trusses of hay (*trussetis feni*) 6s 8d. Carriage of the same 6d. 3 quarters of oats 3s 3d. Total 36s 10½d.

Sixth Saturday   In wages*. Sharpening 1½d. And 2 labourers 18d. And one labourer 10d. And 2 carters 21d. And 8 labourers for one day 12d. 3 trusses of hay bought 18d. 3 quarters . . . bought 3s 6d.

Total 23s 2½d.

Seventh Saturday   In wages*. Sharpening 1½d. And 2 labourers 18d. And one labourer 10d. And 2 carters 21d. 3 quarters of oats 3s 6d.

Total 20s 8½d.

Eighth Saturday   In wages*. Sharpening 1½d. In wages of one labourer 9d. And 2 carters 21d. Hay bought 23¼d. 23 quarters of oats 14s.

Total 31s 6½d.

Ninth Saturday   In wages*. One labourer 9d. And 2 carters 21d. 5 trusses of hay bought with carriage 3s 6d. Item for hay bought 3s 4d. Item for hay bought at Newton (*Niweton*) 2s. Total 15s 7d.

Tenth Saturday   In wages*. And for 2 labourers 20d. And 2 carters 21d. For one axle bought 3d. For putting an axle on a cart 2d. 4 stacks of hay bought (*mullonibus feni emptis*) 24s 1d. 44 trusses of hay carried 2s 9d. Hay bought 21d. Total 36s 9d.

Eleventh Saturday   In wages*. And 2 labourers 20d. And 2 carters 21d. 22 quarters of lime bought 7s 4d. 3 quarters of oats bought 2s 5d.

Total 19s 9d.

Twelfth Saturday   In wages*. Sharpening 1½d. And 2 labourers 20d. And 3 labourers 2s 3d. And 2 carters 21d. For making 8 cart-clouts 8d. Paid to Robert le Hayward for Barley quarry 5s. 2 quarters of oats 20½d.

Total 23s 10d.

Thirteenth Saturday   In wages of four masons 5s 4d. And 2 labourers 20d. And 5 labourers 3s 9d. And 2 carters 21d. 100 laths bought 3½d. 1000 lath-nails (*clavorum ad lathas*) 8d. 4 quarters of oats bought 2s 8¼d.

Total 16s 1¾d.

Fourteenth Saturday   In wages*. And for 2 labourers 20d. And for 5 labourers 3s 9d. And for 2 carters 21d. For hire of the stable at Newton 6d. Farriery for the horses 9d. For horse-shoes with our own iron 15d. For wages of Master Roger the mason for this term 30s. And of dom Robert de Assperton 12s 6d. 4 sacks of oats (*sacc' aveni*) bought 3s 5d.

Total 53s 11½d.

Purchases of stone. The cost of colours, glass and lead (*Empciones petri. Custus picture vitri et plumbi*) 300 stones bought from Hamdon with carriage, from which to make the steps before the high altar (*ad gradus ante summum altare inde faciendis*) 54s 4d. For painting 49 bosses 8 corbels and other portions of the vault (*In xlix clavis viij sursis et aliis particulis volture depinguendis*) together with gold silver azure and other colours bought for the same (*una cum auro argento azuro et aliis coloribus ad idem emptis*) £26. For 1271½ feet of glass bought for the great windows of the front of the New Work and making them together with 2 formes[3] of each side (*In m.cc.lxxj. pedes dim. vitri ad summas fenestras frontis novi operis emptis et faciendis una cum ij formis ex utraque parte*) £29 2s 5½d at 5½d a foot (*pro pede*). For 535 feet of glass for 2 other formes (*In v.c.xxxv. pedes vitri ad alias ij. formas*) £12 5s 2½d, 5½d a foot. For the wages of Master Thomas the plumber with his servant for covering and setting in place the lead over the new fabric for 8 weeks (*In stipendium magistri Thome plumbarii cum garcione suo fundendo et assidendo plumbum super novam fabricam per viij septimanas*) 48s, 6s a week.   Total £72 10s.

Sum total of the whole cost of the fourth term
£96 5s 4½d.

Sum total of the whole cost through the year
£242 5s 6½d.

And there is owing £39 8s 9d.

*   List of wages of named craftsmen is not included here, see pp. 177–9.
1   The quarry at Hamdon (now called Ham Hill) was situated about five miles to the west of Yeovil in Somerset.
2   St Botolph's fair was a market for lead, much of it from Derbyshire, and was held at Boston in Lincolnshire.
3   *forma* is a term used here for the complete glass filling of a window, though elsewhere it is sometimes used to mean both tracery and glass.

2604   1302, 30 September–1303, 29 September

2 membranes, head to tail,: m.1 repaired on right-hand side; m.2 has torn tail and is completely covered with obscuring paper tissue. No contemporary endorsement. Printed: Oliver, extract, p. 380.

(m.1) THE ACCOUNT OF ROBERT DE ASPERTONE CONCERNING THE NEW FABRIC OF THE CHURCH OF THE BLESSED PETER OF EXETER BEGINNING FROM SUNDAY THE MORROW OF ST MICHAEL 1302 UNTIL SUNDAY THE FEAST OF THE SAME MICHAEL IN THE YEAR FOLLOWING.

RECEIPTS

The same [Robert] renders account of £39 8s 9d of arrears of the preceding account. And of £86 18s 8d received from dom Th. de Harpet' chaplain of the lord bishop by 2 tallies. And of £36 from the stewards of the exchequer from the prebend of the canons for Michaelmas, Christmas and Easter terms by 2 bills (*per ij billas*). And of 66s 8d from St Sancreed by the hand of William the clerk. And of 66s 8d from the testament of Master Hamund Parleben. And of 12d from the testament of the wife of John Bosse. And of 2s from the testament of William de Fareweye chaplain (*capell'*). And of 38s from 4 seams of glass sold (*Et de xxxviij.s de iiij summis vit' venditis*). And of £6 13s 4d from the testament of dom Andrew dean of Exeter. And of 24s from the goods of Master Philip de Strode archdeacon of Winchester (*Winton'*). And of 60s from the dignity of the precentor from the past year. And of 64s from the treasurer for his dignity from the past year. And of 38s from the dignity of the chancellor from the past year.

Total of all the receipts with the arrears of the
preceding account £187 13d.

EXPENSES

MICHAELMAS TERM

First Saturday In wages*. He reckons in wages of 2 masons 3s. And 2 labourers 20d. And 5 labourers 3s 9d, 9d each. And 2 carters 21d. 4½ quarters of oats bought for fodder (*empt' ad prebend'*) 3s 10d.

Total 18s 4d.

Second Saturday In wages*. And 2 labourers 20d. And 5 labourers 3s 9d. And 2 carters 21d. 2 barge-loads of stones carried by sea 12s. 4 quarters of oats bought 3s 1d. Total 31s 4d.

Third Saturday In wages*. And one man paving the vestry (*et j homine pavienti vesteriam*) 4s. And 2 labourers 20d. And 2 labourers 18d. And 2 carters 21d. For making 13 cramps (*crampon'*) 120 great nails (*magnis clavis*) from our own iron 8½d. 3 locks bought (*In iij seruris emptis*) 23s. One quarter of wax (*j quarterone cere*) bought for cement 1¾d. One quarter of oats 10d. Total 23s 3¼d.

Fourth Saturday In wages*. And 2 labourers 20d. And one labourer 9d. And 2 carters 21d. 5 boards bought for requirements (*In v bordis ad necessaria emptis*) 10d. 100 seams of sand bought 2s. 4 quarters of oats bought 3s 4d. One barge-load of stones carried 6s. Total 32s 1d.

Fifth Saturday: the time changes In wages*. And 2 labourers 16d. And one labourer 7d. And 2 carters 21d. Sharpening 2½d. One stone of tallow (*j petr' sepi*) bought 14d. 6 trusses of broom for stopping up the high windows (*In vj trussetis miricarum ad summas fenestras stopandis*) 12d. 8 trusses of hay (*feni*) bought 4s ½d. 4 quarters of oats bought for fodder of the cart-horses (*ad prebendam equorum carect'*) 3s 4½d. Total 24s.

Sixth Saturday In wages*. Sharpening 2½d. And 2 labourers 18d. And one labourer 8d. And 2 carters 21d. One barge-load of stones carried 6s. 4 quarters of lime 16d. 2 lbs of cart-tallow (*sepi ad carectam*) 2½d. 7 trusses of broom bought as above 14d. 4 quarters of oats bought 2s 10d.

Total 29s 6½d.

Seventh Saturday In wages*. Sharpening 2½d. 2 labourers 18d. And 4 labourers 2s 8d. And 2 carters 21d. 8½ quarters of lime bought 2s 10d, at 4d a quarter. 3 trusses of broom 4½d. For white-tawing one horse-hide (*In coreo j equi dealbando*) 9½d. Total 31s 9d.

Eighth Saturday   In wages*. Sharpening 3½d. 2 labourers 18d. And 3 labourers 2s. And 2 carters 21d. 1½ lbs of pitch (*picis*) 15d. 125 lbs of tin bought 14s 5d. One barge-load of stones carried 6s. 600 lbs of iron bought 20s 7d. 6 quarters of lime 2s.   Total 66s 3½d.

(m.2) Ninth Saturday   In wages*. Sharpening 1d. And 4 labourers 3s. And 5 labourers 3s 4d. And 2 carters 21d. 5 quarters of lime bought 20d. For paving the south aisle of the new Work (*In ala australi novi operis pavianda*) 8s 6d. 4 quintains of iron for making window-bars (*In iiij quintenis ferri ad barras fenestrarum faciendis*) 14s 8d, at 3s 8d a quintain.

                    Total 51s 2d.

Tenth Saturday   In wages*. Sharpening 2¼d. 4 labourers 3s. And 3 labourers 2s. And 2 carters 21d. 6 quarters of lime 2s. 3 trusses of broom (*miricarum*) 6d. 4½ quintains of iron for making bars for the high windows (*ad barras summarum fenestrarum*) 16s 6d, at 3s 8d a quintain. For making 2 quintains of slabs of iron (*ferri slabbarum*) for the same 8s. For repairing one bucket 1d.   Total 45s 11¼d.

Eleventh Saturday   In wages*. Sharpening 2d. And 4 labourers 3s. And 3 labourers 2s. And 2 carters 21d. For paving 3 steps before the high altar and the area on each side of it (*In iij gradibus ante summam altare et aeram[1] ex utraque parte paviendis*) at task 6s 8d. For making 13 plates (*clippis*) and 7 clouts (*clutis*) and 7 bars for the high altar (*vij barris ad summum altare*) from our own iron 15d. 7 trusses of broom bought 14d. For carrying 2 barge-loads of stones 12s.   Total 46s 11d.

Twelfth Saturday   In wages*. Sharpening 2d. And 4 labourers 3s. And 4 labourers 2s 8d. And 2 carters 21d. For the stable hired at Newton (*Nyweton'*) 6d. Farriery for the horses for the whole term 9d. Horse-shoes (*ferr'*) for the same with our own iron 21d. Cords (*cordic'*) bought 16d. For making 14 bars with our own iron 8d. 1½ quarters of lime bought 6d. In one pavior (*paveario*) with his assistant (*coadjutore*) 2s 2d. In wages of Master Roger the mason for this term 30s. And of Robert de Asperton' 12s 6d.   Total 71s 6½d.

Total of the totals of the first term
£23 12s 1¾d.

CHRISTMAS TERM

First Saturday   In wages of 2 masons for one day 6d. And 2 carpenters 7d. And 8 labourers 12d. And 2 carters 21d for the week (*per septimanam*).
                    Total 3s 10d.
Second Saturday   In carters 21d. 4 trusses of broom 8d.
                    Total 2s 5d.
Third Saturday   In 2 carters 21d. And 3 labourers for 4 days 18d. For working ¾ cwt of iron (*In di. c et quatrone ferri operant'*) for the requirements of the Work 2s 9d. In 3 glaziers (*vitrear'*) for 2 days 16d.
                    Total 7s 4d.
Fourth Saturday   In wages of 2 carters for one week 21d.
                    Total 21d.
Fifth Saturday   In wages of 2 carters 21d. For putting an axle on a cart 2d.   Total 23d.

Sixth Saturday   In wages*. And 2 carters 21d.   Total 5s 2d.

²Seventh Saturday   In wages*. Sharpening 2½d. And 2 labourers 18d.
And 2 carters 21d. For working 3 cwt of iron for the requirements of the
high windows (*In iij.c ferri operant' ad necessaria summarum fenestrarum*)
11s, at 3s 8d a cwt. For making 1100 horse-nails 11d.

                                                            Total 27s ½d.

[Eighth Saturday]   In wages*. And in 2 sawyers (*secator'*) for 4 days 22d.
And 2 labourers 18d. [And 2 carters] 21d. For making one quintain of
iron 3s 8d.   Total 15s 2½d.

[Ninth Saturday]   In wages*. And 2 sawyers for 5 days 2s. 2
labourers 18d. And 2 carters 21d.   Total 13s 10½d.

[Tenth Saturday]   In wages*. And 4 labourers 2s 10d. And 2 carters
21d. . . . 6s. 3 quintains of iron worked (*operat'*) for bars for the high
windows 11s. For . . . . . . repairing carts 2s.   Total² . . .

(m.1d)EASTER TERM

Week 1   In wages of 2 carters 21d. 3000 tiles (*tegularum*) bought 22s 6d, at
7s 6d a thousand. 2 stones of pitch (*petr' picis*) bought 2s. 9½ quarters of
oats 7s 1½d, at 9d a quarter.   Total 33s 4½d.

Week 2   In wages*. . . . and 2 carters 21d.   Total 8s 6d.

Week 3   In wages*. And 2 carters 22d. For glue (*inglueo*) bought 2d.
5 quarters of oats 3s 9d, at 9d a quarter.   Total 14s 8d.

Week 4: there are two feasts   In wages*. And 2 carters 21d. For making
18 wheel-plates (*clippis*) with 4 cart-clouts (*clut' ad carectas*) from our own
iron 12d. One load of twists (*plicarum*) bought 1½d. One barge-load of
stones carried 6s.   Total 21s 5d.

Week 5   In wages*. And 2 labourers 20d. And 2 carters 21d. 1½ quintains of iron for making window-bars (*ad barras fenestrarum*) 5s 6d. 2
quarters of oats bought 19½d.   Total 17s 3½d.

Week 6   In wages*. And 2 carters 21d. For making 3 quarters (*quarter-
onis*) of iron for window-bars 2s 9d. 4 lbs of pitch bought 3½d. Hay bought
11d. 4 quarters of oats bought 3s 4d.   Total 13s 6½d.

Week 7   In wages*. And 2 labourers 20d. And 2 carters 21d. In one
mason (*cement'*) 20d. One quintain of iron for making bars 3s 8d. Hay
bought 12d. 4 quarters of oats bought 3s 4d.   Total 19s 11d.

Week 8   In wages*. 2 carters 21d. 2000 lath-nails (*clavorum ad latas*)
bought 17d. 500 board-nails (*clavorum ad bord'*) bought 17½d. 250 'spik-
nailis' bought 11¼d. 5 quarters of oats bought 4s 2d, at 10d a quarter.

                                                            Total 9s 8½d.

Week 9   In wages*. And 2 labourers 20d. And 2 carters 21d. 3 quarters
of oats 2s 6d.   Total 10s 5d.

Week 10   In wages*. And 2 labourers 20d. And 2 carters 21d. 1100 lbs
of iron bought 23s, at 3s 10d a cwt (*pro centena*). 5 quintains of iron for
making bars 7s 4d. 5 quarters of lime 20d.   Total 42s 2d.

Week 11   In wages*. And 2 carters 21d. For the stable hired at Newton
6d. Farriery for the horses 8d. For their horse-shoes (*ferrura eorumdem*) from

our own iron 18d. 4 quarters of oats 3s 4d. In wages of Master Roger 30s.
And of Robert de Asperton 12s 6d.   Total 54s 6d.

Total of the whole expenses of the third term
£11 5s 6¼d.

MIDSUMMER TERM

Week 1   In wages*. And 2 labourers 20d. 2 quintains of iron for making
window-bars 7s 4d. 100 seams of sand 2s.   Total 12s 8d.

Week 2   In wages*. For 8 quarters of lime 3s 4d, price 5d a quarter. 500
tiles (*teg'*) bought 3s 6d.   Total 11s 4d.

Week 3   In wages*. 4 quarters of lime 18d. 50 seams of [sea?] sand
(*sablonis*) 12d.   Total 12s 3d.

Week 4   In wages*. And 2 labourers 20d. In wages of a smith for ironwork for the door of the choir (*In stipendio fabri pro ferramenta ostii chori*) 6s.
2 quintains of iron for making the requirements of the high windows (*ad
necessaria summarum fenestrarum faciend'*) 7s 4d. One potel of oil bought for
painting (*ad picturam*) 8d. 2 quarters of lime 10d.

Total 24s 2d.

Week 5   In wages*. 4 quarters of lime 18d. 50 seams of sand bought 12d.
Total 4s 6d.

Week 6   In wages of 2 labourers for one day 3½d. 300 lbs of iron bought
11s 6d, at 3s 10½d a cwt.   Total 11s 9½d.

Week 7   In wages*. And 2 labourers 20d.   Total 3s 8d.

Week 8   In wages*. And 2 labourers 20d.   Total 6s 2d.

Week 9   In wages*. And 2 labourers 20d.   Total 9s 8d.

Week 10   In wages*. 100 seams of sand 2s. 150 lbs of [iron] for window-
bars in the aisles of the new Work (*in alis novi operis*) made from our own
iron 5s. 6d.   Total 14s 3d.

Week 11   In wages*. 6 lbs of white lead bought for painting (*In vj lib.
albi plumbi ad picturam emptis*) 22½d, price 3¾d a lb. One potel of oil bought
10d. For making 12 window-bars from our own iron 11d.

Total 6s 1½d.

Week 12   In wages of 2 labourers 20d. 200 lbs of tallow (*sepi*) bought
6s 3d.   Total 8s.

Week 13   In wages of 3 labourers 2s 3d. Three quarters of iron (*In di.
quart. ferri*) for making window-bars 5½d from our own iron.

Total 2s 8½d.

Week 14   In wages of one labourer 10d. . . . making window-bars from
our own iron 4½d. For . . . . . . making great spikes (*magnis spikis*) for the
doors of the choir (*ad hostia chori*) from our own iron 9s 10d. For the stable
hired at Newton for this term 6d. Farriery of the horses for the whole
term 9d. For their horse-shoes from our own iron for the term 14d. In
wages of Roger the mason for this term 30s. And of Robert de Asperton
12s 6d.   Total 55s 11½d.

The cost of glass and pavement (*Custus vitri et pavimenti*)   83 feet of glass
for the 4 high (*summas*) windows £24 16s 4½d, at 5½d a foot (*pro pede*).

380½ feet [of glass] for two windows in the aisles (*ad ij fenestras in alis*) £8 17s 2½d. 11500 tiles bought, and laying them in place (*In xj.m.di. tegularum empt' et in aera¹ ponend'*) in total cost £4 6d, at 7s a thousand (*pro millena*). For making the whole iron trellis of the new Work (*In toto traillicio ferri novi operis*) at task £4 6s 8d. Total £42 9d.

Hay bought for storage, with carriage (*Fen' empt' ad instaurum cum cariagio*) 4 stacks (*mullonibus*) of hay containing 31 trusses (*trussas*) bought 16s. For carrying the same trusses from Withy bridge (*Wighe brigge*) 3s 2¾d, at 1¼d a truss. Total 19s 2¾d.

Total of the whole expenses of the fourth term
£52 2s 2¾d.

Total of the whole receipts as above
£169 19s 1d.

Total of the totals of the whole expenses
£104 14s 7¾d.

And there is owing £82 6s 5¼d. From which the exchequer (*scaccarium*) owes for half the prebend of the canons from Easter term 1303 £12. Item the treasurer from his dignity from the past year 64s. And the chancellor for his dignity from the past year 38s. And thus there is owing clear (*de claro*) £65 3s 5¼d. To be investigated (*Inquiratur*): how much the church of St Sancreed owes the new fabric each year.

* List of wages of named craftsmen is not included here, see p. 180.
¹ *aera*, though it occurs twice, appears to be a spelling error for *area*, which is required by the sense of the context in both cases.
² ... ² The condition of the left-hand side of the roll is bad, and week 11 and the total for the term is lost at the end of the membrane, except for a few names.

2605 1303, 29 September–1304, 29 September

3 membranes: m.1 with slightly damaged surface, backed with paper; m.2 with some holes, partially obscured front and dorse with repair tissue; m.3 in fair condition, repaired on margins.
Endorsed: *Compotus novi operis ecclesie beati Petri Exon' de anno domini m. ccc tercio finiente et intrante quarto.*
Printed: Extract in Oliver, p. 380.

(m.1) THE ACCOUNT OF DOM ROBERT DE ASPERTON WARDEN OF THE NEW WORK OF THE CHURCH OF THE BLESSED PETER OF EXETER FROM THE FEAST OF ST MICHAEL 1303 UNTIL THE SAME FEAST IN THE FOLLOWING YEAR.

Arrears The same [Robert] renders account of £82 6s 5¼d of arrears from the last account.

RECEIPTS

And of £124 18s 8d received from dom Th. de Harpetru chaplain of the bishop of the gift of the bishop [for that year.] And of £24 of the canons' prebend from Easter and Midsummer terms. And of £6 7s 4d from the dignity of the dean. And of 60s from the dignity of the precentor. And of 38s from the dignity of the chancellor. And of 64s from the dignity of the treasurer. And of 6s 8d from the testament of the vicar of Chudleigh (*Chuddelegh'*). And of 6s 8d from the testament of the wife of William Bosset. And of 3s from the testament of dom Robert de Kydelonde. And of 16d of the gift of dom John vicar of Tawton (*Tauton'*). And of 20d of the gift of William Lamprei. And of 4d from the obit of master Barat. And of 3d of the gift of William de Hurneford.

Total of the whole receipt with arrears £246 14s 4¼d.

EXPENSES

MICHAELMAS TERM

Week 1 The same [Robert] reckons in wages of 2 labourers 20d. 4 quarters of lime 18d. 50 seams of sand 12d. 2 cart-wheels (*rotas ad carectam*) bought, with carriage from Taunton 5s 4d. For making rim-plates and bands with nails for the same wheels (*In strakis ligaminibus cum clavis ad easdem rotas*) from our own iron 6s 6d.   Total 16s.

Week 2 In wages of 2 labourers 20d. 50 seams of sand 12d. For working (*operand'*) 100 lbs of our own iron for window-bars 3s 8d.

Total 6s 8d.

Week 3 In wages of one mason 2s. And 2 labourers 20d.

Total 3s 8d.

Week 4 For 4 quarters of lime bought 18d.   Total 18d.

Week 5 For 2000 tiles (*tegularum*) bought and for laying (*assedend'*) them 14s.   Total 14s.

Week 6 In wages of 2 labourers 18d. For working 500 lbs of iron for window-bars 18s 4d, at 3s 8d the 100 (*pro centena*). For working 200 lbs of iron for the same 7s 4d.   Total 27s 2d.

Week 7 For working 200 lbs of iron for window-bars 7s 4d.

Total 7s 4d.

Week 8 In wages of one labourer 9d. 2½ quarters of lime bought 11¼d.   Total 20¼d.

Week 9 In one carpenter 20d. And 2 labourers 18d. 500 lbs of iron bought 17s. For working 300 lbs of iron 11s, at 3s 8d the hundred.

Total 31s 2d.

Week 10 In wages of one carpenter 20d. And 2 labourers 18d. 2 quarters of lime bought 9d. 100 lbs of tin (*stagminis*) bought for solder (*ad solduram*) 12s.   Total 15s 11d.

Week 11 In wages of Master Thomas the plumber with his boy (*cum garcione*) for one week 5s. And 2 labourers 18d. And one carpenter 20d.

Total 8s 2d.

Week 12 In wages of 3 labourers 2s 3d. And of Master Roger the mason for this term 30s. Robert de Asperton 12s 6d. 320 feet of glass bought for 2 formes of the new Work (*ad duas formas novi operis*) £7 6s 8d, at 5½d the foot.   Total £9 11s 5d.

Total of the totals of the expenses of the first term £16 4s . . .

CHRISTMAS TERM

First week before the feast of St. Hilary [13 January]. In wages*. And 3 labourers for 2 days 9d. One man with his boy roofing (*cooperient'*) for 3 days 12d. One quarter of lime 5d. 6 seams of sand 2d.

Total 12s 10½d.

Week 2   In wages*. 3 labourers 2s 3d.   Total 11s 2½d.

Week 3   In wages*. Sharpening 3¼d. And 3 labourers 2s 3d. For 3 quarters of lime 15d.   Total 21s 6½d.

Week 4   In wages*. And 2 men laying stones (*assedentes petras*) for 5 days 2s 1d, 2½d each a day. Sharpening 3d. And 3 labourers 2s 3d. And one roofer and a boy (*cum garcione*) for 2½ days 10d. 11 loads of withies bought for requirements (*xj summis virgarum emptis ad necessaria*) 2s 3½d, at 2½d a load. Straw bought for roofing (*furag' ad coperam'*) 18d. One lock with 2 keys (*j serrura cum ij claviis*) bought for the door leading to the court of the treasury (*hostium versus curiam thesaurarii*) 7d. In wages of 2 carters for one week 21d. 50 horse-shoes (*ferr' ad equos*) bought 3s 6d. 4 [picks?]¹ bought 3s 6d. 14 quarters of oats bought 10s 6d, price 9d a quarter.

Total 39s 9¾d.

Week 5   In wages*. Sharpening 1d. And 3 labourers 2s 3d. 2 carters 21d. One man roofing with straw (*coperient' cum stramine*) for 6 days 12d. 201 quarters of laths bought 6d. 500 board-nails (*clavorum ad bord'*) bought 6½d. One half lb of wax for cement 3¼d. Hay bought at Newton (*Niweton*) 23d.

Total 22s 4¾d.

Week 6   In wages*. Sharpening 1½d. And 4 labourers 3s. And 2 carters 21d. One roofer (*copertor'*) with straw (*stramine*) for 6 days 12d. 2 loads of twists (*plic'*) 5d. ... For making 2 pans (*patellis*) from our own iron 16d. 900 horse-nails bought ready-made (*empt' fac'*) 8d. 22 lbs of cart-tallow (*sepi ad carectam*) bought 19d. 17 lbs of grease (*pinguedinis*) bought 10½d.

Total 27s 2d.

Week 7   In wages*. Sharpening 5d. And 7 labourers 5s 3d, 9d each. 2 carters 21d. For hay 4½d. 2000 lath-nails (*clavorum ad lath'*) 16d. 2 cart-wheels bought with carriage from Taunton 5s 11d.

Total 22s 1½d.

Week 8   In wages*. Sharpening 1d. And 7 labourers 5s 3d. And 2 carters 21d. For 10 boards bought for doors (*ad hostia*) 12d. For making 2 bands (*ligonis*) 3 locks 7 hooks (*gumfis*) and 7 hinges (*vertivellis*) from our own iron 16d. 2 stacks (*mullonibus*) of hay bought 20s 6¼d.   Total 48s 6¼d.

(m.2) Week 9   In wages*. Sharpening 1½d. And 3 labourers 2s 6d. And 4 labourers 3s. And 2 carters 21d. 2 ropes for carts 6d. 6½ quarters of oats 4s 4½d.   Total 39s 2d.

Week 10   In wages*. Sharpening 2d. And 3 labourers 2s 6d. And 5 labourers 3s 9d. And 2 carters 21d. For making 5 cart-clouts 5d. 30 quarters of lime bought 11s 3d, at 4½d a quarter. 300 seams of sand 6s. 2 barge-ropes (*cord' ad barg'*) 20d. 100 lbs of pitch (*picis*) 5s. 20 quarters of oats 15s.   Total 75s 11d.

Week 11: 2 feasts   In wages*. Sharpening 2d. And 3 labourers 2s 6d. And 5 labourers 3s 9d. And 2 carters 21d. For 3 barge-loads of stones carried by sea 12s. 22 quarters of lime 8s 3d, at 4½d a quarter. 100 seams of sand 2s. 5 cart-axles (*axibus ad carectam*) bought 9d. Hay bought at Newton 6d. For strengthening and digging out a certain drain at task (*in quadam cloaca affirmanda et fouranda ad tascam*) 20d. 3 locks bought 7d. One truss of thorn (*spinar'*) 2d. 25 trusses of hay carried 14d. Hire of the stable at Newton 6d. For shoeing horses (*equis ferrand'*) with our own iron for that term 20d. Farriery for the horses for that term 6d. Wages of Master Roger for that term 30s. And of Roger de Asperton 12s 6d.

Total 106s 3½d.

The cost of glass   For 364 feet of glass for making the 2 furthest formes in the aisles of the new Work (*ad ij extremas formas in alis novi operis faciendis*) as for the whole cost (*ut in toto custu*) £8 6s 10d at 5½d a foot.

Total £8 6s 10d.

Total of the whole expenses of the second term £29 13s 10¼d.

EASTER TERM

Week 1   In wages of 2 carters 21d. And of 4 labourers for 3 days 18d. For the expenses of Master Roger to Cor[fe?] to buy stones, going and returning (*eundo apud Co. . . ad petras emendas ut in eundo et redeundo*) 3s.

Total 6s 3d.

Week 2   In wages*. Sharpening and for making 2 mattocks (*ligonibus*) with 2 great hooks (*magnis gumfis*) 13¾d. In wages of labourers 4s 2d, 10d each. And 9 labourers 6s 9d. And 2 carters 21d. 'Wippecord' 4¼d. 28 lbs of pitch 15d. 10 lbs of tallow 18d. For strengthening and oiling a barge (*In bargea affirmanda et unguemda*) 6d. One truss of broom 1d. 38½ quarters of lime 14s 5¼d, at 4½d a quarter. 150 seams of sand 3s.

Total 67s 3½d.

Week 3   In wages*. Sharpening 7d. And 5 labourers 4s 2d. And 9 labourers 6s 9d. And 2 carters 21d. For a certain lock bought 6¼d. 29 quarters of lime bought 10s 10½d, at 4½d a quarter. 250 seams of sand 5s. One cart-horse (*equo ad carectam*) bought 13s 4d.   Total 79s 4¾d.

Week 4   In wages*. Sharpening 8d. In wages of 5 labourers [4] s 2d. And 12 labourers 9s. And 2 carters 21d. 28 quarters of lime 10s 6d. 150 seams of sand . . . For binding one tub 3 buckets . . . (. . . *j tina iij boket' ligand'*) 5½d. For making 4 cart-clouts 4d. Hay bought at Newton with carriage 9s 4d. 2 quarters of oats bought 2s 4d.   Total £4 4s 11½d.

Week 5   In wages*. Sharpening 8½d. In wages of 5 labourers 4s 2d. And 12 labourers 9s. And 2 carters 21d. 16 quarters of lime 6s. 150 seams of sand 3s. One barge-load of stones 6s. 7½ stones of steel (*aceris*) for tools . . . 4 quarters of oats 3s 3d.   Total 70s 9d.

Week 6: 2 feasts   In wages*. Sharpening 8½d. And 2 labourers 17d. And 7 labourers 4s 4½d. And 2 carters 21d. For one load of withies for hurdles (*virg' ad flakes*) 1½d. A sieve (*crib'*) 1d. 3 boards 6d. 6 quarters of lime 2s 3d. 100 seams of sand 2s. 2 barge-loads of stones carried 12s. One pair of cart-wheels bought 5s 8d. 6 collars (*vj color'*) 6d. 3½ quarters of oats 3s 8½d.   Total 73s 11¾d.

Week 7   In wages*. Sharpening 4¾d. In wages of 4 labourers 3s 4d. And 5 labourers 3s 9d. And 2 carters 21d. For one barge-load of stones carried by sea 6s. 12 quarters of lime 3s 9d. 500 horse-nails 5d. 2 quarters of oats 19d. Total 67s 6¾d.

Week 8: and Pentecost In wages of 2 carters 21d. For 400 horse-shoes bought wholesale (*in grosso*) 27s 5½d. 2 pairs of cart-tires (*ligamin' ad carect'*) bought 14s 1¼d. 500 large board-nails bought 20d. 2500 lath-nails bought 22½d. 1000 horse-nails bought 17d. 41 hurdles carried 17d. For putting an axle on a cart 2d. 26 boards for moulds (*ad moldlas*) . . . 250 lbs of iron bought 8s 9d. In expenses of Master Roger the mason with 2 horses and 2 boys going to Lopen to buy various things there (*eundo apud Lopene ad diversas res ibidem emendas*) 2s 6d. 4½ quarters of oats 3s 7¾d. Total 65s 8d.

Week 9 In wages*. Sharpening 7d. And 6 labourers 4s 6d. And 2 carters 21d. For one barge-load of stones carried 6s. 13 quarters of lime 4s 10½d, at 4¼d a quarter. 2 yards of hemp (*virg' canabi*) 5d. 4 quarters of oats 3s 6d. Total 72s ½d.

Week 10 In wages*. Sharpening 8d. And 6 labourers 4s 6d. And 2 carters 21d. For 2 barge-loads of stones carried 12s. 4 quarters of lime 18d. 3 quarters of oats bought 2s 9½d. Total 69s 7¼d.

(m.3) Week 11 In wages*. Sharpening 6½d. And 6 labourers 4s 6d. And 2 carters 21d. For one barge-load of stones carried 6d. For another barge-load of stones carried from Portland (*de Portlonde*) 10s. 6 quarters of lime 2s 3d. For repairing the ironwork of the carts 3½d. 6 quarters of oats 4s 8d. Total 76s 5d.

Week 12 In wages*. Sharpening 7½d. And 6 labourers 4s 6d. And 2 carters 21d. 5 quarters of lime 22½d. For the stable at Newton for that term 6d. For shoeing horses with our own iron 19d. Farriery for the same 6d. 5 quarters of oats 4s ½d. Wages of Master Roger for that term 30s. And of Robert de Asperton 12s 6d. Total 104s 3½d.

Total of the whole expenses of the third term £41 17s . . . d.

MIDSUMMER TERM

First week In wages*. Sharpening 5¼d. And 6 labourers 4s 6d. And 2 carters 21d. For 3 quarters of lime 13½d. 100 seams of sand 2s. One empty cask bought 6d. 3 quarters of oats bought 2s 6d. Total 63s ¾d.

Week 2 In wages*. Sharpening 10d. 7 labourers 5s 3d. 2 carters 21d. For one barge-load of stones carried 6s. 100 loads of stones bought from Barley (*Berlegh'*) 3s 6d. 4 quarters of lime 18d. 3 dressed hides bought for cart-harness (*iij coreis coureatis ad hernes carecte emptis*) 2s 5d. 3 pottles of oil (*potellis pinguedinis*) bought 9d. For cloth? (*In panno*) 2½d. 16 lbs of 'burl' 11d. For mending harness 12d. 10½ quarters of oats bought 8s 9d, price 10d a quarter. Total £4 9s 1½d.

Week 3 In wages*. Sharpening 6d. And 10 labourers 7s 6d, 9d each. And 2 carters 21d. 100 stones from Barley 7s. 13 quarters of lime 4s 10½d, 4½d a quarter. 125 seams of sand 2s 6d. 19 quintains of iron bought for store at Dartmouth (*ad warnesturam apud Dertemiewe*) with carriage of the same there 52s 5d. For carrying the same as far as Topsham (*usque Toppesham*) . . . s. For working 2 cwt of iron (*cc ferri*) for window-bars 7s 4d. For

making 5 wheel-plates for carts 2¾d. 100 alders bought at Shillingford (*In c alnetis apud Schillingeford emptis*) 12s 1d. 6 quarters of oats bought 5s 5d.
Total £8 2s 10¼d.

Week 4   In wages*. Sharpening 6d. And 4 labourers 3s. And 2 carters 21d. For working 100 lbs of iron for window-bars 3s 8d. Hay bought 7s.
Total 77s 2d.

Week 5: 2 feasts   In wages*. Sharpening 5½d. For one barge-load of stones carried 6s. And 7 labourers 4s 4½d, 7½d each. And 2 carters 21d. 14½ quarters of lime 4s 10d, 4d a quarter. 300 stones from Barley 10s 6d. Wages of Adam de Barrington for making the ironwork of one window in the aisle of the new Work from his own iron (*faciente ferramenta j fenestre in alis novi operis de ferro suo proprio*) 40s. 4 great window-bars made from our own iron 8s. Hay 2s 5d. 4 quarters of oats 3s 11d.   Total £6 12s 1d.

Week 6   In wages*. Sharpening 6d. And 4 labourers 3s. And 2 carters 21d. For carrying one barge-load of stones (*j bargea petr' carianda*) 6s. One barge-rope (*corda ad bargeam*) 4d. 12 quarters of lime 4s. For making 10 bars from our own iron 6s. And for making 100 lbs of iron into bars 3s 9d. Hay bought 3s 9d. 5½ quarters of oats 5s 1d.   Total £4 18s 2d.

(m.2d) Week 7   In wages*. Sharpening 7d. And 4 labourers 3s. And 2 carters 21d. For carrying 2 barge-loads of stones 12s. 21 quarters of lime 7s. For making 8 wheel-plates (*clippis*) 4d. For making 10 iron rods for windows (*x virgis ferreis ad fenestras*) 6s. 5 quarters of oats 5s 5d.
Total 100s 2d.

Week 8: 2 feasts   In wages*. Sharpening 5d. And 5 labourers 3s 9d. And 2 carters 21d. For carrying one barge-load of stones 6s. 18 quarters of lime bought 6s. For making 11 iron window-bars 4s 1½d. For carrying 30 alders from Shillingford 15d. 4 sacks (*sacc'*) of oats 3s 3½d.
Total 73s 7¾d.

Week 9   In wages*. Sharpening 4½d. And 7 labourers 5s 3d. And 2 carters 21d. One barge-load of stones carried 6s. 12½ quarters of lime bought 3s 6d. For making 4 cart-clouts and nails 4d. 37 alders carried from Shillingford 17d. For making 100 iron pins (*sprangis ferri*) 4½d. 4 sacks of oats 4s 8d.   Total 72s 8d.

Week 10: 2 feasts   In wages*. Sharpening 2d. And 3 labourers 2s 1½d. And 7 labourers 4s 4½d. And 2 carters 21d. For 4 quarters of lime 16d. 3 sacks of oats 3s 5½d. 20 quarters of oats 16s ¼d.   Total 66s 3d.

Week 11   In wages*. Sharpening 6½d. And 3 labourers 2s 6d. And 7 labourers 5s 3d. And 2 carters 21d. For binding one bucket with iron 4d. For carrying one cart-load of stones from Salcombe (*Saltcomb'*) 18d. 200 loads of stones bought from Barley 7s. 3½ quarters of lime bought 14d.
Total 73s 3½d.

Week 12   In wages*. Sharpening 5¼d. And 4 labourers 3s 4d. And 6 labourers 4s 6d. And 2 carters 21d. Steeling tools (*utensilibus acerandis*) 3½d. For one barge-load of stones carried 6s. 200 loads of stones from Barley 7s. 7 quarters of lime bought 2s 7½d, at 4½d a quarter. 3150 shingles (*cindulis*) bought 3s 8½d. For carrying the same from Topsham 14d. For carrying 2 pairs of cart-tires (*ligamin' ad carect'*) from Petherton (*Pederton*) 8d.
Total £4 8s 6¾d.

(m.3d) Week 13   In wages*. Sharpening 3¼d. And 4 labourers 3s 4d. And 6 labourers 4s 6d. And 2 carters 21d. And one man with his boy roofing over the workhouse for one week (*cooperient' super domum operis per j septimanam*) 2s 4d. 4000 pegs (*cuvellis*) bought 3d. 6 pairs of hinges (*vertivellarum*) bought 14d. 7 boards for the doors (*ad hostia*) 12d. Steeling tools 16d. For repairing and binding (*accuranda et liganda*) a cart with our own iron 18d. For making 5 cart-clouts and 4 wheel-plates 7d. One stone of pitch (*petr' picis*) 12d. One lb of wax for cement 6d. 200 loads of stones bought from Barley 7s. One barge-load of stones carried 6s. 2½ quarters of lime bought 11¼d. 50 seams of sand 12d. 4 sacks of oats bought 2s 11½d.

Total £4 14s 5d.

Week 14   In wages*. Sharpening 5½d. And 4 labourers 3s 4d. And 6 labourers 4s 6d. 100 loads of stones bought from Barley 3s 6d. 100 seams of sand 4s. For one cured horse-hide bought (*In j coreo j equi courato empto*) 22d. 12½ quarters of lime bought 4s 8d, price 4½d a quarter. For wages of Master Thomas the plumber for roofing over the chapel of the Blessed Mary and elsewhere over the new Work for 3 weeks and 3 days (*In stipendio magistri Thome plumbarii cooperient' super capellam beate Marie et alibi super novum opus per iij septimanas et iij dies*) 17s 6d. For the stable hired at Newton for that term 6d. For shoeing horses with our own iron 18d. Farriery for the same 6d. Wages of Master Roger the mason for that term 30s. And of Robert de Asperton 12s 6d.   Total £7 22¾d.

The cost of glass   In wages of Master Walter the glazier for setting the glass of the high gable and 8 high windows and 6 windows in the aisles of the new Work (*In stipendio magistri Walteri le Verr' assident' vitrum summi gabuli et viij summarum fenestrarum et vj fenestrarum in alis novi operis*) £4 10s inclusive (*in grosso*).[2] And for 140 feet of painted glass bought for 2 formes in the new vestry (*in cxl pedes vitri depicti ad duas formas in nova vesteria empta*) 64s 2d, at 5½d the foot. For setting the same 2s.   Total £7 16s 2d.

The cost of stones and the great bosses (*magnorum clavorum*)   For 18 great stones bought at Portland for bosses together with 61 bases and capitals with carriage by sea (*xviij magnis petris apud Portlond ad claves emptis una cum lxj basis et capitrallis cum cariagio per mare*) £4 16s 8d. For carving 30 great bosses (*xxx magnis clavis taillandis*) £7 10s, 5s a boss. For carving 6 bosses in the aisles (*clavis in alis*) 21s. For carving 3 main corbels (*sursis*)[3] 25s 6d. For carving 33 corbels (*corball'*)[3] 11s. For one boat-load of stones bought in total cost 70s.

Purchase of lead   For 3 fothers of lead bought at St. Botolph's fair (*ad nundinas sancti Botolfi*) £8, price the fother 53s 4d. In carriage of the same by sea 17s 3d, 5s 9d the fother.   Total £27 11s 5d.

Cost of hay for storage (*ad warnesturam*)   For 29 stacks of hay bought in various places at various prices (*per loca empta diverso precio*) 108s 7¾d. Carriage of the same 29s 8d. 10 trusses of straw for thatching the stacks (*ad cooperam mullon'*) 21¾d. 3 loads of twists (*plicarum*) bought 5½d. For thatching the haystacks (*mullon' feni*) at task 15d. Hay bought at Newton for storage 12s.   Total £7 3s 10d.

Total of the totals of the expenses of the fourth term £109 4s 9¼d.

Total of the totals of all the expenses through the year £197 14½d.

And there is owing £49 13s 1¾d. From which the treasurer owes from his dignity 68s. And thus there is owing clear £46 9s 1¾d.

* List of wages of named craftsmen is not included here, see pp. 181–2.
1 *picoin?* The reading is uncertain, there is a stroke through the descender of p (=per), but various light random strokes underline words, numbers and phrases in this roll, it may be one of these.
2 The meaning of *in grosso* is not clear, perhaps the cost of the glass is included with the wages in the total.
3 *sursis* are obviously large corbels at 8s 6d each, *corbell'* small ones.

2606/2607   1306, 2 October–1307, 1 October

2 membranes, formerly separated and numbered separately, now brought together again to original form and resewn head to tail; m.1 has very badly damaged head, bad surface and small holes, m.2 has a very badly damaged tail. Both are now repaired with modern parchment and silk gauze.
Endorsed: ... *novi operis ecclesie beati Petri Econ' de* ... *annus nonus*, which indicates that the first year of the new Work was 1298–9.
Printed: Extract, Oliver, p. 380.

(m.1) [THE ACCOUNT OF DOM ROBERT DE AS]PERTON CONCERNING THE NEW WORK OF THE CHURCH OF ST PETER OF EXETER FROM SUNDAY [AFTER THE FEAST OF ST MICHAEL] 1306 UNTIL THE SUNDAY NEXT FOLLOWING [THE FEAST OF THE SAME ST MICHAEL 1307].

RECEIPTS

... £14 11s 7¾d of arrears from the preceding account. ... of dom Thomas de Harpet' of the gift of Thomas the lord bishop ... tally. ... of the prebend of the canons ... ... 4d from the dignity of the dean. ... of the precentor. And of 38s from the dignity of the chancellor. And of 64s from the dignity of the treasurer. And of £10 received from the church of St Sancreed in Cornwall. And of 2s from the testament of dom Roger of Stoke formerly a vicar (*quondam vicarii*) of the church of Exeter. And of 12d from the testament of John Stormel chaplain. And of 5s 10d received from Master J. de Bruton from a certain collection for ... (*de quadam collecta ad ...*) And of 12d from Master Walter de Esse. And of 43s 4d received from Master Roger the mason from stones sold and carried by cart (*de petris venditis et cariag' carecte*) by one tally. And of 12d of the gift of Adam Wolf chaplain. ... ...[1]

Total of the whole of the receipts with arrears £215 13s 9¾d.

EXPENSES

COST OF THE FIRST TERM

Week after Michaelmas   In wages*. Sharpening and steeling of tools 11d. 7 labourers 5s 10d, 10d each. And 6 labourers 4s 6d, 9d each. And 2 carters 22d. 4 quarters of lime bought 16d. For mending a certain auncell

(*In quadam ancora emendenda*) 4d. Hire of one cart carrying timber from Norton to Exeter for 5 turns (*In j carect' locata car' meremium de Norton*[2] *apud Exon' per v vices*) 5s 4d. 5 sacks of oats bought for fodder of the cart-horses (*In v saccis avene ad prebendam equorum carecte emptis*) 5s 4d.

Total 69s 4d.

Second week   In wages*. Sharpening 8½d. 5 labourers 4s 2d, 10d each. And 3 labourers 2s 3d, 9d each. And 2 carters 22d. 4½ quarters of lime 18d. 6 lbs of tallow (*cepi*) 9d. One barge-load of stones carried by sea 6s. 6 sacks of oats 6s 4d.   Total 60s 10½d.

Third week   In wages*. Sharpening 6¼d. 5 labourers 4s 2d, 10d each. 3 labourers 2s 3d, 9d each. And 2 carters 22d. One new cart bound with iron bought (*In j nova carecta ferro ligata empta*) 18s 10d. 3 sacks of oats bought 3s 9d.   Total 64s 8½d.

Fourth week   In wages*. Sharpening 3½d. 5 labourers 4s 2d. 3 labourers 2s 3d. One labourer 6d. 2 carters 22d. 4 trusses of straw (*straminis*) 6d. One load of twists (*plicarum*) 1d. Moss for roofing (*In muso ad coperam*) 5d. One stone of tallow for requirements (*ad necessaria*) 12d. 4 sacks of oats 4s 1d.   Total 41s 5½d.

Fifth week: 2 feasts and the time changes   In wages*. Sharpening 6¼d. In 5 labourers 3s 4d, 8d each. 3 labourers 21d. One labourer 6d. In 2 carters 22d. 6 sacks of oats 7s 2d.   Total 38s 1½d.

Sixth week   In wages*. Sharpening 5½d. And 6 labourers 4s 6d. And 3 labourers 2s. And one labourer 6d. And 2 carters 22d. 5 wheel-plates (*clippis*) made 5d. One stone of pitch 12d. For 'glue' 2d. 2 sacks of oats 2s 1d.   Total 43s 9¼d.

Seventh week   In wages*. Sharpening and steeling tools 23d. And 7 labourers 5s 3d, 9d each. And 3 labourers 2s. And 2 carters 22d. For moss (*In muso*) 3d. One cured ox-hide bought for requirements (*In j coreo bovino courato ad necessaria empto*) 11½d. 3 quarters of grease (*In iij quateron' pinguedinis*) 9d. 2 lbs of 'burl' 1d. One man for 3 days mending cart-harness (*emend' hernes carecte*) 8d. 6 pairs of traces with one rope bought (*In vj paribus trahicum cum j corde emptis*) 2s 1d. 7 quarters of lime 2s 4d, price 4d a quarter. 5 sacks of oats 5s 8d.   Total 45s 10¼d.

Eighth week: 2 feasts   In wages*. Sharpening 8¼d. And 3 labourers 2s. And one labourer 7d. And 2 carters 22d. 10 lbs of grease 16d. 12 quarters of lime 4s. 50 seams of sand 12d. 3 sacks of oats 4s 10d.

Total 40s 10¾d.

Ninth week   In wages*. Sharpening 3¾d. In 6 labourers 4s 6d. In 2 labourers 12d. In 2 carters 22d. For making 55 great spikes (*magnis spikis*) 2½d. 12 quarters of lime 4s. 100 seams of sand 2s. One stone of grease 12d. 3 quarters of oats . . .   Total 43s 10d.

Tenth week   In wages*. Sharpening 8d. And 4 labourers 3s. And 2 carters 22d. 4 trusses of straw 12d. 3 loads of twists (*plicarum*) 10d. For one roofer with his boy 16d. 4000 little wedges for stones (*cuvellarum ad petras*) 4d. 4 sacks of oats bought 4s 9d.   Total 41s 3¼d.

Eleventh week   In wages*. Sharpening 5d. 4 labourers 3s. And 2 carters 22d. 6 lbs of tin 7½d. 100 seams of sand 2s. For one lead-roofer (*copertorio plumbi*) with his boy 4s. 4 sacks of oats 4s 9d.   Total 35s 3¼d.

Twelfth week   In wages of 2 carters 22d. And of 4 labourers 3s. And one
roofer 16d. For tanning one horse-hide (*In corio j equi dealbando*) 9d. One
truss of straw ... For a stable hired at Newton 6d. For farriery for the
horses 9d. For shoeing the same with our own iron 19¼d. For ... quarters
of lime 4s, and so much on account of the high wind? (*et tantum causa
magni venti*). 6 sacks of oats 8s 2d, In wages of Master Roger the mason for
this term 30s. And of Robert de Asperton 12s 6d.   Total 64s 8¼d.

(m.2) For carving 3 great corbels and 18 corbels at task (*In iij surs' xviij
corbellis talliandis ad tascam*) 15s. For cleansing lead from lead ashes
previously smelted (*In plumbo purgando de cineribus plumbi ante fund'*) 2s 2d.
In wages of one plumber founding lead and roofing over the south aisle of
the new Work (*fundantis plumbum et coperientis super alam australem nove
operis*) for 8 weeks 36s, 4s 6d a week.   Total 53s 3d.

Total of the totals of the whole cost of the first term £32 3s 3¾d.

CHRISTMAS TERM

First week   In wages of 2 carters 22d. For 3 sacks of oats 3s 9d.
                                                           Total 5s 7d.

Week 2   In wages*. In one roofer with his boy for 4 days 21d. In one
labourer for the same period (*per idem tempus*) 6d. In wages of 2 carters 22d.
5000 little wedges for stones 5d. 2 sacks of oats 18½d.
                                                           Total 13s ½d.

Week 3   In wages*. For sharpening and steeling of tools 9½d. In one
roofer with his boy for 4 days 21d. In 2 labourers 18d. In 2 carters 22d.
2000 roofing stones (*petrarum ad cooperturam*) bought 3s 6d. 12 quarters of
lime 6s 6d. 25 seams of sand 6d. One cart-horse bought 26s 3½d. 8 quarters
of oats 10s 6d.   Total 69s 11d.

Week 4   In wages*. In sharpening 4½d. In 2 labourers 10d. In 2 carters
22d. In one roofer with his boy 2s 6d.   Total 30s ½d.

Week 5   In wages*. Sharpening 5d. In 2 labourers 18d. In 2 carters 22d.
For ... sacks of oats 5s 7½d.   Total 42s 2½d.

Week 6   In wages*. Sharpening 9¼d. In 2 carters 22d. 20 quarters of
oats 26s 8d.   Total 45s 1¼d.

Week 7   In wages*. Sharpening and steeling of tools ... In 2 carters 22d.
13 lbs of grease 18d. 5 quarters of oats 6s 8d.   Total 34s 9¼d.

Week 8   In wages*. Sharpening and steeling of tools 11½d. For repairing
3 barrows (*civer'*) with iron 7½d. In one carpenter 18½d. In 2 carters 22d.
                                                           Total 28s 9½d.

Week 9: 2 feasts   In wages*. Sharpening and steeling of tools 12d. In one
labourer for 2 days 3d. 2 carters 22d. 16 planking-boards (*bord' ad planchuram*) bought 2s 6½d. 4 loads of withies for hurdles (*virgarum ad flak'*)
bought 6¾d. 700 horse-nails (*clavorum ad equos*) bought 8d.
                                                           Total 33s 4¼d.

Week 10   In wages*. Sharpening and steeling of tools 11d. In one
labourer for 4 days 6d. In 2 carters 22d. 100 horse-shoes (*ferris ad equos*)
5s 6d. 9 loads of withies for hurdles 17d.   Total 44s 6d.

Week 11   In wages*. Sharpening 8½d. In 2 labourers for 3 days 9d. 2 carters 22d. 5 loads of withies for hurdles 10½d. One cart-saddle with all its fittings bought (*In j sella ad carect' cum omne attiro empta*) 11d. 50 seams of sand 12d.   Total 30s 5d.

Week 12   In wages*. Sharpening 10½d. In 2 labourers 20d. In 2 carters 22d. 24 lbs of steel (*aceris*) 13d. 150 loads of stone from Barley (*Berl'*) 5s. For putting on an axle and repairing a cart 3d.   Total 30s 10½d.

Week 13: 2 feasts   In wages*. Sharpening 5½d. For . . . *boket'* bought 4d. 100 loads of stones from Barley 3s 4d. 100 seams of sand 2s. In 2 carters 22d. 3 labourers 2s 1¼d. For a stable hired at Newton 6d. Farriery of the horses 6d. Shoes (*ferrura*) for the same with our own iron 18d. In wages of Master Roger the mason for this term 30s. And of Robert of Asperton 12s 6d.   Total 78s 11d.

Total of the totals of the whole cost of the second term £23 9s 6¼d.

EASTER TERM

First week   In wages of 2 carters 22d. 5 hurdles (*flak'*) bought 7½d. For tanning one horse-hide 8d. 3 sacks of oats 3s 7d.   Total 6s 8½d.

Week 2   In wages*. Sharpening and steeling of tools . . . ¾d. In 2 labourers 20d. 4 labourers 3s. 2 carters 22d. 100 loads of stones from Barley 6s 8d. One barge-load of stones carried by sea 6s. 3 sacks of oats 3s 2d.
                                                         Total 56s 6¾d.

Week 3   In wages*. In sharpening and steeling of tools 17d. And 2 labourers 20d. And 5 labourers 3s 9d. And 2 carters 22d. 600 lbs of iron bought for storage (*ad warnesturam*) 20s 5¼d. 12 lbs of tallow (*sepi*) for the carts 11d. For making 4 cart-clouts . . . d. For mending casks (*tinis*) and buckets 3d. One sieve (*cribr'*) bought 1d. 15 quarters of lime bought 5s. 100 loads of stones from Barley 6s 8d. 100 seams of sand 2s. 6 quarters 2 bushels of oats bought 7s 8¾d.   Total £4 2s 6d.

Week 4   In wages*. Sharpening and steeling of tools 9¼d. In 2 labourers 20d. 5 labourers 3s 9d. 2 carters 22d. For making 10 cart-clouts with nails 10d. 100 loads of stones from Barley 3s 4d. 100 seams of sand 2s. One barge-load of stones carried by sea 6s. 4 sacks of oats 4s 6d.
                                                         Total 53s 9¼d.

Week 5   In wages*. Sharpening 6d. In 2 labourers 20d. 5 labourers 3s 9d. 2 carters 22d. 2 horse-scrapers [curry-combs?] (*strigil' ad equos*) bought 5d. 30½ quarters of lime 10s 2d.   Total 50s 11d.

Week 6: 3 feasts   In wages*. Sharpening 3d. 2 labourers 13d. 6 labourers 3s. 2 carters 22d. One bucket bought 2½d. 4 quarters of oats 5s 7d.
                                                         Total 37s 3d.

Week 7   In wages*. Sharpening and steeling of tools 13½d. In 2 labourers 20d. 6 labourers 4s 6d. In [2 carters] 22d. 100 seams of sand 2s. One barge-load of stones carried by sea 6s. 5 sacks of oats 6s 11d. . . .
                                                         Total 58s [6d?].

Week 8   In wages*. In 2 carters 22d. And 4 labourers for one day 6d. 450 horse-shoes bought 28s . . . d and 9d more in the total (*in toto*). 1000 nails for the same 16d. One barge-rope bought 11s. . . . carried by sea 6s. 36 ridge-tiles (*crestis*) bought 18d. One quarter 3 bushels of oats 22d.

Total 52s 10½d.

Week 9 In wages*. Sharpening and steeling of tools and for making 32 cramps (*cramponibus*) 14d. In 2 labourers . . . 5s 3d. In 2 carters 22d. For 54½ quarters . . . bought 18s . . . at 4d a quarter. . . . for carts bought 6d. For putting an axle on a cart 2d. 6 quarters of oats 8s.

Total 69s 2d.

(m.1d) [Week 10] Sharpening and steeling of tools . . . for 876 feet of boards (*borderiis*) . . . s 7d, at . . . a hundred. In 2 labourers 20d. In 6 labourers 4s 6d. In 2 carters 22d. In . . . sacks of oats 2s 5d.

Total 62s 2½d.

Week 11 In wages*. Sharpening and steeling of tools 10d. And 2 sawyers (*secator'*) for 4 days 20d. And 2 labourers 20d. And 6 labourers 4s 6d. And 2 carters 22d. 150 loads of stones from Barley 5s. 3½ quarters of oats 4s 8d, at 16d a quarter. Total 66s.

Week 12 In wages*. Sharpening 5d. And 2 labourers 20d. And 6 labourers 4s 6d. And 2 carters 22d. 100 loads of stones from Barley 3s 4d. 100 seams of sand . . . For mending a sieve ½d. For mending a bucket 2d. And one load of withies for hurdles . . . 1d. One barge-load of stones carried 6s. 2 quarters of oats 3s. Total 64s 1½d.

Week 13 In wages*. Sharpening and steeling of tools 10d. And 2 labourers 20d. And 6 labourers 4s 6d. And 2 carters 22d. And 200 loads of stones from Barley 6s 8d. 100 seams of sand 2s. For the stable hired at Newton 6d. For shoeing of the horses with our own iron 16d. Farriery of the horses 9d. 3½ quarters of oats 4s 11½d, price 17d a quarter. In wages of Roger the mason for this term 30s. And of Robert de Asperton for this term 12s 6d. Total 105s 11½d.

Total of the totals of the cost of the third term £38 6s 6¾d.

MIDSUMMER TERM

Week 1 In wages*. Sharpening and steeling of tools 13d. And 2 labourers 20d. And 6 labourers 4s 6d. And 2 carters 22d. 100 loads of stones from Barley 3s 4d. 100 seams of sand 2s. 4 sacks of oats 5s 6d.

Total 53s 8d.

Week 2 In wages*. Sharpening 5d. And 2 labourers 20d. And 5 labourers 3s 9d. And 2 carters 22d. 11 quarters of lime 3s 8d, price 4d a quarter. 150 loads of stones from Barley 5s. One barge-load of stones carried by sea 6s. 100 seams of sand 2s. Total 60s 1d.

Week 3 In wages*. Sharpening 7½d. And 2 labourers 20d. And 7 labourers 5s 3d, 9d each. And 2 carters 22d. 100 loads of stones from Barley 3s 4d. 50 seams of sand 12d. 21 quarters of lime 7s, 4d a quarter. One stone of pitch 12d. One cart-rope 10d. 4 sacks of oats 5s 5d.

Total 62s 10½d.

Week 4 In wages*. Sharpening 7d. And 2 sawyers for 1½ days 7d. And one plumber with 2 labourers 5s 7d. And 10 labourers 7s 6d, 9d each. And 2 carters 22d. For one hand-cart hired for carrying timber from Chudleigh to Haldon for one week (*Pro j carro locato car' meremium de Chuddeleighe usque Hagheledon' per j septimanam*) 18s. For carrying 4 great tree-trunks (*magnis lignis*) from Chudleigh to Exeter 7s. 200 loads of stones from Barley 6s 8d. 50 seams of sand 12d. 4 sacks of oats 6s 1d, 18¼d a sack.

Total £4 15s 7d.

Week 5   In wages*. Sharpening 7d. And 2 labourers 20d. And 10 labourers 7s 6d. And 2 carters 22d. For mending 2 buckets 4d. One load of withies for hurdles (*flakes*) 2d. 100 loads of stones from Barley 3s 4d. 10 quarters of oats 14s 2d.   Total 71s 10d.

Week 6   In wages*. Sharpening 4½d. In 11 labourers 9s 2d, 10d each. And 2 carters 22d. 125 loads of stones from Barley 4s 2d. One barge-load of stones carried by sea 6s.   Total 66s 1½d.

Week 7   In wages*. Sharpening and steeling tools 11¼d. And 11 labourers 9s 2d. And 2 carters 22d. 100 stones from Barley 6s 8d.

Total 59s 2¼d.

Week 8   In wages*. Sharpening 2½d. 10 labourers 8s 4d, 10d each. And 2 carters 22d. 125 loads of stones from Barley 4s 2d. One tree-trunk (*ligno*) carried from Chudleigh 2s. One barge-load of stones carried by sea 6s. 10 quarters of oats bought wholesale (*in grosso*) 14s 2d.

Total 71s ½d.

Week 9   In wages*. Sharpening and steeling tools 11d. In wages of 10 labourers 8s 4d, 10d each. And 2 carters 22d. For repairing one bucket 1d. One barge-load of stones carried by sea 6s.   Total 40s 6d.

(m.2d) Week 10   In wages*. Sharpening and steeling of tools 12½d. In wages of 10 labourers 8s 4d, 10d each. And 2 carters 22d. 200 loads of stones from Barley 6s 8d.   Total 53s 8½d.

Week 11   In wages*. Sharpening 4½d. 9 labourers 7s 6d, 10d each. 2 carters 22d. 4 staple-bars for windows (*stapilbarris ad fenestr'*) made from our own iron 2s 6d. One barge-load of stones carried by sea 6s. 200 loads of stones from Barley 6s 8d. 10 quarters of oats 14s 2d.   Total 67s 7½d.

Week 12   In wages*. Sharpening 3d. In 8 labourers 6s 8d. 2 carters 22d. One barge-load of stones carried 6s. For one plumber with his boy roofing over the south aisle (*coperient' super alam australem*) for one week 4s.

Total 43s 10d.

Week 13   In wages*. Sharpening 4d. In wages of one carpenter 22d. And 7 labourers 5s 3d, 9d each. And 2 carters 22d. In one plumber with his boy roofing over the new aisle (*novam alam*) 4s. 4 stones of pitch 4s 4d. For moss 6d. One load of withies for hurdles 2d.   Total 46s 4d.

Week 14   In wages*. Sharpening 5½d. And 9 labourers 6s 9d, 9d each. And 2 carters 22d. In one plumber and his boy roofing over the said aisle 4s. 3 cart-loads of wood carried from Chudleigh 5s. For a stable hired at Newton for this term 6d. For shoeing horses with our own iron for the term 23d. Farriery for the same 6d. In wages of Master Roger the mason for this term 30s. And to Robert de Asperton 12s 6d. 6 sacks of oats 6s 4d.

Total £4 11s 10½d.

The cost of hay   For 15 stacks of hay bought at various prices 74s 7d. For carrying the same stacks containing 128 trusses from various places (*In eisdem mullonibus continentibus vj*^xx^*viij trussis de diversis locis cariandis*)

9s 10d. For making 3 round stacks (*mullonibus rotundis*) with the aid of a labourer 12d. 7 trusses of straw bought for thatching the same 14d. 3 loads of twists (*plicis*) bought 5½d. For one thatcher (*copertor'*) covering the same stacks for a week 12d. 4 stacks of hay bought at Newton 15s. For carrying the same 18d.   Total 104s 6½d.

The cost of iron glass and tiles (*Custus ferri vitri et tegularum*)   For 1600 lbs of iron bought 66s 6d, price 4s 2d a hundred (*centene*) less 2d in the total (*et ij minus in toto*). For carrying the same iron from Topsham (*Tops'*) 6d. 4 seams of glass bought 36s. 131 feet of glass for making (*operand'*) windows 60s 3¼d, at 5½d each foot. 4000 tiles bought 32s. For carrying the same 26s 8d. 168 quarters of lime bought with carriage 49s, price 3½d a quarter.   Total £13 10s 11¼d.

Total of the totals of the whole cost of the fourth term £62 19s 9d.

Total of the totals of the whole cost through the year £156 19s 1½d.

And there is owing £58 14s 8¼d.

---

* List of wages of named craftsmen is not included here, see pp. 182–4.
1 Three or four items of the receipts lost from the damaged membrane.
2 Norton in the parish of Newton St Cyres.

2608   1308, 29 September–1309, 28 September

4 membranes, head to tail; m.1 in poor condition, backed with paper, head and right-hand side badly decayed; mm. 2 and 3 good; m.4 has some holes and a decayed tail, is covered by slightly obscuring tissue, and is the only membrane upon which there are entries on the verso.
Endorsed: *Compotus novi operis ecclesie beati Petri Exon' de anno domini m⁰ccc⁰octavo* . . .
Printed: Extract in Oliver, p.380.

(m.1) [THE ACCOUNT OF DOM] ROBERT [DE A]YSPERTON CONCERNING THE NEW WORK OF THE CATHEDRAL CHURCH OF ST PETER IN EXETER BEGINNING FROM SUNDAY THE FEAST OF ST MICHAEL [1308 ENDING ON] SUNDAY THE VIGIL OF ST MICHAEL 1309

[RECEIPTS]¹

Total of all the receipts with arrears £204 15s 11¾d.

EXPENSES

COST OF MICHAELMAS TERM

The week next after Michaelmas   In wages*. Sharpening and steeling of tools . . . ¾d. And 4 labourers 3s 4d. And 5 labourers 3s 9d. And 2 carters . . .   . . . 200 loads of stones from Barley 7s. 125 seams of sand . . .   . . . 2 loads of tiles (*tegularum*). . . . carried 16d. 10 quarters of oats 12s 6d, price 15d a quarter.   Total 106s 2¾d.

Week 2   In wages*. Sharpening and steeling of tools 6½d. And 4 labourers 3s 4d. And 7 labourers 5s 3d, 9d each. And 2 carters 22d. 100 loads of stones from Barley 7s. 150 seams of sand 3s. One barge-load of stones carried 6s.   Total £4 5s 7½d.

Week 3   In wages*. Sharpening and steeling of tools 11d. And 4 sawyers (*secator'*) 5s 6d, 16½d each. And 4 labourers 3s 4d. And 7 labourers 5s 3d, 9d each. And 2 carters 22d. 350 loads of stones from Barley 12s 3d, at 3s 6d the hundred. 13 hurdles bought 2s. For hire of a cart carrying timber (*merem'*) from Chudleigh for one turn (*una vice*) 16d. Stones carried from Topsham 6d. 50 seams of sand 12d. 4 quarters of oats bought 3s 10½d at 11½d a quarter, and a ½d in addition in the total (*plus in toto*).
                                                       Total 104s 3½d.

Week 4   In wages*. Sharpening 6½d. And 4 labourers 3s 4d. And 9 labourers 6s 9d. And in one plasterer (*dauber'*) with ... 10d. And 2 carters 22d. 100 loads of stones from Barley 3s 6d. 100 seams of sand 2s. ... 200 lbs of iron for manufacturing window bars (*ad barras fenest' fabricand'*) 7s. 64 lbs of pitch bought 2s 5d. ... ... 3s 4½d, at 13½d a quarter.   Total 101s ...

Week 5: in which are three feasts   In wages*. And 4 labourers 2s 8d. And 9 labourers 5s 3d, 7d each. And 2 carters 22d. And ... 2s ¾d. 6 quarters of oats 6s 7d.   Total 45s 6 ...

Week 6: and the time changes   In wages*. Sharpening 5½d. And ... labourers ... , 8d each. And 2 carters 22d. 100 ... for manufacturing window-bars 3s 4d. For ... for manufacturing spikes and cramps (*spikis cramponibus fabricandis*) 21d. For 100 ... For repairing ... harness (*hernes*) ... 9 quarters of oats 9s 5d.   Total ...

Week 7   In wages*. Sharpening ... And 4 labourers 3s. And 9 labourers 6s, 8d each. And 2 carters 22d. For manufacturing 10 staple-bars (*stapel-barr'*) 3s. For 4000 spike-nails (*spikings*) bought 6d. For putting on an axle and strengthening (*affirmanda*) a cart 6d. For carrying one barge-load of stones 6s. 2 quarters 2 bushels of oats ...   Total 53s 2½d.

Week 8   In wages*. Sharpening 7½d. In 4 labourers 3s. In 10 labourers 6s 8d, 8d each. In 2 carters 22d. 15 boards bought 2s 4d. 100 seams of sand 2s. One barge-load of stones carried by sea 6s. For manufacturing 14 bars 2s 6d. 200 laths 5d. 10 pairs of traces bought 4s 2d. 16 hurdles bought 2s 8d. For curing (*courando*) one horse-hide 10d. 4½ quarters of oats 5s 1d.   Total £4 4s ... ½d.

(m.2) Week 9: in which are 2 feasts   In wages*. Sharpening 4½d. In 4 labourers 2s 8d, 8d each. And 10 labourers 5s 10d, 7d each. In 2 carters 22d. In one roofer with his boy 2s 1d. For manufacturing 5 cart-clouts and 4 wheel-plates 6½d. 1000 lath-nails (*clav' ad latas*) bought 10d. 10 empty barrels bought for covering? (*In x doleis vacuis ad coperam emptis*) 5s 10d. 4 quarters of oats 4s 4d.   Total 62s 7¾d.

Week 10   In wages*. Sharpening 6½d. And 4 labourers 3s. And 10 labourers 6s 8d, 8d each. And 2 carters 22d. One barge-oar (*remo ad bargiam*) bought 5d. 7 quarters of oats 8s 2d, 14d a quarter.
                                                        Total 63s 4d.

Week 11   In wages*. Sharpening and steeling of tools 9d. And 4 labourers
3s. And 10 labourers 6s 8d, 8d each. And 2 carters 22d. For manufacturing 7 bars 22d. 3 quarters of oats bought 3s 6¾d.   Total 62s ¼d.

Week 12   In wages*. Sharpening 6½d. And 4 labourers 3s. And 10
labourers 6s 8d. And 2 carters 22d. 500 board-nails bought 18d. For repairing cart-harness 11d. 6½ quarters of oats bought 7s 7d, price 14d a
quarter. For the hire of a stable at Newton for the quarter 6d. For horse-
shoes (*ferr' equorum*) from our own iron for the term 2s 3d. Farriery 9d. In
wages of 3 glaziers setting in the glass formes in the aisles of the new Work
(*In stipendiis assedendent' formas vitreas in alis novi operis*) for 2 weeks and 4
days 13s 4d. For the fee (*in feodo*) of master Roger the Mason for this term
30s. And of Robert de Aysperton 12s 6d.   Total £6 5s 11d.

Total of the whole expenses of the first term £49 10s 5¾d.

COST OF CHRISTMAS TERM

First week in the feast of Christmas   In wages*. And to 6 labourers for
the same period [2 days] 18d. And 2 carters 22d.   Total 4s 6d.

Week 2   In wages*. And 6 labourers for one day 9d. And 2 carters for
one week 22d. One cart-horse bought 9s ¼d. 4½ quarters of oats bought in
bulk (*in grosso*) 5s ½d.   Total 17s 9d.

Week 3   In wages*. And 4 labourers for 2 days 12d. And one mason and
one roofer for one day 6d. And 2 carters 22d. For repairing some ironwork
with one nail? bought for the same (*In quadam ferr' emend' cum j clave ad
eandem empta*) 2d.   Total 12s 3¾d.

Week 4   In wages*. Sharpening 2d. And 4 labourers for 5 days 2s 6d.
And 2 carters for a week 22d. 2000 lead-nails (*clavorum ad plumbum*)
bought 4s 6d. For mending sieves (*cribris*) 2d. 9 quarters of oats bought in
bulk (*in grosso*) 10s.   Total 48s 1¾d.

Week 5   In wages*. Sharpening 6½d. And 4 labourers 3s. And 2 carters
22d. For an axle bought and for fitting it and strengthening the cart
(*In j axea ad carectam empta et in eadem axeanda et affirmanda*) 6d. Tallow for
solder (*In sepo ad solduram*) 2d. 4 quarters of oats 4s 6d, 13½d a quarter.
                Total 38s 7d.

Week 6   In wages*. Sharpening 8d. In 4 labourers 2s 10d, 8½d each. In 2
carters 22d. One quarter of oats 12d.   Total 32s 6½d.

Week 7   In wages*. Sharpening 2d. In 2 carters 22d. For curing one
horse-hide 9½d. 4 quarters of oats 4s 6d.   Total 33s 6d.

Week 8   In wages*. Sharpening 4d. In one labourer 9d. In 2 carters 22d.
3 quarters of oats 3s 7d.   Total 32s 8½d.

Week 9   In wages*. Sharpening 6½d. In 4 labourers 3s. In 2 carters 22d.
For a certain saw (*In quadam serr'*) bought 3d. 1½ quarters of oats 21d.
                Total 38s 9½d.

Week 10   In wages*. Sharpening and steeling of tools 13¼d. In 4 labourers
3s. And 2 carters 22d. 5 quarters of oats 6s 2½d.   Total 43s 3d.

Week 11   In wages*. Sharpening 8d. And 2 labourers 18d. And 3
labourers 2s. And 2 carters 22d. 3 cart-axles bought 6d. For putting an

axle on a cart and strengthening it 3d. For repairing harness 2d. Grease 6d. One barge-rope bought 8s 9d. One horse bought 15s 2¼d. 6½ quarters of oats bought in bulk (*in grosso*) 7s 3¼d. Total 77s 10¾d.

Week 12: and the time changes. In wages*. Sharpening 9d. And 4 labourers 3s. And 2 labourers 20d. And 2 carters 22d. Tallow for solder 1d. Total 57s 1d.

Week 13 In wages*. Sharpening 9d. And 3 labourers 2s 6d. And 5 labourers 3s 9d. And 2 carters 22d. For strengthening a cart-wheel with iron (*In una rota carecte ferro affirmanda*) 18d. For curing a horse-hide 8d. Candles (*candel'*) for the carts for the term 8d. 3 quarters of oats 3s 4½d. Total 66s 1½d.

Week 14: and 2 feasts In wages*. Sharpening 3½d. And 3 labourers 2s 3d. And 5 labourers 3s 4d. And 2 carters 22d. For strengthening tubs and a 'boket' 10d. 1100 lbs of iron bought 55s, 5s a hundred. For hiring a stable at Newton 6d. For shoeing horses with our own iron for the term 22d. For their farriery 6d. 4 quarters of oats 4s 9½d. For the fee of Master Roger the mason 30s for the term and of Robert de Aysperton 12s 6d. Total £7 5s 10¼d.

Total of the whole expenses of the second term £32 9s ½d.

(m.3) COST OF EASTER TERM

Week 1 In wages of 2 carters 22d. For repairing cart-harness 4d. 3 quarters of oats bought 3s 7¾d, price 14d a quarter. Total 5s 9½d.

Week 2 In wages*. Sharpening 7½d. In 3 labourers 2s 6d. In 6 labourers 4s 6d, 9d each. In 2 carters 22d. One barge-load of stones carried by sea 6s. 150 loads of stones bought from Barley 5s 3d. For one sieve bought, and mending others 1d. 150 board-nails bought 6½d. For 4½ quarters of oats 4s 1d, price 14d a quarter. Total 76s 11d.

Week 3 In wages*. Sharpening 4¾d. In 3 labourers 2s 6d. In 6 labourers 4s 6d. In 2 carters 22d. 100 loads of stones from Barley 3s 6d. One load of withies for hurdles 2½d. One bleached hide (*coreo albo*) bought for harness 4d. 6½ quarters of oats bought 7s 7d, price 14d a quarter. Total 62s ¼d.

Week 4 In wages*. Sharpening 4d. In 3 labourers 2s 6d. In 6 labourers 4s 6d. In 2 carters 22d. 5 quarters of oats bought 5s 6¼d. Total 55s 10¼d.

Week 5: and 2 feasts In wages*. Sharpening 5d. In 3 labourers 2s 3d, 9d each. In 6 labourers 4s, 8d each. In 2 carters 22d. 2 barge-loads of stones carried by sea 12s. Total 54s 9¾d.

Week 6: and 2 feasts In wages*. Sharpening 4¼d. And 3 labourers 2s 3d, 9d each. And 6 labourers 4s, 8d each. And 2 carters 22d. For binding one tub 1d. Tallow for solder 1d. In 9 labourers carrying lead-ashes to the Exe for washing and carrying them back to Kalendarhay (*In ix operarios portant' cineres plumbi apud Exe ad lavand' et reportand' apud Kalendereheie*) 13½d, 1½d each. In wages of 10 men helping the plumber to smelt the lead from the said ashes for one day (*In stipendiis x hominum iuvant' plumbar' ad fundendum plumbum de dictis cineribus per j diem*) 20d. For 2 bellows hired for the same purpose (*In ij flatis ad idem locatis*) 2s. In the wages of Master Thomas the plumber and his boy about the said work 5s. For 125 loads of stones from Barley 4s 4½d. 3 loads of stakes (*pelorum*) bought 6d. 8 loads of fencing (*clausture*) 14d. One bundle of withies (*In j fess' virgarum*) 1½d. Charcoal (*in carbone*) 14d. 400 lath-nails 4d. 4 quarters of oats 4s 8d.

Total 68s 2d.

Week 7   In wages*. Sharpening 5½d. And 4 labourers 3s 4d. And 5 labourers 3s 9d. And 2 carters 22d. 2 trusses of fencing 3½d. 100 board-nails 2½d. 225 loads of stones from Barley 7s 10½d. One barge-load of stones carried 6s. 5 quarters of oats 5s 10d.   Total 73s.

Week 8: Pentecost   In wages of 2 carters 22d. One cart-horse bought 27s. 200 horse-shoes with nails bought 15s 6d. 100 board-nails bought 3s 4d. 2000 lath-nails bought 17d. In expenses of one boy carrying the same iron goods from Lopen fair (*In expensa unius garcionis cariantis dicta ferramenta de nundinis de Lopene*) 4d. One potel of grease bought 5d. 'Burl' for harness 2d. For repairing harness 2d. 7 quarters of oats 7s 9d.

Total 57s 11d.

Week 9   In wages*. Sharpening 5½d. And 4 labourers 3s 4d. And 8 labourers 6s. And 2 carters 22d. 50 loads of stones from Barley 21d. 4 quarters of lime 18d. 550 seams of sand 12s 4½d, 2s 3d a hundred.

Total 70s 8d.

Week 10   In wages*. Sharpening 7½d. And in 4 labourers 3s 4d. And 8 labourers 6s. And 2 carters 22d. 6 quarters of lime 2s 3d, 4½d a quarter. One cart-horse bought 16s. 3 quarters of oats 3s 10½d.

Total 75s 6d.

Week 11   In wages*. Sharpening 6d. And 2 sawyers 2s 9d. And 4 labourers 3s 4d. And 5 labourers 3s 9d. And 2 carters 22d. 17 quarters of lime 6s 4½d, price 4½d a quarter. 100 loads of stones from Barley 3s 6d. One barge-load of stones carried by sea 6s. 6 quarters of oats 6s 11d.

Total 78s ½d.

Week 12   In wages*. Sharpening 6d. And 2 sawyers 2s 9d. And 4 labourers 3s 4d. And 5 labourers 3s 9d. And 2 carters 22d. 13 quarters of lime 4s 10½d, 4½d a quarter. For a stable hired at Newton for this term 6d. For shoeing horses with our own iron for the term 16d. Farriery of the same 6d. One quarter of oats 19d. For the fee of Master Roger the mason for the term 30s. And of Robert de Aysperton 12s 6d.

Total 106s 6½d.

Total of the whole cost of the third term £39 5s 2¾d.

(m.4) COST OF MIDSUMMER TERM

Week 1   In wages*. Sharpening 5d. In 3 labourers 2s 6d. In 3 labourers 2s 3d. In 2 carters 22d. For manufacturing 14 crampons (*In xiiij pegonibus fabricandis*) 7d. For carrying one barge-load of stones 6s. 3 quarters of lime 14½d. 7 quarters of oats 8s 8½d.   Total 64s 3d.

Week 2   In wages*. Sharpening 4½d. In 3 labourers 2s 6d. In 3 labourers 2s 3d. In 2 carters 22d. 63 seams of sand 15d. 10 quarters of lime 3s 9d, 4½d a quarter. For making 11 wheel-clouts with nails 11d. For putting an axle on a cart and strengthening it 4d. 2 quarters of oats 2s 5d.

Total 48s 11½d.

Week 3   In wages*. Sharpening 4d. In 3 labourers 2s 6d. In 2 labourers 18d. In 2 carters 22d. 5 quarters of lime 22½d, 4½d a quarter. Tallow for solder 1d. 4 quarters of oats 5s 4½d.   Total 36s 10½d.

Week 4   In wages*. Sharpening 5½d. In 2 labourers 20d. In 2 labourers 18d. In 2 carters 22d. For 25 loads of stones from Barley 10½d. 4 quarters of oats 4s 8d.   Total 41s.

Week 5: 2 feasts   In wages*. Sharpening 8½d. In 2 labourers 17d. In 2 labourers 15d. In 2 carters 22d. One load of withies 2d. Cart-grease 2d. In a painter for priming the bosses of the vault (*In j pictor' ad primandum claves volture*) 2s. 5 quarters of oats bought in bulk (*in grosso*) 7s 10d.

Total 40s 7d.

Week 6   In wages*. Sharpening 3¼d. In 2 labourers 20d. In 2 labourers 18d. In 2 carters 22d. In one painter (*pictor'*) 2s. One barge-load of stones carried by sea 6s. 2 quarters of oats 2s 10d.   Total 46s 1¼d.

Week 7   In wages*. Sharpening and steeling of tools 9½d. In one painter 2s. In 2 labourers 22d. In 2 labourers 20d. In 2 carters 22d. 4 quarters of oats 6s 8d.   Total 46s 7½d.

Week 8   In wages*. Sharpening and steeling of tools 11¾d. In wages of the said painter 2s. And 2 labourers 22d. And 2 labourers 20d. And 2 carters 22d. For repairing a bucket 1d. 7 quarters of oats bought in bulk 10s 4d.   Total 57s 9¾d.

Week 9   In wages*. Sharpening 5½d. And 2 labourers 22d. And 4 labourers 3s 4d. And one boy (*garcione*) 6d. In 2 carters 22d. One barge-load of stones carried 6s.   Total 54s 2d.

Week 10   In wages*. Sharpening 4½d. And 2 labourers 22d. And 6 labourers 5s. And 2 carters 22d. In one plasterer (*daubeour*) with his boy 2s 10d. 4 quarters of oats 4s 4½d.   Total 50s 10d.

Week 11   In wages*. Sharpening and steeling of tools 10d. In 2 labourers 22d. In 6 labourers 5s. In 2 carters 22d. In one plasterer with his boy 2s 10d. 9½ quarters of lime 3s 11½d, 5d a quarter. One barge-load of stones carried by sea 6s. For mending a barrow (*cribris*) 1d. 4 quarters of oats 5s 4d.   Total 73s 5½d.

Week 12   In wages*. Sharpening 4½d. In 2 labourers 20d. In 11 labourers [8s] 3d, 9d each. In 2 carters 22d. 11 quarters of lime 4s 7d, 5d a quarter. One great bucket (*magno buketo*) bought 6d. 100 seams of sand 2s. In one plasterer with his boy 2s 10d. For tanning one horse-hide 9d. 5 quarters of oats 6s 4½d.   Total 70s 11d.

Week 13   In wages*. Sharpening 4½d. In 2 labourers 20d. In 11 labourers 8s 3d, 9d each. In 2 carters 22d. 27 quarters of lime 11s 3d, 5d a quarter. 500 roofing stones (*petras ad copertur'*) bought 11d. For one roofer with his boy roofing over the house in Kalendarhay (*In j copertor' cum garcione suo coperient' super domum de Kalenderehaye*) for the week 2s 6d. For fitting 3 formes of glass in the south part of . . . of the new Work (*In iij formis vitri assedend' in australi parte . . . novi operis*) 6s. For manufacturing 94 lbs of iron for bars for the said windows and formes (*ad barras fenest' predict' et formarum*) 3s . . . d. 3 quarters of oats 3s 11½d.   Total 50s . . .

Week 14   In wages*. Sharpening 4d. In one plasterer with his boy 2s 10d. In 2 labourers 20d. In 10 labourers 7s 6d, 9d each. In 2 carters 22d. 2

ropes bought for the work (*ad op'*) 7s 8d. 23 quarters of lime bought 9s 7d, 5d a quarter. For the stable hired at Newton 6d. For shoeing horses with our own iron for this term 23d. Farriery for them 6d. 5 quarters of oats 6s 6d. For the fee of Master Roger for this term 30s. And of Robert of Aysperton 12s 6d. **Total 118s 2d.**

(m.4d.) Further (*adhuc*) to Midsummer term

The cost of colours and oil for priming the bosses of the vault (*Custus colorum et olei ad claves volture primendas*) 1½ lbs of red lead (*rubei plumbi*) bought 9½d. 12 lbs of white lead (*blank plumb'*) bought 5s, at 5d a lb. And 21 lbs of the same bought on another occasion (*alia vice*) 7s 10d, 4½d a lb. And one lb of sinoper (*cinopol*) bought 2s 9d, and one ounce 2¾d. 3½ lbs of varnish (*vernise*) 21d. 7 gallons one quart of oil bought 11s 3d, price 18½d a gallon (*lagene*) and 1d more in the total. **Total 29s 7¾d.**

The cost of lead and the roofing of the Work (*copertur' operis*). 111 fotmels of lead bought with carriage and at total cost £13 17s 6d, price 2s 6d the fotmel. For wages of Master Thomas the plumber and his boys for their work at task £8. **Total £21 17s 6d.**

The cost of hay 11 stacks of hay near the park of 'Athelingebeare' (*iuxta parcum de Athelingebeare*) containing 52 trusses bought in bulk (*in grosso*) 44s 6d. For their carriage to Exeter 4s 4d. And 3 stacks of hay bought at Newton with carriage 13s 3d. Paid to the executors of the lord Thomas bishop of Exeter for . . . lime lately bought in bulk (*Soluto executoribus domini Thome Exon' episcopi pro . . . calc' nuper in grosso empto*) 110s. **Total £8 12s 1d.**

Total of the totals of the whole cost of the fourth term £73 . . . 11¾d.

Total of the totals of the whole cost through the year £194 10s 8¾d.

And there is owing £10 5s 3d.

Memorandum of 100s owed from the testament of Master Adam le Blound from his legacy and his executors R. de Otery and W. Bonde.

Item of 38s owed from the dignity of the chancellor for the present year. Item memoranda of money assigned by R. Barat.

* List of wages of named craftsmen is not included here, see pp. 185–7.
¹ Receipts section completely torn away, total only remains.

2609 1309 [Michaelmas]–1310 [Michaelmas]

A fragment only survives, part of one membrane, apparently the final one of the account. It is defective and very badly damaged throughout the small part of it which remains, and covered on both sides with very obscuring tissue.
Endorsement: *Compotus novi operis ecclesie beati Petri Exon' de anno domini m ccc°nono intrante usque decim' exeunt'*
Printed: Extract in Oliver, p.380.

[NO HEADING]

[EXPENSES]

[Michaelmas and nearly all of Christmas term lost]

[CHRISTMAS TERM]

(m.1) [Week 12?]   Entries include: For making 4 cart-clouts 4d. .... *In
v quarteriis ... In ... gumf' et clavis empt' vjd ...*

Total £4 10s 2½d.

[Week 13?]   Entries include: Sharpening and steeling of tools 22½d. ....
And 2 labourers 20d. And 13 labourers ... And 2 carters 22d. For ...
slabs of iron bought 5s 6¼d. ... 8 trusses of hay at Newton ... 28½
quarters of lime bought 14s 3d.   Total £6 20¼d.

[Week 14?]   Entries include: Sharpening and steeling of tools 15d. ....
And 2 labourers 20d. And 17 labourers ... *barr' fenestr'* ... For making 2
buckets 4d. For binding the same with iron ...   Total £6 22½d.

[Week 15?]   In wages*. Sharpening and steeling of tools 17d. And 2
labourers 20d. And 17 labourers 12s 9d. And 2 carters 22d. 2 trusses of
broom 5d. 18 quarters of lime 9s. 650 seams of sand 13s, 2s a hundred.
Tallow for solder 1d. One lb of iron for the requirements of the Work of
the fabric 22d. For the stable hired at Newton for this term 6d. For shoeing
horses with our own iron 22d. Farriery for them 9d. 5 sacks (*saccis*) of oats
7s 2d. In wages of Master Roger the mason for this term 30s. And of
Robert of Asperton' 12s 6d.   Total £8 21d.

Cost of glass and the stalls (*Custus vitri et stallorum*) For 482 feet of glass
bought for the 2 formes of the high Work as in their length and breadth
together with 112 feet of glass for their tracery (*In iiij^c iiij^{xx}ij ped' vitri ad
ij formas summi operis ut in longitudine et latitudine earundem unacum cxij ped'
vitri ad hernesia earundem emptis*) £16 21d, 6½d a foot. 53 feet of glass for the
tracery of the third forme (*ad hernesiam iij^{cie} forme*) 28s 8½d, price as above.
For setting in (*assesend'*) the whole of the said glass 8s.

In wages of Master John de Glaston' removing the stalls (*removent' stall'*)
for 14 weeks 52s 6d, 3s 9d a week.   Total £20 10s 11½d.

Total of the totals of the cost of the second term £74 19s 5¾d.

EASTER TERM

Week 1 of the third term   In wages of 2 carters 22d. 3 cured hides bought
for cart-harness (*ad carect' hernes'*) and other requirements 21d. Cloth
(*panno*) for the same 3d. Grease 6d. Thread ¼d. For mending harness 9¾d.
11 trusses of hay bought 16s. For carrying them 10d. 5 quarters of oats
bought 8s 4d, price 20d a quarter.   Total 30s 4d.

Week 2   In wages*. Sharpening and steeling of tools 10¾d. And 2
labourers 20d. And 12 labourers 9s. And 2 carters 22d. 7½ quarters of
lime 3s 9d. 350 seams of sand 7s. 2 quarters of oats 3s.

Total £4 5s 2¾d.

Week 3   In wages*. Sharpening 7½d. And 2 labourers 20d. And 12
labourers 9s. And 2 carters 22d. 9 quarters of lime 3s 6d. 350 seams of
sand 7s. In one plasterer (*dauber'*) 18d. Withies for hurdles (*virgis ad flak'
et ad hard'*) 3½d. 3 quarters of oats 5s 6d.   Total £4 5s 1d.

Week 4   In wages*. Sharpening 8d. And 3 labourers 2s 6d. And 12 labourers 9s. And 2 carters 22d. For newly making 2 mattocks (*ligon'*) and mending other mattocks 10d. For ... 1d. 9 quarters of lime 4s 6d. 200 seams of sand 4s. 5 quarters of oats 9s 2d.   Total £4 6s 10d.

Week 5   In wages*. Sharpening 10d. And 3 labourers 2s 6d. And 10 labourers 7s 6d. And 2 carters 22d. 4 metal rings (*anulis de metallo*) for the columns 4s. For making 8 crampons 6d. 6 quarters of lime 3s. 400 seams of sand 8s. 8 marble columns bought for the chapel (*In viij columpnis marmor' emptis ad capellam*) 22s. 5 quarters of oats 9s 2d, price 22d a quarter.   Total 113s 7d.

[MIDSUMMER TERM]

(m.1d) [Rest of Easter term and 11 weeks of Midsummer term lost.]

[Week 11]   A few words only remain: ... *merem' apud Chuddel'* ...

Week 12   Entries include: ... In one labourer in the quarry 11d ... And 2 carters 22d ... 1100 laths 3s 8d, price 4d a hundred ... One horse bought 24s 9d ... *In v quarteriis* ...

Week 13   Entries include: Sharpening ... And 4 labourers there 3s ... For one barrow (*civera*) ... In 2 carters 22d. ... 2000 lath-nails 16d ... For shoeing horses with our own iron 22d. For their farriery 9d ... And to Robert de Ayspert' 12s 6d. In wages of Master John de Glaston for 11 weeks ... *et magne crucis* ... 35s 9d, ... of stalls, clock and other things (*stallorum oralog' et al*).

The cost of hay for storage (*Custus feni pro warnestura*)   For 18 stacks of hay bought in various places and at various prices £6 5s. For the same containing 148 trusses ... 9d. 8 trusses of thatching straw (*furag' ad coperam*) for the large stack made by the labourers on the cathedral Work 20d. 6 stacks of hay bought at Newton with carriage 16s 4d. Item 2 stacks of hay bought there with carriage 8s 3d.

                    Total £8 3s ... d.

The cost of glass   482 feet of glass bought for 2 formes of the high Work (*formas summi operis*) together with 53 feet of glass for the tracery (*hernesiam*) of the third forme £14 9s 9½d, 6½d for each foot. For setting in the same glass 6s and not more here because more is reckoned for glass ... as he shows in the margin of this roll.   Total £14 15s 9¾d.

The cost of lead and iron   3 fothers of lead bought at St. Botolph's fair £9 12s, price ... 64s. For weighing marking and paying custom on (*ponderant' signand' et custrumand'*) the same at the same fair and then carrying it to the water and transporting (*ad aquam ibidem portand' et cariand'*) 3s 9d. For carrying the same lead ... to Topsham 18s. For receiving the same lead from the boat (*de navi recipiend'*) and carrying it to land 17d. For carrying the same to Exeter 3s 3d. 1000 lbs of iron bought 40s, price 4s a hundred. And 600 ... lbs of [iron] ... 23s 10d, price 3s 8d a hundred.   Total £14 2s 3d.

Purchase of marble stone and Caen stone (*petre de marbre et petre de Kain*) 2 boat-loads (*naveatis*) of Caen (*Kain*) stone £12 4s. Item paid to William Canon of Corfe for marble £26 13s 4d.

Total £38 17s 4d.

Total of the cost of the fourth term £148 3s ¾d.

Total of the totals of the cost for the year £336 19s 11¼d.

And thus the expenses exceed the receipts by £70 3¼d.

Note: The bad condition of this roll makes it impossible to compile wage lists of named craftsmen. For those names which it has been possible to abstract, see p. 212.

2610 1310, 27 September–1311, 3 October

> 5 membranes, head to tail; m.1 has flaking surface and some loss of left hand margin, and is covered completely by opaque tissue; m.2 good, but both margins partly obscured by tissue; m.3 has bad surface with small holes, and is covered by opaque tissue; m.4 is good; m.5 has flaking surface with holes.
> Endorsed: *.b. Compotus novi operis ecclesie beati Petri Exon' et veteris operis de anno domini m⁰ccc⁰x⁰ intrante xj . . .*
> Printed: Extract in Oliver, pp.380–1.

(m.1) [THE ACCOUNT OF ROBERT DE] AS[PERTON] WARDEN OF THE NEW WORK AND OF THE OLD CHURCH OF THE BLESSED PETER OF EXETER FROM THE SUNDAY NEXT BEFORE THE FEAST OF ST MICHAEL 1310 TO THE SUNDAY AFTER THE FEAST OF ST MICHAEL [1311].

RECEIPTS

The same renders account of 8s 2d of rents of assize for the year as he shows in certain particulars (*per quasdam particulas*). And of £124 18s 8d received of the gift of Walter the lord bishop by the hands of dom Thomas de Harpet[re] by one tally. . . . And of . . . of the canons' prebend. And of £6 6s 4d . . . And of 64s from the dignity of the treasurer for the year. And of 60s from the dignity of the precentor for the year. And of £8 from Master J. de Upavene . . . And of £150 received from the same Master J. of the same . . . by tally. And of £7 13s 4d from dom J. parson of Powderham (*Pouderham*) from a collection in the archdeaconry of Exeter by a letter for the alms of the faithful (*de collecta in archidiacon' Totton per j litteram de elemos' fidel'*). And of £12 5s 8d from dom William vicar of Dean (*Dene*) from a collection in the archdeaconry of Totnes (*Totton'*) by a letter for the alms of the faithful as above. And of £4 3s 5d from dom Simon rector of the church of Arlington (*Alrington*) from a collection in the archdeaconry of Barnstaple by a letter for alms. And of 100s of the gift of Master Michael de Berham chancellor of the lord archbishop (*cancellar' domini arch'*) by the hand of the lord bishop. And of £16 from the church of St Erth (*Lanho*) in Cornwall assigned to the fabric. And of 10s from the testament of Master David de Molton. And of 13s 4d from the sale of a

silver cup (*j cipho arg'*) of his gift ... And of 2s from the testament of
Thomas late rector of the church of Bratton. And of 22s from the sale of 2
old horses. And of 13s 4d from free-stone (*franchea petra*) old glass and a
certain old set of traces (*trahic'*) sold by the lord treasurer. And of 16s from
stone and old timber sold [to/by?] the precentor (*vend' precentor'*). And of
26s from Whitsuntide offerings in the nave of the church. And of 7s 3d
from offerings on 1 August (*ad gulam Augusti*). And of 12s 6d from the red
chest (*de rubea arka*). And of 6s 10d from offerings at the feet of old Peter
(*ad pedes veteris Petri*).

Total of the whole receipts £385 9s 10d.

EXPENSES

(m.2) COST OF MICHAELMAS TERM

Surplus (*Superplus'*)[1] The same reckons in surplus of the preceding
account £70 4¼d.

Week 1   In wages*. Sharpening and steeling of tools 14½d. In one
labourer in the quarry 11d. In 2 labourers there 20d. In 4 labourers there
3s. And 5 labourers on the Work 4s 2d, 10d each. And 2 carters 22d. And
2 sawyers for 5 days 2s 3½d, 5½d each. 11 boards of poplar (*pupiller*) for
making centerings (*cintern'*) 16d. 200 board-nails bought 7d. 2000 lath-
nails bought 16d. For 2 quintains of iron for manufacturing bars for the
windows of the new chapel (*ad barras fenest' nove capelle fabricand'*) 7s. For
making 8 cart-clouts with nails 8d. For carrying 25 loads of Caen stones
(*xxv chargiis petrarum de Kain*) from Topsham 25s. For carrying 7 cart-loads
of marble (*vij chargiis de marbre*) from Topsham 6s 8d. Wages of J. Cuyl-
labole[2] carrying stones from the quarry with his cart for 4 trips (*per iiij
vices*) 12s. In 2 labourers at Topsham helping to load stones (*iuvant' ad
chargiend' petras*) for the week 2s. For covering the new masons' lodge with
stones at task (*In nova loggea cementar' cum petris ad tascam coperiend'*) 6s 8d.
4½ quarters of oats 6s, price 16d a quarter.   Total £7 4s 9d.

Week 2   In wages*. Sharpening and steeling of tools 15½d. In one
labourer in the quarry 11d. In 2 labourers there 20d. In 4 labourers there
3s. And 2 sawyers 2s 9d. And 6 labourers 5s. And one labourer 9d. And 2
carters 22d. For one quintain of iron for manufacturing window-bars 3s
6d. For making 500 board-nails 8d. For making 150 large nails (*major'
clav'*) 4d. For manufacturing 30 hooks (*gumphis*) with as many hinges
(*vertivellis*) and 14 staples (*stapellis*) for the new lodge (*loggiam*) 3s. 100
loads of stones from Barley 4s. In one man and his cart carrying stones
from the quarry for 6 trips 18s. 2½ quarters of oats 3s 4d, price 16d a
quarter.   Total 110s 5½d.

Week 3   In wages*. Sharpening and steeling of tools 13d. In one labourer
in the quarry 11d. In 2 labourers there 20d. In 4 labourers there 3s. In 6
labourers on the Work 5s. In one labourer for 3 days 5d. In 2 carters 22d.
500 lath-nails bought 7½d. 2 quintains of iron for manufacturing window-
bars 7s. Withies (*virgis ad hardas*) bought 3d. In one carpenter felling 2
oak-trees (*prosternent' ij quercos*) at Newton 6d. 5½ quarters of oats 7s 4½d,
price 16d a quarter and ½d more in the total.   Total £4 6s 1d.

Week 4 In wages*. Sharpening and steeling of tools 12½d. In one labourer in the quarry 11d. In 2 labourers there 20d. In 4 labourers there 3s. And 4 labourers 3s 4d. And 3 labourers 2s 3d. And 2 carters 22d. 26½ quarters of lime 13s 3d, price 6d a quarter. One load of stones from Barley 2s 3d. For 2 trusses of straw for roofing 5½d. For 2 bundles of twists (*fessis plicarum*) 3d. 13 boards bought to serve for requirements (*serviendis ad necessaria*) 2s. 2 quintains of iron for manufacturing bars 7s. For carrying 2 cart-loads . . . from Norton . . .   Total £4 19s 6d.

Week 5 In wages*. Sharpening 12d. In one labourer in the quarry 11d. In 2 labourers there 20d. In 4 labourers there 3s. And one carpenter at Norton 2s. And the other carpenter there 21d. And the third there 18d. And 2 sawyers for 3 days 19d. And 8 labourers on the Work 6s 8d. And 2 labourers 18d. And 2 carters 22d. For one quintain of iron for manufacturing bars 3s 6d. For making 8 cart-clouts 8d. For mending springs (*sprang'*) and locks 3d. 100 loads of stones from Barley 4s 6d. 4½ quarters of lime 2s 3d. For 'wippecord' 2½d. 7 quarters of oats 11s 1½d, price 19d a quarter and ½d more in the total.   Total 102s 2d.

Week 6: and the time changes In wages*. Sharpening 11¾d. In one labourer in the quarry 10d. In 2 labourers there 18d. In 4 labourers there 2s 8d. In 2 carters 22d. And 7 labourers 5s 3d, 9d each. And 4 labourers 2s 8d. 2 quintains of iron for manufacturing window-bars 3s 6d. For manufacturing 4 cart-clouts with 2 linches (*linch'*) 5d. 50 alders bought from Walter de Breynton 8s. For carrying one boat-load (*naveata*) of Corfe stones from Topsham to Exeter 6s 8d. In one labourer helping to load carts (*iuvant' ad cariand' carect'*) at Topsham 9d. For making 13 hooks 3d.   Total £4 4s 2½d.

Week 7 In wages*. Sharpening 10¾d. In one labourer in the quarry 10d. In 2 labourers 18d. In 4 labourers there 2s 8d. And 5 labourers 3s 9d. And 4 labourers 2s 8d. And 2 carters 22d. For one sack (*sacco*) 10½d. For manufacturing 2 quintains of iron 7s. 100 loads of stones from Barley 4s 6d. 4 trusses of straw (*furag'*) 9d. 8 quarters of oats 12s 8d, price 19d a quarter.   Total £4 9s.

(m.3) Week 8 In wages*. Sharpening and steeling of tools 13½d. In one labourer in the quarry 10d. In 2 labourers there 18d. In 4 labourers there 2s 8d. And 5 labourers 3s 9d. And 4 labourers 2s 8d. And 2 carters 22d. 4 trusses of roofing straw 11¼d. 3 bundles of twists 3d. 50 loads of stones from Barley 2s 3d. 4 cart-axles of ash (*de freno*) bought 12d. For making 2 iron pieces for requirements (*ferris ad necess'*) 4½d.   Total . . . s 3d.

Week 9 In wages*. Sharpening and steeling of tools 11½d. In one labourer in the quarry 10d. In 2 labourers there 18d. In 4 labourers there 2s 8d. And 5 labourers on the Work 3s 9d. And 4 labourers 2s 8d. And 2 carters 22d. And for 4 trusses of straw (*straminis*) 13½d. 4 bundles of twists 4½d. Pitch for cement . . . 8d. 2½ quarters of oats 3s 10½d, price 19d a quarter.   Total 69s 4¾d.

Week 10 In wages*. Sharpening 16½d. In wages of one labourer in the quarry 10d. And 2 labourers there 18d. And 4 labourers there 2s 8d. In 5 labourers on the Work 3s 9d. In 6 labourers there . . . s. In 2 carters 22d. In one glazier mending breaks in the windows (*In j. vitrear' emendant' breckas fenest'*) for 3 weeks 4s. 1500 lath-nails bought 12½d. For repairing tools at the quarry 7½d. For curing the hide of one horse [dead] on account of the murrain (*In coreo j equi proven' de morina couriando*) 10d. 6 seams of red sand 6d. For carrying one boat-load of stones from Topsham to Exeter 6s 8d. For carrying 2 cart-loads of timber from Norton 4s. One sieve 1¼d. Tallow for lead 1d. For manufacturing 4 cart-clouts and 2 wheel-clamps (*gropis*) 4½d. Total £4 19d.

Week 11   In wages*. Sharpening and steeling of tools 13¾d. In one labourer in the quarry 10d. In 2 labourers there 18d. In 4 labourers there 2s 8d. In 5 labourers 3s 9d. In 6 labourers 4s. And 2 carters 22d. For making 2 cart-clouts 6d. 42 lbs of tallow for candles in the stables and other requirements 2s 5d. 10 lbs of tin bought for solder 2s 2d. For carrying 3 barge-loads of stones from the quarry to Topsham 22s 6d, 7s 6d each barge-load. For carrying a fourth barge-load thence to Topsham 4s 6d. 6½ quarters of oats 10s 10d, price 20d a quarter. 2 trusses of straw 5d.

Total 105s 6d.

Week 12   In wages*. Sharpening 16½d. In one labourer in the quarry 10d. In 2 labourers there 18d. In 4 labourers there 2s 8d. And 5 labourers 3s 9d. And 6 labourers 4s. And 2 carters 22d. In wages of one man with his draught beast and dray hauling 4 barge-loads of stones (*In stipend' j hom' cum affro suo et dragea tractant' iiij bargeat' petrarum*) from the quarry to the sea at task 2s 4d. For carrying 4 cart-loads of timber from Norton 8s. 8 loads of firewood (*buste*) bought for founding lead 2s. 1200 horse-nails bought 12d. For mending buckets 1¾d. Moss bought for lead (*ad plumbi*) 4d. Total 76s 5½d.

Week 13   In wages*. Sharpening 6¾d. In 6 labourers 2s 4d, 4½d each. In 6 labourers 2s. In 2 carters 22d. 100 quarters of lime 35s 8d, price 4¼d a quarter and 3d more in the total. 6 seams of glass bought 72s 2½d. For cutting 17 floor-boards at Chudleigh at task (*In xvij bordis ad planchuram apud Chuddelegh ad tascam secand'*) 4s. For carrying 2 barge-loads of stones from the quarry to Topsham 16s. One boat-load of Caen stones bought (*In j naveata petrarum de Kain empt'*) 106s 8d. In wages of Master Thomas the plumber with his boy covering over the chapel of St Paul's tower (*super capellam turris sancti Pauli*) and founding lead for the same work for 3 weeks 15s. 4½ quarters of oats 7s 7d, price 20d a quarter, and 1d more in the total. For the stable hired at Newton for this term 6d. Farriery for the horses 9d. For shoeing horses with our own iron for this term 22½d. For the fee of Master W. the mason for this term 33s 4d. And of Robert de Asperton 12s 6d. Total £16 7s 3½d.

Total of the totals of the whole cost of the first term £72 5s 4¾d.

Total of the surplus (*superplus'*) £70 4¼d.

CHRISTMAS TERM

Week 1   In wages of 2 carters 22d. Total 22d.

Week 2   In wages*. 2½ quarters of oats 4s 2d. Total 7s 8½d.

Week 3   In wages*. Sharpening 7¾d. In one labourer in the quarry 10d. In 2 labourers there 18d. In 4 labourers there 2s 8d. In one pavior (*paveour*) with his boy paving in the quire (*pavient' in choro*) 3s. In 3 labourers on the Work 2s 3d. In 7 labourers there 4s 8d, 8d each. In 2 carters 22d.

For making one lock with 5 keys to the postern door into the treasurer's court (*In j serura cum v clav' ad ostium posterne versus curiam thesaurar'*) 20d. For making 600 horse-nails and 100 board-nails 6d. 2 bundles of twists 1½d. 14 boards bought for moulds (*ad moldas*) 14d. 4½ quarters of oats 7s.

Total 60s 9d.

Week 4   In wages*. Sharpening 8¾d. In one labourer in the quarry 10d. In 2 labourers there 18d. In 4 labourers there 2s 8d. And one pavior with his boy 3s. And 5 labourers 3s 9d. And 8 labourers 5s 4d. And 2 carters 22d. For making 4000 board-nails 4d. 2 lbs of wax for cement 15d. Twists 1¾d. For mending 2 saws (*serr'*) 2½d. 3½ quarters of oats 5s 10d, price 20d a quarter.   Total 66s 6d.

Week 5   In wages*. Sharpening and steeling of tools 12½d. In one labourer in the quarry 10d. In 2 labourers there 18d. In 4 labourers there 2s 8d. In 6 labourers on the Work 4s 6d. In 5 labourers there 3s 9d. In 2 carters 22d. For making 700 board-nails and horse-nails 7d. In one pavior with his boy 3s. 2 trusses of straw 7d. Twists 1¼d. In wages of one roofer with his boy roofing over the houses of Kalendarhay (*Kalendereheye*) for the week 2s 1d. 7 quarters of oats 11s 8d, price 20d a quarter.

Total 70s 7d.

Week 6   In wages*. Sharpening and steeling of tools 2s 5½d. In one labourer in the quarry 10d. In 2 labourers there 18d. In 4 labourers there 2s 8d. In one pavior and his boy 3s. In 6 labourers on the Work 4s 6d. In 5 labourers 3s 4d. In 2 carters 22d.   Total 58s 10½d.

Week 7   In wages*. Sharpening 15d. In one labourer in the quarry 10d. In 2 labourers there 18d. In 4 labourers there 2s 8d. In 6 labourers on the Work 4s 6d. In 5 labourers there 3s 4d. In 2 carters 22d. In wages of one man with his boy roofing over the house (*domum*) in Kalendarhay (*de Kalendereheye*) for 6 days 2s 6d. For making 1200 board-nails and horse-nails 12d. For one *truss'* . . . 3d. Withies and twists (*virg' et plicis*) 4½d. For manufacturing 16 cart-plates 8d. One key to the door into the treasury court (*clav' ad hostium versus curiam thesaur'*) 3d. For pitch 4d. 5 quarters of oats 8s 8d, price for one quarter 20d and the rest of the others 21d.

Total 68s 6d.

(m.4) Week 8   In wages*. Sharpening and steeling of tools 9½d. In one labourer in the quarry 10d. In 2 labourers there 18d. In 4 labourers there 2s 8d. In 4 labourers on the Work 3s 1d. 5 labourers 3s 4d. In 2 carters 22d. In one roofer working over the lodges (*super loggeas*) for 6 days with his boy 2s 6d. Withies for hurdles 1d. For manufacturing (*fabricand'*) 2 hooks 4 springs 3d. 6 pairs of traces (*trahicum*) bought 5s. 4 quarters of oats 7s 6d, 20d a quarter. One quarter of oats 18d.

Total 59s 4d.

Week 9: 2 feasts   In wages*. Sharpening 9¾d. In one labourer in the quarry 10d. In 2 labourers there 18d. In 4 labourers there 2s 8d. In 4 labourers on the Work 2s 6d. In 5 labourers 2s 9¾d, [   ][3] each. In 2 carters 22d. 2 quarters of oats 2s 8d.   Total 48s 8d.

Week 10   In wages*. Sharpening 15½d. In one labourer in the quarry 10d. In 2 labourers there 18d. In 4 labourers there 2s 8d. In 8 labourers 6s 8d. In 7 labourers 4s 8d. In 2 carters 22d. For lengthening joining up and steeling 3 mattocks (*In iij ligon' elong' adiacend'*[4] *et acerand'*) 6d. For making

4 cart-clouts with nails 4d. For carrying 2 barge-loads of stones from Sal-combe to Topsham 15s 4d. 2 cart-wheels bought at Taunton with car-riage 6s. 5 quarters of oats bought at various prices 8s 11½d.

Total £4 16s 6d.

Week 11   In wages*. Sharpening and steeling of tools 14½d. In one labourer in the quarry 10d. In 2 labourers there 18d. In 4 labourers 2s 8d. In 5 labourers on the Work 3s 9d. In 7 labourers 4s 8d. And 2 carters 22d. In one painter priming the bosses of the chapels (*deprimand' claves capellarum*) 3s. For one gallon of oil (*lagena olei*) 2s. For equipping the axles of the large crane and pulley with our own iron (*In axibus magne verne et poleis proprio ferro et armand'*) 12d. 4 quarters of oats 6s 10d.

Total 77s 3½d.

Week 12   In wages*. Sharpening 14d. In one labourer in the quarry 11d. In 2 labourers there 20d. In 4 labourers there 3s. In 4 labourers on the Work 3s 4d. In 8 labourers 6s. In 2 carters 22d. Pitch for cement 14d. For carrying 2 barge-loads of stones from the quarry to Topsham 15s 4d.

Total £4 11s 8d.

Week 13   In wages*. Sharpening and steeling of tools 16½d. In one labourer in the quarry 11d. In 2 labourers there 20d. In 4 labourers there 3s. In 5 labourers 4s 2d. In 8 labourers 6s. In 2 carters 21d. For carrying one barge-load of stones from the quarry to Topsham 7s 8d.

Total 66s 4½d.

Week 14   In wages*. Sharpening 14d. In one labourer in the quarry 11d. In one labourer there 20d. In 4 labourers there 3s. In 5 labourers on the Work 4s 2d. In 8 labourers there 6s. In 2 carters 22d. 2 sieves 3d. For binding and strengthening of tubs and buckets 3d. 8 lbs of tin (*stagminis*) bought for solder 18d. For tallow for the same 1d. For removing stones from the quarry to the sea with the help (*cum auxilio*) of labourers 2s 8d. For carrying one barge-load of stones from the quarry to Topsham 7s 8d.

Total 75s 6d.

Week 15   In wages*. Sharpening 13½d. In one labourer in the quarry 11d. In 2 labourers there 20d. In 4 labourers there 3s. In 5 labourers 4s 2d. In 7 labourers 5s 3d. In 2 carters 22d. 6 lbs of cart-grease 9d. For the stable hired at Newton for this term 6d. Farriery for the horses 9d. For shoeing the same with our own iron 2s 1d. 10 quarters of oats 23s 4d, price 2s 4d a quarter. For the fee of Master William the mason for this term 33s 4d. And of Robert de Aysperton 12s 6d.

Total £6 17s ½d.

Purchase of iron with the cost of the same   For 3 quinterns of iron bought from John Sleghe 15s. For working the same iron for window-bars of the new chapels (*ad barras fenestrarum novarum capellarum*) and for iron work of the glass of 2 high windows (*ferramenta vitri duarum summarum fenestrarum*) 10s 6d, 3s 6d a quintain. Item for 2 quintains of iron for manufacturing bars (*ad barr' fabric'*) 7s. . . . [quin]tain of our own iron for manufacturing the same 10½d. Pitch (*pice*) 9d. 468 lbs of iron bought at Topsham with carriage 17s 8d.   Total 51s 9½d.

The cost of glass   For 615 feet of finished glass (*vitri perfecti*)[5] bought for the 2 high formes of the new Work (*ad duas summas formas novi operis*)

£16 13s 1½d, 6½d a foot. In wages of Master Walter the glazier (*le verrator*) with his two boys setting (*assedent'*) the said glass for 2 weeks 6s.

Total £16 19s 1½d.

Total of the totals of the whole cost of the second term £69 8s ¾d.

EASTER TERM

Week 1   In wages of 2 carters 22d. 3 cured hides bought for cart-harness 14d. 17 lb of grease bought 2s 1½d, price 1½d a lb. For 'burl' 10½d. In one man mending harness for 4 days 12d. For strengthening 'strakis' of carts 6d. 4 quarters of oats 8s 8d, price 2s 2d a quarter.   Total 16s 2d.

Week 2   In wages*. Sharpening 11¾d. In one labourer in the quarry 11d. In 2 labourers there 20d. In 5 labourers there 3s 9d. And 7 labourers 5s 10d. And 10 labourers 7s 6d, 9d each. And 2 carters 22d. 5½ quarters of oats 12s 10d, price 2s 4d a quarter.   Total 79s ¾d.

(m.5) Week 3   In wages*. Sharpening and steeling of tools 16½d. In one labourer in the quarry 11d. In 2 labourers there 20d. In 5 labourers there 3s 9d. In 7 labourers working on the Work (*In vij operar' in operar' in opere*) 5s 10d. In 9 labourers 6s 9d, 9d each. In 2 carters 22d. For carrying boards from Chudleigh 9d. For . . . withies for hurdles 1½d. One iron crow (*crowa ferrea* . . .) bought 2s 6d. For making 5 hooks and repairing and steeling 2 mattocks with work on 5 wheel-plates (*ij ligon' emendend' et acerand' cum opere v clippis*) . . . 8½d. For carrying one cart-load of timber from Norton . . . 120 large Caen stones (*petr' de Kain*) bought 28s 6d. For carrying the same from Topsham with the aid of our own cart (*cum auxilio proprie carecte*) 2s. 22 trusses of hay bought at Sidbury (*Sidebiri*) 13s 4d. For carrying the same to Newton (*La Nyweton*) 2s 9d, 1½d a truss. Paid to a certain (*cuidam*) Master William de Schoverwille mason coming from Salisbury to visit the new Work (*de Sar' venient' ad visitandum novum opus*) 20s by order of the treasurer (*precepto thesaurarii*).

Total £7 4s 4d.

Week 4: 2 feasts   In wages*. Sharpening and steeling of tools 13¼d. In one labourer in the quarry 10d. In 2 labourers there 18d. In 5 labourers there 3s 4d. And 6 labourers 4s 6d, 9d each. And 9 labourers 6s 8d each. In 2 carters 22d. 2 ropes of 36 fathoms (*teys*) bought 4s. In wages of a smith repairing a sledge[6] (*draggeam*) and lengthening an iron crow (*elongant' crowam ferream*) 8d. 2 shafts (*lomon'*) for carts bought 3d. One hand-barrow (*civera portativa*) bought 1d. One cart-horse bought 40s 1d.

Total 102s 10d.

Week 5   In wages*. Sharpening and steeling of tools 18d. In one labourer in the quarry 11d. In 2 labourers there 20d. In 5 labourers there 3s 9d. In 8 labourers 6s 8d. In 7 labourers 5s 3d, 9d each. In 2 carters 22d. For making 7 wedges (*weggis*) 7d. For making 26 iron crampons (*pegon' ferreis*) for bosses (*ad claves*) 6d. For making 26 horse-shoes with nails 6d. For making one new mattock 5d. For making 4 cart-clouts with nails 4s. For making 6 wheel-plates (*clippis*) with 12 dowels 8d, and strengthening a cart with them. 7½ quarters of oats 17s 6d, price 2s 4d a quarter.

Total £4 5s 1½d.

Week 6   In wages*. Sharpening and steeling of tools 16d. In one labourer
in the quarry 11d. In 2 labourers there 20d. In 5 labourers there 3s 9d.
In 8 labourers on the Work 6s 8d. In 8 labourers there 6s. In 2 carters 22d.
For working 2 quintains of iron for one pair of wheel-tires with clamps,
dowels, bands, nails and other requirements for new cart-wheels, with the
making of one mattock and steel bought for the same, and binding and
fastening the said wheels[7] (*In ij quinter' ferri fabricand' ad j par ligam' cum
gropis doel' bendis clavis et aliis necessariis ad novas rotas carecte cum factura j
ligonis et acere ad idem empt' et lig' inde et affirmant' dictas rotas*) 8s 10d. 8 lbs of
tin bought for solder 13½d. Tallow for the same 1½d. For carrying hurdles
(*flakis*) from Huxham (*Hokesham*) 9d. One iron hammer (*ham'*) for making
lead pipes 8d. One cart-axle bought 6d. For putting it on a cart and
strengthening it 4d. 3 quarters of oats 7s, price 2s 4d a quarter.
                                                      Total £4 8s 1d.

Week 7   In wages*. Sharpening and steeling of tools 14½d. In one
labourer in the quarry 11d. In 2 labourers there 20d. In 5 labourers there
3s 9d. In 8 labourers on the Work 6s 8d. In 9 labourers there 6s 9d. In 2
carters 22d. One barge-load of stones carried from the quarry to Topsham
7s 8d. 18 lbs of tallow bought for requirements 2s 3d. For making 600 lead-
nails 6d. 10 lbs of tin for solder 20d. 5 quarters of oats 12s 6d, 2s 6d a
quarter.   Total £4 13s 11½d.

Week 8: the feast of Pentecost   In wages of 2 carters 22d. 200 horse-
shoes with nails bought at Lopen fair 14s. 1000 horse-nails bought there
17d. 16 lbs of steel bought there 10d. 3 lbs of tin bought for solder 6d.
For expenses of one boy and one horse carrying the said iron work from
the said fair 16d. For 8 labourers carrying ashes of lead for washing
(*portand' cineres plumbi ad lavand'*) for 2 days 2s, 1½d a day each.
                                                      Total 21s 11d.

Week 9   In wages*. Sharpening and steeling of tools 16½d. In wages of
one labourer in the quarry 11d. And 2 labourers there 20d. And 5 labourers
there 3s 9d. In 6 labourers on the Work 5s. In 9 labourers there 6s 9d. In
2 carters 22d. For mending one scraper (*strigulo*) 1d. For repairing and
widening (*elargiendis*) the roads near Wonford on account of (*causa*) the
carts 2d. In one carpenter for one day 4½d. 10 quarters 5 bushels of oats
28s 4d, price 2s 8d a quarter.   Total 102s 10d.

Week 10   In wages*. Sharpening 16½d. In one labourer in the quarry
11d. In 2 labourers there 20d. In 5 labourers 3s 9d. In 6 labourers on the
Work 5s. In 10 labourers there 7s 6d. In 2 carters 22d. For making 5
clouts and 11 wheel-plates for the carts 10½d. For 2 rafts? hired for founding lead from lead ashes (*In ij flotis*[8] *locatis ad plumbum de ciner' plumbi
fund'*) 2s. 10 lbs of tin bought for solder 10d. For grease for the said rafts 4d.
For a certain boat (*In quadam navi*) with stones from Corfe discharging
(*discarkiand'*) at Topsham 3s 5d.   Total £4 11d.

Week 11   In wages*. Sharpening 14½d. In one labourer in the quarry
11d. In 2 labourers there 20d. In 5 labourers there 3s 9d. In 6 labourers
on the Work 5s. In 10 labourers there 7s 6d. In 2 carters 22d. One tub
bought and binding another 8d. 2 small tubs bought 4d. For steeling tools
at the quarry 9d. For carrying one boat-load of stones (*batello petrarum*)
from the quarry to the sea 2s. In one plasterer (*daubour*) with his boy 4s 4d.

100 quarters of lime bought with carriage 50s. For the stable hired at Newton for this term 7½d. For shoeing horses with our own iron 14d. Farriery of the horses 9d. 3 quarters of oats 6s 8d, price 26½d a quarter and a ½d less in the total. For the fee of Master William the mason for this term 33s 4d. And of Robert de Aysperton 12s 6d.

Total £9 2s 1d.

Total of the totals of the whole cost of the third term £49 17s 4¾d.

(m.4d) MIDSUMMER TERM

Week 1   In wages*. Sharpening and steeling of tools 14½d. And one labourer in the quarry 11d. And 2 labourers there 20d. And 5 labourers there 3s 9d. And 6 labourers on the Work 5s. And 10 labourers there 7s 6d, 9d each. And 2 carters 22d. One pair of cart-shafts (*limon' ad carect'*) bought 22d. 7 quarters of oats 14s 7d.   Total £4 19s 7½d.

Week 2   In wages*. Sharpening and steeling of tools 13d. In one labourer in the quarry 11d. In 2 labourers there 20d. In 5 labourers there 3s 9d. In 6 labourers on the Work 5s. In 6 labourers there 4s 6d. In 2 carters 22d. For making 4 cart-clouts 4d. In wages of one plasterer for one day 5d. 2 quarters of oats 4s.   Total 70s 6d.

Week 3   In wages*. Sharpening and steeling of tools 18½d. In one labourer in the quarry 11d. In 2 labourers there 20d. In 5 labourers there 3s 9d. In 6 labourers on the Work 5s. In 8 labourers there 6s. In 2 carters 22d. For steeling 3 mattocks and making 3 hooks 6d. For making 8 wheel-plates and 2 linches (*linthis*) 5d. 400 lead-nails bought 8d. 300 tack-nails bought 4d. 6 metal rings (*annilis de metallo*) bought from John le Hornere for marble columns (*ad columpnas marmoreas*) 12s. 4 quarters of oats 8s 4d.

Total £4 8s 10d.

Week 4   In wages*. Sharpening 13½d. In one labourer in the quarry 11d. In 2 labourers there 20d. In 5 labourers there 3s 9d. In 6 labourers on the Work 5s. In 8 labourers there 6s. In 2 carters 22d. For making 100 lead-nails 1d. For making 100 'spikis' 2d. For carrying 100 large stones from the quarry to the sea 2s. In 2 sawyers (*secator'*) 2s 6d.

Total 72s 2½d.

Week 5   In wages*. Sharpening and steeling of tools 18½d. In one labourer in the quarry 11d. In 2 labourers there 20d. In 5 labourers there 3s 9d. In 7 labourers on the Work 5s 10d. In 3 labourers there 2s 3d. In 2 carters 22d. In 2 sawyers 2s 9d. For carrying one barge-load of stones from the quarry to Topsham 7s 6d. For making 200 lead-nails 2d. For tallow for solder 2d. 4 quarters of oats 8s 2d.   Total £4 13s ½d.

Week 6   In wages*. Sharpening and steeling of tools 11½d. In one labourer in the quarry 11d. In 2 labourers there 20d. In 5 labourers there 3s 9d. In 10 labourers on the Work 8s 4d. In 2 labourers there 18d. In 2 carters 22d. 2 lbs of steel bought 14d. 500 lead-nails bought 11d. 18 lbs of tallow bought for requirements 2s 1d. For moss 4d. For putting an axle on a cart 2d. 5 quarters of oats 12s 6d, price 2s 6d a quarter.

Total 79s ½d.

Week 7   In wages*. Sharpening and steeling of tools 10½d. For 2 labourers in the quarry 22d. In 2 labourers there 20d. In 4 labourers there 3s. In

8 labourers on the Work 6s 8d. In 2 labourers there 18d. In 2 carters 22d. One cart-axle bought 6d. For mending one tub and 2 buckets 3d. For putting an axle on a cart and strengthening it 4d. For red sand for founding over lead (*In rubea arena ad plumbum suprafundend'*) 2s. Tallow for solder 1d. 3 quarters of oats 6s.   Total 67s 7½d.

Week 8   In wages*. Sharpening and steeling of tools 16½d. In wages of 2 labourers in the quarry 22d. And 2 labourers there 20d. And 4 labourers there 3s. For 8 labourers on the Work 6s 8d. In 4 labourers there 3s. In 2 carters 22d. For carrying one cart-load (*carectata*) of stones from the quarry to Exeter 3s 6d. 2 quarters of oats 3s.   Total 67s 1½d.

Week 9   In wages*. Sharpening and steeling of tools 17d. In 2 labourers in the quarry 22d. In 2 labourers there 20d. In 4 labourers there 3s. In 8 labourers on the Work 6s 8d. In 2 labourers there 18d. In 2 carters 22d. For making 8 hooks 8d. For carrying 6 cart-loads (*charg'*) of Corfe stones from Topsham to Exeter 5s, 10d each. In one plasterer (*dealbatore*) 2s. 4 quarters of oats 8s.   Total £4 5s 10½d.

Week 10   In wages*. Sharpening and steeling of tools 11½d. In 2 labourers in the quarry 22d. And 2 labourers there 20d. And 4 labourers there 3s. In 9 labourers on the Work 7s 6d. And 3 labourers there 2s 3d. In 2 carters 22d. 50 loads of stones from Barley 2s. For carrying 2 barge-loads of stones from the quarry to Topsham 12s. One cart (*carro*) hired for carrying Corfe stones from Topsham to Exeter for 13 trips (*per xiij vices*) 9s 9d, for each turn (*pro quolibet turno*) 9d. 3 quarters of oats 3s 8d.

                    Total £4 17s 5½d.

(m.5d) Week 11   In wages*. Sharpening 14¼d. In 2 labourers in the quarry 22d. In 2 labourers there 20d. In 4 labourers there 3s. In 8 labourers on the Work 6s 8d. In 3 labourers 2s 3d. In 2 carters 22d. In one roofer with his boy roofing over various houses for 5 days 2s 1d. 9 quarters of lime 4s 6d. For carrying one barge-load of stones by sea from the quarry to Topsham 6s. 14 lbs of lard (*pingued' porc'*) bought for requirements 2s 2d. For making 6 iron hooks 6d. For carrying 3 cart-loads (*carrat'*) of marble (*marbr'*) from Topsham 2s 3d. One quarter of oats 12d. 50 alders for requirements bought from Walter de Breyngton 8s.

                    Total £4 18s 5¼d.

Week 12   In wages*. Sharpening 16d. And 2 labourers in the quarry 22d. And 2 labourers there 20d. And 4 labourers there 3s. And 8 labourers on the Work 6s 8d. And 2 labourers there 18d. And 2 carters 22d. For 100 laths bought 4d. For making 52 iron springs (*sprangis ferri*) 3d. 8 quarters of oats 9s 8d.   Total 78s 7d.

Week 13   In wages*. Sharpening 16¾d. In 2 labourers in the quarry 22d. In 2 labourers there 20d. In 4 labourers there 3s. In 8 labourers on the Work 6s 8d. In 4 labourers there 3s. In 2 carters 22d. In one roofer over the cloister (*super claustrum*) with his boy for 4 days 20d. In one labourer for the same for the same time 6d. For manufacturing 2 cart-clouts with 2 axle-plates (*hurter'*) 4d. 125 quarters of lime bought with carriage 62s 6d, 6d a quarter. One cart-horse bought 31s 1d. 4 quarters of oats 4s 1d.

                    Total £8 9s 3¾d.

Week 14   In wages*. Sharpening and steeling of tools 13¾d. In 2 labourers in the quarry 22d. In 2 labourers there 20d. In 4 labourers there 3s. In 6

labourers on the Work 5s. In 3 labourers there 2s 3d. In 2 carters 22d. For
3½ quintains of iron for manufacturing window-bars 15s 9d, 4s 6d a quintain (*pro quintero*). 2 ropes 34 fathoms (*tesiarum*) in length bought 3s 6d. A
hide bought for harness (*ad hernes*) 4d. For mending harness 3d. For manufacturing 36 springs (*sprangis*) for moulds (*ad moldas*) and one lynch (*linthe*)
5d. For 3 keys (*clavis*) bought with the repair of one lock 4d. 50 loads of
stones bought from Barley 2s. 5 pairs of traces bought 2s 2¼d. 7000 roofing
stones (*petrarum ad coperiend'*) bought 9s 7½d, price 16½d a thousand. For
the stable hired at Newton 7½d. Farriery for the horses 9d. For shoeing
them 18d. 6 loads of alders carried from Brenton (*Breyngtone*) 10d. In
wages of Master William the mason 33s 4d. And of Robert de Asperton'
12s 6d. For the rent of the house of the master of the Work for the year
32s. In wages of the collector of rents (*collect' redd'*) 12d.

Total £9 3s 5d.

Cost of Corfe marble (*Custus petre marmor' de Corf'*)   For payment made to
William Canoun for marble stone of Corfe for columns (*In solucione fact'
Will' Canoun pro petra marmor' de Corf' ad columpnas*) £35 2s 8d. And not
more this year because the same William received £26 13s 4d in the previous year.   Total £35 2s 8d.

Purchase of hay with the cost of the same   For 214 trusses of hay bought
£6 12s 5d at various prices. For carrying the same from various places
25s 6½d. For making one large stack from them 3s 10d. 12 trusses of
thatching straw (*furag' ad coperturam*) bought 2s 6d. Twists bought for the
same 6d. 4 stacks of hay bought at Newton with carriage 18s 6d. 9 trusses
of old (*veteris*) hay bought at Sidbury 5s 6d. For carrying the same to
Newton 13½d. For distributing the same by gift (*In eodem in dono allocando*)
6d.   Total £9 10s 5d.

Purchase of iron and lead   17 quintains of iron bought 76s 6d, 4s 6d a
quintain. For carrying the same from Topsham 10d. 2 fothers (*fotheres*)
of lead bought at St Botolph's fair (*in nundinis sancti Botulfi*) £6 8s. For
weighing and marking (*ponderand' signand'*) the same lead at the same
fair and carrying it to the water 2s 8d. For carrying the same by sea to
Topsham 12s 6d. For unloading (*deponend'*) the same from the boat and
carrying it to land 16d. For carrying the same to Exeter 2s 6d.

Total £11 4s 4d.

Total of the whole cost of the fourth term £122 6s 7d.

Total of the totals of the whole cost for the year with £70 4¼d of
surpluses of the preceding account £383 17s 8½d.

And thus he owes 22s 1½d.

---

* List of named craftsmen is not included here, see pp. 187–91.
1 *Superplus'* set against receipts is a surplus of debt from the previous year's account, and
  so in fact a deficit and not a surplus.
2 Alternative reading *Cnyllabolle*.
3 MS leaves blank.
4 The meaning of *adiacend'* is uncertain in this context.
5 This is the only occurrence of *vitri perfecti*, perhaps meaning that the glass was bought
  ready-made to fit the tracery?
6 The meaning is uncertain, perhaps a dray?
7 Two separate entries seem to have been run together here.
8 The meaning of *flotis* is uncertain.

Editor's note: A special effort was made in 1310 to raise funds through the diocese for the cathedral building. Bishop Stapeldon by a statute *ad subveniendum fabricam ecclesie Exon'* ordered a clerical subsidy of 6d in the mark for resident clergy and 12d in the mark for non-resident clergy to be levied for three years; the dean and chapter were exempted because they were already donating a share of their dignities and prebends every year. In the same year, religious houses offered participation in their divine celebrations to all persons assisting the fabric of the cathedral; documents issued by nine of these monasteries all dated 31 July 1310 offering this benefit in exactly similar terms survive among the Chapter archives (D. & C. MSS 3625 fo.s 29–30; and 2139–2144).

2611   1312, 29 September–1313, 29 September

> 4 membranes, originally head to tail, but now separate, as the weight of their paper repair has retorn the repaired sewing; m.1 is in fair condition, backed with paper; m.2 is very bad, large holes over all the surface, covered completely by obscuring tissue; m.3, badly flaking surface and numerous holes, covered completely by tissue; m.4 has a badly flaking surface, backed with paper.
> Endorsed: *D. Compotus novi operis beati Petri de anno domini m⁰ccc⁰xij⁰ intrante xiij⁰.*
> (Repeated on tail of the roll).
> Printed: Extract in Oliver, p.381.

(m.1) THE ACCOUNT OF ROBERT DE ASPERTONA WARDEN OF THE WORK OF THE CHURCH OF THE BLESSED PETER OF EXETER FROM THE FEAST OF ST MICHAEL 1312 TO THE FEAST OF ST MICHAEL 1313.

RECEIPTS

The same [Robert] renders account of 23s 7¼d [altered from 19s 8½d] from arrears of the preceding account. Of £124 18s 8d of the instalment of the gift of Walter the lord bishop concerning the fabric (*de dono dom Walteri episcopi de portione ips' contingent' ad fabricam*). And of £48 from the prebend of the canons for the year. And of £7 7s 4d from the dignity of the dean for the year. And of 60s from the dignity of the precentor for the year. And of 64s from the dignity of the treasurer. He does not pay for the chancellor. And of £90 received from Master John de Upavene from the voluntary subsidy (*gratuito subsidio*) assessed through the diocese in Devon (*in episcopatu Devon*) by one tally. And of £16 from the church of St Erth (*Lanaho*) in Cornwall. Of £20 of the gift of master J. de Bruweton. And of 10s of the gift of Jordan de Venella. And of 50s from the vicar of Dean (*Dene*) from the collection of indulgences (*indulgenciarum*) in the archdeaconry of Totnes (*Totton'*). And of 7s from the reeve (*preposito*) of Lawhitton (*Lawitton*) in Cornwall for 2 fotmels and 4 stones of lead sold to him for the bishop's requirements. And of 7s 2d of rents of assize for the year. And of 31s from Whitsuntide offerings in the nave of the church. And of 7s 4d from offerings on 1 August (*ad gulam Augusti*). And of 19s 6d from the proceeds of the red chest for the year. And of 5s 3d from the proceeds at the feet of old St Peter for the year.

Total of all the receipts with arrears of the preceding amount £319 10s 10¼d [altered from £324 6s 8½d].

EXPENSES

(m.2) MICHAELMAS TERM

Week 1   In wages*. Sharpening (*bateria*) and steeling and whetting (*acerand'*
et acuand') of tools 10d. In 2 labourers in the quarry 22d. In 2 labourers
there 20d. In 6 labourers there 4s 6d. In 6 labourers on the Work 5s. In
5 labourers there 3s 9d, 9d each. And 2 carters 22d. 10 quarters of lime
5s. 6 quarters of oats 6s 6d.   Total £4 6s.

Week 2   In wages*. Sharpening 13d. In 2 labourers in the quarry 22d.
In 2 labourers there 20d. [In 6 labourers] there 4s 6d. In 8 labourers on
the Work 6s 8d. In 6 labourers there [4]s 6d. In 2 carters 22d. In wages of
William de Monteacuto for 4 days carving 2 capitals and one head of
free stone (*talliant' ij capitrall' et unum capud franch' petre*) 20d. 6 quarters
of lime 3s. 5 quarters of oats 6s 8d.   Total £4 7s 6½d.

Week 3   In wages*. In 2 labourers in the quarry 22d. In 2 labourers
there 20d. In 6 labourers [there 4s 6d. In 8 labourers on the Work 6s] 8d.
In 6 labourers there 4s 6d. In 2 carters 22d. In wages of W 7
quarters of lime 3s 6d. One load of withies 3d. For ...   ... bought 6d.
                                                             Total £4 2s 9d.

Week 4   In wages*. In wages of William de Monteacuto carving one
great corbel one great boss and 2 bab[wins?] at task (*taillant' j magnam
sursam j magn' clavem et ij bab ... ad tascam*) 5s. Sharpening of tools 10¾d.
In 2 labourers in the quarry 22d. In 2 labourers there 20d. 6 labourers
there 4s 6d. In 8 labourers on the Work 6s 8d. In 5 labourers there 3s 9d.
In 2 car[ters 22d]. ...   ... bought, with the smith's work (*empt' cum
opere fab'*) 22d. For making 4 cart-clouts with nails 6d. ... labourers 2s.
14 quarters of lime 7s. For repairing buckets and other utensils ...
                                                             Total 100s 6¾d.

Week 5: 2 feasts, All Saints and All Souls [1 and 2 November]   In
wages*. ...   ... In 2 labourers there 18d. In 6 labourers 4s. In 4
labourers on the Work 3s. In 3 labourers there 2s. In 2 carters 22d. For
carrying 2 barge-loads of stones from the quarry to Topsham by sea 12s.
For [carving] 2 great corbels (*sursis*) at task ... 4s. 15 oak boards bought
for requirements 4s 4d. One rope bought for drawing water (*ad aquam
tractand'*) 1½d.   Total 70s 3½d.

Week 6   In wages*. In one labourer in the quarry ...   ... In 2 labourers
there 18d. In [6] labourers there 4s ...   ... In 2 carters [22d]. For ...
carving ... corbels and 3 marble capitals at task (*In ... sursis et iij
capitrell' marmor' ad tascam tailland'*) 4s 6d. ... [One roofer] with his boy
roofing over the cloister ... (*... cum socio suo cooperiend' super claust' ...*)
for 4 days 20d. 4 quarters of lime 2s. ...   Total 68s 8½d.

Week 7   In wages*. Sharpening and renewing (*renovand'*) and steeling of
tools 15 ... In 2 labourers in the quarry 20d. In 2 labourers there 18d.
In 6 labourers there 4s. In 6 labourers on the Work ... In 2 carters 22d.
3 pairs of cart-traces 2s 2d. For making 8 wheel-caps (*clippis*) 4d. ...   ...
                                                             Total 63s 6d.

Week 8: 2 feasts, Dedication of the Church and St Katherine [21 and 25
November]   In wages*. Sharpening 9d. For ... tools 7d. In 2 labourers
in the quarry 18d. In 2 labourers there 16d. In 6 labourers there 3s 6d.

7d each. In 4 labourers on the Work 2s 8d. In 4 labourers there 2s 4d. In 2 carters 22d. 3 quarters of oats 3s 3d. Total 51s 5¼d.

Week 9   In wages*. Sharpening 10d. In one labourer in the quarry 10d. . . . 18d. In 6 labourers there 4s. In 4 labourers on the Work 3s. In 3 labourers there . . . In 2 carters 22d. 2 trusses of straw (*furagii*) . . . In one man roofing over the lodges (*loggeas*) for 3 days 6d. . . . locks bought for the chambers of the warden (. . . *serrur' ad cameras custo . . . empt'*) with other locks for the same 8d. One cart-horse . . . 3 quarters of oats [3] s 3d. Total £4 19s ½d.

Week 10   In wages*. Sharpening 8½d. In 2 labourers in the quarry 20d. In 2 labourers there 18d. In 6 labourers there 4s. In . . . labourers on the Work 4s 6d. In 3 labourers there 2s. In 2 carters 22d. 1000 lead-nails . . . 6 lbs of . . . for carts 9d. 8 lb . . . 9d. . . . 6 poplar boards for centerings (*ad cinternas*) 6d. For . . . (*ad plumb'*) 4d. 7 quarters of oats 7s 7d. Total 65s.

Week 11   In wages*. Sharpening 11¾d. In . . . labourers in the quarry 20d. And 2 labourers 18d. And 6 labourers 4s. And 6 labourers on the Work 4s 6d. And . . . labourers there 2s. . . . 8 trusses of straw bought 20d. One load of twists 3d. In one roofer (*copercore*) for 6 days 13½d. . . . Total 63s ½d.

Week 12   In wages*. Sharpening 9½d. In 2 labourers in the quarry 20d. In 2 labourers there [18]d. In . . . labourers there . . . In 6 labourers on the Work 4s 6d. In 3 labourers there 2s. In 2 carters 22d. 14 quarters of lime 7s. 50 large stones carried from the quarry 13s. For a certain large hammer for breaking stones (*In quodam magno mart' ad petr' frangend'*) . . . 3d. 3 . . . of straw bought 7½d. In wages of Master Thomas the plumber with his boy roofing and working over the Work (*cooperient' et operant' super opus*) for 2 weeks 10s. For the stable hired at Newton [for this term] 7½d. Farriery for the horses 9d. For shoeing with 7 dozens (*dozenis*) of iron 14d. 6 quarters of oats 6s 6d. Wages of Master W. the mason for this term 33s 4d. And of Robert de Aspertona [12s] 6d. Total £6 12s 6d.

Total of the totals of the expenses of the first term £48 7s 5½d.

(m.3) CHRISTMAS TERM

Week 1   In wages of 2 carters [at?] Christmas 22d. Total 22d.

Week 2   In wages of 2 carters 20d. 4 quarters of oats 4s 8d. Total 6s 4d.

Week 3   In wages*. Sharpening 7½d. In 2 labourers in the quarry 20d. In 2 labourers there 18d. In 6 labourers there 4s. In 6 labourers on the Work 4s 6d. In 3 labourers there 2s. In 2 carters 22d. In one man mending holes in the public roads on account of the carts (*In j homine emendent' breccas viarum forensicarum causa carecte*) for 4 days 5d. For making 8 wheel-plates for carts 4d. 'Wippecord' 4d. 2 ropes for carrying trusses (*ad fess' port'*) 2d. 15 alder boards for centerings 19d. 6 quarters of oats 6s 6d. Total 47s 2¼d.

Week 4   In wages*. Sharpening 9½d. In 2 labourers . . . 22d. In 2 labourers there 20d. In 6 labourers there 4s. In 6 labourers on the Work

4s 6d. In 3 labourers there 2s. In 2 carters 22d. ... ... bought for harness 8d. For mending ... 4 quarters of lime 2s. 4 quarters of oats 7s 2d. Total 53s 8½d.

Week 5   In wages*. Sharpening 8¼d. In one labourer 10d. In 2 labourers there 18d. In 4 labourers there 2s 8d. In 6 labourers on the Work 4s 6d. In 3 labourers there 2s. In 2 carters [22d]. For making ... cart-clouts 4d. Red sand ... 6 quarters of oats 7s 1d. Total 50s ½d.

Week 6   In wages*. Sharpening ... ½d. In one labourer in the quarry 10d. In 2 labourers there 18d. In 4 labourers there 2s 8d. In 7 labourers on the Work 5s 3d, 9d each. In 3 labourers ... 2s. In 2 carters 22d. For making one mattock (*ligone*) 3d. 2 sieves bought 1½d. 4 quarters of oats 4s 8d. Total 59s 7d.

Week 7   In wages*. Sharpening 9¼d. In 2 labourers in the quarry 20d. In 2 labourers there 18d. In 4 labourers there 2s 8d. In 6 labourers [on the Work] 4s 6d. In 3 labourers there 2s. In 2 carters 22d. For manufacturing 3 cart-clouts 8d. One axle bought and put on a cart 6d. 5 quarters of oats 5s 10d. Total 52s 4d.

Week 8   In wages*. Sharpening 9½d. ... labourers in the quarry ... In 2 labourers there 18d. In 4 labourers there 2s 8d. In 6 labourers on the Work ... In 3 labourers ... In 2 carters 22d. 6 slabs (*slabbis*) of iron bought 18d. For binding vessels (*vasis*) 8d. 7 quarters of oats 8s 2d, at various prices (*diverso precio*). Total 55s 11d.

Week 9: 2 feasts, St Peter's Chair and St Mathias [22 and 24 February]   In wages*. Sharpening 9d. In 2 labourers ... In 2 [labourers] there 16d. In 4 labourers there 2s 4d. In 6 labourers on the Work 4s. In 3 labourers there 21d. In 2 carters 22d. In ... t[russes] of thatching straw (*straminis ad cooperam*) 4d. For twists (*plicis*) 4d. In one roofer over the lodges (*super loggeas*) for 3 days 7½d. 3 quarters of oats 3s 6d. Total 43s 5½d.

Week 10   In wages*. In 2 labourers in the quarry 20d. In 2 labourers there 18d. In 5 labourers there 3s 4d. In 6 [labourers] ... ... 4s 6d. In 3 labourers there 2s. In 2 carters 22d. 6 quarters of lime 3s. For 6 trusses of straw 12d. For twists 4d. In one roofer for 3 days 6d. 36 lbs of pitch for cement 2s 7½d. 9 lbs of wax 5s 3d, 7d a lb. For ... 2s 2d. Total 62s 4¼d.

Week 11   In wages*. Sharpening 10½d. In 2 labourers in the quarry 20d. In 2 labourers ... In 5 labourers there 3s 4d. In 6 labourers there on the Work 4s 6d. In 4 labourers there 2s 8d. In 2 carters 22d. For manufacturing 36 ... for moulds (*ad mouldas*) 4d. 50 slabs (*slabbis*) of iron bought 11s 6¾d. ... One [pair of cartwheels] bought with carriage from Taunton 6s. For making 6 wheel-plates 3d. 2 trusses of straw 5d. In one roofer for the week 9d. 200 ... nails bought 4d. Withies 4½d. 6 quarters of oats 7s. Total 74s 11d.

Week 12: And the time changes   In wages*. Sharpening 8¼d. For 2 labourers in the quarry 20d. In one labourer there 10d. In 5 labourers there 3s 9d. In 7 labourers on the Work 5s 10d. In 4 labourers there 3s. In 2 carters 20d. For carrying 100 large stones (*grossis petris*) from the quarry to the sea with the aid of labourers (*cum auxilio operariorum*) 2s. For carrying 2 barge-loads of stones from the quarry to Topsham by sea 11s.

For making . . . for carts 4d. For mending public roads on account of the carts (*In viis extraneis causa carecte emendend'*) 12d. For putting on a cart-axle 3d. For mending and binding 2 tubs 4d. 3 quarters of oats 3s 6d.

Total 79s 1½d.

Week 13   In wages*. Sharpening 11½d. And 2 labourers in the quarry 22d. And 2 labourers there 20d. And 4 labourers there 3s. And 7 labourers on the Work 5s 10d. And 3 labourers there 2s 3d. And 2 carters 22d. For making a pair of tires (*j pari ligamen'*) for new cart-wheels and for fixing them with the aid of the old tire (*et assedend' cum auxilio veteri ligamen'*) 7s 7d. For manufacturing 4 cart-clouts 4d. For making 4 . . . 2d. One bucket bought and for binding it with iron 6½d. For making a great hammer for breaking stones (*grosso martello ad petras frang'*) 4d. For manufacturing and fixing the ironwork of a wheel above the choir vault in order to hang a chandelier in the choir (*In ferrament' j rote super volturam chori causa corone pendend' in choro fabricand' et affirmand'*) 16d. For making a brass 'tresel' for the same 8d. For carrying a barge-load of stones by sea from the quarry 5s 5d. For carrying 100 large stones to the water 2s. 5 quarters of oats 5s 10d.

Total £4 10s 8d.

Week 14   In wages*. Sharpening 13½d. And 2 sawyers for one day 6d. In 2 labourers in the quarry 21d. In 2 labourers there 20d. In 4 labourers there 3s. In 7 labourers on the Work 5s 10d. In 4 labourers there 3s. In 2 carters 22d. For making a certain . . . of lead for the wheel on the vault above the high altar (*In quodam . . . plumbi ad rotam super volturam summi altaris*) 4d. For strengthening the ironwork of the same wheel (*In ferramentis eiusdem rote affirmand'*) 8d. For carrying 100 great (*grossis*) stones from the quarry to the sea 2s. For carrying a barge-load of stones from the quarry to Topsham 5s 6d. 3 quarters of oats 3s 6d.

Total 77s 5½d.

Week 15   In wages*. Sharpening 16½d . . . In 2 labourers in the quarry 21d. In 2 labourers . . . . . . 5 labourers there 3s 9d. In 7 labourers on the Work 5s 10d. In 4 labourers there 3s. In 2 carters 22d. For digging out and quarrying 6 great stones in [   ]¹ quarry 18d. For mending tools at the quarry (*In utens' quarere . . . endend'*) 8d. For manufacturing and fixing 6 large pegs and 10 bands with nails to the new crane (*In vj magnis cuvellis et x bend' cum clavis ad novam vernam fabricand' et assedend'*) 18d. For cart-grease 4½d. For carriage of one load (*charg'*) of stones from Topsham 8d. 8 quarters of lime 4s. [3] quarters of oats 3s 6d.

Total £4 3s 9d.

Week 16   In wages*. Sharpening 9d. In 2 labourers in the quarry 22d. And 2 labourers there 20d. And 5 labourers there 3s 9d. And 7 labourers on the Work 5s 10d. And 3 labourers there 3s. And 2 carters 22d. For 1½ quintains of lead for making window-bars 4s 6d. For strengthening a bucket with iron 3d. For putting an axle on a cart 3d. 6 quarters of lime 3s. For discharging (*disarcandanda*) one boat-load (*naviata*) of stones from Corfe at Topsham 12d. For the stable hired at Newton for this term 7½d. For shoeing horses with 9 dozen shoes (*ix dudenis ferrorum*) 15d . . . (m.4). Candles for the stable for this term 7d. For farriery for the horses 9d. For the fee of William le Luve for this term 33s 4d. And of Robert de Aysperton 12s. 3 quarters of oats 2s 6d.

Total £6 9s 9½d.

Total of the whole of this term £47 18s 5¾d.

EASTER TERM

Week 1 : Easter   In wages of 2 carters 22d. And . . . labourers for 3 days 20d. For one large barge carried with stones to Topsham from the quarry 10s. 4 bushels of oats 7½d.   Total 16s 1½d.

Week 2   In wages*. Sharpening 9½d. . . . And one labourer in the quarry 11d. And 2 labourers there 20d. And 5 labourers there 3s 9d. And 7 labourers on the Work 5s 10d. And 3 labourers there . . . And 2 carters 22d. For one quintain of iron for manufacturing window-bars (*ad barr' fenestrarum fabricand'*) 3s. 9 quarters of lime 4s 6d. For carrying 100 large (*grossis*) stones to the sea 2s. 12 boards of poplar bought 12d. 6 quarters of oats bought 7s, price 14d a quarter.   Total 78s 8½d.

Week 3: in which are 2 feasts   In wages*. And of Richard Digon carving 2 large bosses at task (*talliant' ij magnas claves ad tascam*) 2s 9d. Sharpening 6½d. And 2 labourers in the quarry 20d. And 2 labourers there 18d. And 6 labourers there 4s. And 7 labourers on the Work 5s 3d, 9d each. And 4 labourers there 2s 8d. And 2 carters 22d. For making 4 cart-clouts 4d. For making 12 . . . for the same 2d. One quintain of iron for manufacturing window-bars 3s. 18 quarters of lime 9s. For mending sieves 2½d. 3 quarters of oats 3s 6d.   Total 70s 10¾d.

Week 4   In wages*. Sharpening 11d. In 2 labourers in the quarry 22d. In 2 labourers there 4s 6d. In 8 labourers on the Work 6s 8d. In 4 labourers there 3s. In 2 carters 22d. For removing 100 large stones from the quarry to the sea 2s. For carrying one large barge-load of stones from the quarry to Topsham 12s. 36 elders bought for requirements 6s 8d. 13 quarters of lime 6s 6d. 5 quarters of oats, price 14d a quarter.
                    Total £4 17s 7d.

Week 5   In wages*. Sharpening 15½d. In 2 labourers in the quarry 22d. In 2 labourers there 20d. In 6 labourers there 4s 6d. In 8 labourers on the Work 6s 8d. In 4 labourers there 3s. In 2 carters 22d. One large iron hammer (*uno magno malleo ferreo*) bought 2s 7d. For mending tools at the quarry 12½d. For carrying 2 barge-loads of stones from the quarry by sea 11s. For removing 200 large stones from the quarry to the water 4s. 4 cart-tyres (*tyibus ad carectam*) bought 12d. 50 elders bought at Nether Exe (*Nitherexe*) 7s. For their carriage to Exeter 5s. For carrying 36 alders lately bought at Langacre (*Langakre*) to Exeter 6s 4d. 8 quarters of lime 4s. 5 quarters of oats 5s 10d.   Total 119s 11d.

Week 6   In wages*. Sharpening 10d. In 2 labourers in the quarry 22d. In 2 labourers there 20d. In 6 labourers there 4s 6d. In 8 labourers on the Work 6s 8d. In 4 labourers there 3s. In 2 carters 22d. For carrying 5 loads (*charg'*) of stones from Topsham 4s. For carrying 2 barge-loads of stones from the quarry to Topsham 11s. 6 quarters of lime 3s. For mending 2 padlocks (*pendul'*) and one lock for the door of the choir (*serrura ad ostium chori*) and other ironwork (*ferramentis*) 10d. For making 4 crampons 2d. 4 quarters of oats 4s 8d.   Total £4 13s 4d.

Week 7   In wages*. Sharpening 13½d. In 2 labourers in the quarry 22d. For 2 labourers there 20d. In 6 labourers there 4s 6d. In 8 labourers on the Work 6s 8d. In 4 labourers there 3s. In 2 carters 22d. 4 quarters of lime 2s. For moving 150 large stones from the quarry to the sea 3s. For carrying one barge-load of stones from the quarry to Topsham 5s 7d.

One pair of cart-wheels bought with carriage from Taunton 5s 9d. For binding them with our own iron . . . For making 4 clouts and 6 crampons . . . 3d. 60 poles (*cheveronibus*)² and 60 hurdles (*flakis*) bought 7s. And 60 poles bought 9s 6d. 6 quarters of oats 7s.   Total 117s 1½d.

Week 8: feast of Pentecost   In wages of 2 carters 22d. In 4 labourers for 3 days collecting withies at Stoke wood and making other requirements 20d. 360 horse-shoes with nails bought at Lopen 22s . . . . . . 3000 horse-nails bought there 2s 3d. 12 slabs of iron bought 3s 6d. . . . board-nails bought 20d. For the expenses of 2 men with 2 horses going to and bringing back from Lopen the said iron work including fair-toll (*tolneto in nundinis*) 18d. For the purchase of a window and fixing it in the canons' bread-house (*In j fenestra empta et eam in domo panis canonicorum assedenda*) 14d.

Total 36s 1d.

Week 9   In wages*. Sharpening 14d. In 4 sawyers 5s 6d. In 2 labourers in the quarry 22d. In 2 labourers there 20d. In 6 labourers there 4s 6d. In 8 labourers on the Work 6s 8d. In 4 labourers there 3s. In 2 carters 22d. In 6 labourers at Chudleigh (*Chudd'*) for 3 days 3s. For making 6 cart-clouts 6d. 6 quarters of lime 3s. 6 quarters of oats 8s.

Total £4 11s 3d.

Week 10   In wages*. Sharpening 14d. In 2 labourers in the quarry 22d. In 2 labourers there 20d. In 6 labourers there 4s 6d. In 8 labourers on the Work 6s 8d. In 4 labourers there 3s. In 2 carters 22d. In 2 sawyers 2s 3d. In 2 sawyers for 3 days 15d. For 2 barge-loads of stones carried from the quarry to Topsham 11s. For 3 cart-loads (*charg'*) of stones carried from Topsham to Exeter 2s 6d. For moving 100 great stones from the quarry to the water 2s. 2 hides? (. . . *core'* . . .) bought for harness 4s 1d. 18 lbs of 'burl' bought 12d. Grease 7d. For repairing harness 10½d. One pair of cart-shafts (*j pari limonum ad caractam*) bought 18d. For making 8 springs 6 dowels and 4 'lonths' (*viij sprang' vj doel' et iiij lonth*) 6d. 8 quarters of lime 4s. For the stable at Newton for this term 7½d. Farriery for the horses 9d. For shoeing them 9d. 2 quarters of oats 2s 8d. For the fee of Master William Loive 33s 4d. And of Robert de Asperton' 12s 6d.

Total £7 13s 1d.

Total of the totals of the third term £43 14s 1¼d.

(m.2d) MIDSUMMER TERM

Week 1   In wages*. And 2 sawyers 2s 9d. And 2 labourers in the quarry . . . . . . 20d. And 4 labourers there 3s. In 8 labourers on the Work 6s 8d. And 6 labourers there 4s 6d. In 2 carters 22d. 90 alders bought for requirements near (*iuxta*) Newton 18s 11d, price 2½d each and 2d more in the total. One rope of 30 fathoms (*tesiis*) bought 7s. 12 lbs of lard (*uncti porcorum*) 18d. For making 4 bands and 2 clouts 6d. 10 quarters of lime 5s. 4 quarters of oats 3s [6d].   Total 117s 3d.

Week 2   In wages*. . . . in the quarry 22d. In 2 labourers there 20d. In 4 labourers there 3s. In 7 . . . . . . In 2 sawyers 22d. 100 loads of stones from . . . 4s. . . . 3 quarters of oats bought 4s.   Total £4 . . . 1½d.

Week 3   In wages*. For sharpening 13d. In 2 labourers . . . . . . labourers there 2s. In 8 labourers on the Work 6s 8d. In 7 labourers there . . . In 2 carters 22d. In payment for . . . alders to . . . the bishop and removing them from his place (*In . . . alnetis . . . episc' prosolvend' et de loco suo extrahend'*) 22d. 32 lbs of tallow bought 2s 8d. For 18 lbs . . . 11d. 38 quarters of lime 19s. In 2 sawyers at Chudleigh (*Chuddelee*) 2s 9d. For carrying . . . cartloads of . . . from Chudleigh to Exeter 7s 6d. For making and fixing one cart-strake (*j straka ad carectam fac' et assedend'*) 12d . . . . . . 6 quarters of oats 7s 6d, price 15d a quarter. Total . . .

Week 4   In wages*. Sharpening 12½d. In 2 labourers in the quarry 22d. In 2 labourers in the quarry 20d. In 3 labourers there 2s 2d. In 3 labourers . . . 2s 3d. In 8 labourers on the Work 6s 8d. In 6 labourers there 4s 6d. In 2 carters 22d. 50 loads of stone . . . 36 quarters of lime 18s. For carrying 4 cartloads of timber from Chudleigh to Exeter 10s. One rope with 3 pairs of traces bought 5s. For making 6 cart-clouts 6d. For moving 200 large stones from the quarry to the sea 4s, with the assistance of labourers (*cum auxilio operariorum*). One calf-hide (*coreo j vituli*) bought for harness 5d. For cloth?³ (*panno*) 4d. For mending a cart-collar (*colar'*) 3d. 2 quarters of oats 2s 8d. Total 104s 7½d.

Week 5   In wages*. Sharpening 11d. In 2 labourers in the quarry 22d. In 3 labourers there 2s . . . In 3 labourers there . . . 6d. In 9 labourers on the Work 7s 6d. In 5 labourers there 3s 9d. . . . 22d. For carrying . . . from the quarry to Topsham 12s. For moving 100 great (*grossis*) stones to the water . . . 28 quarters of lime 14s. For carrying 20 . . . of timber from C[hudleigh] to Haldon (*Hagenedon'*) 20s. For manufacturing 24 dowels (*doulis*) 4 wheel-plates (*clippis*) and strengthening 3 cart-strakes . . . For mending other things 1½d. For mending tools at the quarry 7d. 6 quarters of oats 7s . . . at various prices. Total 117s 3½d.

Week 6   In wages*. . . . In 2 labourers in the quarry 22d. In 3 labourers there 2s 6d. In 3 labourers there 2s 3d. In 9 labourers on the Work 7s . . . . . . labourers there 4s 6d. In 2 carters 22d. 14 quarters of lime 7s. 36 slabs of iron bought 7s 6d, price . . . 6 quarters of oats 9s 6d, price 19d a quarter. Total £4 4s.

Week 7   In wages*. Sharpening 8½d. In 2 labourers in the quarry 22d. In 3 labourers there 2s 6d. In 3 labourers there 2s 3d. In 9 labourers on the Work 7s 6d. In 6 labourers there 4s 6d. In 2 carters 22d. And 2 sawyers 2s 4d. For 150 large stones and 81 smaller stones bought in bulk from Caen (*In cl magnis petris et iiij*ˣˣ *j minoribus petris de Kain in grosso emptis*) 12s. For 50 large 'gobbets' (*gobettis*) from Caen bought separately on another trip (*alia vice per se*) 13s 3d. 14 quarters of lime 7s. 2 quarters of oats 3s. Total £4 19s 10½d.

Week 8   In wages*. Sharpening 9¾d. In 2 labourers in the quarry 22d. In 2 labourers there 20d. In 3 labourers there . . . In 8 labourers on the Work 6s 8d. In 6 labourers there 4s 6d. . . . For carrying 4 . . . to Exeter 6s. For 2 axles . . . putting them on carts [2d] . . . For one potel (*potello*) of oil for the same 4d. 4 quarters of oats 4s 7d. Total £4 4¾d.

Week 9   In wages*. Sharpening 8½d. In 2 labourers in the quarry 22d. And 3 laboures there 2s 6d. And 3 labourers there 2s 3d. And 8 labourers on the Work 6s 8d. And 6 labourers there 4s 6d. And 2 carters 22d. And 6 labourers there 4s 6d. And 2 carters 22d. And 6 quarters of oats 7s 8d at various prices. Total 73s . . . ½d.

Week 10   In wages*. Sharpening 5¾d. In 2 labourers in the quarry 22d. In 3 labourers there 2s 6d. In [3] labourers there 2s 3d. In 8 labourers on the Work 6s 8d. In 5 labourers there 3s 9d. In 2 carters 22d. And 2 saw-yers 2s 3d. 4 quarters of lime 2s . . .   . . . 21s. 6 quarters of oats 7s 1½d.

Total £4 12s 7¼d.

(m.3d) Week 11   In wages*. In 2 labourers in the quarry 22d. In 3 labourers there 2s 6d. In 3 labourers there 2s 3d. In 8 labourers on the Work 6s 8d. In 6 labourers there 4s 6d. In 2 carters 22d. In 2 sawyers 2s 2d. . . . to Corfe (*apud Corf'*) . . . For making one mattock (*ligon'*) 3d. For making 12 large spikes (*grossis spikis*) for the high (*summ*) . . . . . . 3d. 2 quarters of lime 12d. 5 quarters of oats 5s 10d.

Total 62s 2½d.

Week 12   In wages*. Sharpening 8½d. In 2 labourers in the quarry 22d. In [3 labourers] there 2s 6d. In 3 labourers there 2s 3d. In 8 labourers on the Work 6s 8d. In 6 labourers there 4s 6d. And 2 carters 22d. And 2 sawyers 2s 2d. For carrying 3 cart-loads of timber from Chudleigh to Exeter 10s. 4 quarters of lime . . . 4 quarters of oats 4s 4d [?].

Total 79s 3½d.

Week 13   In wages*. Sharpening 9d. In 2 labourers in the quarry 22d. In 3 labourers there 2s 6d. In 3 labourers there 2s 3d. In 13 labourers on the Work 10s 10d. In 6 labourers there 4s 6d. In 2 carters 22d. And for carrying 3 cart-loads (*charg'*) of timber from Chudleigh to Exeter 7s . . . d. For carrying 2 cart-loads of timber from Haldon (*Hagledon*) to Exeter . . .   . . . 5s 6d a thousand (*pro millena*).   Total 107s.

Week 14   In wages*. Sharpening . . . In 2 labourers in the quarry 22d. In 3 labourers there 2s 6d. In 3 labourers there 2s 3d. In 12 labourers on the Work 10s. In 7 labourers there 5s 3d. In 2 carters 22d. And 2 sawyers 2s 3d. 1000 large board-nails bought 2s 6d. For making 8 wheel-plates with 12 d . . . 7d. For making 4 cramps 2d. For 2 . . .   . . . bought 8s 6d. For carrying 24 loads of alders from Newton to Exeter 4s. For the stable hired at Newton for this term 7½d. Farriery of the horses for this term 9d. For shoeing the horses with 11 dozens for the term 22d. For the fee of William Luve master of the Work for this term 33s 4d. And of Robert de Asperton 12s 6d. For the house of the said Master William hired for the year 32s. In wages of the collector of the rents of the Work of the Blessed Peter for the year . . .   . . . oats . . .   Total £8 9s.

The cost of lead for founding ashes, and solder (*Custus plumbi de cineribus fundendis et soldurie*).   In wages of Master Thomas the plumber and his boy supervising (*existent' ultra*) the washing of ashes of lead in the Exe (*apud Exam*) for 3 days 3s. For their wages for founding 36 fotmels of lead from the said ashes for one week 5s. In wages of one smith (*fabri*) . . . for 3 days 9d. Charcoal (*carbon'*) 2s 8d. For drinks (*in potationibus*) for the labourers concerned in washing the ashes (*circa cineres lavand'*) 6d. And founding the ashes 12d . . . Timber bought for new bellows (*ad nov' flat'*) 8d. Iron 16d. In wages of a smith for balances?[3] (*pendulis*) and other requirements 10d. For 100 nails 3d. For curing the hide of a horse [dead] due to murrain (*proven' de morina*) together with grease for the same . . . For making the said bellows (*flat'*) at task 3s.   Total . . .

Cost of the wall (*muri*) by Broadgate[4] (*iuxta la Brodeyete*) 100 loads of stones from Barley 4s. In one mason for 3 weeks ... ... (*altera ... dom'*) ... 5s 7d, 22½d a week. In 2 masons for one week 2s 8d. In the same for 2 weeks 6s 4d, 20d each a week. In one mason for one week 22½d. In 3 labourers for 2 weeks 4s 6d, 9d each a week. Total 25s.

Cost of timber for the bishop's throne (*Custus meremii ad sedem episcopi*)

In wages of Master Thomas de Winton being at Norton and Chudleigh (*Chuddelea*) for the purpose of looking over timber and concerning the felling of timber (*ad providend' merem' et circa merem' prosternend'*) for one week 3s. In wages of William de Membiri carpenter for 3 days 13½d. And Richard de Brugges 10½d. And J. de la Wichie 9d. And R. Prodomme 9d. And 2 sawyers 8d. In wages of the said Master Thomas for another week 3s. And William de Membiri carpenter 2s 3d. And Robert Grosp and John Loch 3s 8d. And Richard de Briggis Walter Unfrey and Alexander de Holecomb 5s 3d, 21d each. And Thomas Ata Wichie 19d. And J. Prodomme and J. Schere 3s. And 2 sawyers 2s 6d. And 2 sawyers 2s 3d. And one sawyer 15d. And 2 sawyers 20d.

Week 3 In wages of Master Thomas 3s. And Robert de Galmeton carpenter 2s 2d. And J. Loch 22d. And 2 sawyers 2s 6d. And 2 sawyers 2s 2d.

Week 4 In wages of Master Thomas 3s. And 2 sawyers 2s 6d. For carrying timber to the water at Norton and submerging it (*In merem' apud Norton ad aquam cariand' et mergend'*) 10d. Paid to the said Master Thomas for his expenses in returning home (*in recessu eius versus patriam suam*) 5s.

Week 5 In wages of W. de Membiri 2s 3d. And Robert de Galmeton for the said week 13d. And Benedict Scrogeyn 12d. And Robert Crop 11d. And in one man felling timber (*prosternent' merem'*) for 2½ days 12½d.

Week 6 In wages of William de Menbiri 2s 3d. And Benedict Scrogeyn 20d. And R. Prodomme 18d.

Week 7 In wages of W. de Menbiri 2s 3d. And Crop Penung' 22d. And 8 labourers at Norton for hauling the timber out of the mill-pool there (*ad merem' ibidem de stagno molendini extraend'*) 4s, 6d each. For carrying all the timber from Norton to Exeter *in grosso* 36s 2d.

Week 8 For 2 sawyers at Chudleigh 2s 8d. For raising a certain great tree-trunk for sawing there (*In quodam magno ligno ibidem levand' ad secatur'*) 5d. In one carpenter for sawing 2 tree-trunks (*ad ij ligna quarand'*) 2s. And one carpenter for various weeks 12d. For carrying certain planks (*tabulis*) to the water 1d. For 2 sawyers for half a week 15d.

Week 9 In 2 sawyers for one week 2s 2d.

Weeks 10, 11 In 2 sawyers 4s 6d.

Week 12 In 2 sawyers 2s 6d. And in 2 sawyers 2s 3d. And in 2 sawyers for various weeks 14½d.

Total £6 12s 8½d.

Purchase of hay with the cost of the same For 7 stacks of hay bought at Clyst 44s 6d ... Price ... of 6 stacks 6s 3d each, and of one stack 6s. For carrying 74 trusses of hay from Clyst to Exeter 9s 3d, 1½d a truss. 6 trusses of thatching straw (*furagii ad cooperam*) bought for the large stack 11½d. 2 loads of twists 4d. For thatching the stack (*In mullone cooperiendo*) 7d. 3

stacks of hay bought at Newton 16s 8d, at various prices. For carrying them 18d. For hay deposited in buildings there (*in domibus ibidem loc'*) 4½d. 3 small stacks of hay bought at Newton 8s 10d.   Total £4 2s.

Cost of Corfe stone, glass, tin and rings   [Cancelled: 138 feet of columns (*columpnar'*) of Corfe marble bought 115s, 10d a foot. And carrying them from Topsham 4s. Written over: allowed in the previous roll (*allocatur in rotulo prev'*)]. 100 lbs of tin bought for solder 13s. 2 seams of glass bought 20s. 3 large metal rings bought (*magnis annulis de metallo*) 16s.

Total 49s [altered from £8 8s].

Sum total of the fourth term £85 4s 10½d [altered from £90 3s 10d].

Total of the totals of the whole cost for the year
£225 4s 11d [altered from £231 3s 1d].

And he owes £94 5s 11¼d [altered from £73 3s 7½d].

* List of wages of named craftsmen is not included here, see pp. 191–3.
1 MS leaves blank.
2 For the meaning of *cheveron'* as poles for scaffolding rather than rafters, see Colvin, *Building Accounts* p.13 n.4.
3 Meaning uncertain.
4 Broadgate was one of the main gates of the Close.

2612   1316, 26 September–1317, 25 September

> 4 membranes, head to tail; m.1 has large holes in its upper part and is completely covered with obscuring tissue; mm. 2–4 are in sound condition. Some lines throughout the roll are partially or wholly obscured by galls.
> Endorsed: *Compotus operis ecclesie beati Petri de anno domini m⁰ccc⁰xvj intrante xvij.*
> Printed: Extract in Oliver, p. 381.

(m.1) THE ACCOUNT OF JOHN DE SCHYREFORD CHAPLAIN WARDEN OF THE WORK OF THE CHURCH OF THE BLESSED PETER OF EXETER FROM THE SUNDAY BEFORE THE FEAST OF ST MICHAEL 1316 TO THE SAME SUNDAY IN THE FOLLOWING YEAR.

RECEIPTS

The same renders account of £124 18s 8d of the gift of the lord bishop for the year. And of £48 from the prebend of the canons for the year. And of £17 of the fruits (*de fructibus*) of the church of St Erth in Cornwall (*Lanuduho in Cornub'*). And of £6 7s 4d from the dignity of the dean. And of 64s from the dignity of the treasurer (*de dygnitate Teserer*). And of £10 from the executors of Master Ralph Germeyn late (*nuper*) precentor of Exeter. And of 40s from the executors of Master Peter de Sc . . . And of 5s from the tomb (*tumba*) . . . le Archedeakene. And of . . . from the testament of Walter Lovecoc. And of 6d from Master W. Vealdy. And of 2d from the obit (*de obitu*) of Eustace (*Eustachii*). And of 10 . . .   . . . from the testament of Robert Kytel. And of 5s from the testament of Master Stephen de Martinho. And of 53s 4d . . . Roger de Oteri. And of 6s 8d from the

testament of dom R . . . rector of Goodleigh (*Godelegh'*). And of . . . . . .
8d. And of 4s from the testament of the rector of Ashton (*Assereston*). And
from the burial (*fossato*) of R. the precentor 3s 8d. And from the burial
(*fossato*) of . . . (Clifford?) . . . . . . Gatepede. And of 12d from the testament of Adam . . . . . . Kylkenny. And of 20s from one stone sold (*de j
lapide vend'*). . . . from the testament of dom Richard de Kareton rector of
. . . . . . of Master Henry de Stoford. And of 40s 4d . . . from the treasurer
for a certain (*quodam*) . . . And of 12d from the testament of William
(*Cornuset?*) And 3d received . . . And of 2s 9d from Master Richard de
Morestestri. And of 26s 1d from the red chest . . . from Whitsuntide offerings (*de obventionibus pentecostalibus*). And of 6s 6d on 1 August (*gula
Augusti*). And of 5s for timber sold . . . And of 12d for the carriage of one
cask of wine from Exeter to Clyst bridge (*xij.d pro car' j dolei vini de Exon'
usque Cliste brygge*). And of 16s? for 2 carts hired at Colyford (*Coliford'*).
And of 13s 4d for the carriage of one cask of wine to Torrington (*Torriton*).
And of 3s for the carriage of a cask to N . . . And of 10s for 2 casks to
Sidford (*Sydford*). And of 20s for the carriage of a corpse to Stockey (*pro
car' funus usque Stokehaye*). And of the dignity of the [chancellor] 38s. And
of the arrears of the account of corn bought at Cheriton (*de arreragia
compoti bladi empti apud Churytone*) 29s 3d. And of . . . Hugh de la Pole from
a certain penitent (*de quodam penitent'*). And of 8s 2d from the rent of tenements in Exeter for the year.

Total £229 15s 10½d [altered from £228 6s 7½d].

EXPENSES

Default of rent (*Defectus redd'*) . . . of Chambernon 2s because it is not
leased (*quia non locat'*). Item for default of rent of the tenement of Jesse in
'Combestret' 6d because it is burned (*quia crematum est*). Item default of
rent of the tenement of H. Lovecock . . . Item in default of rent . . . in
'Combestret'. Total 3s 7d.

Surplus (*Superplus*) . . . in allowance . . . for surplus of the account of
the preceding year £19 18s 11d. Item for minor expenses (*minut' expens'*)
. . . in the account of the same year 24s 3d. Total £21 3s 2d.

MICHAELMAS TERM

Week 1 In wages*. Sharpening of tools 2d. In one labourer in the quarry
11d. The other labourer there 9d. In 4 labourers on the Work 3s 4d. And
one labourer there 9d. In 4 carters 4s 2d. Hay bought from the adminis-
trators of John de Hamaco late rector of the church of Ch . . . Paid for
the equipment for carrying certain timber from Lustleigh to Chudleigh
and Teignbridge (*Soluto pro hernis cuiusdam merem' cariand' de Lusteleghe
usque Chuddeleghe et Teingebrigge*) 20s. Sharpening . . . . . . empty casks
bought, 8d a cask. In wages of Robert de Galmeton for making centerings
(*cinternas*) 2s 2d. In one labourer . . . , 5d a day. 2 hooks and 2 hinges
(*gumfis et vertivellis*) bought for requirements (*ad necessaria*) 3d. Fodder of
10 cart-horses for a week 6 quarters 4½ bushels, that is, to each horse for a
day and a night one half bushel 1 peck.

Total 74s 6d by tally against Master Thomas.

Cost of carpentry in the said week   In wages*. In 2 sawyers at Lustleigh 2s 6d. And 2 sawyers on the Work 2s 8d. 50 great nails bought for rafters (*ad cheveron*') 9d.

Total 13s 5d by tally against William the carpenter.

Week 2   In wages*. Sharpening and mending saws with two nails bought for them 7d. In one labourer in the quarry 11d. And the other labourer there 9d. In 4 labourers on the Work 3s 4d. And one labourer there 9d. And 4 carters 4s 2d. In Robert de Galmeton the carpenter for making centerings 2s 2d. And one sawyer for the same 2s 9d. 200 iron spikes bought for centerings 9d. 1500 smaller iron spikes (*minor' spikis ferreis*) bought for the laths of the high work (*ad lath' summi operis*) 4s 6d. For binding a pot (*bussello*)[1] with our own iron 5d. For binding 2 tubs 4d. 3 barge-loads of timber carried from Chudleigh to Haldon (*Hagheledon*) 3s. 6 fotmels of lead bought in the town (*in villa*) 12s 6d. Fodder [as above].

Total 54s 5d by tally against Master Thomas.

Cost of carpentry in the said week   In wages*. And one carpenter 19d. And 2 sawyers for 2 days 10d.

Total 8s 8d by the said tally against W.

Week 3   In wages*. Sharpening 2d. In wages on one labourer in the quarry 11d. And one labourer there 9d. And 4 labourers on the Work 3s 4d. And one labourer there 9d. And 4 carters 4s 2d. And one . . . for the same work for the above-named week and this one 2s. And 2 sawyers 2s 9d. For binding and strengthening 2 new cart-wheels with our own iron tires (*strakis*) 2s 3d. For one roofer with his boy roofing over various places (*In j copercore cum garcione suo coperient' per diversa loca*) 2s 6d. 1000 wedges (*cuvell'*) bought 1d. Fire-wood (*busca*) bought for founding lead 3s. One lb of lard (*uncti porcini*) for solder 2d. Fodder [as above].

Total 42s 6d.

Cost of carpentry in the said week   In wages*. In 2 sawyers 2s 9d. For 30 great spikes bought in the said week 3d.   Total 17s 6d.

Week 4   In wages*. Sharpening and steeling of tools 12d. In one labourer in the quarry 11d. And the other labourer there 9d. In 4 labourers on the Work 3s 4d. In 4 carters 3s 10d. And R. de Galmeton for centerings 2s 2d. In one carpenter for the same 12d. 100 iron spikes bought for the same 5d. 4 pairs of cart-traces (*traicum ad carectas*) 2s 3d. 'Wippecord' 3d. 2 oat-sacks bought for putting inside carts (*in ij saccis ad avenas carect' infra ponend' emptis*) 16d. 14 lbs of lard bought for the carts 21d. 2 new cart-wheels bought at Taunton 6s. 1500 lead-nails (*clavorum ad plumb'*) bought from W. de Crockerewille 3s 9d, 3d a hundred. 500 lead-nails bought from the smith of Clyst 20d, 2d a hundred, because they are worth less than the others (*minor valor' aliorum*). 600 spike-nails (*clavorum spicorum*) bought for the laths of the high roof (*summe coperture*) 21d, $3\frac{1}{2}$d a hundred. 2 small cart-clouts bought . . . In wages of one roofer with his boy roofing over the cloister (*super claustrum*) 2s 6d. In one boy helping the same (*iuvant' ad idem*) 10d. 10 pegs (*pinnis*) 1d. Fodder [as above].

Total 53s $2\frac{1}{4}$d.

For carpentry in the said week   In wages*. And 2 sawyers for half a week 15d. 30 large spikes bought 3d.   Total 13s 4d.

Week 5   In wages*. Sharpening of tools $2\frac{3}{4}$d. In one labourer in the quarry 11d. And the other labourer there 9d. In 4 labourers on the Work

3s 4d. In 4 carters 3s 10d. And R. de Galempton making centerings 2s 2d. And the other carpenter at the same 12d. In 2 sawyers 2s 9d. 2000 nails bought for the high roof (*ad summam coperuram*) 4s 8d. 2000 lead-nails bought 5s. One empty cask bought for covers (*ad cuveras*) with its binding 12d. One tree-trunk bought at Combe-in-Teignhead (*In j ligno apud Comeheved empto*) 3s. 5 ash-trees bought at Dunchideock for cart-axles (*In v fraccinis apud Dunschidiok ad axeas carrectarum emptis*) 5s. In one roofer with his boy over the cloister 2s 6d. For pins (*pinis*) 1d. In one labourer for the same 10d. For tempering 26 lbs of steel 12d. For binding 3 'boket' with our own iron 12d. Fodder [as above].   Total 58s 7¾d. Carpentry in the said week   In wages*. And 4 sawyers 5s 6d. Iron nails bought 2d.   Total 16s 6d.

Week 6: the feast of All Saints [1 November] and the time changes and 2 feasts   In wages*. Sharpening 3½d. In one labourer in the quarry 7¼d. And the other labourer there 6¼d. In 4 labourers on the Work 2s 4d, 7d each. And R. de Galempton for centerings 18d. And the other carpenter 8½d. 3000 great lath-nails bought for the high roof (*summ' copertu'*) 7s, 2s 4d a thousand. 10 lead-nails bought 2s 6d. For manufacturing one great hammer (*martello*) for the quarry 8d. For three sheets? (*lodic'*)[2] bought 1d. One cart-horse bought at Week fair (*in nundinis de Wike*) 5s 11d. 2 hooks and hinges bought for a certain door (*quoddam ostium*) 3½d. For repairing the ironwork of one cart 10d. [cancelled: Fodder of 11 cart-horses for a week 7 quarters 1½ bushels and one peck etc.]. Fodder withdrawn because it is included in the cost of the tabulature.   Total 36s 10½d. Carpentry in the said week   In 2 sawyers at Lustleigh 23d. And 2 sawyers for half a week 13¾d. 50 great nails bought for rafters (*cheverones*) 11d.   Total 10s 1¾d.

(m.2) Week 7   In wages*. Sharpening and steeling of tools 10d. In one labourer in the quarry 9½d. And the other labourer there 8d. In 4 labourers on the Work 3s. And one labourer there 7d. In 4 carters 3s 10d. In wages of R. de Galmeton carpenter making centerings 22d. And the other carpenter for the same 10d. 18 quarters of lime 9s. 2000 spikes bought 5s 10d, 3½d a hundred. 1000 lead-nails bought 2s 6d. 2000 nails bought for the high support (*ad summam laturam*) 4s 8d. For making and binding 11 new buckets 18d. In one man cleansing the cloister and gutters (*purgant' in claustro et in goteris*) for 4 days 4d. Fodder for 11 cart-horses 7 quarters one bushel and one peck, to each horse for a day and a night one half bushel and one peck.   Total 54s 1¾d. Cost of carpentry in the said week   In wages*. In 4 sawyers 4s 7d.

Total 13s 8½d.

Week 8   In wages*. Sharpening and steeling of axes (*secur'*) 7¼d. In one labourer in the quarry 9½d. In the other labourer there 8d. In 4 labourers on the Work 3s. In one labourer there 7d. Nothing concerns carters here because they are in the altar account. In one carpenter 10d. And 2 sawyers 2s 4d. One long rope 60 fathoms in length (*in longitudine lx tes'*) bought for the grab (*robinet*) 8s 11½d. 1400 lath-nails bought for high roof (*summe coperture*) 3s 4d. 1000 lead-nails bought from the smith at Clyst (*Clist*) 2s. 2000 horse-nails (*clavis equinis*) bought in a greater quantity (*per maiorem numerum*) 3s. 1000 horse-nails made from our own iron 10d. 500 tack-nails (*clavis ad tack'*) made for the carts 5d. 24 cart-clouts bought

16d. 12 horse-shoes bought 12d. 6 empty casks 4s. 4 hinges with hooks bought for the doors in the high gallery (*ad ostia in summ' alur'*) 14d. For binding a new cart with iron bought in advance (*ferro de preemptione*) 2s 4d. 1 lb of 'burle' bought for the carts 12d. 9½ quarters of lime bought 4s 9d.   Total 69s 11½d.

Week 9   In wages*. Sharpening and steeling of tools 2¼d. In one labourer in the quarry 9½d. In the other labourer there 8d. In 3 labourers on the Work 2s 3d. In one labourer there 7d. In 4 carters 3s 10d. In one carpenter making[3] the galleries and other requirements at task (*In j carpent' fac' aluras et alia necessaria ad tascam*) 2s 6d. In one mason refitting the altar of St Stephen in the quire (*In j cementar' redrescent' altare sancti Stephani in choro*) for 1½ days 5d. In 2 sawyers for one day 5d. In wages of one man cleansing the gutters and the cloister (*goteras et claustrum*) for 4 days 4d. For binding a wheelbarrow 3d. 9600 little wedges (*cuvell'*) bought for the roof 7d. 9 quarters of lime bought 4s 6d. 3 latches (*lachet'*) and 9 iron staples (*stapellis ferreis*) made for the three gates of the close (*ad iij portas clausi*) 3d. For distributing (*partiand'*) 60 horse-shoes 4d. 1000 lead-nails bought 2s. Fodder of 10 cart-horses for this week 6 quarters 4½ bushels, to each for a day and a night one half bushel and 1 peck.
                                                                              Total 32s 10d.

Week 10   In wages*. Sharpening 2d. In one labourer in the quarry 9½d. And the other labourer there 8d. In 3 labourers on the Work 2s 3d. In one labourer there 7d. In 4 carters 3s 10d. 10 quarters of lime bought 5s. For 50 great iron spikes (*grossis spikis ferr'*) bought 4½d. For 2 iron latches with their fittings (*cum omni attiro*) bought for certain doors (*ostia*) 4½d. In one labourer bringing up (*adjacent'*) stones for 3 days 9d. For one rope bought for drawing water (*ad aqua in traend'*) 4d. Fodder [as above].
                                                                              Total 28s ¾d.
Cost of carpentry in the said week   In wages*. And 2 sawyers 2s 3½d. Paid to W. de Menbiri carpenter for courtesy (*ad facessiam*) for his labour, by order of the stewards of the exchequer 10s.   Total 16s 10d.

Week 11   In wages*. Sharpening 2d. In one labourer in the quarry 9½d. And the other labourer there 8d. In 4 labourers on the Work 3s. In 4 carters 3s 10d. 1000 lead-nails bought 2s. Fodder [as above].
                                                                              Total 26s 4¾d.

Week 12   In wages*. Sharpening of tools 17¾d. In one labourer in the quarry 9½d. And the other labourer there 8d. In 4 labourers on the Work 3s. In 4 carters 3s 10d. In 2 sawyers for 3 days 14d. 50 great spikes bought 6d. 1000 lead-nails bought 2s. In 2 roofers with one boy for 3 days 19d. 15 feet of ridge-tiles (*crestearum*) bought 5d. In one pavior (*paviator'*) paving in the cloister for one day 4d. One large hide and 2 smaller tanned hides bought for the requirements of the carts 2s 11¼d. One gallon of grease bought for the same 11d. 1½ stones of 'burle' bought 14d. In one man tanning the said hide for 1½ days 3d. 7 empty casks bought 4s 8d, price 8d each. For their carriage 3d. Fodder [as above].
                                                                              Total 41s 10¾d.

Week 13: 2 feasts, St Thomas the apostle [21 December] and Christmas
    In wages*. Sharpening and steeling and whetting (*acerand' et acuand'*) of tools 3½d. In one labourer in the quarry 8d. And one labourer there 7d.

In 4 labourers on the Work 2s 6d. In 4 carters 3s 10d. And 2 sawyers for 3 days 12d. For putting an axle on a cart 3d. One small tanned hide bought 4d. For making 6 horse-collars (*colar'*) 12d. 7 lbs of mutton fat (*cepi ovini*) bought 7d. One gallon of grease 11d. Steel (*acere*) bought 2½d. 9 quarters of lime 4s 6d. For repairing and steeling tools at the quarry for the whole quarter 8d. For the stable hired at Newton for this term 7½d. Farriery of the horses for this term 9d. For shoeing horses with 14 dozens of horse-shoes (*ferror'*) 2s 4d. 6 horse-shoes bought 6d. Candles bought for the stable for the whole term 7d. For a stable hired at Colyford (*Coliford*) 4d. 2 hinges and an iron bolt (*bolto*) bought for a lectern (*descam*) in the choir 2½d. For the fee of Master Thomas the mason for this term 33s 4d. And of John de Schireford warden of the Work (*custodis operis*) 12s 6d. Fodder [as above]. For a certain building hired at Newton in which to place hay for the previous year (*ad imponendum fenum pro anno preterito*) 12d. For curing one horse-hide 9d.   Total £4 20¼d.

Cost of lead   One fother of lead of 24 fotmels bought at Topsham from Stephen Gorwet 50s. For founding 27 fothers of both new and old lead and laying it on the church (*plumbi tam de nove quam de veteri fundend' et super ecclesiam adiacend'*) £6 17s 6d, 5s a fother. In expenses of Thomas the plumber in coming and returning once from Glastonbury (*veniend' et redeundo semel de Glaston*) 4s.   Total £9 11s 6d.

Purchase of oats for fodder of the horses   41 quarters of oats bought at various prices as is shown in a certain note annexed to this present account (*ut patet per quadam particulatam presenti compoto annexam*) 77s 3d, by one tally by himself. Item for 22 quarters 6½ bushels 1 peck of oats bought from Cheriton (*Churiton*) 34s 3d, price 18d a quarter.

Total 111s 6¼d [altered from 77s 3d] by one tally.

Receipts of oats and expenses in the fodder of the horses   He renders account of 9 quarters of oats from the remainder over the account of the immediately preceding year. And of 41 quarters previously bought (*de preemptione*). And of 22 quarters 6½ bushels 1 peck produced from Cheriton.

Total 72 quarters 6½ bushels 1 peck.

From which for fodder of 10 cart-horses from Sunday before Michaelmas for ten weeks 65 quarters 5 bushels, by week 6 quarters 4 bushels and ½ 'sak', to each horse each week 5 bushels 1 peck, that is, to each horse for a day and night ½ bushel 1 peck. And for fodder of 11 horses for one week 7 quarters 1½ bushels 1 peck. Memorandum that he does not reckon more on this account because he reckons for 2 weeks on the altar account (*super compoto tabule*).

Total 72 quarters 6½ bushels 1 peck, and is equal (*et equ'*).

Total of the defaults of rent 3s 7d. Total of the surplus of the preceding account £21 3s 2d. Total of the account of the Work for the preceding term £42 6s 7d by one tally against Master Thomas the mason. Total of carpentry (*carpentrie*) for the same term 110s 1¼d by one tally. Total cost of the purchase of oats 77s 3d by one tally.

Total of the totals of the whole cost with the surplus of the
preceding account £74 14s 11½d [altered from £72 7s 1¼d].

CHRISTMAS TERM

Week 1: after Christmas Day   In wages of 2 carters 2s. And of one carpenter for 2 days mending carts 7d. In one man mending cart-harness for one day 2d. Fodder of 10 horses [as above].   Total 2s 9d.

(m.3) Week 2   In wages*. Sharpening of tools 2¾d. In one labourer in the quarry 9½d. And the other labourer there 8d. In 3 labourers on the Work 2s 3d. In 4 carters 3s 10d. 2 stones of beef tallow (*cepi bovini*) bought 2s 8d. One stone of lard (*uncti porcorum*) bought 2s. In one man mending a forme for one day 2d. Fodder [as above].   Total 23s 3¾d.

Week 3   In wages*. Sharpening 7¼d. In one labourer in the quarry 9½d. And the other labourer there 8d. In 3 labourers on the Work 2s 3d. In 4 carters 3s 10d. 9 quarters of lime 4s 6d. For one man hired to carry lead ashes to the water for one day 1½d. In wages of a plumber with his boys and other assistance founding 67 fotmels and one stone of lead from the said ashes 4s. 8 traces (*trahic'*) weighing 54 lbs bought for the carts 4s 6d, price 1d a lb. For a 'wippecord' bought 2d. For repairing carts and making 2 axle-plates (*hurteris*) 7d. 7 quarters of charcoal (*carbonis*) bought for founding the said ashes and lead 4s 8d, 8d a quarter. For one pot (*olia*) bought for cement ¼d. Fodder [as above].   Total 39s 6¾d.

Week 4   In wages*. Sharpening 5¼d. In one labourer in the quarry 9½d. In the other labourer there 8d. In 3 labourers on the Work 2s 3d. In 4 carters 3s 10d. 13 quarters of lime 6s 6d. 15 loads of clay bought for plastering (*In xv summis gliris ad plastrand' emptis*) 3d. Fodder [as above].
Cost of lead   52 fotmels of lead bought 104s, price 2s each. For founding 4 fothers (*fotheres*) of lead and placing it over the church (*super ecclesiam ponend'*) 20s. One weight (*pondere*) bought and the other mended for weighing various things 7s.   Total £7 19s 7½d.

Week 5   In wages*. Sharpening 5d. In wages of one labourer in the quarry 9½d. And the other labourer there 8d. In 3 labourers on the Work 2s 3d. In 4 carters 3s 10d. 8½ quarters of lime 4s 3d. One horse-collar (*colorio*) bought 1d. Fodder [as above]. In wages of one plumber for one week 5s.   Total 28s 9¼d.

Week 6   In wages*. In one labourer in the quarry 9½d. In the other labourer there 8d. In 3 labourers on the Work 2s 3d. In 4 carters 3s 10d. 1000 lead-nails bought 2s. Fodder [as above].   Total 26s 5¼d.

Week 7   In wages*. Sharpening 6d. In one labourer in the quarry 9½d. In the other labourer there 8d. In 3 labourers on the Work 2s 3d. In 4 carters 4s. In wages of one plumber with his boy for 2 weeks in stripping off the old lead roof and setting the same with their solder over the chapel of the Blessed Mary (*eradnand' veteram coperturam plumbi et ponend' eandem cum solduram eiusdem super capellam beate Marie*) 10s. In one carpenter making moulds and forms (*moldas et formas*)[4] for 2 weeks 2s 6d. And one carpenter for half a day 2½d. For making 2 barrels (*barillis*) for oil with the binding of one 'boket' 9d. One iron pan (*patella ferrea*) bought 16d. Paid for making one image, named the Saviour (*Soluto pro j ymagine faciendo nomine Salvator*) 3s. 17½ quarters of lime bought 8s 9d. 100 lead-nails bought 2½d. For mending a certain old pan 2d. Fodder of 11 cart-horses 7 quarters 1½ bushels 1 peck, to each [as above].   Total 46s 7¼d.

Week 8   In wages*. Sharpening 8d. In one labourer in the quarry 9½d. In one labourer there 8d. In 3 labourers on the Work 2s 3d. In one labourer there 7d. In 4 carters 4s. 13 quarters of lime 6s 6d. In wages of one plumber with his boy over the old roof (*super veteram coperturam*) 5s. For making 1300 horse-nails 13d. 2 stones of mutton and goat tallow (*cepi ovin' et caprin'*) bought 2s 6d. 2 stones of lard (*lardar' porcorum*) bought 3s 1d, 2¼d a lb. For priming 17 great stone bosses and assessing them for gilding[5] (*In xvij magnis clavis de petr' primand' apprestand' usque ad aurum*) 20s 5d, 14½d each. 10 lead-nails 2s. Fodder [as above].   Total 61s ¾d.
Cost of carpentry of the exchequer vault (*cumuli scaccarii*) in the said week In wages*. And 2 sawyers for 5½ days 2s 1d.
Total 5s 7½d by one tally against W. the carpenter.

Week 9: 2 feasts, St Peter's Chair and St Mathias [22 and 24 February]
   In wages*. Sharpening 4¾d. In one labourer in the quarry 7¼d. In the other labourer there 6¼d. And three labourers on the Work 22½d. In 4 carters 4s. 14½ quarters of lime 7s 3d. 6 iron cramps bought for a lead gutter-pipe (*ad quadam pipam plumbeam goteri*) 6d. For making 12 halter-rings (*anulis ad capist'*) 2d. 12 lbs of 'burl' bought for the carts 8d. For repairing one scraper (*strig'*) 2d. One iron bolt for mending the dean's lectern in the quire (*bolto ferreo ad descam decani in choro emendendo*) 1d. Fodder [as above].   Total 25s 9¾d.
Cost of 'carpentrie'   In wages*. And 2 sawyers 2s 1d. For mending one saw (*seca*) ½d.   Total 5s 1d.

Week 10   In wages*. Sharpening 4d. In one labourer in the quarry 9½d. In 3 labourers there 2s. In 3 labourers on the Work 2s 3d. In 2 carters 2s because 2 others are shown in the altar account (*compote tabule altar'*). In wages of R. de Galmeton for centerings 22d. 11 quarters of lime bought 5s 6d. 6 seams of red sand (*rubei arene*) bought for the lead 3d. 4 wooden covers[2] (*lodic' ligneis*) bought for the masons (*ad cementar'*) 1d. 2 small ropes for centerings (*minut' cord' ad cinternas*) bought 3d. One half-bushel measure of wood bought for measuring oats 2¼d. 6 halters (*capust'*) made from our own hide (*de proprio coreo*) 4d. For steeling the hoof of one horse (*In pede j equi aceractand'*) 1d. One bolt and staple bought for a certain stall in the choir (*bolto cum stapello ad quandam stalleam in choro empto*) 2d. For another bolt with a round plate (*placa rotunda*) and other iron fittings made for the high wooden bosses (*ad summas claves lapideas fac'*) 11d. Ironwork bought for the new lenten veil (*ferramentis veli quadragesimale novis emptis*) 18d. In wages of John le Hoppere for working the metal (*pro opere metalli*) of the same veil, and for the metal 3s 6d. Fodder of 4 cart-horses 2 quarters 6 bushels, to each [as above], and not more here because he reckons the fodder of 7 horses in the altar account.   Total 36s 9½d.
Carpentry in the same week for the Work of the church   In wages*. And 2 sawyers 2s 6d, and another sawyer for 3 days 18d.
Total 10s 7d.

Week 11   In wages*. Sharpening of tools 3¾d. In one labourer in the quarry 9½d. In 3 labourers there 2s. In 5 labourers on the Work 3s 9d. In 4 carters 4s. And 2 sawyers for 3 days 15d. 12 quarters of lime 6s. One cart-rope (*lod' corda*) of 32 fathoms (*tesiis*) bought 2s 3d. 2 smaller ropes bought 6d. One tanned hide bought for cart-saddles (*ad panella carect'*) 7d. Grease bought for the same 3d. Hempen string (*filo canabe*) bought for the same and other requirements 4d. For 1½ yards of cloth (*panni*) for . . . 4d. In wages of one man making cart-saddles (*panell'*) for 2 days 4d. In wages of Master Thomas the plumber for founding 3 fothers of lead and laying it above the exchequer 15s. 500 nails bought for the same 12d. For 200 large board-nails bought 14d. One iron 'chake' bought with 6 nails for the same 1d. Fodder of 11 cart-horses 7 quarters 1½ bushels 1 peck, to each [as above].   Total 58s 3½d.

Cost of carpentry for the Work.   In wages*.   Total 6s 7d.

Week 12: the time changes to longer days (*in long'*) In wages*. Sharpening of tools 6d. In one labourer in the quarry 18d. And the other there 11d. In 4 labourers there 3s 2d. In 6 labourers on the Work 5s. In 4 carters 4s. And 2 sawyers for 2 days 12d. 15½ quarters of lime 7s 9d. 2 dozen iron cart-clouts bought 3s. 500 great nails for centerings (*cinternas*) and other requirements bought 2s 1d. 6 bundles of woodland moss for roofing with lead over the exchequer⁶ (*vj fessis musei silvestri ad cooperturam plumbi super scaccarium*) 6d. Fodder [as above].   Total 51s 4d.

Cost of carpentry for the same week In wages*. For a gratuity (*curialitate*) given to John Norreys on account of the carriage of timber with carts from Canonteign (*Tein' canonicorum*) across his land (*ultra terram suam*) 6d, that is, in wine. In 2 sawyers 2s 6d.   Total 12s 6¼d.

Week 13 In wages*. Sharpening 6½d. In one labourer in the quarry 16½d. In the other labourer there for 2 weeks 2s 8d. In 2 labourers there 22½d. In 3 labourers there 2s 3d. In 6 labourers on the Work 5s. In one labourer there 8d. In 4 carters 4s. And R. de Galmeton for making centerings 2s 2d. 16 quarters of lime 8s. 200 loads of stones from Barley 8s. Fodder of 10 cart-horses 6 quarters 4½ bushels, to each [as above]. And no more here because he reckons one horse with murrain (*moreyna*).   Total 56s 3½d.

Cost of carpentry In wages*. In 2 sawyers for the whole week 2s 6d.   Total 5s 8d.

Week 14 In wages*. Sharpening and steeling of axes 3¼d. In 2 labourers in the quarry 2s 8¼d. In 2 labourers there 22½d. In 3 labourers there 2s 3d, 9d each. In 6 labourers on the Work 5s. In one labourer there 8d. And R. de Galmeton making centerings and other necessities 2s 2d. In 4 carters 4s. 500 loads of stones from Barley 20s. 20 quarters of lime 10s. For sharpening and mending tools at the quarry for this term 9½d. In wages of Master Thomas the plumber with his boy for a day founding lead 10d. For the stable hired at Newton for this term 7½d. For a building hired for storing oats 3d. Farriery of the horses for this term 9d. For shoeing horses with 16½ dozen made from our own iron 2s 9d, 2d a dozen. For curing one horse-hide 5d. Candles for the stable for the whole term 2d. For strengthening a cart-binding called a 'strake' 2d. For making 600 tack-nails from our own iron 6d. For painting (*depictand'*) one stone boss on the vault (*clav' lapideo ad voutur'*) 14d. For the fee of Master Thomas the mason for this term 33s 4d. And of John of Schyreford the warden of the Work 12s. Fodder [as above].   Total £6 2s 5¼d.

Carpentry in the same week In wages of 2 sawyers 2s 6d.

                                                      Total 2s 6d.

(m.4) Purchase of oats The same renders account for 98 quarters and 3½ bushels produced from Cheriton £7 7s 7¾d. The same renders account of 98 quarters 3½ bushels bought above (*de super emptis*).

Total is shown (*patet*).

Expenses of oats   In fodder of 10 horses for 8 weeks as he shows in his account above 52 quarters 4 bushels, to each etc. Item in fodder of 4 horses for one week 2 quarters 5 bushels. And of 11 horses for 5 weeks 36 quarters ½ bushel and 1 peck, to each etc. and not more here because he reckons 7 horses for one week on the account of the tabulature of the high altar.   Total 91 quarters 2½ bushels. And 7 quarters 2 bushels remain. Total of the Work for the said term £36 19s 2d. Total of carpentry 48s 6¾d. Total of oats £7 7s 7¾d.

Total of the whole Work with carpentry and oats £47 15s 4½d.

EASTER TERM

Week 1: feast of Easter   In wages*. Sharpening 1½d. In 2 labourers in the quarry 10½d. In 5 labourers on the Work 2s 1d. In 4 carters 4s. 150 loads of stones from Barley 6s. 9½ quarters of lime 4s 9d. Fodder of 10 horses [as above].   Total 25s 7½d.
Carpentry   In wages of 2 sawyers for 4 days 20d.

Total 20d by the same tally as above.

Week 2   In wages*. Sharpening and steeling of tools 8½d. For making 2 large buckets for mortar (*boket ad morter'*) and binding them with our own iron 3s 4d. In one labourer in the quarry 12d. And the other labourer there 11½d. And the third labourer there 10d. In 3 labourers there 2s 3d. In 4 carters 4s. In 7 labourers on the Work 5s 10d. 9 quarters of lime bought 4s 9d. Fodder [as above].   Total 48s 4d.

(m.1d) Week 3   In wages*. Sharpening and [steeling] of axes 5½d. In one labourer in the quarry . . .   . . . there 11½d. . . . labourers there 10d. In 3 labourers there 2s 3d. In 4 carters 4s. In 6 labourers on the Work 5s. In one labourer there 8d. For 51 iron nails? . . . bought . . .   . . . For 7 quarters of lime 3s 6d. Fodder [as above].   Total 54. . . .

Week 4   In wages*. Sharpening 4½d. In one labourer in the quarry . . . And the other labourer there 11d . . .   . . . 3 labourers there 2s 3d. In 4 carters 4s. In 7 labourers on the Work 5s 10d. For 25 . . . lime 13s 3d. For 14 iron slabs (*slabbis*) bought 2s 9d. Fodder [as above].

Total 53s ½d.

Week 5: 2 feasts, Invention of the Holy Cross and St John at the Latin Gate [3 and 6 May]   In wages*. Sharpening and steeling of axes 6d. . . .   . . . the other labourer there 9d. In [3] labourers there 22½d, 7½d each. In 8 labourers . . .   . . . at Crediton (*Criditon*) 8s 8d. In 4 carters 4s. . . . For 100 stones carried from the quarry to the sea 2s. Fodder . . .

Total 44s 3½d.

Week 6   In wages*. Sharpening and steeling of axes 7¼d. In one labourer in the quarry 12d. And the other labourer . . .   . . . 3 labourers . . .   . . . 2s 3d. In 7 labourers on the Work 5s 10d. In one labourer there 8d. In 4 carters 4s. In wages . . . and W. Laci carpenters making scaffolding (*faciend' scheffot'*) 4s. . . . 18 quarters of lime 9s. Fodder for 10 horses [as above].   Total 51s 11½d.

Week 7   In wages*. Sharpening and steeling of axes 7½d. In one labourer in the quarry 12d. In the other labourer there . . . . In 3 labourers there . . . In 5 labourers on the Work 4s 2d. In 5 labourers there 3s 9d. . . . For making one tub . . . 23½ quarters of lime 11s 9d. For binding 2 buckets with our own iron 8d. . . .   . . . Fodder of horses . . .

Total 55s 10d . . .

Week 8: Pentecost   In wages of 4 carters 4s. 500 large horse-shoes (*ferr'*) bought at Lopen . . . 31s 6d. 2 cart-bindings (*ligam' ad carrect'*) with their fittings (*cum apparatu*) 21s 1½d. 4 dozen cart-clouts 7s 8d. 3 dozen cart-clouts 3s 4d. One horse bought 24s. . . . 5d. In expenses of . . . going and returning for 3½ days 4s, that is, to Lopen with 4 horses . . . repairing other things 4½d. 4 quarters of lime 2s. Fodder . . .   Total £5 3s 4d.

Week 9   In wages*. Sharpening and steeling of axes 8¼d. In one labourer in the quarry 12d. And the other labourer there . . . 3 labourers there 2s 3d. In 5 labourers on the Work 4s 2d. In 5 other labourers there 3s 9d. In 4 carters . . . 7 pairs of cart-traces weighing 38 lbs . . . 26½ quarters of lime 23s 3d. In 2 carters . . . 2 sawyers for 4½ days 23d. Fodder of 11 cart-horses 4 quarters 6½ bushels.   Total 63s 3½d.

Week 10   In wages*. In one plasterer plastering the new vault (*nova voutura*) 21d. Sharpening and steeling of axes 4¼d. In one labourer in the quarry 12d. And the other labourer there 11d. In 3 labourers there 2s 3d. In 4 carters 4s. In 4 labourers on the Work 3s 4d. In 3 labourers there 2s 3d. 2 iron pins (*pynnis*) and making and binding 28 bands called 'grotes' for the carts from our own iron 20d. 14 scaffold-nails (*clav' ad scaffot'*) 11d. One large barge-load of stones set down (*locat'*) at Topsham 14s. 800 stones called 'pendauns' carried from the quarry to the sea 4s 8d. For aid in loading the said barge 5d. 27½ quarters of lime 13s 9d. 2 fotmels and 2 stones of lead bought 4s 3d. For making . . . horse-nails and 200 spikes 12d. Fodder [as above].   Total 76s 4½d.

Week 11   In wages*. In one plasterer 22d. Sharpening and steeling of axes 4¼d. In one labourer in the quarry 12d. And the other labourer there 11d. In 3 labourers there 2s 3d. In 4 labourers on the Work 3s 4d. In 2 labourers there 18d. 2 iron wedges for the pulleys (*covellis ferr' pro poleyes*) 2½d. For painting 24 bosses for the vault (*xxiiij clavibus pro voutur' depytand'*) 23s, for each boss 14½d. 300 nails for strengthening centerings (*ad cinternas firmand'*) 10 . . . For 6 brass wheels which are called 'trokeles' for the pulleys (*vj rotis eneis que dicuntur trokeles pro poleyes*) 3s. Fodder for one horse for a week 3½ bushels.   Total 75s 7¼d.

Week 12   In wages*. And one plasterer 22d. Sharpening and steeling of axes 7½d. In one labourer in the quarry 12d. And the other labourer there 11d. In 3 labourers there 2s 3d. In 4 labourers on the Work 3s 4d. In 2 labourers there 18d. Hay bought 7s 3d. For three trees bought at Melhuish (*Melehydis*) 26s 6d. For shoeing horses with 23 shoes (*ferr'*) bought from the smith 23d. And making and strengthening 4½ dozens from our own iron (*de ferramento nostro proprio*) 2s 3d. And 12 dozens of iron (*ferr'*) 2s. For the stable hired at Newton for this term 10½d. Farriery for the horses 9d. For binding one vat (*cuva liganda*) 2d. For 12 oak boards (*bordis de quercu*) bought, 10 feet in length 3s 8d. 11½ quarters of lime 10s 9d. For the fee of Master Thomas de Witteneye for this term 33s 4d. And of John de Scherford warden of the Work 12s 6d. In 2 carters 2s. One pair of cart-wheels bought at Canonsleigh (*Canounelegh'*) 5s. 2 large barge-loads of stones from Salcombe quarry carried to Topsham 28s. For binding one bucket 1d. 100 loads of stones from Barley 4s. Fodder of 6 horses 2 quarters 5 bushels.   Total £8 9s 8½d.

Purchase of oats   He reckons 56 quarters 1½ bushels of oats bought from Cheriton £4 4s 4¼d.

> Total of the Work for the said term £45 8s 5½d [altered
> from £41 4s 2d] with carpentry by tally.

Oats   He accounts for 7 quarters 2 bushels of oats remaining from the previous term and of 56 quarters 1½ bushels previously bought.

> Total 63 quarters 3½ bushels.

He expends from this as he shows in the above roll 63 quarters 3½ bushels and is equal.

MIDSUMMER TERM

Week 1 : after the feast of St John Baptist [24 June]   (m.2d) In wages*. And one plasterer (*plaustrator'*) 22d. Sharpening and steeling of axes and 6 rings and 4 . . . 17½d. In one labourer in the quarry 12d. And the other labourer there 11d. In 3 labourers there 2s 3d. In 4 labourers on the Work 3s 4d. In 2 labourers there 18d. One barge-load of stones from the quarry to Topsham 14s. One pair of cart-wheels 8s 8d. For carrying 100 large stones from the quarry to the sea and 200 'pendent' 2s 10d. For assistance there in loading (*carciand'*) the said barge 6d. Sharpening there for the whole term 6d. 6 boards of ash (*tabulis de fraxill'*) bought 15d. For unloading (*discharkyand'*) 2 barges at Topsham 12d. In 4 carters 4s. 200 nails bought 9½d. 20 quarters of lime 10s. 400 laths bought for the canons' bread-house (*pro domo panis canonicorum*) 12d. 200 'latnayles' 2d. 1000 wedges (*kevillis*) 1d. In one roofer for the same for 2 days 6d. For his boy for the same time 3d. Fodder of 11 horses 4 quarters 6½ bushels.

> Total £4 10d.

Week 2   In wages*. In one plasterer 22d. For binding 2 carts with iron 4s. For putting axles on the same and making them with other appurtenances (*cum aliis pertinent' faciend'*) 8d. In 4 carters 4s. In one labourer in the quarry 12d. And the other labourer there 11d. In 3 labourers there 2s 3d. In 4 labourers on the Work 3s 4d. In 4 other labourers there 3s. Sharpening and steeling of axes 4½d. 226 loads of stones from Barley 9s. 23 quarters of lime 11s. Paid for 28 fothers (*foder'*) of timber carried from Lustleigh (*Lostelegh*) to Chudleigh 36s 9d. 20s in the roll . . .   . . . Fodder [as above].   Total £5 2½d.

Week 3   In wages*. Sharpening and steeling of axes 4½d. In one labourer in the quarry 11d. In 3 labourers there 2s 3d. In 4 carters 4s. In 4 labourers on the Work 3s 4d. In 5 labourers there 3s 9d. One rope weighing 10 lbs 10d. 'Vippecord' 2d. In assistance in loading one barge at the quarry 6d. 21 quarters of lime 10s 6d. In 13 carters hired to carry stones from Salcombe quarry to Blackdown (*la Blakedoune*)[7] 21s 8d, 20d each. Fodder [as above].   Total 72s 4½d.

Week 4   In wages*. Sharpening and steeling of axes 3¼d. In one labourer in the quarry 11d. In 3 other labourers there 2s 3d. In 4 carters 4s. In 4 labourers on the Work 3s 4d. In 6 other labourers there 4s 6d. In 24 carters hired to carry stones from Salcombe quarry to Blackdown 40s, for each carter 20d. 22 quarters of lime 11s. And to William de Mambiri carpenter felling a tree at Melhuish (*Melehywis*) for 2 days 9d. Paid to William de Harcomb' for 5 fothers (*foderes*) of timber carried from Chudleigh to Holloway (*Holewaye*) 6s 3d, 15d for each fother. For making new hinges (*vertivello de novo*) for the gate which leads towards the Dominican friars with hooks and other fittings (*cum gouffis et aliis pertinent'*) 10d. Fodder [as above].   Total £5 13¼d.

Week 5   In wages*. Sharpening and steeling of axes 9¼d. In one labourer in the quarry 11d. In 3 other labourers there 2s 3d. In 4 carters 4s. In 5 labourers on the Work 4s 2d. In 5 other labourers there 3s 9d. And 2 sawyers 2s 6d. For one cart with one carter (*Pro j caragio cum j carect'*) from Blackdown to Exeter 20d. For putting an axle on a cart 3d. 25 quarters of lime 12s 6d. 19 loads of stones from Silverton (*Sylfortone*) that is, 'pendeuns',[8] carried to Exeter 2s. Fodder [as above].   Total 71s 8¼d.

Week 6   In wages*. In one plasterer for 2 weeks 3s 8d . . . Sharpening and steeling of axes 5½d. In one labourer in the quarry 11d. In 3 other labourers there 2s 3d. In 4 carters 4s. In 5 labourers on the Work 4s 2d. In 4 other labourers there 3s. In 11 carters of stone (*carect' petr'*) hired to carry stones from Salcombe quarry to Blackdown 18s 4d. In labourers in the quarry 9d. And 2 sawyers for one day 5d. 23 quarters of lime 11s 6d. For 400 'pendaunz' stones bought at Silverton (*Sylferton*) 8s 6d. For their carriage, that is for 27 loads 2s 9¾d. Fodder [as above].
                                              Total £4 5s 2¾d.

Week 7   In wages*. In one plasterer 22d. Sharpening and steeling of axes 4½d. In one labourer in the quarry 11d. In 4 labourers there 3s. In 4 carters 4s. In 5 labourers on the Work 4s 2d. In 3 labourers there 2s 3d. And 2 sawyers 2s 6d. And 2 other sawyers for 3½ days 12d. In 2 labourers on the Work for one day 3d. For 500 'pendaunz' stones from Silverton 10s. For their carriage, that is for 58 loads 6s ½d. 27 quarters of lime 13s 6d. For making 2 bands with nails (*ligaminis cum clavibus*) for the bell called Marie 3d. Fodder [as above].   Total 73s 5d.

Week 8   In wages*. And one plasterer 22d. Sharpening and steeling of axes 3d. In one labourer in the quarry 11d. In 4 labourers there 3s 4d. In 4 carters 4s. In 4 labourers on the Work 3s 4d. In 3 other labourers there 2s 3d. And 2 sawyers 2s 6d. For putting an axle on one cart 3d. For assistance (*ausilio*) in raising timber at Melhuish (*Melehydis*) 1d. For carriage of one cart from Chudleigh to Exeter 2d. 21 quarters of lime 10s 6d. For 450 'pendaunz' stones from Silverton 9s and their carriage 5s 5d, that is for 52 loads. Fodder [as above].   Total 68s.

Week 9   In wages*. And one plasterer 22d. Sharpening and steeling of axes 4½d. In one labourer in the quarry 11d. In 4 other labourers there 3s 4d. In 4 carters 4s. In 4 labourers on the Work 3s 4d. And 2 sawyers 2s 6d. For putting an axle on a cart 3d. For one pair of cart-wheels bought at Taunton 6s 3d. 19 quarters of lime 9s 6d. For 400 'pendaunz' 4s, for their carriage 4s 9½d, that is for 46 loads. For fodder [as above].
                                              Total 62s 10½d.

Week 10   In wages*. And one plasterer 22d. Sharpening and steeling of axes 4½d. In one labourer in the quarry 11d. In 3 other labourers there 2s 6d. In 4 carters 4s. In 4 labourers in the quarry 3s 4d. In 2 labourers there 18d. For putting axles on 2 carts 7d. 21 quarters of lime 10s 6d. For 400 'pendaunz' 4s, for their carriage 3s 9d. One barge-load of stones from the quarry to 'la Sege' 14s. One load (*chargio*) of timber carried from Lustleigh (*Lostleye*) to Chudleigh 2s. 26 lbs of tallow bought 2s 2d. Fodder [as above].   Total 68s 8½d.

Week 11   In wages*. And one plasterer 22d. Sharpening and steeling of tools 1¾d. In one labourer in the quarry 11d. In 3 other labourers there 2s 6d. In 4 carters 4s. In 5 labourers on the Work 4s 2d. In 2 labourers there 18d. For putting an axle on a cart 3d. 3 loads (*charg'*) of timber carried from Chudleigh to Haldon (*Haladon*) 3s 9d. For assistance in loading (*chargiandum*) timber at Haldon for a whole week 12d. 24 quarters of lime 12s. For 300 'pendaunz' 3s. For their carriage 3s 10¼d, that is for 37 loads from Silverton. 2 cart-loads from the quarry set down at Blackdown 3s 4d. Fodder [as above].   Total 61s 3d.

Week 12   In wages*. And one plasterer 22d. Sharpening and steeling of axes 3d. In one labourer in the quarry 11d. In 3 other labourers there 2s 6d. In 4 carters 4s. In 3 labourers on the Work 3s 4d. In one labourer there 9d. For binding a bucket ½d. 350 'pendaunz' 3s 6d. For their carriage 3s 7¾d, that is for 35 loads. One barge-load of stones from Salcombe quarry to 'la Sege' 14s. For assistance in discharging (*discarkiand'*) the said barge 3d. Fodder [as above].   Total 54s ¼d.

(m.3d) Week 13   In wages*. Sharpening and steeling of axes 4d. In 4 carters 4s. In one labourer in the quarry 11d. In 3 labourers there 2s 6d. In 4 labourers on the Work 3s 4d. In 2 labourers there 18d. And 2 sawyers 2s 6d. 23 quarters of lime 11s 6d. For the stable hired at Newton for this term 12d. For repairing the same stable 4d. One key for the gate which is against the bishop's gate (*In j clave ad portam qua est contra portam episcopi*) 1d. Farriery of the horses for this term 9d. For the fee of Master Thomas de Witteneye for this term 33s 4d. And of John de Schyreford warden of the Work 12s 6d. Sharpening for Salcombe quarry for this term 6d. One barrow (*civer'*) bought 4d. For assistance in loading 2 barges 6d. 100 large stones and 200 'pendaunz' carried from the quarry to the sea 3s 4d. For shoeing horses with 12½ dozens 19d. For making 12 horse-shoes with our own iron 6d. And for one horse-hide bought 2s 3d. And for a drag made by John le Noreys in his meadow and for corn, with 2 carts carrying timber from Canonsteign wood[9] (*pro trag' facta Joh' le Noreys in prato suo et in blado cum ij carect' car' meremium de bosco de Canouneteyn'*) 2s. 15 lbs of 'burl' 11d. 350 'pendaunz' stones 3s 6d. For their carriage in 36 loads 3s 9d. Fodder [as above].   Total £5 14s 11d.

Cost of the bishop's throne (*Custus sedis episcopi*)   Paid to Robert de Galmeton and his associate (*socio suo*) for making the bishop's throne at task (*pro factura sedis episcopi ad tascam*) £4. [Crossed out: And to Nicholas the painter for images 11s].   Total £4.

Cost of hay   34 stacks of hay bought in various places at various prices as he shows in certain details (*per quasdam particulas*) £7 5s 9½d. 107 trusses carried from Rockbeare (*Rokebeare*) to Exeter 17s 10d, for each truss 2d. 32 trusses carried from West Clyst (*Clist Moysen*) to Exeter 4s, for each truss 1½d. 30 trusses from Sowton (*Clist Fometoum*) carried to Exeter 3s 9d, for each truss 1½d. 8 trusses carried from Rewe to Exeter 12d. 86 trusses carried from 'Athelyngebeare' (*Adelyngebeare*) to Exeter 10s 9d, for each truss 1¼d. 66 trusses carried from Greendale (*Grendel*) to Newton 2s, for each truss 2d. For wages of 11 men for 2 days making one great stack in Kalendarhay (*Calendernehaye*) 16½d, 1½d each. 13 loads of straw bought in the town for thatching the stack 2s 5¾d. Twists for the same 10½d. For a man thatching the said stack for 5 days 15d. For his servant (*serviente suo*) for 5 days 7½d.   Total £10 8¾d.

Purchase of oats   The same reckons 2 bushels 1 peck of oats bought from Cheriton 5¼d. And for 36 quarters 5½ bushels of oats bought after Pentecost £8 14s 9d. Item for 26 quarters 7 bushels of new oats bought 51s 8½d.
                                              Total £11 6s 10¾d.

Total of the whole expense of the said term £76 2s 3d.

Oats   He renders account of 63 quarters 6½ bushels 1 peck bought above. From this he expends above 61 quarters 6 bushels. And 2 quarters ½ bushel 1 peck remain.

[Cancelled: Total £11 5s 6d except the oats from Cheriton. Total of all the oats from Cheriton £13 17s 6d. From which he reckons in fodder of 20 cart-horses for 6 weeks 45 quarters 7½ bushels, to each horse etc. And in fodder of 11 horses for 18 weeks 50 quarters ½ bushel, one half bushel to each horse and not more here because he reckons 15 horses for two weeks on the altar account.]

Total of oats bought except from Cheriton 63 quarters 3 bushels by 2 tallies. Total of oats from Cheriton 185 quarters by tally. Total of all the receipts of oats for the whole year, with 9 quarters of the remainder on the account, 185 quarters from Cheriton and 104 quarters 3 bushels previously bought (*de preemptione*), as he shows in details on the said schedule 298 quarters 3 bushels. Total of the whole expense except oats £65 6s 4½d by tally.[10] Total of all the oats bought including the oats from Cheriton £25 3s.

Total of the whole expenses for the year £244 12¼d.

Item for 7 quarters 2 bushels of oats bought from Cheriton with expenses for cart-horses beyond their usual fodder (*consuet' prebend'*) by the oath of Thomas the mason 10s 10½d.

And thus the true total of the whole expenses is £244 11s 10¾d.

And the total of the whole receipts is £229 15s 10½d. And thus the expenses exceed the total of the receipts by £14 16s ¼d, which is owed to him. And he is allowed for wages in the previous year by grace as a supplement 50s. And thus he is owed in general (*universo*) £15 6s ¼d.

*   List of wages of named craftsmen is not included here, see pp. 194–5.
1   A bushel measure for oats.
2   The meaning is uncertain without any context to indicate their use.
3   Making [woodwork] for the galleries must be implied.
4   *Forma* is used here in a different sense from that of the formes of windows.
5   W. St John Hope in his notebook suggested that the meaning of this phrase is the preparation of the great bosses for gilding. This is obviously the general implication, but *apprestand'* suggests also the estimation of the amount of gold which would be required for application after priming.

⁶ This entry explains the purpose of the various purchases of moss found elsewhere in the accounts.
⁷ *La Blakedoune* is not satisfactorily identified. It appears to be a staging or storage place for stones to be carried to Exeter from Salcombe and Beer quarries by the overland route.
⁸ 'pendeuns' (and variants on this spelling) were stones usually from the quarry at Silverton which were largely used for infilling of vaulting.
⁹ Two entries appear to have been combined in one here.
¹⁰ This entry seems to be misplaced. If it applies to the Midsummer term, it is incorrect according to the preceding Midsummer totals.

2612A   Altar account: 1316, 6 June–1317, 25 September

> 2 membranes, head to tail, with a small docket sewn to the head; very good condition. This roll was previously numbered 2625 in error because it was filed out of sequence. 2625 is now a cancelled number.
> No contemporary endorsement.

(m.1) THE ACCOUNT OF JOHN DE SCHYREFORD WARDEN OF THE WORK OF THE CHURCH OF THE BLESSED PETER OF EXETER FROM SUNDAY NEXT BEFORE THE FEAST OF ST BARNABAS THE APOSTLE 1316 UNTIL THE SUNDAY NEXT BEFORE THE SAME FEAST IN THE FOLLOWING YEAR. AND FROM THAT SAME SUNDAY UNTIL THE SUNDAY BEFORE THE FEAST OF ST MICHAEL NEXT FOLLOWING [1317] FOR FOURTEEN WEEKS.

RECEIPTS

He renders account of £66 4s 8d received from dom W. de Doun' and W. de Pederton by one tally.   Total £66 4s 8d.

EXPENSES

Cost of Caen stone (*petr' de Kain*)   One boatload of stones in which are contained 162 'gobbets' and 108 coins bought inclusive (*una naviata petrarum in qua continebantur clxij gobetti et cviij koynge in grosso empto*) £6 13s 4d. 40 loads (*charg'*) of the said stones carried from Topsham to Exeter 26s 8d, 8d a load.   Total £8 by one tally from himself (*de se*).

Week 1: feast of St Barnabas [11 June] and weeks 2 and 3   In wages*.
                          Total of the said 3 weeks 12s 6d by one tally.
Week 4   Total 6s 3d by one tally.
Weeks 5, 6, 7   Total 6s 3d [each week].
Week 8   Total 7s 5d.
Weeks 9, 10, 11   Total 8s 7d [each week].
Week 12   In wages*. 20 Welsh boards bought for moulds (*xx bordis Walens' ad moldas emptis*) 4s 1d.   Total 12s 8d.

Week 13   In wages*. 2 iron pulleys and 2 brass trundle-wheels bought (*ij poleis ferreis cum ij trendellis eneis emptis*) 6s 8d. Sharpening tools (*In utensilia bateranda*) 1d.   Total 15s 4d.

Week 14   In wages*. Sharpening 1d.
                                        Total 8s 8d [corrected from 15s 4d].

Week 15   In wages*. Sharpening 3¾d. In wages of 3 men in Beer quarry 2s 2d.   Total 11s ¼d.

Week 16   In wages*.   Total 13s 1d.

Week 17: the feast of St Michael   In wages*. Sharpening 1¼d. In one labourer in Beer quarry (*in quarera de la Beara*) for 2 weeks 3s. And 3 labourers there for 2 weeks 5s, 10d a week each.   Total 21s 2¼d.

Week 18   In wages*. Sharpening 1d. In one labourer in Beer quarry 18d. And 3 labourers there 2s 6d.   Total 17s 2d.

Week 19   In wages*. And one labourer in Beer quarry 18d. And one mason there 2s. And 3 labourers there 2s 6d. Sharpening [   ].[1]
                                                 Total 19s 1d.

Weeks 20, 21   In wages*. In one labourer in Beer quarry 18d. In 3 labourers there 2s 6d.   Total 17s 1d [each week].

Week 22: the feast of All Saints [1 November] and the time changes   In wages*. And 4 carters 3s 10d. And one labourer in the said quarry 12½d. And 2 labourers there 14½d, 7¼d each. Fodder of 11 cart-horses for this week 7 quarters 1½ bushels one peck, that is, to each horse for a day and a night half one bushel one peck.
                         Total 15s 3d, except the purchase of oats.

(m.2) Week 23   In wages*. And one labourer in Beer quarry 15d. And 2 labourers there 16d.   Total 13s 8d.

Week 24   In wages*. In one labourer in Beer quarry 15d. In 2 labourers there 16d. For a dayn of land leased as well as the digging of stones (*In j daina terre locata tam petrarum fod'*) 12d. In 2 boys (*garcionibus*) assisting in digging stone for one day 2½d. In one turner (*turnero*) for 3 days 12d. And 4 carters 3s 10d. Fodder of 11 horses [as above].
                                                 Total 19s 7½d.

Weeks 25, 26   In wages*. In one labourer in Beer quarry 15d. In 2 labourers there 16d.   Total 15s 3d [each week].

Week 27   In wages*. For repairing tools (*utensilibus*) 1d. In one labourer in Beer quarry 15d. In 2 labourers there 16d. 2 chains bought for the high altar-table (*ij cathenis ad summam tabulam emptis*) 5s 6d.
                                                 Total 20s 10d.

Week 28   In wages*. In one labourer in Beer quarry 15d. And 2 labourers there 16d.   Total 15s 3d.

Week 29: 2 feasts, St Thomas the apostle [21 December] and Christmas   In wages*.   Total 11s 5¾d.

Week 30   In wages*. In one labourer in the quarry 15d. The other labourer there 8d.   Total 14s 7d.

Week 31   In wages*. In one labourer in Beer quarry 15d. The other labourer there 8d.   Total 14s 7d.

Week 32   In wages*. In one labourer in Beer quarry 15d. The other labourer there 8d. Sharpening of tools 1d.   Total 15s 5d.

Weeks 33, 34   In wages*. In one labourer in Beer quarry 15d. The other labourer there 8d. Sharpening 1d.   Total 18s ½d each week.

Week 35   In wages*. Sharpening 1d. In one labourer in Beer quarry 15d. The other labourer there 8d. For 25 Irish boards (*bordis Ybern'*) bought for the requirements of the altar-table (*ad necessaria tabule*) 5s.

Total 23s ½d.

Week 36   In wages*. Sharpening ½d. One labourer in the quarry 15d. The other labourer there 8d. For 26 boards carried from Teignmouth (*de Teingemiwe*) 8d.   Total 18s 8½d.

Week 37: 2 feasts, St Peter's Chair and St Mathias [21 and 24 February]
   In wages*. Sharpening 1d. In one labourer in the quarry 12½d. And the other labourer there 7d.   Total 15s 1¼d.

Week 38   In wages*. In one labourer in the quarry 15d. And the other labourer there 8d. In 2 carters for this week 2s. Sharpening 1d. Fodder of 7 cart-horses carting stones for that week 4 quarters 4½ bushels 1 peck, to each horse [as above].   Total 20s ½d.

Week 39   In wages*. In one labourer in Beer quarry 15d. And the other labourer there 8d. Sharpening tools 1d.   Total 16s 3½d.

Week 40: the time changes   In wages*. Sharpening ½d.

Total 14s 4½d.

Week 41   In wages*. Sharpening ½d.   Total 17s 1½d.

Week 42   In wages*. Sharpening 2½d.   Total 16s 3½d.

Week 43   In wages*. Sharpening ½d. 3 labourers in the quarry for 3 days 16d.   Total 7s 5d.

Week 44   In wages*. Sharpening 2d.   Total 16s 2d.

Week 45   In wages*. Sharpening 1¾d.   Total 16s 8¾d.

Week 46   In wages*. Sharpening 1d.   Total 16s 8d.

Week 47: 2 feasts, Invention of the Holy Cross and St John before-the-Latin-Gate [3 and 6 May]   In wages*. Sharpening 1½d.

Total 13s 8½d.

Weeks 48, 49   In wages*. Sharpening 1d.

Total 16s 8d [each week].

Week 50   In wages*. For 4 gudgeon-pins for one engine (*gogoinis ad j ingenium*) for Beer quarry 4d. Sharpening ¾d.   Total 16s 11¾d.

(m.1d) Week 51   In wages*. For repairing and making a road-way (*vico*) from Beer quarry to the sea, as well as carting stones 3s. Sharpening 2d. And one labourer in Beer quarry 12d.   Total 26s 9d.

Week 52   In wages*. And 4 labourers in Beer quarry 3s 4d. And 2 labourers there 18d. For 4 carters 4s. For hay bought for cart-horses 4s. For 5 iron wedges (*veggis ferreis*) for the quarry 12d. Fodder of 10 horses 4 quarters 3 bushels. Sharpening 1d.   Total 34s 8d.

Week 53   In wages*. In 3 labourers in Beer quarry 2s 6d. And one labourer there 9d. And 2 carters 2s. For making one great hammer

(*magno martello*) 3d. Sharpening 1d. For 2 barge-loads of stones from Beer quarry to Topsham 28s 6d. Fodder of 5 horses 2 quarters 1½ bushels.
Total 55s 4d.

Week 54   In wages*. In 3 labourers in Beer quarry 2s 6d. One labourer there 9d. Sharpening 1d.   Total 24s 8d.

Week 55   In wages*. In 3 labourers in the quarry 2s 6d. And one labourer there 9d. Sharpening 1d.   Total 24s 8d.

Week 56   In wages*. In 3 labourers in Beer quarry 2s 6d. And one labourer there 9d. Sharpening 1d.   Total 24s 8d.

Week 57   In wages*. And 3 labourers in the quarry 2s 6d. And 3 labourers in Beer quarry 2s 3d. Sharpening 1½d. For 100 large stones carted from Beer quarry to the sea 3s 6d.   Total 26s 6½d.

Week 58   In wages*. In 3 labourers in Beer quarry 2s 6d. And one labourer there 9d. Sharpening and steeling of axes (*securis acerandis*) 4½d. Paid for 18 cart-loads of stone from Beer quarry to Blackdown (*usque la Blakedoune*) 45s.   Total 68s 3½d.

Week 59   In wages*. In 3 labourers in Beer quarry 2s 6d. And one labourer there 9d. Sharpening and steeling of axes 1d. For one cart hired from Beer quarry to Blackdown 2s 6d. For making one hammer 6d. For one large barge (*bargea*) of stones from Beer quarry to 'La Sege' 14s.
Total 40s.

Week 60   In wages*. 3 labourers in Beer quarry 2s 6d. In one labourer there 9d. Sharpening and steeling of axes 1d. Paid for one dayn of land at Beer quarry 12d.   Total 24s.

Week 61   In wages*. In 3 labourers in Beer quarry 2s 6d. One labourer there 9d. For assistance (*in ausilio*) in loading a barge 6d. Sharpening ½d.
Total 23s 5½d.

Week 62   In wages*. Sharpening ½d. In 3 labourers in Beer quarry 2s 6d. For one barge of stones from Beer quarry to 'La Sege' 10s.
Total 31s 10½d.

Weeks 63, 65   In wages*. In 3 labourers in Beer quarry 2s 6d. Sharpening ½d.   Total 18s 6½d [each week].

Week 64   In wages*. 3 labourers in Beer quarry 2s 6d. Sharpening [   ].[1]
Total 18s 6d.

Week 66   In wages*. 3 labourers in Beer quarry 2s 6d. Sharpening ½d. Sharpening for Beer quarry for the whole term 6d.
Total 19s ½d.

Purchase of oats (*Empcio avene*)   For 25 quarters 4½ bushels 1 peck 67s 4½d.   Total 67s 4½d.

Oats   He renders account of 25 quarters 4½ bushels 1 peck of oats bought above which were expended above and nothing remains (*et nichil remanet*).
Total of the whole expense £69 19s 9½d.

And thus the total of the expense exceeds the total of the receipts by 75s 1½d.

Attached docket:
The purchase of oats for fodder for the cart-horses towards the cost of the

table (*in custa tabule*) for various weeks. 4 quarters 7 bushels 9s 2d. 5 quarters 6 bushels 12s 1d. 3 quarters 2 bushels 7s 8d. 4 quarters ½ bushel 18d. 4 quarters 4½ bushels 1 peck 10s 8½d. 6 quarters 4½ bushels of oats 26s 3d.

Total of quarters 25 quarters 4½ bushels 1 peck

Total of money (*den'*) 67s 4½d.

---

* List of wages of named craftsmen is not included here, see pp. 196–7.
1 MS leaves blank.

2613 1317, 26 September–1318, 1 October

4 membranes, head to tail. The whole roll is not badly decayed but so thoroughly stained down the whole right-hand side as to have washed away the writing, which cannot now be read by ultra-violet light, and many portions are also almost or wholly obscured by galls; m.1 complete, mm.2 and 3 covered completely by obscuring tissue, m.4 complete.
Endorsed: *Compotus Iohannis de Schireford capellani custod' operis ecclesie . . . dominica proxima ante festum sancti Michaelis . . . usque ad dominicam proximam post festum sancti Michaelis . . .*
Printed: Extract in Oliver, p. 381.

(m.1) THE ACCOUNT OF JOHN DE SCHIREFORD CHAPLAIN WARDEN OF THE WORK OF THE CHURCH OF THE BLESSED PETER OF EXETER FROM THE SUNDAY BEFORE THE FEAST OF ST MICHAEL 1317 UNTIL THE SUNDAY FOLLOWING THE FEAST OF ST MICHAEL IN THE NEXT YEAR.

RECEIPTS

The same renders account of £124 18s 8d of the lord bishop . . .
[The rest of this section is so faded and obscured by galls as to yield only a few incomplete and isolated sums of money].

EXPENSES

Default of rent [illegible].
(m.2) Surplus [illegible].

MICHAELMAS TERM

Week 1   Entries include: . . . labourers on the Work 2s 6d. In 4 other labourers there 3s . . .

Week 2   Entries include: . . . 3 other labourers there 2s 3d. . . . labourers in the quarry 11d. And 2 other labourers there . . . 20 quarters of lime 10s. . . .

Week 3   Entries include: . . . one plasterer . . . labourers . . . 24 quarters
of lime 12s. 450 'pendant' stones . . . 4s 6d, and their carriage . . .
Total 68s 2½d.

Week 4 [illegible].   Total 2s.

[Week 5]   Entries include: . . . labourers in the quarry 11d. In 2 other
labourers there 20d. In 3 labourers on the Work . . . horse-hide bought
for the requirements of the carts 15d. One rope for . . . 500 'pendaunz'
5s, with carriage . . . Fodder for 11 horses 4 quarters 6½ bushels.

Week 6: 2 feasts, All Saints and All Souls [1 and 2 November] and the
time changes   Entries include: Sharpening 2d. In one labourer in the
quarry 7¾d. In 2 other labourers there . . .   . . . on the Work 16¾d. In 5
other labourers there 2s 7¼d. . . . sawyers 21d. 4 lbs of wax bought for
cement 2s. For making buckets . . . Fodder [as above].
Total 50s 2 . . .

Week 7   Entries include: Sharpening 2¼d. In one labourer . . . 2 carters
4s. In one plasterer 18½d. In 3 labourers on the Work 2s 3d . . . 2 sawyers
. . . 500 'pendaunz' 5s 6d. . . .   Total 75s 11d.

Week 8   Entries include: Sharpening and steeling of axes 6¾d. . . . In
3 carters 3s 2d. In one plasterer 18½d . . . 19 quarters of lime 9s 6d.
Fodder for 9 horses 3 quarters 7½ bushels.

Week 9: 2 feasts, Dedication of the Church and St Katherine [21 and
25 November]   Entries include: . . . one plasterer 18½d. In 3 labourers
on the Work 2s 3d. In 2 labourers there 15d. In one labourer in the quarry
. . . For binding a cask (*tino*) 1d. 18 quarters of lime 9s. . . . 'Wyppecord'
3d. For sawing 463 feet at task 3s 5½d. . . .   Total 42s 1¼d.

[Week 10]   Entries include: Sharpening 2¼d. In one labourer in the
quarry 9½d. In 2 other labourers . . . In 4 labourers on the Work 3s. . . .
(m.3) 2 stones of beef tallow (*cepi bovin'*) bought . . .
Total 27s 4¾d.

[Week 11]   Entries include: . . . In one labourer in the quarry 9½d. In
2 other labourers . . . In 4 labourers on the Work 3s. 6½ quarters of lime
. . .

Week 12   Entries include: Sharpening and steeling of axes 8d. In one
labourer . . . In 4 labourers on the Work 3s. One pair of wheels . . . For
sharpening for Salcombe quarry 5d. . . . from the church of St Erth
granted to the lord king 5s 8d. One stone of 'burl' bought 11d. . . . For
sawing 350 feet at task 2s 7½d. . . .   Total 35s 4½d.

Week 13   Entries include: Sharpening and steeling of axes 8½d. In one
labourer in the quarry 9½d. . . . 4 labourers on the Work 3s. . . . For
shoeing horses with 11 dozen . . . 20d . . . For a stable 4d. Farriery for the
horses 9d. For the fee of Master Thomas de Wyteney . . .   . . . Schyreford
warden of the Work 12s 6d. 20 quarters of lime 10s. For putting an axle on
a cart. . . . One barge-load of stones from Salcombe quarry set down
(*locatis*) at 'la Sege' 14s. . . . For sawing 300 feet . . .
Total £4 17s 1½d.

Purchase of oats for fodder   66 quarters and 1 bushel bought £6 4s 2¾d,
from which in fodder for 10 horses for one week 4 quarters 3 bushels, to

each horse for a day and a night half a bushel. And for fodder ... of 9 horses for 2 weeks 7 quarters 7 bushels and not more because he reckons ...

Total 41 quarters 1 bushel, and there remains ...

Total of default of rent 3s 1d. Total of the surplus of the said account ...

Total of the Work for the said term £35 ... Total of the purchase of oats £6 4s 2[¾]d.

Total of the totals of the whole cost and surplus ...

CHRISTMAS TERM

Week 1: one feast, Christmas   Entries include: ... And one plasterer 18½d. ... For sharpening and steeling of axes ...   Total 19s ...

Week 2   Entries include: ... And one labourer in the quarry 9½d. And 2 other labourers there 18d. ... For sharpening and steeling of axes 5¼d. In 4 labourers on the Work 3s. One sack (*sacco*) bought ...   ... lard for the engines (*porcinis pro ingeniis*) 3s.   Total 23s 7d.

Week 3   Entries include: In one labourer in the quarry 9½d. And 2 other labourers there 18d. ... and steeling of axes 3¼d. In 4 labourers on the Work 3s. Paid for the maintenance (*pro procuratione*) ...   ... for the church of St Erth (*Lanandriho*). For sawing 335 feet at task 2s 6d.

Total 25s 6d.

Week 4   Entries include: ... steeling of axes 3d. In one labourer in the quarry 9½d. In 2 other labourers there 18d ... 4 labourers on the Work 3s. In one plumber soldering over the old vestry (*In j plumbar' soldiend' super veterem vestiarum*) for one week 18d. ... sawing 200 feet 20¼d.

Total 21s 11¼d.

Week 5   Entries include: ... steeling of axes 3½d. In one labourer in the quarry 9½d. In 4 labourers on the Work 3s. ... 100 lbs of tin for solder (*stagnis pro soldur'*) ... In one plumber soldering over the church (*soldient' super ecclesiam*) for one week 18d.   Total 34s 10½d.

Week 6: with cost of lead   Entries include: ... In one labourer in the quarry 9d. In 2 other labourers there 18d ... For carrying one great tree-trunk (*magno ligno*) from Norton to Exeter 2s. 60 fotmels of lead bought £6 8s 3d. ... for roofing the tower of the church (*cooperiendum turrim de ecclesia*) 18d. In one man mending a window in St Mary's chapel (*capellam beate Marie*) 12d. ... sawing at task 2s 7½d.

Total £7 5s 7½d.

Week 7   Entries include: ... Sharpening and steeling of axes 2½d. In one labourer in the quarry 9½d. In 2 other labourers there 18d. In 4 labourers in the quarry 3s. ... 100 stones carried from the quarry to the sea ... And one man mending a glass window in the new Work 18d. ... 100 lead-nails bought (*clavis pro plumbo empt'*) 3d. Fodder of 9 horses ... more because of the length of the journey.   Total 26s ¼d.

Week 8: 2 feasts   Entries include: In 2 carters 2s. In 3 labourers on the Work 22½d. In one labourer in the quarry 8d. ... In one plumber 15d. And one man mending glass windows (*fenestras vitreas*) in the new Work 15d. In a roofer ... the lodge in which dom Walter lives (*logeam in quam dominus Walterus inhabitat*) for 2 days and the other lodge 8d. ...

Sharpening 3¾d . . . sawing at task (*thascam*) 18d. Fodder of 9 horses 4 quarters 3 bushels. Total 21s 9½d.

Week 9   Entries include: . . . and steeling of axes 17¼d. In one labourer in the quarry 9½d. In 2 other labourers there 18d. . . . In 2 carters 2s. In 4 labourers on the Work 3s. In one plumber 18d. . . . 'Vippecord' 2d. For putting an axle on a cart 3d. Tempering 13 lbs of steel 6½d. . . . For one man . . . Kalendarhay (*Kalendarenehaye*) 12d. One barge-load of stones from Salcombe to 'la Sege'. . . . In one roofer roofing over the cloister (*cooperient' super claustrum*) 12d. For his colleague (*coadjutori*) 8d. . . . Fodder [as above]. Total 44s 10[½]d.

Cost of images for the bishop's throne (*imag' ad sedem episcopi*)   For carving 6 images for the bishop's throne (*In vj imagin' talliand' pro sede episcopi*) 32s. Total 32s.

Week 10   Entries include: . . . sharpening 2¼d. In one labourer in the quarry 9½d. In 2 other labourers there 18d. . . . carters 2s. In 3 labourers on the Work 2s 3d. In one plumber mending the chapter house (*emendend' domum capituli*) 18d. . . . 10 quarters of lime 5s. For making 1100 horsenails 11d. For sawing 400 feet . . . Fodder [as above]. Total 31s 9¼d.

(m.3) Week 11: the time changes   Entries include: . . . and steeling of axes 4d. In one labourer in the quarry 11d. In 2 other labourers there . . . In 2 labourers on the Work 2s 6d. . . . mending glass windows (*emend' fenestras vitreas*) 2s. In 2 sawyers sawing 300 [feet] at task 2s . . . [Fodder as above]. Total 28s 8d.

Week 12   Entries include: . . . and steeling of axes 3½d. In one labourer in the quarry 11d. In 2 labourers there 20d. In wages of 2 carters . . . In 3 labourers on the Work 2s 6d. For wages of Crockernewelle for the larger bell (*pro majore campana*) . . . Fodder [as above]. Total 28s 7½d.

Week 13   Entries include: In one labourer in the quarry 11d. In 2 labourers there 20d. In 2 carters 2s . . . In wages of Stephen the smith for making 42 dowels 5 long and 15 smaller clamps for carts (*xljj doulis v longas gropas xiiij minores pro carectis*) . . . Fodder [as above]. Total 21s 6¾d.

Week 14   Entries include: . . . In one labourer in the quarry 11d. In 2 labourers there 20d. In 2 carters 2s. . . . Sawing 350 feet at task 2s 7½d. And one plasterer 22d. Fodder [as above]. Total 24s 11¼d.

Week 15   Entries include: . . . And one labourer in the quarry 11d. In 2 labourers there 20d. In 2 carters 2s. And 2 sawyers sawing 250 feet 22½d. And one plasterer . . . . . . of iron for the bell, and for making marble columns because of the fall of the newly-made window, for lighting a candle . . . (*ferri pro campan' et ad faciend' columpnas marmoreas pro casu fenestri noviter facti ad illuminand' cereum* . . .)[1] . . . In wages of W. Crokernewille for making the said formes (*formas*) and mending the clapper of the bell (*emendant' percussor' campane*) 5s 6d. 100 nails . . . In wages of one glazier mending glass and setting it in the said forme 4d. Solder for the same 2d. . . . Fodder of 9 horses 3 quarters 7½ bushels. Total 37s 11¼d.

Week 16   Entries include: For sharpening and steeling of axes 7½d. In one labourer in the quarry 11d. In 2 other labourers there 20d. . . . In

3 labourers on the Work 2s 6d. And one plasterer . . . 18½d. And 2 sawyers sawing 300 feet 27d, 9d a hundred. 6 quarters of lime 3s. In carriage
of stones . . . 2s. For repair of the labourers' tools in the quarry (*in emendacione instrumentorum operariorum in quarera*) 6d. For the stable at Newton
12d. Farriery for the horses . . . horseshoes 18d. Candles for the stable for
this term 4d. 4 pairs of cart-traces . . . 'Vippecord' 2d. For making 400
'tacnailes' 4d. For the fee of Master Thomas 33s 4d. And of J de Sch
. . . [12s] 6d. . . . Fodder [as above].   Total £4 3s 2d.

Week 17   Nothing here because it is reckoned in the altar account in
the week of Christmas.

Purchase of oats   He accounts for 25 quarters of oats previously bought
(*de preemptione*). And for 54 quarters of oats bought for £5 10¾d for fodder
of 9 horses for 3 weeks 13 quarters one bushel . . . a week in the roll of
details (*particular'*), that is, to each horse for a day and a night a half bushel
and 3½ bushels more a week on account of the length of the journey [etc].
And for fodder of 9 horses for 7 weeks 27 quarters 4½ bushels and not more
because he reckons . . . for 7 weeks on the altar account.

Total of oats bought 40 quarters 5½ bushels, and of the remainder . . . of
the preceding quarter. [Cancelled: Total expenses of oats 40 quarters
5½ bushels]. Total of oats £5 10¾d. Total cost of the Work for the said term
£32 12s . . .

Total of the whole cost of the preceding term £37 13s 5¾d.

EASTER TERM

Week 1: feast of Easter   Entries include: . . . In 2 labourers for 3 days
10d. In carters 2s. . . . sawing 180 feet 16d. One pair of cart-wheels bought
at Petherton (*Pederton*) 5s 2d. . . . seeking them at Petherton (*querent'
easdem apud Pederton*) 4d. Fodder of 9 horses 3 quarters 7½ bushels, to each
horse half a bushel.   Total 28s 2½d.

Week 2: 3 feasts   Entries include: . . . one man plastering for 3 days 11d.
Sharpening and steeling of axes 4¾d. And 2 sawyers sawing 150 feet of
board (*bord'*) 13½d. In 3 labourers on the Work 15d. In 2 carters . . .
. . . labourer in the quarry for 3 days 5½d. In 2 other labourers there 10d.
For putting an axle on a cart 3d. 400 *clavis ad* . . . Fodder [as above].
                    Total 16s 6d.

Week 3   Entries include: . . . and one labourer in the quarry 11d. In 2
other labourers there 20d. In 2 carters 2s. . . . In 3 labourers on the Work
2s 6d. In 2 sawyers sawing 300 feet 2s 7d. For repair of carts 8d . . . 50
seams of sand 12d. For 20 loads of 'pendent' carried from Silverton 2s 6d,
1½d a load. For 15 loads of . . . , 1¼d a load. Fodder [as above].
                    Total 33s 2¾d.

Week 4   Entries include: . . . Sharpening and steeling of axes and
mending one lock (*serrura*) 4¾d. . . . In 3 labourers on the Work 2s 6d. In
2 sawyers in the wood (*in bosco*) for 4 days 20d. And one labourer on the
Work . . . In 2 carters 2s. In one plumber for one day 3d. One lb of solder
bought 1½d. 2 linch-pins (*lincis*) and 2 bands (*bendis*) . . . 4d. In one plasterer
for 2 days 7d. In one labourer in the quarry 11d. In 2 other labourers
there 20d. . . . '[pen]danz' carried from Silverton to Exeter 4s 10½d. For

carriage of 36 loads of the same 4s 6d, 1½d a load. 9 quarters of lime 4s 6d. 150 'bornayles' bought for centerings 4½d. Fodder [as above].

Total 50s 3½d.

Week 5   Entries include: . . . Sharpening and steeling of axes 4d. In 3 labourers on the Work 2s 6d. In one labourer there 9d. And the other labourer there 8d. and the third labourer (*tercio operario*) there 8d . . . In one glazier 2s. In one plasterer 22d . . . In 2 other labourers [in the quarry] 20d. In 2 carters 2s. For carrying 22 loads of 'pendens' from Silverton quarry to Exeter . . . For carrying 21 loads of 'pendic' from the same 2s 2¼d. 11 quarters of lime 5s 6d. 400 'pend' stones bought 4s. Fodder [as above].

Total 54s 1¼d.

Week 6   Entries include: . . . Sharpening and steeling of axes 2¾d . . . And 2 labourers [on the Work] 18d. And one labourer there 8d. And in one man helping carters to load up in the wood (*carkiand' in bosco*) 13d. And one plasterer and one mason 3s 8d. And one glazier (*verrator'*) 2s. One labourer in the quarry 11d. And 2 other labourers there . . . And 2 carters 2s. For making a gudgeon (*gouygone*) for a bell 8d. One grozing iron (*grusor'*) and solder bought 5d. Board-nails for the well (*pro fonte*) . . . 4d. For binding 2 buckets and one tub 2½d. 500 'pend' 5s 6d. For carrying 27 loads of the same from Silverton to Exeter 2s 9¾d, 1¾d a load. For carrying 37 loads of the same from the same place 4s 7½d, 1½d a load. 16 quarters of lime 8s 3d. Fodder [as above].

Total 61s ½d.

Week 7:   Entries include: . . . Sharpening and steeling of axes 3¼d. In 3 labourers on the Work 2s 6d. In 2 labourers there 18d. And one labourer there 8d. In one plasterer and one mason . . . And one glazier 2s. In one labourer in the quarry 11d. In 2 other labourers there 20d. In 2 carters 2s. . . . One large hammer (*magno martello*) for Salcombe quarry 6d. For 800 'pend' 8s. 73 loads of the same carried . . . , 1½d a load. 15 quarters of lime 7s 9d. For carrying 24 cart-loads (*car'*) from Salcombe quarry to Blackdown 36s, 18d [a load]. Fodder [as above].

Total £4 19s 2¾d.

Week 8: feast of Pentecost   Entries include: . . . In wages of 2 carters 2s. 150 horse-shoes bought at Lopen fair 14s 7d. And 300 of iron . . . 8 dozens of cart-clouts 16s. 45 of the same clouts 3s 9d. 4000 horse-nails 6s. For 27 . . . of iron bought there 8s 6d. In expenses of J. de Schyreford going to Lopen with 4 horses for one day and remaining there for one day and returning for 1½ days 3s 9d. For fodder [as above].

Total 76s 7d.

Week 9   Entries include: . . . Sharpening and steeling of axes 4½d. . . . and one plasterer 22d. And one glazier 2s. In 4 labourers on the Work 3s 4d. In 3 labourers there 2s 3d. In one labourer . . . 11d. In 2 labourers there 20d. In 2 carters 2s. 15 quarters of lime 7s 6d. 600 'pend' stones 6s. For carrying 42 loads . . . 5s 3d. 4 quarters of charcoal (*carbon'*) bought for smelting lead ashes (*pro ciner' plumbi fundend'*) 2s 4d. For carrying 27 cart-loads from Salcombe quarry to Blackdown 39s. Farriery for the horses for this term 9d. For the fee of Master Thomas 33s 4d. And of J. de [Schy]-reford 12s 6d. For the stable hired at Newton 12d. For sharpening for Salcombe quarry 3d. For shoeing horses . . . dozens of our own iron 14d. For packing? for glass (*In get'² pro vitro*) 2½d. For fodder [as above].

Total £7 5s 4¼d.

Oats remaining   Item he renders account for 38 quarters 2½ bushels from the preceding quarter of the remainder (*de remanenti*) from which in fodder of 9 horses for 9 weeks . . . 3½ bushels and 2 quarters 7 bushels remain.   Total is shown (*summa patet*)

The total of the cost of the Work of the said quarter £28 4s 6½d.

(m.2d) MIDSUMMER TERM

[Week 1]   Entries include: . . . In 2 labourers . . . 2 carters 2s . . . And 3 labourers on the Work . . . 44 loads . . . stones from the quarry to 'la Sege' . . . Fodder [etc].   Total 56s 5d.

[Week 2] [illegible]   Total 75s 8½d.

[Week 3]   Entries include: . . . Sharpening 3½d. In one labourer in the quarry 11d . . . In one other glazier for 5 days 20d. . . . In 3 other labourers there 2s 3d. . . . For binding a cart-wheel (*ligatione j rot' pro quadam carect'*) 8½d. . . . Fodder [etc].   Total . . . s 10¼d.

[Week 4]   Entries include: . . . Sharpening and steeling of axes 7¼d. . . . . . . glazier 6s. In one man . . . the said glaziers 2s 6d. In 3 other labourers there 2s 3d. . . . For 59 loads of the same from Silverton . . .
Total . . . s 5¾d.

[Week 5]   Entries include: . . . Sharpening 3¼d. In one labourer in the quarry 11d. In 4 labourers . . . 2 carters 2s. In 3 labourers on the Work 2s 3d. In 2 labourers there 18d. . . . 18 quarters of lime 9d. . . .

[Week 6] [illegible]   Total £5 6s 5½d.

[Week 7]   Entries include: . . . In one labourer in the quarry 11d. In 4 other labourers there 3s 4d. . . . 5 quarters of lime 2s 6d. Fodder etc.
Total 29s 7½d.

[Week 8]   Entries include: . . . Sharpening and steeling of axes 6½d. . . . In one labourer there 9d. In 2 carters 2s. In 4 labourers on the Work . . . For carrying stones from the quarry to the sea 3s 3d. 3 barge-loads of stones from the quarry . . . For newly making . . . for St Peter's well[3] (*pro fonte sancti Petri*) 12d. 6 quarters of lime 3s. And one labourer on the Work . . . Stones bought at Silverton for the well 8d. For fodder [etc].
Total 69s ½d.

[Week 9]   For carving 18 wooden bosses (*Pro xviij clavis lygneis talliandis*) £6.   Total is shown (*patet*).
. . . Sharpening and steeling of axes 12d. . . . And one labourer in the quarry 11d. In 4 other labourers there 3s 4d. In one labourer there . . . In one labourer there 8d . . . Fodder [etc].   Total 41s 11d.

[Week 10]   Entries include: Sharpening and steeling of axes 6¼d. . . . In one labourer in the quarry 11d. In 4 other labourers there 3s 4d. In one labourer . . . In one labourer there 8d. 1000 laths bought 2s [6d]. . . . repairing carts 12d. 11 quarters of lime 2s 6d. . . . For making [58] bars for glass windows with our own iron 3s 9d. . . . Fodder [etc].
Total 60s 6¼d.

Week 11   Entries include: . . . Sharpening and steeling of axes 4¼d. . . . and 2 sawyers 2s 6d. In one labourer in the quarry 11d. In 4 other labourers there . . . In 2 carters 2s. In 4 labourers on the Work 3s 4d. In one labourer there 8d. For founding [one bell][4] with 5 lb of brass bought (*cum v li er' empt' et fundend'*) 3s 1d . . . carried from 'la Sege' to Exeter 10d. For one roofer with his servant for one day . . . carriage from the quarry to Blackdown . . . Fodder [etc].   50s 4¼d.

(m.3d) [Week 12]   Entries include: . . . Sharpening 6½d. . . . In 2 other labourers there 20d. In one labourer there 9d. In 2 carters . . . One load from the quarry to Blackdown 20d. . . . 10 quarters of lime 5s. . . . For 4 shingles (*singul'*) 2d. . . . 172 lbs of iron for making iron work . . . Fodder [etc].   Total 62s ½d.

[Week 13]   Entries include: . . . And 2 sawyers 2s 6d. . . . In one labourer in the quarry 11d. In 4 other labourers there 3s 4d. In one labourer there 9d. . . . In 4 labourers on the Work 3s 4d. In one labourer there 8d. 2 loads (*car'*) carried from the quarry to Exeter 6s . . . 8 quarters of lime 4s. For mending 2 tubs 2d. Fodder [etc].   Total 47s 7d.

[Week 14]   Entries include: . . . For sharpening and steeling of axes 3d. . . . And 2 sawyers 2s. . . . [In one labourer] the quarry 11d. In 4 other labourers there 3s 4d. In one labourer there 9d. In 2 carters 2s. In 3 labourers on the Work . . . For the stable at Newton for this term 12d. For the fee of Master Thomas for this term . . . and of J. de Schyreford 12s 6d. For farriery for the horses 9d. For 100? . . . for ironwork . . .[5] 8 quarters of lime 4s. For shoeing horses with 11½ dozens from our own iron (*propriis ferris*) 23d. One pair of wheels . . . . . . for windows (*pro fenestr'*) 12d. For their carriage 8d. . . . Fodder etc.   Total £9 16s 10d.

[Purchase of hay] . . . bought in various places £8 9d. For carrying 38 trusses from Rockbeare (*Rokebere*) to Exeter 6s. . . . For carrying 167 trusses from West Clyst (*Clist Moyson*) and Sowton (*Clist Fometoun*) 20s 10½d, 2d a truss. And for carrying . . . trusses from Greendale (*Grendel*) to Exeter 6s 2d, 2d a truss. For carrying 89 trusses from Duryard (*Dureherde*) to Exeter 6s 7d . . . In wages of 5 men for 4 days making one great stack in Kalenderhaye 2s 8d . . . for a roofer for thatching (*cooperient'*) the said stack . . . Twists for the same 15d. . . . with his colleague (*coadiutore suo*) 7d.   Total £11 15s.

[Purchase of oats]   . . . from the preceding quarter . . . £14 18s ¾d. . . . for 14 weeks 55 quarters one bushel, to each horse for a day and a night half a bushel and thus there remains . . .

[Purchase of glass]...[Item 629 weys][6] of white glass bought at Rouen (. . . *de albo vitro empt' apud Rotomagens'*) £15 14s 9d. Item 203 weys of coloured [glass] (*ij*^c *iij peys de color'*) [£10 3s].[6] For a barge hired to carry the said glass from Sutton to Exeter 10s.   Total £26 7s 9d.

For making [240 feet][6] of glass from our own glass 52s 6d [altered from 52s 9d] for each foot of white . . . . . . 56 feet of coloured (*color'*) glass . . . Total 52s 6d.

[Purchase of marble]   . . . [38][6] . . . of marble for the galleries (*marmor' ad aluras*) between the great altar and the choir (*inter magnum altarem et chorum*) [altered from *magni altaris*] with capitals and bases for the same (*cum capitrall' et basis ad idem*) £10 8s, 5s 6d for each . . . [Cancelled: . . . for 4 columns for 'la Poulpyte' 18s, in part payment of 8 marks].

Total £10 8s.

... [54 ... 6 great capitals (*liiij chev* ... *vj magn' capitrill'*)][6] 32 pairs of capitals 6 large corbels (*xxxij parum capitrill' vj magn' surs'*) 8 ... for his work (*pro opere suo*) 108s 4d.   Total £15 10s.

Total of the whole term £127 10½d. Total with oats £131 18s 11¼d. Total of all the totals £255 4s 10¼d.

And he ought to answer for £18 13s 3½d, from which he is allowed £14 11s 2¼d owed to him from the altar roll ... And thus he ought to answer for £4 2s 1½d clear (*de claro*).

Note: The bad condition of this roll makes it impossible to compile wage lists of named craftsmen. For those names which it has been possible to abstract, see p. 212.

[1] The passage is badly damaged, but the reading of this part is clear, though it is difficult to make sense of it. Three separate items are run together, and *ad faciend' columnas* .. *noviter facti* seems to record damage caused by the fall of a window resulting in the need to replace columns?

[2] The meaning of *get' pro vitro* is very doubtful. MLW gives a meaning connected with guarding for *waita/geyta*, so possibly this may mean protective packing?

[3] St Peter's well, which is the *fons* referred to on several occasions, was the chief source of the water supply of the Close, brought from St Sidwell's spring in the capitular manor outside Eastgate through underground passages which still exist. The earliest existing 'plat' of the Close, of late sixteenth century date, shows the well as a small circular building near the north-west corner of the cathedral.

[4] A passage defaced by galls: W. St John Hope in notes made in 1915 has a reading of *campan'* which is now illegible.

[5] A passage defaced by galls: Hope as above has a reading of an item *iij[c] ferri empt' apud Dertemuth*? which is now entirely illegible.

[6] A passage defaced by galls: Hope as above has readings 'Item 629 weys', '£10 3s', '240 feet', '38' and *liiij chev'* ... *vj mag' capitrill'*, all of which are now totally illegible.

2614 1318, 1 October–1319, 30 September

3 membranes, head to tail, good condition.
Endorsed: *Compotus Johannis de Shireford capellani custodis ecclesie beati Petri Exon' a dominica proxima post festum sancti Michaelis anno domini m°ccc°xviij usque ad eandem dominicam anno revoluto.*
Printed: Extract in Oliver, p. 381.

(m.1) THE ACCOUNT OF JOHN DE SCHYREFORD CHAPLAIN WARDEN OF THE WORK OF THE CHURCH OF THE BLESSED PETER OF EXETER FROM SUNDAY NEXT AFTER THE FEAST OF ST MICHAEL 1318 TO THE SAME SUNDAY IN THE FOLLOWING YEAR.

Arrears The same renders account of £4 2s 1½d of arrears from the preceding account.

RECEIPTS

And of £124 18s 8d received from dom. Walter Daumarle of the gift of the lord bishop for the year. And of £48 from the canons' prebend for the year.

And of £17 from the church of St Erth (*Lananduho*) in Cornwall. And of £6 8s 4d from the dignity of the dean. And of 64s from the dignity of the treasurer. And of 60s from the dignity of the precentor. And of 38s from the dignity of the chancellor. And of 33s 11¼d from the red chest. And of 26s 4½d from Whitsuntide offerings. And of 6s 1½d on 1 August (*ad gulam Augusti*). And of [   ].¹ And of £10 from the testament of Master Richard of Morcestr'. And of 100s from the testament of dom. John Tholiron'. And of 13s 4d from the testament of dom Thomas late rector of Dartington (*Dertingnton*). And of 2s from the testament of dom Richard rector of the church of Petertavy (*Thavi sancti Petri*). And of 5s of the testament of James de Mohun. And of 12d from the testament of Richard de Mavygg'. And of 12d from the testament of Henry Pers'. And of 2d from the rector of Talaton (*Taleton*). And of 2s from the treasurer. And of 10d from him from a certain dead man (*de quodam mortuo*). And of 6s 8d from the testament of Richard Coling. And of 20s from the testament of Benedict Bastard in Cornwall. And of [   ].¹ And of [   ].¹ And of 13d from people confessing, through the penitentiary (*de confitentibus per penitentiar'*). And of 2d from the obit of Eustace. And of 8s 2d from rent of assize for the year. And of 15d from 3 old wheels. And of 10d from withdrawal of a labourer (*de retractione operar'*).

Total of receipts £230 10¾d.

EXPENSES

Default of rent (*Defectus redditus*)   The same reckons in default of rents for Chambernoun's tenement 2s, because it is not leased and he cannot distrain (*Idem computat in defectu redditus in tenemento Chambernoun ijs quia non locatur nec potest distringere*). Item in default of the tenement of Henry Lovecoc 12d because it is not leased. Item in default of one house in 'Comestrete' because it is burned (*cremat'*) 6d and of a certain area there 1d.   Total 3s 7d.

(m.2) [MICHAELMAS TERM]

Week 1 after the feast of St Michael [29 September]   In wages*. Sharpening 4¼d. And 2 sawyers for 4 days 20d. In one labourer in the quarry 11d. In 4 other labourers there 3s 4d. In one labourer there 9d. In 2 carters 2s. In 3 labourers on the Work 2s 6d. In one labourer there 8d. For carrying one cart-load (*cariagio*) from the quarry to Exeter 3s. For carrying one cart-load from Blackdown (*la Blakedoun'*) to Exeter 18d. For making 8 iron bars for windows (*barris ferri pro fenestris*) 12d. For making 300 nails for glass windows (*fenestris vitreis*) 6d. For carrying 5 trusses of broom (*miritis*) 5d. 12 quarters of lime 6s. Fodder of 9 horses 3 quarters 7½ bushels, to each horse ½ bushel by day and night.   Total 50s 3¼d.

Week 2   In wages*. Sharpening 3¼d. And 2 sawyers for 2 days 10d. In one labourer in the quarry 11d. In 4 other labourers there 3s 4d. In one labourer there 9d. In 2 carters 2s. In 3 labourers on the Work 2s 6d. In one labourer there 8d. For oxen (*in bob'*) hired for carrying one great tree-trunk (*magnum lignum*) from Norton to Exeter 2s. 4 hinges with hooks and nails for 2 doors to the galleries (*In iiij vertivellis cum gumfis et clavibus pro ij hostiis ad aluras*) 13d. 8 quarters of lime 4s. Fodder of 9 horses, 3 quarters 7½ bushels. Total 42s 10¼d.

Week 3   In wages*. Sharpening and steeling of axes 3¾d. And 2 sawyers 2s 6d. In one plumber 2s. In one labourer in the quarry 11d. In 4 other labourers there 3s 4d. In one labourer there 9d. In 2 carters 2s. In 3 labourers on the Work 2s 6d. In 2 other labourers there 18d. For carrying 3 cart-loads from the quarry to Exeter 9s. 12 quarters of lime 6s. For making 600 'tackenayles' 6d. One large rope called a hawser (*que dicitur* 'hauter') weighing 200 lbs bought 15s. 5 *gaddis* of iron bought at Callington (*Kalstinesdon'*) 6s 6d. For fodder [as above]. Total 71s 3¾d.

Week 4   In wages*. Sharpening 5¾d. And 2 sawyers 2s 6d. In one labourer in the quarry 11d. In 4 other labourers there 3s 4d. In one labourer there 9d. In 2 carters 2s. In 3 labourers on the Work 2s 6d. In one labourer there 8d. For making 16 cramps (*cramponibus*) for the gallery (*alura*) 4d. For making ironwork for the bell called Walter 8d. In one roofer with his servant 2s 6d. For carrying one cart-load from Blackdown to Exeter 18d. 7 quarters of lime 3s 6d. 66 feet of ridge-tiles for a house in which the oats for the horses' fodder are stored 21d. Fodder [as above]. Total 41s 10¾d.

Week 5: 2 feasts, All Saints and All Souls [1 and 2 November] and the time changes.   In wages*. Sharpening 3¾d. And 2 sawyers 20d. In one labourer in the quarry 7¾d. In 4 other labourers there 2s 5d, 7¼d each. In one labourer there 6¼d. In 2 carters 2s. In 3 labourers on the Work 22d. In one labourer there 6d. In one roofer roofing over the 'le tracour'[2] for 2 days 8d. 7 quarters of lime 3s 6d. Fodder [as above].
Total 26s 11½d.

Week 6   In wages*. Sharpening 5¼d. And 2 sawyers 2s. In one labourer in the quarry 9½d. In 4 other labourers there 2s 8d. In one labourer there 7½d. In 2 carters 2s. In 3 labourers on the Work 2s 1½d. In 2 other labourers there 14d. Repair of carts 4d. 25 large spikes bought 5d. For making ironwork for one window in the new Work (*In ferrament' pro j fenestra in novo opere faciend'*) 6d. 10 quarters of lime 5s. Fodder [as above]. One large barge hired for carrying stones from the quarry to 'la Sege' 16s 5¼d.
Total 56s 9½d.

Week 7   In wages*. Sharpening 3¼d. And 2 sawyers 2s 1d. And in 2 glaziers setting in one forme of glass (*Et ij verrator' inponendum j formam vitri*) 3s 4d. In one labourer in the quarry 9½d. In 4 other labourers there 2s 8d. In one labourer there 7½d. In 2 carters 2s. In 3 labourers on the Work 2s 1½d. In 2 other labourers there 14d. In one roofer roofing over the lodges and cloister (*super logeas et claustrum*) for 2 weeks 4s 2d. For making 120 lbs of iron for ironwork for glass (*pro ferrament' vitri*) 3s 4d. For binding a certain cart with new bands and making them with our own iron 6s. For painting 10 heads for the new galleries in the choir (*In x capit' depyctand' ad novas aluras in coro*) 4s. For making 2 iron cases with 4 hooks for the same galleries (*In ij cassis ferreis faciend' ad easdem aluras cum iiij gumfis*) 2s 8d. For carrying 2 cart-loads from Blackdown to Exeter 3s. 7 quarters of lime 3s 6d. Fodder [as above]. Total 62s 11¼d.

Week 8   In wages*. And 2 sawyers 21d. For sharpening 3¾d. In one labourer in the quarry 9½d. In 4 other labourers there 2s 8d. In one labourer there 7½d. In 2 carters 2s. In 4 labourers on the Work 2s 10d. In 2 other labourers there 14d. In one roofer with his servant 21d. For making 5 iron cases for the glass windows for the new galleries in the choir (*In v cassis ferreis faciendis pro fenestris vitreis ad novas aluras in choro*) 6s 8d. 26 loads of stones from Barley 9s. 10 quarters of lime 5s. For wages of Michael the glazier for placing and fixing glass in the new galleries (*ponend' et affirmand' vitrum in novis aluris*) 17d. 1000 pins for roofing-stones (*pinis pro petris ad coopertur'*) 1d. Fodder [as above].   Total 55s 2¼d.

Week 9   In wages*. Sharpening 3¼d. And 2 sawyers 2s 1d. And one glazier mending windows (*emendend' fenestras*) and fixing the galleries (*et affirmand' aluras*) in the choir 20d. In one labourer in the quarry 9½d. In 4 other labourers there 2s 8d. In one labourer there 7½d. In 2 carters 2s. In 4 labourers on the Work 2s 10d. In one labourer there 7d. 100 loads of stones from Barley 6s. 8 quarters of lime 4s. 4 stones of steel bought 4s. For binding (*ligacione*) of one cart 2s 10d. For making 47 lbs of iron for cramps for the galleries 15d. Fodder [as above].   Total 53s 11½d.

Week 10   In wages*. Sharpening 8¼d. And 2 sawyers 2s 1d. And one labourer in the quarry 9½d. In 4 other labourers there 2s 8d. In one labourer there 7½d. In 3 carters (*carectariis*) 2s. In 4 labourers on the Work 2s 10d. In 2 other labourers there 14d. In one roofer roofing over the lodge in Kalendarhay (*Calendernahaye*) 6d. Twists for the same 3d. For making 120 dowels (*doulys*) for the carts 12d. 3 troughs (*gatis*) bought for the Work 3d. 11 cart-loads (*cariagiis*) from Salcombe quarry to Blackdown 16s 6d. Sharpening for the quarry 12d. For mending 3 barrows 7d. 50 'talstones' carried from the quarry to the sea 12d. And in the same way (*eodem modo*) for carrying 150 'pendanz' 10½d. 6½ quarters of lime 3s 3d. 154 loads of stones from Barley 6s 2d. Fodder [as above].   Total 65s 5½d.

Week 11   In wages*. Sharpening 2d. And 2 sawyers 2s 1d. In one labourer in the quarry 9d. In 4 other labourers there 2s 8d. In one labourer there 7½d. In 2 carters 2s. In 4 labourers on the Work 2s 10d. In 2 other labourers there 14d. 6 quarters of lime 3s. For making 900 horse-nails 9d. 3 cramps for the galleries 5d. In one glazier placing one forme of glass in the vestry to St Edmund's altar (*ad ponendum j formam vitri in vestiario ad altar' sancti Edmundi*) and other requirements for a week 18d. Fodder [as above].   Total 38s 5½d.

Week 12   In wages*. Sharpening 6¼d. And 2 sawyers 2s 1d. In one labourer in the quarry 9½d. In 4 other labourers there 2s 8d. In one other labourer there 7½d. In 2 carters 2s. In 4 labourers on the Work 2s 10d. In 2 other labourers there 14d. 11 stones of beef and mutton tallow and lard (*coreis bovin' multon' et porcin'*) bought for solder, carts and other requirements 20s 2d, 22d a stone. 6 pairs of cart-traces bought 2s 5d. For the iron binding of a small cart (*In ligatur' j ferrea parve carecte*) 2s. 15 lbs of tin bought for solder 20d. 6 cart-loads with hire of carts (*In vj cariagiis cum carect' locat'*) from the quarry to Blackdown 9s. Farriery for the horses for this term 9d. For shoeing horses with 12 dozens (*dozenis*) of our own iron 2s. Candles for the stable for this term 5½d. For the fee of Master Thomas for this term 33s 4d. And of John de Schyreford the warden of the Work 12s 6d. For the stable hired at Newton for this term 12d. For mending the ironwork for 2 bells in St Paul's tower 6d. 7 quarters of lime

3s 6d. For making 900 horse-nails 9d. For painting 9 heads in the new galleries (*capit' depitandis in novis aluris*) 4s. Fodder [as above].

Total £6 10s 7¼d.

Total of the Work of the said term £34 16s 7¾d, except oats.

Oats in arrears   He renders account of 12 quarters 2 bushels from the remainder of the preceding account.

Purchase of oats for the horses' fodder   73 quarters 6 bushels of oats bought 78s 2½d.   Total 78s 2½d.

From which in fodder of 9 horses for 12 weeks 47 quarters 2 bushels viz. to each horse by day and night one half bushel. And thus 38 quarters 6 bushels remain.

CHRISTMAS TERM

Week 1: in which Christmas falls on Monday   In wages of 2 carters 2s. Fodder of 9 horses 3 quarters 7½ bushels.   Total 2s except oats.

Week 2: 2 feasts, the Circumcision and Epiphany [1 and 6 January]   For wages*. And 2 sawyers 21d. In one labourer in the quarry 8d. In 4 other labourers there 2s 4d. In one other labourer there 6½d. In 2 carters 2s. In 3 labourers on the Work 22½d. Fodder [as above].   Total 22s 9d.

Week 3   In wages*. Sharpening 6d. And 2 sawyers 2s 1d. In one labourer in the quarry 9½d. In 4 other labourers there 2s 8d. In one other labourer there 7½d. In 2 carters 2s. In 3 labourers on the Work 2s 1½d. 7 quarters of lime 2s 11d. 207 lbs of tin bought for solder 26s 8d. One horse-hide bought 16d. 4 quarters 3½ bushels of charcoal (*carbon'*) for founding lead-ashes (*pro cineribus plumbi fundend'*) 2s 7d, price 7d a quarter. Fodder [as above].

Total 60s 7d.

Week 4   In wages*. Sharpening 8d. And 2 sawyers 2s 1d. In one labourer in the quarry 9½d. In 4 other labourers there 2s 8d. In one other labourer there 7½d. In 2 carters 2s. In 3 labourers on the Work 2s 1½d. In one other labourer there 7d. 2 horse-hides for the carts 3s 8d. 6 quarters of lime 2s 11d. Fodder [as above].   Total 37s 3d.

(m.3) Week 5   In wages*. And sharpening 4½d. And 2 sawyers 2s 1d. In one labourer in the quarry 9½d. In 5 other labourers there 3s 4d. In one other labourer there 7½d. In 2 carters 2s. In 2 labourers on the Work 17d. In one other labourer there 7d. One rope for tying carts 8d. 'Wyppe-cord' 3d. For repair of carts 8d. Fodder [as above].   Total 33s 9½d.

Week 6   In wages*. Sharpening and one lock newly bought for the Broadgate (*la Brodezete*) 11½d. And 2 sawyers 2s 1d and mending one saw (*serra*) 1d. In one labourer in the quarry 9½d. In 5 other labourers there 3s 4d. In one labourer there 7½d. In 2 carters 2s. In 3 labourers on the Work 2s 1½d. In one other labourer there 7½d. For carrying 6 loads of marble stones (*petr' marmor'*) from 'la Sege' to Exeter 6d. For carrying 2 cart-loads from the quarry to Exeter 10s. Fodder [as above].

Total 46s 4½d.

Week 7   In wages*. For sharpening and steeling of axes 6½d. And 2 sawyers 2s 1d. In one labourer in the quarry 9½d. In 4 other labourers there 2s 8d. In one other labourer there 7½d. In 2 carters 2s. In 3 labourers on the Work 2s 1½d. In one labourer there 7d. In one glazier setting glass in the new Work (*ad sedend' vitrum in novo opere*) 18d. For making 26 cramps 10d. Fodder [as above].   Total 36s 11½d.

Week 8   In wages*. Sharpening 5d. And 2 sawyers 2s 1d. In one labourer in the quarry 9½d. In 4 other labourers there 2s 8d. In one other labourer there 7½d. In 2 carters 2s. In 3 labourers on the Work 2s 1½d. In 2 other labourers there 14d. 2000 'spykys' 6s 8d. 12000 'latnailes' 11s 2d. 5 quarters of lime 2s 1d. 7 loads of withies 2s 4d. 200 loads of stones from Barley 8s. 3 stones of 'burlis' 2s 6d. Fodder [as above].

Total 68s 8d.

Week 9: the feasts of St Peter's Chair and St Mathias [22 and 24 February] In wages*. And 2 sawyers 21d. Sharpening 6¼d. In one labourer in the quarry 8d. In 4 other labourers there 2s 4d. In one labourer there 6½d. In 2 carters 2s. In 3 labourers on the Work 22½d. In one labourer there 6d. 3 quarters of lime 15d. 8000 'pynnis' for roofing the houses 6d. Paid to dom Richard Kyng for a certain chamber in the church (*Soluto domino Ricardo Kyng pro quadam camera in ecclesia*) by order of the lord treasurer (*theserar'*) 2s 9¼d. 26 loads of stones from Barley 12d. Paid to Crockerne-wille for making ironwork for 2 large glass formes in the nave of the church (*ad ij magnas formas vitreas in navi ecclesie*) 9s 9d. For making 700 horse-nails 7d. Fodder [as above].   Total 44s 8d.

Week 10   In wages*. And 2 sawyers 2s 1d. And 2 glaziers for setting and fixing one large glass forme in the nave of the church 3s 4d. In one labourer in the quarry 9½d. In 4 other labourers there 2s 8d. In one labourer there 7½d. In 2 carters 2s. In 3 labourers on the Work 2s 1½d. In one labourer 7d. Sharpening 3¼d. 100 seams of sand 2s. For making one saw for sawing stones (*pro petris serrand'*) 12d. Fodder [as above]. 2 fothers (*foderes*) and one fotmel of lead bought with carriage £5.

Total £7 8¼d.

Week 11   In wages*. And 2 sawyers 2s 1d. In one labourer in the quarry 9½d. In 4 other labourers there 2s 8d. In one labourer there 7½d. In 2 carters 2s. In 3 labourers on the Work 2s 1½d. In one labourer there 7d. For painting and gilding 19 heads in the new galleries (*In xix capit' depyctand' et deaurand' in novis aluris*) 8s. For making 40 cramps 14d. Sharpening 12½d. 200 seams of sand 4s. Fodder [as above].

Total 51s 11½d.

Week 12: and the time changes   In wages*. Sharpening 6¼d. And 2 sawyers 2s 6d. In one labourer in the quarry 11d. In 4 others 3s 4d. In one labourer there 9d. In 2 carters 2s. In 3 labourers on the Work 2s 6d. In one labourer there 9d. One iron plate for mixing colours (*In j plata ferr' pro color' molend'*) 12d. For one 'houna' and 21 large 'spyks' 10d. For making 500 horse-nails 5d. 126 seams of sand 2s 6d. Fodder [as above].

Total 48s 1¼d.

Week 13   In wages*. Sharpening 1d. And 2 sawyers (*sereator'*) 2s 6d. In one labourer in the quarry 11d. In 4 other labourers there 3s 4d. In one labourer there 9d. In 2 carters 2s. In 3 labourers on the Work 2s 6d. In one labourer there 9d. One ox-hide and 3 pig-skins bought for the carts 5s 7d. For grease and for cleansing (*mundriand'*) the same 16d. For colour?[3] bought for glass (*In color' empt' pro vitro*) 10d. 8 loads of withies for making hurdles (*virg' pro flakys faciendis*) 2s. 100 loads of stones from Barley 4s. Fodder [as above].   Total 56s 8d.

Week 14   In wages*. Sharpening and steeling of axes 12¼d. And 2 sawyers 2s 6d. In one labourer in the quarry 11d. In 4 other labourers there 3s 4d. In one labourer there 9d. In 2 carters 2s. In 3 labourers on the Work 2s 6d. In one labourer there 9d. In 2 roofers roofing over St John's tower (*cooperient' super turrim sancti Iohannis*) 2s 6d. For newly making and tying the binding of one cart (*In ligature j carecte de novo faciendo et ligando*) 6s 2d. 2 pairs of spokes (*radiis*) bought for carts 20d. 200 loads of stones from Barley 8s. 2½ quarters of lime 12½d. For making 8 hooks for 'la pulpytte' (*In viij gumfis faciendis pro la pulpytte*) 6d. Fodder [as above].
                                            Total 63s 8¾d.

Week 15   In wages*. And 2 sawyers 2s 6d. In one labourer in the quarry 11d. In 4 other labourers there 3s 4d. In one labourer there 9d. In 2 carters 2s. In 3 labourers on the Work 2s 6d. In one labourer there 9d. One large barge of stones from the quarry to 'la Sege' 14s. For the fee of Master Thomas for this term 33s 4d. And of John de Schyreford warden of the Work 12s 6d. For the stable hired at Newton for this term 12d. Farriery for the horses 9d. For shoeing the horses with 12 dozens 2s. For making 11 shoes and shoeing with them (*In xj ferr' faciend' et ferrand'*) 6d. For candles for the stable for this term 1½d. For sharpening and steeling of axes for the Work and the quarry 10d. Fodder of 9 horses 3 quarters 7½ bushels and 6 quarters more for the whole term on account of the length of the journey from Beer quarry.   Total 106s 9½d.

Total of the Work for the whole quarter £41 1¾d except the tabulature of the high altar and oats.

Oats remaining and previously bought (*de preemptione*)   He renders account of 38 quarters 6 bushels of the remainder of the preceding quarter. And of 33 quarters purchased before, 38s 9d.
                                    Total in money (*denar'*) 38s 9d.

Total of quarters of oats 71 quarters 6 bushels. From which there is in fodder of 9 horses for 15 weeks 59 quarters ½ bushel viz. to each horse for a day and a night half a bushel and 6 quarters more in the whole term on account of the length of the journey from Beer quarry. Total expenses of oats 55 quarters ½ bushel and 6 quarters 5½ bushels remain.

EASTER TERM

Week 1 in the feast of Easter   In wages of 2 carters 2s. For fodder of 9 horses 3 quarters 7½ bushels.   Total 2s except oats.

Week 2   In wages*. In one labourer in the quarry 11d. In 4 other labourers there 3s 4d. In one other labourer there 9d. In 2 carters 2s. In 3 labourers on the Work 2s 6d. In one labourer there 9d. 18000 lath-nails 18s. 8 quarters of lime 3s 4d. For making 22 cramps for the galleries 10d. Sharpening 3d. Fodder [as above].   Total 60s 3d.

Week 3   In wages*. In one labourer in the quarry 11d. In 4 labourers there 3s 4d. In one labourer there 9d. In 2 carters 2s. in 3 labourers on the Work 2s 6d. In one labourer there 9d. 2100 lbs of iron bought at

Topsham (*Thoppesham*) 76s 8d. For carrying the same 8d. Sharpening 6¼d. For making ironwork for one glass forme in St John's chapel (*pro j forma vitrea in capella sancti Iohannis*) 20d. Fodder [as above].

Total 116s 8¼d.

(m.2d) Week 4: 2 feasts, SS. Philip and James and the Invention of the Holy Cross [1 and 3 May]   In one labourer in the quarry 9½d. In 4 other labourers there 2s 8d. In one labourer there 7d. In 2 carters 2s. In 3 labourers on the Work 2s 1½d. In one labourer there 7d. 'Vyppecord' 2d. 8 quarters of lime 2s 11d. Fodder [as above].   Total 36s 5½d.

Week 5   In wages*. Sharpening 4d. In 3 carpenters felling trees (*prosternent' arbor'*) at Norton 6s 6d. In 2 sawyers 2s 6d. In one labourer in the quarry 11d. In 4 other labourers there 3s 4d. In one labourer there 9d. In 2 carters 2s. In 3 labourers on the Work 2s 6d. In one labourer there 9d. Ironwork viz. hooks (*gumfis*) and other requirements for 'la pulpyte' 16d. 2 quarters of lime 10d. 100 loads of stones from Barley 4s. In one glazier setting (*ponend'*) glass in St John's chapel 2s. Fodder [as above].   Total 53s 4d.

Week 6   In wages*. And 2 sawyers 2s 6d. And one labourer in the quarry 11d. And in 4 other labourers there 3s 4d. In one labourer there 9d. In 2 carters 2s. In 3 labourers on the Work 2s 6d. In one labourer there 9d. 5 quarters of lime 2s 1d. Sharpening 3½d. Fodder [as above].

Total 47s 4½d.

Week 7   In wages*. In 2 sawyers 2s 6d. In one labourer in the quarry 11d. In 4 other labourers there 3s 4d. In one labourer there 9d. In 2 carters 2s. In 3 labourers on the Work 2s 6d. In one labourer there 9d. 100 feet of ridge-tiles (*crest'*) for the house in Kalenderhay 2s 1d. Sharpening 1¼d. 2 quarters of lime 10d. Fodder [as above].

Total 42s 10½d.

Week 8: feast of Pentecost   In wages of 2 carters 2s. 400 large horse-shoes bought at Lopen fair 35s. In expenses of J. de Schyreford for 3½ days with 3 horses 2s. 6 dozens of cart-clouts bought there 10s. For 1000 horse-nails bought there 20d. Fodder [as above].   Total 50s 8d.

Week 9   In wages*. And one labourer in the quarry 11d. In 4 other labourers there 3s 4d. In one labourer there 9d. In 2 carters 2s. In 3 labourers on the Work 2s 6d. In one labourer there 9d. In 13½ quarters of lime 5s 7½d. For sharpening 6½d. In putting axles on 2 carts 6d. For making a lectern (*desca*) before (*coram*) Master William Kylkenny in the quire 4d. For one plumber for the week 2s. For 9 pig-skins (*pell' porcinis*) for the requirements of the carts with grease and trimming (*ornacione*) 7s 8d. For binding of 2 buckets 3d. 3½ fothers (*fodris*) of lead bought at Teignmouth (*Teygnemue*) £8 3s 5d. 10000 lath-nails 8s 7d. Fodder [as above].   Total £11 3s 8½d.

Week 10   For wages*. In one labourer in the quarry 11d. In 4 other labourers there 3s 4d. In one labourer there 9d. In 2 carters 2s. In 3 labourers on the Work 2s 6d. In one labourer there 9d. 250 loads of stones from Barley 10s. For sharpening 6½d. 5½ quarters of lime 2s 3½d. 6 pairs of cart-traces 3s. For carriage of one large cart-rail? (*scal'*) from Powderham (*Pouderam*) to 'la Sege' 6d. Fodder [as above].

Total 51s 8d.

Week 11   In wages*. And one carpenter 22d. And 2 sawyers 2s 6d. In one labourer in the quarry 11d. In 4 other labourers there 3s 4d. In one labourer there 9d. In 2 carters 2s. In 3 labourers on the Work 2s 6d. In one labourer there 9d. For sharpening and ironwork for one window beyond the door of the cloister (*fenestra ultra hostium claustri*) 5s 1d. 5 quarters of lime 2s 1d. 250 loads of stones from Barley 10s. 325 seams of sand 6s 6d. 11300 'sclatchis' stones for the houses in Kalenderhay 11s 6d. For carrying the same 4s 3d. 4 gallons of grease for the requirements of the carts 18d. For carrying 2 cart-loads from Blackdown to Exeter 3s. For carrying one cart-load of timber from Norton to Exeter 20d. Farriery of the horses for this term 9d. For the stable hired at Newton 12d. For the fee of Master Thomas 33s 4d. And of John de Schyreford the warden 12s 6d. 2 sieves 2d. For shoeing horses with 10½ dozens of our own iron 21d. For sharpening for the quarry for the whole term 12d. For fodder as above.

Total £6 17s 11d.

Total of the whole quarter except oats and the tabulature
£41 2s 11¼d.

Oats remaining from the preceding quarter 6 quarters 5½ bushels. And by purchase 55 quarters 4 bushels price 71s 10d.

Price 71s 10d.

From which in fodder of 9 horses for 11 weeks 43 quarters 2½ bushels, viz. to each horse for a day and a night half a bushel, and 3 quarters more in the whole term on account of the length of the journey, and thus 15 quarters 7 bushels remain.

MIDSUMMER TERM

Week 1 after the feast of St John Baptist [24 June]   For wages*. And one carpenter 22d. And 2 sawyers 2s 6d. In one labourer in the quarry 11d. In 4 other labourers there 3s 4d. In one labourer there 9d. In 2 carters 2s. In 3 labourers on the Work 2s 6d. In one labourer there 9d. Sharpening 7d. 6 quarters of lime 2s 6d. For making 10 cart-collars 2s. In one glazier setting one glass forme beyond the cloister door (*ad ponen' j formam vitream ultra hostium claustri*) 18d. For binding vats 6½d. For carrying 3 cart-loads of timber from Norton to Exeter 5s. Fodder of 8 horses 3 quarters 4 bushels.

Total 53s 11½d.

Cost of marble (*Custus marmorei*)   He reckons for 4 columns with bases sub-bases and capitals (*in iiij columpnis cum basis subbasis capitrall'*) £5 6s 8d. Item for 243 feet of marble steps (*marmoreis grad'*) for 'la pulpytte' £4 10s 3½d, 4½d a foot. Item for 2 altars with marble frontals and other fittings (*Item pro ij altar' cum frontelis marmor' et aliis aparat'*) 26s 8d. Item released to William Canoun £4 by order of the lord dean and chapter out of courtesy (*ex cutialitate*).

Total £15 3s 7½d.

Week 2   In wages*. And one carpenter 22d. And 2 sawyers 2s 6d. In one labourer in the quarry 11d. In 4 other labourers there 3s 4d. In one labourer there 9d. In 2 carters 2s. In 3 labourers on the Work 2s 6d. In one labourer there 9d. 9 boards bought 2s 7½d. 3½ stones of 'burlis' 2s 11d. 7 quarters of lime 2s 11d. 150 'spykys' and 2 hinges and sharpening 15½d. Fodder [as above].

Total 51s 7d.

Week 3   In wages*. In one labourer in the quarry 11d. In 4 labourers there 3s 4d. In one labourer there 9d. In 2 carters 2s. In 3 labourers on the Work 2s 6d. In one labourer there 9d. In one labourer for 3 days 3½d. In one glazier for the week in setting glass in the church 2s. For carrying 3 cart-loads (*chargiis*) of timber to Exeter 5s. 3 quarters of lime 15d. For making 800 horse-nails 8d. 100 seams of sand 2s. For making ironwork for 3 glass formes (*in ferramento pro iij formis vitreis*) 3s 8d. 3 yards of canvas (*In iij vlnis de canevase*) for the requirements of the carts 9d. Fodder [as above].   Total 50s 11d.

Week 4   In wages*. In one labourer in the quarry 11d. In 4 other labourers there 3s 4d. In one other labourer there 9d. In 2 carters 2s. In 3 labourers on the Work 2s 6d. In 3 other labourers there 2s 3d. For 'vippe-cord' 4d. Sharpening 6½d. 3 quarters of lime 15d. 150 loads of stones from Barley 6s. 250 seams of sand 5s. For making 2 hinges with 4 iron bolts and one lock 2s 2d. For carrying 4 cart-loads (*cariagiis*) of timber from Norton to Exeter 6s 8d. Fodder [as above].   Total 63s 1½d.

(m.3d) Week 5   In wages*. In one labourer in the quarry 11d. In 4 other labourers in the quarry 3s 4d. In one labourer there 9d. In 2 carters 2s. 200 seams of sand 4s. 4 loads of withies 9d. Sharpening 4¼d. 65500 tiling stones (*In lxv m^{lis} et v^c petris tegulinis*) for the roof of a house in Kalenderhay 65s 2d. 300 feet of ridge-tiles (*crestis*) 7½d. Ironwork for one forme in the chapel of St Paul (*In ferramenta pro j forma in capella sancti Pauli*) 3s 1d. Fodder [as above].   Total 100s 9d.

Week 6   In wages*. In one labourer in the quarry 11d. In 4 other labourers there 3s 4d. In one labourer there 9d. In 2 carters 2s. In one rope called a 'hautour' weighing 160 lbs 7s. For 12000 lath-(*latthis*) nails 10s. Sharpening 2½d. 2 barge-loads (*bar'*) of stones from the quarry to 'la Sege' 23s 8d. 7½ quarters of lime 3s 1½d. Fodder [as above].

                                                                 Total 68s 7d.

Week 7   In wages*. In one labourer in the quarry 11d. In 4 other labourers there 3s 4d. In one labourer there 9d. In 2 carters 2s. For carry-ing 8 cart-loads (*cariag'*) of timber from Norton to Exeter 13s 4d. Sharpen-ing 1¼d. 2 horses bought at Priddy (*Pridie*) 74s. For curing one horse-hide 5d. 100 loads of stones from Barley 4s. For sawing (*serrand'*) 250 feet at task 22½d. Fodder [as above].   Total 118s 3¾d.

Week 8   In wages*. And 2 carters 2s. 14000 'pynnis' for tiling stones 14d. For roofing the house in Kalendarhay (*Calenderreaye*) at task 46s 8d. For sawing 312 feet 2s 3½d. Fodder [as above]. Sharpening 1½d.

                                                                 Total 67s 8d.

Cost of glass   For making one forme of glass at task in St Paul's tower which contains (*continet*) 120 feet of which 24 feet is coloured glass in the said forme (*unde de color' in eadem forma xxiiij ped'*) 26s viz. for white [glass] 2½d a foot, coloured [glass] 3d (*de colori iijd*). And for 2 large formes in the nave of the church (*et de ij magnis formis in navi ecclesie*) which contain 440 feet of which 112 feet are coloured [glass] £4 16s 3d, costing per foot as above (*capient' pro pede ut supra*). And one forme beyond the door of the cloister (*ultra hostium claustri*) which contains 69 feet, which are all white [glass] 14s 4½d. And one forme near the bread-house (*iuxta domum panis*) contains 101 feet of which 16 feet are coloured 21s 8½d. And one forme in

St Edmund's chapel (*Et j forma capelle sancti Edmundi*) which contains 36 feet 9s. And one forme in St Paul's chapel which contains 120 feet of which 28 feet are coloured (*unde de colore xxviij ped'*) 26s 1½d. And 2 other formes in the same chapel contain 86 feet 17s 11d. And one forme in St John's chapel (*Et j forma in capell' sancti Iohannis*) contains 120 feet of which 10 feet are coloured 25s 5d. And 2 other formes in the same chapel contain 86 feet 17s 11d. And 2 windows in the exchequer (*Et ij fenestr' in scaccar'*) contain 13½ feet 2s 10d. In one glazier setting in the forme in St Paul's chapel and the exchequer (*In j verrator' ad ponendum formam in capell' sancti Pauli et in scaccario*) 2s. And in courtesy (*in curialitate*) to the glazier by order of the treasurer 6s 8d.   Total £13 6s 2½d.

Week 9   In wages*. In 2 carters 2s. 3 rings for marble columns (*In iij anulis pro columpnis marmor'*) 7s. For carrying 4 cart-loads of timber from Norton to Exeter 6s 8d. For making 300 'tacnayles' 3d. Fodder [as above]. One barge-load of stones carried from the quarry to Exeter 6s 6½d.

                    Total 37s 10½d.

Cost of hay   For 26 stacks of hay bought in various places 103s 6d: 221 trusses for Clyst (*Clistes*) Butterford (*Boterford*) Sowton (*Fometoun*) and West Clyst (*Clistes Moysen*) carried to Exeter 27s 7½d, 1½d a truss. 20 trusses from Rockbeare carried to Exeter 3s 4d. 60 trusses carried from Greendale to Newton 10s. For making a large stack in Kalendarhay (*Lendernahaye*) 2s. Straw for roofing 2s 5d. Twists 10d. In one roofer covering over the said stack for 5 days 15d. For his servant for the same time 10d.   Total £7 11s 9½d.

Week 10   In wages*. In 2 carters 2s. For sawing (*serrand'*) 350 feet at task 2s 7½d. One roofer over the cloister (*super claustrum*) and his servant 2s 6d. 2 loads (*chargiis*) of timber carried from Norton to Exeter 10s. Fodder [as above].   Total 18s 7½d.

Week 11   In wages*. In 2 carters 2s. In one roofer over the cloister and his servant 2s 6d. For sawing 300 feet at task 2s 3d. Fodder [as above].

                    Total 13s 3d.

Week 12   In wages*. In 2 carters 2s. For sawing 350 feet 2s 7½d. 1500 laths (*latchis*) for the house in Kalendarhay 13s 9d. Fodder [as above].

                    Total 24s 10½d.

Week 13   In wages*. In 2 carters 2s. For sawing 300 feet 2s 3d. For 2 cart-loads (*cariag'*) of timber from Norton 5s. Fodder [as above].

                    Total 13s 6d.

Week 14   In wages*. In 2 carters 2s. For the fee of Master Thomas for this term 33s 4d. And of J de Shyreford the warden 12s 6d. For the stable hired at Newton 12d. Farriery for the horses 10d. For curing one horse-hide 6d. One bridle for the axles of the carts (*In j freno pro exiles cariartis*) 8d. For shoeing horses with 12½ dozens 2s 1d. Fodder [as above].

                    Total 57s 2d.

Total of the whole quarter £73 21¼d except oats and the altar.

Oats remaining and purchased   He renders account of 15 quarters and 7 bushels remaining from the preceding quarter. And of 44 quarters 4 bushels purchased for 58s 7d.   Total 58s 7d.

From which there is in fodder of 8 horses for 14 weeks 49 quarters, to each for a day and a night half a bushel and 4 quarters more in the whole term and 7 quarters 3 bushels remain.

Total of the whole expenses £202 13s 3½d.

And he owes £27 7s 7¼d which were allowed him at the end of his account for the tabulature of the great altar as he shows in the same account, and he is here quit (*quietus*).

---

* List of wages of named craftsmen is not included here, see pp. 197–8.
1 MS leaves blank.
2 'le tracour' probably means the tracing-house.
3 Since all coloured glass was purchased, the meaning of this entry is not clear.

2615 Altar account: 1318, 1 October–1319, 30 September

> One membrane, good condition.
> Endorsed: *Compotus Johannis de Schireford capellani custodis operis de expensis factis pro ornatu altar' de anno domini m°ccc°xvij a dominica post festum sancti Michaelis usque ad eandem dominicam anno revoluto.*

(m.1) THE COST OF THE ALTAR VIZ. THE STONE TABULA-TURE FROM SUNDAY AFTER THE FEAST OF ST MICHAEL 1318 UNTIL THE SAME SUNDAY IN THE FOLLOWING YEAR 1319.

[RECEIPTS]

The same [John] renders account of £12 23¾d received from dom William de Doune and dom William de Pederton by tally.

[EXPENSES]

[MICHAELMAS TERM]

First week   In wages*. Sharpening 4½d.   Total 19s ½d.

Week 2   In wages*. In 3 labourers in Beer (*Ber*') quarry 2s. Sharpening 2¼d. One cart-load carried from Blackdown (*Blakedoune*) to Exeter 18d.
Total 24s 8¼d.

Week 3   In wages*. 2 cart-loads carried from Blackdown to Exeter 3s. Sharpening 2d.   Total 15s 6d.

Week 4   In wages*. Sharpening 1½d.   Total 12s 5½d.

Week 5: the feast of All Saints [1 November], the time changes and 2 feasts   In wages*. Sharpening 1½d.   Total 10s 5½d.

Weeks 6, 8, 9, 10, 11   In wages*.   Total 5s 7d [each week].

Week 7   In wages*.   Total 3s 6d.

Week 12   In wages*. Sharpening 6½d.   Total 6s 1½d.

Total of the whole quarter 119s 8¼d.

[CHRISTMAS TERM]

Week 2: after Christmas, 2 feasts, the Circumcision and Epiphany [1 and 6 January]   In wages*.   Total 4s 9d.

Weeks 3, 4, 6, 7, 8, 10   In wages*.   Total 5s 7d [each week].

Week 5   In wages*. For carrying 5 great stones from Beer quarry to Exeter 25s.   Total 30s 7d.

Week 9: 2 feasts, St Peter's Chair and St Mathias [22 and 24 February] In wages*.   Total 5s 7d.

Week 10   In wages*.   Total 2s 11½d.

Week 11   In wages*.   Total 3s 6d.

Week 12   In wages*.   Total 4s.

Week 13   In wages*. For carrying 3 great stones from Beer quarry to Exeter 15s.   Total 19s.

Week 14   In wages*.   Total 20d.

Week 15   In wages*. For one cart-load (*cariag'*) carried from Blackdown to Exeter 18d. And sharpening for the whole term 7d.

Total 3s 9d.

Total for the whole quarter 103s 8¾d.

EASTER TERM

Weeks 1,[1] 2   In wages*.   Total 6s 6d [each week].

Week 3   In wages*.   Total 5s 7d.

Week 4   In wages*.   Total 7s 10d.

Weeks 5, 6   In wages*.   Total 9s [each week].

Item to John de Bannebiri for 3 vaults carrying the canopy of the high altar at task (*pro iij vouter' portand' tabernaculum in maiore altar' ad thascam*) 100s.   Total is shown (*summa patet*).

Week 8: after Pentecost   In wages*. For 2 great carts (*cariag'*) carrying from Beer quarry to Exeter 10d.   Total 18s 6d.

Week 9   In wages*.   Total 4s 6d.

Week 10   In wages*. For one cart-load (*cariagio*) carried from Beer quarry to Blackdown 2s 6d.   Total 7s.

Total of the whole quarter £8 14s 5d.

(m.1d) MIDSUMMER TERM

Weeks 1, 2, 3, 4   In wages*.   Total 4s 6d [each week].

Week 5   In wages*. In 2 labourers 20d. In 3 other labourers 2s 3d.

Total 17s 2d.

Week 6   In wages*. In one labourer 10d. In 3 other labourers 2s 3d. 100 seams of sand 2s. 100 loads of stones from Barley 4s. 7 quarters of lime 2s 11d. Sharpening 2d.   Total 25s 3d.

Week 7   In wages*. In one labourer 10d. In 3 other labourers there 2s 3d. In sharpening ¾d. 225 stones from Barley 9s. 8 quarters of lime 3s 4d. 225 seams of sand 4s 6d.   Total 39s 4¾d.

112 *Exeter Cathedral Fabric Accounts*

Week 8   In wages*. In one labourer in Beer quarry 11d. In 4 other labourers there 3s 4d. In one labourer there 9d. In one labourer on the Work 10d. In 3 other labourers there 2s 3d. 100 loads of stones from Barley 4s. 10 quarters of lime 4s 2d. Sharpening 1¼d.

Total 37s 6¾d.

Week 9   In wages*. In one labourer in the quarry 11d. In 4 other labourers there 3s 4d. In one labourer there 9d. For one labourer on the Work 10d. In 3 other labourers there 2s 3d. 7 quarters of lime 2s 11d. Sharpening 3¼d.

Total 33s 11¼d.

Week 10   In wages*. In one labourer in the quarry 11d. In 4 other labourers there 3s 4d. In one labourer there 9d. 7 quarters of lime 2s 11d. For one labourer on the Work 10d. In 3 other labourers there 2s 3d. Sharpening 1½d.

Total 43s 9½d.

Week 11   In wages*. And one labourer in the quarry 11d. In 4 other labourers there 3s 4d. In one labourer there 9d. In one labourer on the Work 10d. In 2 others 18d. 3 quarters of lime 15d.

Total 39s 4d.

Week 12   In wages*. In one labourer in the quarry 11d. In 4 other labourers there 3s 4d. In one labourer there 9d. In one labourer on the Work 10d. In 2 other labourers 18d. 6 quarters of lime 2s 6d.

Total 40s 8d.

Week 13   In wages*. In one labourer in the quarry 11d. In 4 other labourers there 3s 4d. In one labourer there 9d. In one labourer on the Work 10d. In 3 other labourers there 2s 3d. 7 quarters of lime 2s 11d.

Total 32s 11d.

Week 14   In wages*. In one labourer in the quarry 11d. In 4 other labourers there 3s 4d. In one labourer there 9d. In one labourer on the Work 10d. In 3 other labourers there 2s 3d. For making 3 great iron bars 4 pulleys (*poleyes*) 2 iron rods (*virgis ferr'*) 2 hinges (*vertivellis*) and sharpening for the high (*maiorem*) altar 19s 7d. 4 quarters of lime 20d. For one plumber (*plumbar'*) for one day 4d. Glue bought 3s 1½d.

Total 63s 4½d.

Total £19 11s 9¼d for the whole term.

Total of the whole expenses £39 9s 7d.

And there is owing to him £27 7s 7¼d. For which sum he is satisfied (*sibi satisfactum est*) by his arrears in his account of the fabric of the church for the present year, which arrears reach this same sum, as is shown in that same account. [Cancelled: Total £39 9s 7d].

* List of wages of named craftsmen is not included here, see pp. 198–9.
1 Margin: *post dominica in octavis Pasch' qu' cantatur office quasimodo geniti*, the only occasion that a week is dated by the Sunday office.

2616   1319, 30 September–1320, 28 September

2 membranes, head to tail, good condition.
Endorsed: *Compotus Johannis de Shyreford capellani custodis operis ecclesie beati Petri Exon' de dominica proxima post festum sancti Michaelis anno domini millesimo ccc°xviij usque ad* . . .
Illegible under galls but appears the same as the account heading.
Printed: Extract in Oliver, pp. 381–2.

(m.1) THE ACCOUNT OF JOHN DE SCHYREFORD CHAPLAIN
WARDEN OF THE WORK OF THE CHURCH OF THE BLESSED
PETER OF EXETER FROM SUNDAY AFTER THE FEAST OF
ST MICHAEL 1319 TO THE SUNDAY BEFORE THE FEAST OF ST
MICHAEL 1320.

RECEIPTS

The same [John] renders account of £124 18s 8d of the gift of the bishop
for the year. And of £48 from the canons' prebend for the year. And of
£17 from the church of St Erth (*Lananduho*) in Cornwall. And of £6 7s 4d
from the dignity of the dean for the year. And of 60s from the dignity of
the precentor. And of 64s from the dignity of the treasurer. And of 38s
from the dignity of the chancellor. And of [   ].[1] And of 12d for the carriage of a pipe of wine (*j pype vini*) from Exeter to Bishop's Clyst (*Clist
episcopi*). And of 8s 2d of rents of assize for the year. And 27s 1d from Whitsuntide offerings. And of 27s 10½d from the red chest (*de rubea archa*). And
of 8s 1d on 1 August (*ad gulam Augusti*). And of 2s 2d received from the
treasurer for stone and fire-wood (*busc'*). And of 3s from the sale of old
cart-wheels. And of 3d received from dom Richard de Brayle for one
stone sold to him. And of 13d from the gift of dom William de Alresford.
And of 3s from arrears of rent from Chambernoun's house. And of 35s
from the testament of Henry de Broke in part payment of 7 marks, that is
for Christmas and Easter terms. And of 4s from the testament of J. de la
Wode. And of 4s from the testament of John Lange. And of 6s 8d from
Master Walter de Bodmyna. And of 12d from the testament of Beatrice de
la Roche. And of 2s 10d from the executors of dom Ralph de Tyverton
chaplain. And of 8d for the grave (*fossat'*) of the vicar of *Nymet'*. And of 2d
from the obit of Eustace. And of 6d from John de Sparkewyll' chaplain.
And of 12d received from the stewards for lead for the well (*plumbo ad
fontem*). And of 11s received from them for carriage of timber to the suc-
centor's house (*ad dom' succentoris*). And of 45s 10d from the same for the
felling and carriage (*prosternacione et car'*) of timber for the gates of the close.
And of 20s from the testament of Master John Dyrewine. And of 6s 8d by
order of the executors of master Ralph de Stokes deceased from the goods
of the same Ralph.

Total £215 9s 1¼d.

EXPENSES

Default of rents   He reckons in default of the tenement of Henry Lovecok
within the south gate 12d, because no-one lives there or can be distrained.
And of 8d from 2 tenements in Combe St (Comestrete).

Total 20d.

COST OF MICHAELMAS TERM

Week 1   In wages*. And 2 carters 2s. For carrying 2 cart-loads (*cariag'*)
of timber from Norton to Exeter 3s 4d. For loading (*charg'*) them 5½d.
Fodder of 8 horses 3 quarters 7 bushels. And 3½ bushels more for the week
in augmentation (*ad incrementum*) on account of the length of the journey
(*propter longitudinem itineris*).   Total 12s 2½d.

Week 2   In wages*. In 2 carters 2s. For sawing (*serrand'*) 225 feet 20¼d. In one plumber for one day 4d. For binding 3 buckets and one tub 4½d. Fodder of 8 horses 3 quarters 4 bushels, that is to each horse for a day and a night one half bushel. And 3½ bushels more each week on account of the length of the journey from Beer quarry.   Total 10s 10¾d.

Week 3   In wages*. And 2 carters 2s. For sawing (*serrand'*) 300 feet 2s 3d. In one labourer on the Work 10d. And 3 other labourers there 2s 3d. 6000 pins (*pinnis*) for the roofs of the houses in Kalendarhay 9d. 6½ quarters of lime 2s 8½d. Fodder [as above].   Total [17s 2¼d].

Week 4   In wages*. And 2 carters 2s. For sawing 300 feet 2s 3d. One labourer on the Work 10d. 2 labourers 2s 3d. 6000 pins for roofing stones (*petris tegular'*) 9d. 3 quarters of lime 17½d. Fodder [as above].

Total 19s 7½d.

Week 5: 2 feasts, All Saints and All Souls [1 and 2 November]   In wages*. And 2 carters 2s. Item for sawing 125 feet 11¼d. In one labourer on the Work 8½d. In 3 other labourers there 22½d. 6000 pins 9d. 2 quarters of lime 10d. Fodder [as above].   Total 14s 1¾d.

Week 6: here the time changes   In wages*. And 2 carters 2s. And for sawing (*serrant'*) 275 feet 2s ¾d. And in one labourer on the Work 8½d. And in 3 other labourers there 22½d. 3 quarters of lime bought 15d. And in one roofer with his servant for 2 days 10d. Fodder [as above].

Total 17s 5¼d.

(m.2) Week 7   In wages*. And 2 carters 2s. One labourer on the Work 8½d. And 3 other labourers there 22½d. 2000 laths for the house in Kalendarhay 5s. 3000 pins for roofing 4½d. Paid to W. Allegate for 24 feet for roofing beyond the agreement (*ultra pactum*) 10s 6d. In one roofer roofing over the cloister for 2 days 8d. In the other roofer there with 2 servants for the whole week 2s 7d. In one plumber soldering (*soldiend'*) gutters 3d. Paid to Crokkernewill' for 500 lbs of iron for making large bars for 'la Pulputte' 15s 5d. Item for one barge-load of stones from the quarry to 'la Sege' 8s 5d. For sawing 268½ feet at task 2s. Fodder [as above].

Total 59s 3d.

Week 8   In wages*. And 2 carters 2s. And one labourer in the quarry 9d. And 4 other labourers there 2s 10d. In one labourer there 7½d. In one roofer with 2 servants roofing over the cloister 2s 7d. In one labourer on the Work 8½d. In 3 other labourers there 22½d. Sharpening for the quarry 15d. One rope for binding carts 10d. For binding one bucket 1d. Fodder [as above].   Total 23s 10d.

Week 9   In wages*. And 2 carters 2s. In one labourer in the quarry 9d. In 4 other labourers there 2s 10d. In one other labourer there 7½d. In one roofer with 2 servants roofing over the cloister 2s 7d. In one labourer on the Work 8½d. In 3 other labourers there 22½d. For digging and making the grave of William Briwer the lord bishop[2] (*In fosso fodiando et faciendo dom' Willelmi Briwere episcopi*) 9d. 1000 laths bought 2s 6d. One sack bought for fodder 10d. 3 quarters of lime 15d. Sharpening 6d. Fodder [as above].

Total 27s 6d.

Week 10   In wages*. And 2 carters 2s. In one labourer in the quarry 9d. In 4 other labourers there 2s 10d. In one other labourer there 7½d. In one labourer on the Work 8½d. In 3 other labourers there 22½d. 2½ quarters of lime 12½d. 2 horse-hides bought for the requirements of the carts 4s 5d. 4 stones of beef and mutton tallow (*cepi bovin' et multon'*) bought for the carts, engines and solder 6s 8d. 44 fotmels of lead bought £4 9s 2d, together with their carriage (*una cum cariacione eiusdem*). Fodder of 9 horses 4 quarters 3 bushels [as above]. Total £6 1[4?]s 4½d.

Week 11   In wages*. And 2 carts 2s. In one labourer in the quarry 9d. In 4 other labourers there 2s 10d. In one other labourer there 7½d. In one labourer on the Work 8½d. In 3 other labourers there 22½d. 2 quarters of lime 10d. Sharpening 4¼d. Glue bought 5¼d. Fodder of 9 horses [as above]. Total 22s 6½d.

Week 12   In wages*. And 2 carters 2s. In one labourer in the quarry 9d. In 4 other labourers there 2s 10d. In one other labourer there 7½d. In one labourer on the Work 8½d. In one other labourer there 7d. For 8 ashes (*fraxinis*) bought for making cart-axles 4s 10d. In payment made to the stewards of the exchequer for arrears from the house of Master Thomas the mason £4 7s 4d before the feast of Christmas in the aforesaid year. Item for mats for the chapter-house (*natis pro domo capituli*) 10d. For the fee of Master Thomas the mason for this term 33s 4d. And of John de Schyreford warden of the Work 12s 6d. For the stable hired at Newton for this term 12d. Farriery of the horses 9d. For shoeing horses with 10½ dozens of our own iron 21d. For making 1500 horse-nails 16d. 'Wippecord' 6d. Candles for the stable for the whole term 6d. Sharpening 7¾d. 10 quarters of lime 4s 2d. Fodder of 9 horses [as above]. Total £8 9s 1¼d.

Total of the whole quarter except oats and the tabulature of the high (*maioris*) altar £25 13s 10¼d [altered from £25 6s 7¼d].

Oats remaining and purchased[3]   Item he renders account of 7 quarters 3 bushels remaining from the preceding year. And in purchase 48 quarters 3 bushels price 55s 11½d. From this, for fodder of 8 horses for 9 weeks 39 quarters 3½ bushels, each horse for a day and a night taking half a bushel, and 3½ bushels more each week on account of the length of the journey from Beer quarry. And for fodder of 9 horses for 3 weeks 13 quarters 1 bushel, to each horse as above. And thus 7 quarters 1½ bushels remain. From which there are 4 quarters in augmentation (*in incremento*). And 7 quarters 1½ bushels remain as above.

Total of the purchase of oats 55s 11½d.

COST OF CHRISTMAS TERM

Week 1: in which the feast of Christmas falls on Tuesday   In wages of 2 carters 2s. Fodder of 9 horses 4 quarters 3 bushels and 3 bushels more in augmentation.[4]   Total 2s.

Week 2   In wages*. And 2 carters 2s. And one labourer in the quarry 9d. In 4 other labourers there 2s 10d. In one labourer there 7½d. In one labourer on the Work 8½d. In one other labourer there 7d. Fodder [as above]. Sharpening 4½d.   Total 17s 1d.

Week 3   In wages*. And 2 carters 2s. And one labourer in the quarry 9d. In 4 other labourers there 2s 10d. In one labourer there 7½d. In one labourer on the Work 8½d. In one other labourer there 7d. Sharpening 3¾d. Fodder [as above].   Total 18s 3¼d.

Week 4   In wages*. And 2 carters 2s. And one labourer in the quarry 9d. In 4 other labourers there 2s 10d. In one labourer there 7½d. In one labourer on the Work 8½d. In one labourer there 7d. 3 quarters of lime 15d. Sharpening 3½d. Fodder [as above].   Total 19s 6d.

Week 5   In wages*. In 2 carters 2s. In one labourer in the quarry 9d. In 4 other labourers there 2s 10d. In one labourer there 7d. In one labourer on the Work 8½d. In one other labourer there 7d. 6 pairs of cart-traces 2s 6d. 48 wheel-spokes (*radiis*) for carts bought 20d. 8½ quarters of lime 3s 6½d. For fodder [as above].   Total 25s 7½d.

Week 6   In wages*. And 2 carters 2s. In one labourer in the quarry 9d. In 4 other labourers there 2s 10d. In one labourer there 7½d. In one labourer on the Work 8½d. In the other labourer there 7d. Glue bought at Hampton 4s 4½d. 9 quarters of lime 3s 9d. For binding one tub and 2 buckets 5½d. Sharpening 2½d. Fodder [as above].   Total 26s 9d.

Week 7   In wages*. In one labourer on the Work 8½d. In one other labourer there 7d. For making 2 pairs of traces (*traicarum*) for the carts 4s 6d. For making 800 'tackenayles' 8d. Fodder [as above].
                                                               Total 11s 5d.

Week 8   In wages*. In one labourer on the Work 8½d. In the other labourer there 7d. Fodder [as above].   Total 9s 11d.

Week 9   In wages*. In one labourer on the Work 8½d. In one other labourer there 7d. Fodder [as above].   Total 9s 11d.

Week 10   In wages*. In one labourer on the Work 8½d. In one other labourer 7d. For 2 barge-loads from the quarry with stones to 'La Sige' 20s. Fodder [as above].   Total 26s 3d.

Week 11   In wages*. In one labourer in the quarry 7d. For binding 2 carts 5s. For putting an axle on a cart 3d. For one rope bought for the well 2½d. For one roofer with his servant for 4½ days 22½d. For one pair of cart-wheels bought at Taunton with carriage 7s 9d. Fodder [as above].
                                                               Total 20s 7½d.

Week 12   In wages*. In one labourer on the Work 8d. In one roofer roofing over 'le trasour' for 3 days 15d. Payment made to the stewards for the tithes of the church of St Erth granted to the lord king (*Solutione facta senescall' pro decima ecclesie de Lananduo domino regi concesse*) for 2 terms 11s 4d. 8s for the rent of the mason's house for the Christmas term. And 33s 4d paid to Master Thomas the mason for his fee for this term. 8d for making 800 horse-nails from our own iron. Fodder [as above].   Total 65s 6d.

Week 13   In wages*. In one labourer on the Work 10d. In one other labourer there 8d. In one roofer with his servant 2s 6d. For a barrow bought 12d. Sharpening 1¼d. Fodder [as above].   Total 15s 6¼d.

Week 14   In wages*. In one labourer on the Work 9d. In one other labourer there 7d. For the stable hired at Newton 12d. Farriery of the horses 9d. For shoeing horses with 11 dozens of our own iron 22d. For the fee of the warden (*custod'*) for this term 12s 6d. For one roofer with his servant 2s 6d. Candles for the stable 3d. 4 quarters of lime 20d. Fodder [as above].   Total 30s 6½d.

Total of the whole quarter except the tabulature and oats
£14 18s 11d.

Oats remaining and purchased   Item he renders account of 7 quarters 1½ bushels remaining from the second preceding quarter. And in purchase 57 quarters 2 bushels price £4 4s 10d. From this, for fodder of 9 horses for 14 weeks 61 quarters 2 bushels, that is, to each horse etc., and 3 bushels more each week on account of the length of the journey from Beer quarry And thus 3 quarters 1½ bushels remain.

Total of money (*argenti*) £4 4s 10d.

(m.1d) COST OF EASTER TERM

Week 1: feast of Easter   In wages*. And 2 labourers on the Work 10d. For repairing tools for the quarry 12d. Fodder of 9 horses 4 quarters 6 bushels as he shows below.   Total 4s 10½d.

Week 2   In wages*. In one labourer on the Work 10d. In one other labourer there 8d. For making 600 horse-nails 6d. Fodder [as above].
                                                    Total 9s 5d.

Week 3   In wages*. In one labourer on the Work 10d. In one other labourer there 8d. Sharpening 2d. For binding one bucket 1½d. For hempen thread (*filo canabe*) for carts 2d. One quarter of lime 5d. Fodder of 9 horses [as above].   Total 12s 1½d.

Week 4   In wages*. In one labourer on the Work 20d. In 2 other labourers there 16d. In 2 sawyers 2s 6d. For one carpenter hired at Norton for 2 days 6d. For mending 2 sieves 1½d. In one plumber 2s. For making 100 lead-nails 2d. 2 quarters of lime 10d. Fodder [as above].
                                                    Total 21s ½d.

Week 5: in which are 2 feasts, SS Philip and James and Holy Cross [1 and 3 May]   In wages*. In 5 labourers on the Work 3s 6½d. And 2 sawyers 2s 1d. In one plumber 20d. And his servant 8d. In 2 glaziers (*verrator'*) for mending the old glass in St John's tower (*pro veteri vitro emendendis in turr' sancti Iohannis*) 3s 4d. One pan (*patella*) bought for glue and cement 14d. Fodder [as above].   Total 22s 5¾d.

Week 6   In wages*. In 6 labourers on the Work 4s 3d. In one glazier for 3 days 12d. 11 lbs of white lead (*blamplu'*) 2s 10d. Oil for the same 8d. Sharpening 9d. One quarter of lime 5d. In one labourer 8½d. For one man hired for loading (*carkiand'*) carts 3d. Fodder of 10 horses 4 quarters 6 bushels.   Total 22s 8¾d.

Week 7   In wages*. And 2 masons 3s. In one roofer 12d. In 7 labourers on the Work 5s 10d. One gallon of oil for priming (*aprimand'*) wooden bosses (*claves ligneas*) 2s 2d. 2 alders bought for scaffolding (*scaffot'*) 1d. One horse bought 46s 8d. 3300 lbs of iron bought at Topsham £6 12s. For 2 locks 2 hinges with keys (*clav'*) for the same and in sharpening 18d for the gate in Kalendarhay. For 300 laths bought 9d. Fodder [as above].
                                                    Total £9 7s 1d.

Week 8: feast of Pentecost   In 4 carters 4s. 600 horse-shoes and 30 iron pieces (*ferr'*) bought with nails at Lopen 52s 10½d. 4000 horse-nails 4s 9½d. 6 dozen (*duodenis*) cart-clouts 5s 1d. 2 cart-saddles 6d. In expenses of John de Schyreford for a day in going and 2 days in staying and 1½ days in returning with 4 horses and 3 men 2s 6d. 80 loads of stones from Barley 3s. Fodder as above.   Total 72s 9d.

Week 9   In wages*. In 6 labourers on the Work 5s. 2 alders 2d. 11½ quarters of lime 4s 9½d. For binding vats (*cuvis*) 7d. Sharpening 4½d. Fodder [as above].   Total 20s 8d.

Week 10   In wages*. In 6 labourers on the Work 5s. 8 alders for scaffolding (*pro scaffot'*) 6d. 10 quarters of lime 4s 2d. Fodder [as above].
                                                Total 19s 10d.

Week 11   In wages*. In 6 labourers on the Work 5s. 5 quarters of lime 2s 1d. 2000 pins (*pynnis*) 2d. In 2 sawyers 2s 6d. Sharpening 5d. 1000 laths 2s 6d. For making 2 great bars for 'La Pulepytte' weighing 400 lbs 12s 4d. Fodder [as above].   Total 39s 1d.

Week 12   In wages*. And 6 labourers on the Work 5s. 10½ quarters of lime 4s 4½d. 25 boards bought 4s. 5 alders bought 6d. One cart-rope and 6 pairs of traces weighing 56 lbs 4s. For the stable hired at Newton for this term 12d. Farriery of the horses 9d. 1000 'spykes' bought 3s 1d. For sawing 250 feet at task 22½d. For [sawing] 50 feet of 'aysselers' at task 20d. For shoeing horses with 11 dozens of our own iron 22d. For the fee of Master Thomas for this quarter 33s 4d. And of John de Schyreford 12s 6d. For binding one vat (*cuva*) 3d. Sharpening 4d. One fother of lead bought 46s. Fodder [as above].   Total £6 8s 7d.

Total of the whole quarter except the tabulature and oats £29 3d.

Oats remaining and purchased   Item he renders account of 3 quarters 1½ bushels of the remainder of the previous quarter. And in purchase 81 quarters 3 bushels price £7 6s 2d. From this, in fodder of 10 horses for 12 weeks 55 quarters 1 bushel, that is, to each horse etc., and 3 bushels more each week on account of the length of the journey from Beer quarry. And thus 29 quarters 3½ bushels remain.

Total of money £7 6s 2d.

COST OF MIDSUMMER TERM

Week 1   In wages*. And 6 labourers on the Work 5s. 2 sacks bought for the horses' fodder 11d. 4 lbs of steel bought 3s 4d. 4 alders 3d. For making 700 nails for cart-clouts 6d. Sharpening and steeling of axes 7½d. Fodder of 10 horses 4 quarters 6 bushels as above.   Total 23s 1½d.

Week 2   In wages*. And 6 labourers on the Work 5s. For [sawing] 88 feet of 'aysselers' at task 3s. 20 quarters of lime 8s 4d. One horse bought 10s. For binding one cart 15s 1d. For one pair of cart-wheels 6d. For sawing 360 feet at task 2s 9½d. Sharpening 7d. For making one 'tripod' 3d. Fodder [as above].   Total 63s 5½d.

Week 3   In wages*. And 5 labourers on the Work 4s 2d. In 2 sawyers for 4 days 20d. 12 alders for scaffolding (*schaffot'*) 11d. 16 weys (*peysses*) of coloured glass (*de vitro colorato*) 20s 8d. And 8 weys of white glass (*In viij peysses de albo vitro*) 5s 4d. 3 quarters of lime 15d. Sharpening 11d. Fodder [as above]. Total 45s 6d.

(m.2d) Week 4   In wages*. In 5 labourers on the Work 4s 2d. In 2 sawyers for 3 days 15d. In one plumber for 9 days 2s 8d. For making 100 feet of 'ayssel' at task 3s 4d. 8 quarters of lime 3s 4d. Sharpening 7½d. Fodder [as above]. Total 27s 2½d.

Week 5—2 feasts: St Mary Magdalene and St James [22 and 25 July]   In wages*. In 6 labourers on the Work 4s 3d. In 2 sawyers for one day 5d. In one plumber for 2 days 8d. Sharpening 4d. 100 large spikes bought 10d. One horse bought 14s 4d. Fodder of 11 horses 4 quarters 6 bushels. Total 36s ½d.

Week 6   In wages*. In 4 labourers on the Work 3s 4d. In 2 other labourers there 18d. 1000 'spykes' bought 4s. 2 pairs of traces 8d. 26 loads of stones from Barley 12d. For binding a vat (*cuvis*) 3d. 9 quarters of lime 3s 9d. Sharpening 3d. In 2 sawyers 2s 1d. Fodder [as above]. Total 36s 7d.

Week 7   In wages*. In 4 labourers on the Work 3s 4d. In 2 other labourers there 18d. Sharpening 8¼d. For skinning one horse and curing the said hide (*In j equo excoriando et dicto coreo corriando*) 6d. 10½ quarters of lime 4s 4½d. 100 loads of stones from Barley 4s. 2 brass pulley-wheels (*In ij rotis eneis pro poleyes*) 11d. Fodder [as above]. Total 37s ¾d.

Week 8   In wages*. In 4 labourers on the Work 3s 4d. In 2 other labourers there 18d. In 2 sawyers 2s 6d. For binding one cart 16s. And to William Frensch for making 3 new reliquaries (*Et Willelmi Frensch fac' iij nova feretra*) 3s 2d. Timber for the same 3s. 6 boards and 150 large 'spykes' for the same 2s 3d. 7 quarters of lime 2s 11d. For binding one large chest (*magna arca*) with our own iron 12d. 50 loads of stones from Barley 22d. For binding one tub 2d. Fodder [as above]. Total 59s 5d.

Week 9   In wages*. In 5 labourers on the Work 4s 2d. In 2 other labourers there 18d. 9 quarters of lime 3s 9d. Sharpening 5¼d. For making 4 hinges (*vertiwellis*) for 'la pulpite' 2s. For making iron bands nails and other requirements for one great bell called Jesus (*j magna campana vocatur Jesus*) 2s 6d. 15 boards bought 3s 1d. 2½ lbs of white lead (*albo plumbo*) 10d for the image of the bishop's throne (*pro ymaginibus sedis episcopi*). Fodder [as above]. Total 40s ½d.

Week 10   In wages*. In 5 labourers on the Work 4s 2d. In 2 other labourers there 18d. In 2 masons (*lathomis*) 3s. In one roofer with his servant 2s 6d. For 3000 pins for roof-stones (*pinnis pro petris tegulinis*) 3d. 500 loads of stones from Barley 18s 4d. In payment made to Crockernewille for 324 lbs of iron for bars for 'la pulpitte' 9s 3d. 11 quarters of lime 3s 7d. Fodder [as above]. Total 65s 3d.

Week 11   In wages*. And 2 masons 3s. In 4 labourers on the Work 4s 2d. In 2 other labourers there 18d. For one roofer with his servant 2s 6d. 425 loads of stones from Barley 15s 7d. For 2 barges hired (*bargiis locatis*) from Beer quarry to 'la Sege' 21s 4d. 4 alders 6d. 6 lbs of wax for cement 3s 2d. For making 2000 horse-nails 20d. 9 quarters of lime 3s 9d. Fodder of 9 horses 4 quarters 6 bushels. Total 78s 11d.

Week 12   In wages*. And 2 sawyers 2s 6d. And one roofer with his servant 2s 6d. And one mason 18d. In 5 labourers on the Work 4s 2d. In 2 other labourers there 18d. 250 loads of stones from Barley 9s 2d. 10 quarters of lime 4s 2d. For making 100 spikes 6d. Fodder of 11 horses 4 quarters 6 bushels.   Total 55s 11d.

Week 13   In wages*. And 2 sawyers 2s 6d. And one roofer with his servant 2s 6d. In 6 labourers on the Work 5s. 13 boards of poplar (*pypeler*) 21d. 26 weys (*peys*) of coloured glass and 20 weys (*peys*) of white glass 23s 8d. 6 quarters of lime 2s 6d. 5000 pins of roof-stones 5d. 226 loads of stones from Barley 8s 3d. For 2000 laths 5s. Fodder [as above].
                                                                          Total 72s 8d.

Cost of hay   25 stacks of hay bought in various places at various prices £3 5s 3d. For carriage of the same 39s 6d. viz: For carriage of 100 trusses from Greendale to Newton 16s 8d. And carrying 183 trusses to Exeter from Greendale, Bishop's Clyst and Duryard (*Dureherd*) 22s 10d.
                                                                     Total £6 4s 9d.

Week 14   In wages*. In 2 sawyers 2s 6d. In one roofer with his servant 2s 6d. In 5 labourers on the Work 4s 2d. In one labourer there 9d. In payment made to the stewards for rent of the house of Master Thomas 16s, for the terms of Easter and Midsummer. For the stable hired at Newton 12d. For the fee of Master Thomas for this term 32s 4d. And of J. de Schyreford 12s 6d. For 'wyppecord' and hempen thread for the requirements of the carts 10d. Sharpening 10½d. 200 loads of stones from Barley 7s 4d. 14 quarters of lime 5s 10d. For shoeing horses with dozens (*duodenis*) of our own iron 2s 9d. Farriery of the horses 9d. Fodder [as above].
                                                                   Total 110s ½d.

Total of the whole quarter [cancelled: except oats and the tabulature of the high altar] £43 15s 11¾d.

[Cancelled: Oats remaining from the preceding quarter   There remains 29 quarters 3½ bushels of the remainder. And 57 quarters 6 bushels of oats previously bought for £4 17s 5d. From this, for fodder of 11 horses for 14 weeks 56 quarters 4 bushels, to each horse etc. And thus the remainder is 20 quarters 5½ bushels].

Total of money £4 17s 5d.

Total of the whole quarter with oats £48 13s 4¾d.

Purchase of oats   57 quarters 6 bushels of oats bought for the whole term
                         Total £4 17s 5d as is shown by the tally.

Total of both (*utriusque*) £48 13s 4¾d.

Expenses of oats   He reckons in 29 quarters 3½ bushels from the remainder of the previous term. And surplus purchase 57 quarters 6 bushels.
                                          Total 87 quarters 1½ bushels.
From which are expended in the above weeks 66½ quarters. And there remains 20½ quarters.

Total of the totals of the whole year £132 14s 4½d.

And he owes £82 14s 8¾d, allowed to him in his account of the tabulature of the high altar of the same year. And thus he is quit here.

* List of wages of named craftsmen is not included here, see pp. 199–200.
1 MS leaves blank.
2 A new grave was made for Bishop Briwer (d.1244) probably because the progress of the building necessitated moving the position of his original one.
3 The cumbrous method of accounting for the fodder for the horses is very much confused in this year's accounts. Here the totals for oats in the Michaelmas term are incorrect.
4 The number of bushels is altered in each weekly total throughout Christmas and Easter terms, and the figures of numbers of horses and their ration are equally confused. However, the quarterly total for oats is rationalized at the end of Easter term to a correct figure.

2617 Altar account: 1319, 30 September–1320, 28 September

One membrane, good condition.
Endorsed: *Compotus Johannis de Schyreford capellani custodis operis beati Petri Exon' de custu tabulator' lapid' maioris altar' dicte ecclesie Exon' a dominica proxima post festum sancti Michaelis anno domini millesimo ccc⁰xix⁰ usque ad dominicam proximam ante festum sancti Michaelis anno domini m⁰ccc⁰ vicesimo.*

(m.1) THE ACCOUNT OF JOHN DE SHIREFORD CHAPLAIN WARDEN OF THE WORK OF THE BLESSED PETER OF EXETER CONCERNING THE COST OF THE STONE TABULATURE OF THE HIGH ALTAR OF THE SAID CHURCH OF EXETER FROM SUNDAY AFTER THE FEAST OF ST MICHAEL 1319 UNTIL THE SUNDAY BEFORE THE FEAST OF SAINT MICHAEL 1320.

COST OF MICHAELMAS TERM

Week 1 In wages*. In one labourer in Beer quarry 11d. In 4 other labourers there 3s 4d. In one other labourer there 9d. In one labourer there 10d. In 3 other labourers there 2s 3d. 3½ quarters of lime 17½d. Sharpening 4¼d. 3 fotmels of lead bought for the high (*maior'*) altar 6s. For making one iron trough for founding lead about the altar (*patell' ferri faciend' ad fundendum plumb' circa altar'*) 8d. For carrying 2 barge-loads of stones from the quarry to 'la Sege' 20s.   Total 65s.

Week 2 In wages*. In one labourer in the quarry 11d. In 4 other labourers there 3s 4d. In one labourer there 9d. In one labourer on the Work 10d. In 3 other labourers there 2s 3d. Sharpening 6½d. 7½ quarters of lime 3s 1½d. 2 ropes weighing 109 lbs bought 7s. 60 lb of iron bought for bars for the great altar (*barr' ad magnum altare*) 11s.   Total 60s 8d.

Week 3 In wages*. Sharpening 4½d. In one labourer in the quarry 11d. In 4 other labourers there 3s 4d. In one labourer there 9d. One pot for glue (*olla pro visco*) ½d.   Total 36s 4d.

Week 4 In wages*. In one labourer in the quarry 11d. In 4 other labourers there 3s 4d. In one labourer there 9d. For priming of one great table (*In apprimacione unius magne tabule*) 3s 4d.   Total 35s 7d.

Week 5: the feast of All Saints [1 November] In wages*. In one labourer in the quarry 9d. And in 4 other labourers there 2s 10d. And in one labourer there 7½d.   Total 27s 1d.

Week 6   In wages*. And in one labourer in the quarry 9d. In 4 other labourers there 2s 10d. In one labourer there 7½d. Sharpening for the 3 preceding weeks 11¼d.   Total 26s 2¼d.

Week 7   In wages*. In one labourer in the quarry 9d. In 4 labourers there 2s 10d. In one labourer there 7½d. Sharpening and steeling axes (*secur' acerandis*) 5½d.   Total 25s 8½d.

Week 8   In wages*.   Total 19s 2½d.

Week 9   In wages*. One fother of lead containing 24 fotmels bought for the high altar (*j fodera plumbi continente xxiiij fotmell' empta pro maiore altari*) 48s.   Total 65s 6½d.

Week 10   In wages*. For 500 lbs of iron bought for the high altar 22s 10d.
                                                     Total 40s ½d.

Week 11   In wages*. 48 lbs of pitch for cement 4s. For priming one door with 2 layers of white lead (*In j hostio aprimando cum ij asisis de blankplum'*) 2s.   Total 25s 2½d.

Week 12   In wages*. 2 barge-loads of stones from Beer quarry to 'La Sege' 28s. Sharpening for Beer quarry for the whole term 13d.
                                                     Total 48s 3½d.

Total of the whole quarter £23 14s 10¼d.

COST OF CHRISTMAS TERM

First week after Christmas   In wages*.   Total 13s 4½d.

Weeks 2, 3   In wages*.   Total 20s 10½d [each week].

Week 4   In wages*.   Total 17s 1½d.

Week 5   In wages*.   Total 19s 2½d.

Week 6   In wages*. In 2 carters 2s. And one labourer in Beer quarry 9d. In 4 other labourers there 2s 10d. In one labourer there 7½d. Sharpening 4½d.   Total 31s 3½d.

Week 7   In wages*. And in 2 carters 2s. In one labourer in the quarry 9d. In 4 other labourers there 2s 10d. In one labourer there 7½d. Sharpening 5½d. One quarter of lime 5d.   Total 31s 9½d.

Week 8   In wages*. And 2 carters 2s. In one labourer in the quarry 9d. In 4 other labourers there 2s 10d. In one labourer there 7½d. For making 6 great bars of iron weighing 448 lbs for the high altar 12s 4d.
                                                     Total 43s 3d.

Week 9   In wages*. And in 2 carters 2s. In one labourer in the quarry 9d. In 4 other labourers there 2s 10d. In one labourer there 7½d. Sharpening 5½d. In one plumber for 3 days 9d.   Total 30s ¼d.

Week 10   In wages*. And 2 carters 2s. In one labourer in the quarry 9d. In 4 other labourers there 2s 10d. In one labourer there 7½d. Sharpening 3½d.   Total 31s 2½d.

Week 11: the time changes   In wages*. And 2 carters 2s. And in one labourer in the quarry 11d. And in 5 other labourers 4s 2d. Sharpening 2¾d.   Total 32s 6¼d.

Week 12   In wages*. And 2 carters 2s. And in one labourer in the quarry 11d. And in 5 other labourers 4s 2d.   Total 36s 10d.

Week 13: 2 feasts   In wages*. In 2 carters 2s. In one labourer in the quarry 9d. In 5 other labourers there 3s 6d. Sharpening 4d.
                                                        Total 31s 3½d.
            Total of the whole quarter £17 19s 8¼d.

COST OF EASTER TERM

First week: the feast of Easter   In wages*. In one labourer in the quarry 5½d. In 5 other labourers there 2s 1d. 2 quarters of lime 10d. Sharpening 1d.
                                                        Total 20s 4d.

Week 2   In wages*. In 2 carters 2s. In one labourer in the quarry 11d. In 5 other labourers there 4s 2d. In 2 sawyers (*serrator'*) 2s 1d. 3 quarters of lime 15d.   Total 37s 8d.

Week 3   In wages*. And in 2 carters 2s. In one labourer in the quarry 11d. In 5 other labourers there 4s 2d. 3 lbs of wax bought for cement (*cer' emp' pro cement'*) 20d. Sharpening 6d.   Total 39s.

Week 4   In wages*. In 2 carters 2s. In one labourer in the quarry 11d. In 5 other labourers there 4s 2d. For aid in loading carts at Norton (*In auxilio ad chargiand' carectas apud Norton'*) for one week 11d. In sharpening 8d.   Total 38s 5d.

Week 5: 2 feasts, SS Philip and James and Holy Cross [1 and 3 May]   In wages*. In 2 carters 2s. In one labourer in the quarry 9d. In 5 other labourers there 3s 6½d. Glue bought 2d. One quarter of lime 5d.
                                                        Total 31s 9d.

Week 6   In wages*. In 2 carters 2s. In one labourer in the quarry 9d. In 5 other labourers there 3s 6½d.   Total 31s 2d.

Week 7   In wages*. In 2 carters 2s. In one labourer in the quarry 11d. In 5 other labourers there 4s 2d. 8 quarters of lime 3s 4d. Ironwork of one engine (*Pro ferramento j ingenii*) 12d.   Total 41s 2d.

Week 8   In wages*. In 4 carters 3s 10d. In one labourer in the quarry 11d. In 5 other labourers there 4s 2d. For repair of one cart 8d.
                                                        Total 39s 4d.

Week 9   In wages*. In 4 carters 3s 10d. In one labourer in the quarry 11d. For 3 other labourers 2s 6d. For repair of one cart 12d. Sharpening and steeling of axes 12d.   Total 39s.

(m.1d) Week 10   In wages*. In 3 carters 3s 10d. In one labourer in the quarry 11d. In 2 other labourers there 20d.   Total 34s 2d.

Week 11   In wages*. In 4 carters 3s 10d. In one labourer in the quarry 11d. In one other labourer there 10d. Sharpening 4½d. Sharpening at the quarry for this term 9d.   Total 32s 5½d.
            Total of the whole quarter £19 4s 5½d.

COST OF MIDSUMMER TERM

Week 1   In wages*. In 4 carters 3s 10d. In one labourer in the quarry 11d. In one other labourer there 10d.   Total 30s 10d.

Week 2   In wages*. In 4 carters 3s 10d. In one labourer in the quarry 11d. In one other labourer there 10d. For carrying 100 large stones from the quarry to the sea 2s.   Total 32s 10d.

Week 3   In wages*. In 4 carters 3s 10d. In one labourer in the quarry 11d. In 2 other labourers there 20d.   Total 29s 8d.

Week 4   In wages*. In 4 carters 3s 10d. In one labourer in the quarry 11d. In 4 other labourers there 2s 6d.   Total 26s.

Week 5: 2 feasts, St Mary Magdalene and St James [22 and 25 July]   In wages*. In 4 carters 3s 10d. In one labourer in the quarry 9½d. In 2 other labourers there 17d. For hooping a barrow (*In ligatione j civeris*) 6d.
                                                          Total 26s.

Week 6   In wages*. And in 4 carters 3s 10d. In one labourer in the quarry 11d. In 7 others there 5s 10d.   Total 33s 10d.

Week 7   In wages*. In 4 carters 3s 10d. In one labourer in the quarry 11d. In 4 other labourers there 3s 4d.   Total 31s 4d.

Week 8   In wages*. In 4 carters 3s 10d. In one labourer in the quarry 11d. For 4 other labourers there 3s 4d. For making 6 iron bars for the canopy of the great altar (*vj barris ferri pro tabernaculo magni altaris*) 2s. Sharpening 2½d.   Total 33s 6½d.

Week 9   In wages*. In 4 carters 3s 10d. In one labourer in the quarry 11d. In 4 other labourers there 3s 4d.   Total 31s 4d.

Week 10   In wages*. In one labourer in the quarry 11d. In 4 carters 3s 10d. In 4 labourers in the quarry 3s 4d. Sharpening 4½d.
                                                          Total 34s 2½d.

Week 11   In wages*. And 4 carters 3s 10d. In one labourer in the quarry 11d. In 4 other labourers there 3s 4d. For 1065 lbs of iron bought 41s 6d. Sharpening 3d.   Total 75s 7d.

Week 12   In wages*. In 4 carters 3s 10d. In one labourer in the quarry 11d. In 4 other labourers there 3s 4d. Sharpening 4¾d.
                                                          Total 34s 2¾d.

Week 13   In wages*. In 4 carters 3s 10d. In one labourer in the quarry 11d. In 4 other labourers there 3s 4d. Sharpening 3d.
                                                          Total 31s 10d.

Week 14   In wages*. In 4 carters 3s 10d. In one labourer in the quarry 11d. In 4 other labourers there 3s 4d.   Total 29s 1d.

Total of the whole quarter £24 3¾d.

Total of the totals of the whole year £84 19s 3¾d.

This sum he is owed, of which he has received from the arrears of his account of the cost of the fabric of the same year £82 14s 8¾d. And thus he is still owed 44s 7d.

---

* List of wages of named craftsmen is not included here, see pp. 200–2.

2618 1320, 28 September–1321, 27 September

3 membranes, head to tail; m.1 is torn, with defective right-hand margin, repaired with paper; mm.2 and 3, good condition.
Endorsed: . . . [ca]pellani custodis operis de anno xx⁰
Printed: Extract in Oliver, p. 382.

(m.1) THE ACCOUNT OF JOHN DE SCHIREFORD WARDEN OF THE WORK OF THE CHURCH OF THE BLESSED PETER OF EXETER FROM SUNDAY BEFORE THE FEAST OF ST MICHAEL 1320 UNTIL THE SAME SUNDAY IN THE FOLLOWING YEAR 1321.

RECEIPTS

The same [John] renders account of £124 18s 8d of the gift of the lord bishop for the year. And of . . . And of £48 from the prebend of the canons for the year. And of £17 from [the church of St Erth].¹ And of £6 7s 4d from the dignity of the dean. And of 60s from the dignity [of the precentor].¹ And of 38s from the dignity [of the chancellor].¹ And of 8s 2d from rents of assize for the year. And of 8s from arrears of a tenement . . . And of 41s 1d from Whitsuntide offerings. And of 6s 10d on 1 August (*festo advincula sancti Petri*). And 32s 3d from the red chest. And of 6s 8d from one old horse . . . And of 3s for carriage of one pipe of wine from Exeter to Crediton (*Crydyton*). And of 5d for one small piece of lead. And of 2s for 3 old wheels sold. And of 12d for carrying 2 heads (*capitibus*) . . . And of 100s from the testament of dom John Strange. And 13s 4d from the testament of Master . . . And of 2s from the testament of dom Richard vicar of Kenton. And of 6d from the testament of Richard Spealte. And 2d from the obit of Eustace. And of 35s from the testament of Henry de . . . in part payment of 7 marks. And of 6s 8d from Vincent . . .

Total of the whole receipts £217 14s 1½d.

Memorandum concerning one basin and ewer (*pelvi et lavator'*) remaining from the gift of Andrew the chaplain.

EXPENSES

Surplus   He reckons in surplus of the preceding account he is owed 44s 7d.   Total 44s 7d.

Default of rent   The same reckons in default of the tenement of Henry Lovecok within the south gate 12d because no-one lives there nor can be distrained. And of 8d from 2 tenements in 'Combestrete'.

Total 20d.

(m.2) COST OF MICHAELMAS TERM

Week 1   In wages*. And one carpenter for 1½ days 6½d. In 5 labourers on the Work 4s 2d. In one labourer there 9d. In 2 sawyers 2s 6d. In one roofer with his servant 2s 6d. 50 loads of stones from Barley 22d. 7 quarters of lime 2s 11d. Sharpening 5d. 13 gallons one quart of oil 18s 9d. For making 2 tubs and 2 buckets 8d. 3000 pins 3d. 2 bowls (*gatis*) 2d. Fodder of 11 horses 5 quarters 2½ bushels, each horse receiving for a day and night ½ bushel, and 3½ bushels more in augmentation on account of the length of the journey from Beer quarry.   Total 61s ½d.

Week 2   In wages*. And 2 sawyers for 5 days 2s 1d. In one roofer with his servant 2s 6d. In 5 labourers on the Work 4s 2d. In one labourer there 9d. 2 cart-wheels 6s. For making 600 horse-nails 6d. In one plumber 2s. 2 quarters of lime 10d. Sharpening 2¾d. Fodder [as above].

                                                         Total 38s 11¾d.

Week 3   In wages*. And 2 carpenters 4s. And 2 sawyers 2s 6d. In one roofer with his servant for 5 days 2s 1d. In 5 labourers on the Work 4s 2d. In one other labourer there 9d. Fodder [as above].   Total 37s 5d.

Week 4   In wages*. And 4 carpenters 8s. And 2 sawyers 2s 6d. In 5 labourers on the Work 4s 2d. In one labourer there 9d. 15 quarters of lime 6s 3d. 2000 'pynnis' 2d. Sharpening 5d. 2 lbs of white lead 12d. 7 pairs of traces 3s. Fodder [as above].   Total 48s.

Week 5: in which are 2 feasts, SS Simon and Jude and All Saints [28 October and 1 November]   In wages*. In 3 labourers on the Work 2s 1½d. 5½ quarters of lime 2s 3½d. 2000 laths 5s. In one plasterer plastering one shed (*logeam*) 2s 6d. Fodder [as above].   Total 25s 11½d.

Week 6   In wages*. In 2 sawyers for 2 days 9d. In one roofer with his servant 2s 1d. In 4 labourers on the Work 2s 10d. In one labourer there for 4 days 5½d. 6 quarters of lime 2s 6d. Sharpening 6¾d. For making 6 bolts of iron for the vault (*voutur'*) 3s 4d. In exchange (*in exambiacione*) of one horse 18s 2d. 3000 roofing stones (*petris tegulinis*) 4s 7½d. Fodder [as above].   Total 54s 3¼d.

Week 7   In wages*. In one roofer with his servant 2s 1d. In 5 labourers on the Work 3s 6½d. For making 3 'bockets' 6d. 4000 roofing-stones 6s 2d. 7000 'pynnis' 7d. 60 feet of tiles (*tegulis*) 18d. 7 quarters of lime 2s 11d. For making 2 planes (*planis*) 5d. Fodder [as above].

                                                         Total 27s 9½d.

Week 8: purchase of colours   In wages*. In one roofer with his assistant (*adjutor'*) 2s 1d. In 3 labourers on the Work 2s 1½d. For sharpening 1½d. 100 lbs of white lead bought by the lord [bishop?] in London 18s. 500 foils of gold bought in the same place by the lord [bishop?] 19s 2d. 16 gallons (*lagen'*) of oil for painting (*pro pictur'*) 21s 6d. 2 quarters of lime 10d. Fodder [as above].   Total 78s 9d.

Week 9   In wages*. In 4 labourers on the Work 2s 10d. Sharpening 2d. 2 quarters of lime 10d. 6 lbs of mutton- and goat-tallow (*cepi multoninis caprinis*) for carts, engines and solder 7s 6d. 10000 large 'spykis' for the vault 10s. Fodder [as above].   Total 37s 1d.

Week 10   In wages*. In 4 labourers on the Work 2s 10d. Sharpening 5d. 4 quarters of lime 20d. 300 'spyks' for the vault 13½d. 4500 'lathnauyls' 3s 4½d. Oil bought 4d. Fodder [as above].   Total 27s 2d.

Week 11   In wages*. In 4 labourers on the Work 2s 10d. 5 quarters of lime 2s 1d. In one glazier (*verrator*) 12d. Sharpening 12d. Ironwork for one bell in St Paul's tower (*In ferramentis pro j campana in turr' sancti Pauli*) 12d.

100 'spyks' for the vault 6d. For making 1100 horse-nails 11d. Glue 1½d. Candles for the vault (*candel' pro voutur'*) 7d. Fodder [as above].

Total 25s 2½d.

Week 12   In wages*. In 4 labourers on the Work 2s 10d. In one roofer for 2 days with his servant 5d. One pickaxe (*pekassis*) 1 large iron hammer (*magno martello ferri*) 1 crow (*crouwa*) and 4 iron wedges (*weggis ferr'*) bought 3s 4d. In one plumber for 3 days 12d. One horse-hide bought 14d. 200 'spyks' for the vault 12d. For making 1000 small 'spyks' from our own iron 12d. For binding a bucket 1d. 6 quarters of lime 2s 6d. For sharpening with making 12 cramps for the gallery (*alur'*) 12½d. Fodder [as above].

Total 28s 3½d.

Week 13: in which the feast of Christmas falls on Thursday   In wages*. In 3 labourers on the Work 12¾d. For binding a cart with our own iron 6s. 200 lbs of tin bought for solder, with carriage 29s 10d. For the fee of Master Thomas for this term 33s 4d. And of J. de Schyreford the warden 12s 6d. For the stable hired at Newton for this term 12d. Farriery of the horses 9d. For shoeing the horses with 10½ dozens 21d. Sharpening 6d. 4 quarters of lime 20d. Candles for the stable for this term 3d. Fodder [as above].

Total £4 11s 3¼d.

Total of the whole quarter £29 14s ¾d.

Purchase of oats   58 quarters 2 bushels for the term 62s 1d.

Total 62s 1d.

Total of both with surplus and default of rent £34 9s 6¾d
[altered from £34 7s 10¾d].

Expenses of oats   He reckons 19 quarters 5½ bushels of the remainder from the previous year. And 58 quarters 4 bushels of previous purchase (*super emptione*).

Total 78 quarters 1½ bushels.

From this were expended for the 13 above weeks 69 quarters ½ bushel. And 9 quarters one bushel remain.

(m.3) COST OF CHRISTMAS TERM

Week 1: after Christmas   In wages of 2 carters 2s. Fodder of 8 horses 3 quarters 7 bushels [as above]. And he accounts here for 2 horses with murrain (*in morina*) and one horse sold (*in vendicione*).

Total 2s.

Week 2   In wages*. In 3 labourers on the Work 2s 1½d. Glue bought 2d. Sharpening 3d. 100 spikes for the vault 6d. Fodder [as above].

Total 19s 2½d.

Week 3   In wages*. And 2 glaziers 3s 4d. In 4 labourers on the Work 2s 10d. In 2 sawyers 2s 1d. 2 quarters of lime 10d. For binding 2 buckets 3d. Sharpening 3d. Ironwork for 6 glass windows in St Paul's tower (*In ferrament' pro vj fenestris vitreis in tur' sancti Pauli*) 12d. For making 2 images 2s 10d. Fodder [as above].

Total 29s 7d.

Week 4   In wages*. And 2 glaziers for 2 days 13d. In one plumber for 2 days 8d. 6 quarters of lime 2s 6d. Furze (*jampnis*) bought 4¼d. One horse-hide bought 13d. In one labourer on the Work 8d. In 4 other labourers there 2s 10d. 200 spikes 2s. Sharpening 2d. Fodder [as above].

Total 28s 11¼d.

Week 5   In wages*. And 2 sawyers 2s 1d. In 5 labourers on the Work 3s 6d. For 7 pig-skins for making cart-collars (*In vij coreis porcinis pro coleria carecte facientibus*) 2s 1d. Grease for the same 18d. In one tanner (*coreator'*) 4d. 3 stones of 'burl' 2s for the same. For 2 tilers (*tegulator'*) for 2 days 12d. For sawing (*serrand'*) 125 feet 11d. For making 400 horse-nails 4d. 3½ quarters of lime 17½d. For one roofer with his servant for one day 5d. 300 large spikes for the vault 4s 6d. 100 smaller (*minor'*) spikes for the same 3d. For binding 2 barrows 8d. 2 large iron bolts for the vault 2s. One lb of wax candles (*candelarum de cera*) 7d. One rope 10d. Fodder [as above].

Total 42s ½d.

Week 6   In wages*. And 2 sawyers 2s 1d. In 5 labourers on the Work 3s 6d. 3½ quarters of lime 17½d. Sharpening 3d. Fodder [as above].

Total 24s 8½d.

Week 7   In wages*. And 4 sawyers 4s 2d. In 5 labourers on the Work 3s 6d. 2 quarters of lime 10d. One lb of vermilion ('vermylloun') 1 lb of verdegris 2s 2d. And one lb of vermilion (*werm'*) 5d. For repair of one cart 9½d. One yard of woven linen (*j wlna lenee tele*) for painting (*pro pictur'*) 3d. One hide 3d. Fodder [as above].

Total 30s 11½d.

Week 8   In wages*. And 4 sawyers 4s 2d. In 4 labourers on the Work 2s 10d. 2½ quarters of lime 12½d. In one glazier for 3 days 10d. Sharpening 7d. In payment made [to] the stewards for the tithes granted to the lord king for one year, that is by the said lord?[2] 11s 4d. Item to the same for the rent of the house of Master Thomas for Michaelmas and Christmas terms 16s. Fodder [as above].

Total 55s 4½d.

Week 9   In wages*. And 4 sawyers 4s 2d. In 4 labourers on the Work 2s 10d. One hide for the requirements of the carts 7d. 3½ quarters of lime 17½d. In one plumber with his servant soldering above the church (*soldiand' super ecclesiam*) for 4 days 15d. Fodder [as above].

Total 28s 10½d.

Week 10   In wages*. And 4 sawyers 4s 2d. In 4 labourers on the Work 2s 10d. 2 quarters of lime 10d. 24 stones (*pet'*) of timber bought from dom William de Alreford 46s 8d. One lb of vermilion ('wermylloun') and one lb of red lead ('rogeplum') 18d. Fodder [as above].   Total 74s 7d.

Week 11   In wages*. In 4 labourers on the Work 2s 10d. In one labourer there for one day 1¼d. One lb of vermilion 14d. For sharpening and other requirements for the tabulature of the high altar (*pro tabul' sum' altar'*) 14½d. For making 1000 horse-nails 10d. For sawing 550 feet at task 4s 1½d. Fodder [as above].   Total 28s 10½d.

Week 12: the time changes   In wages*. In 4 labourers on the Work 3s 4d. In 3 other labourers there 2s 3d. One rope for binding carts 10d. 'Vippecord' 6d. One saddle with 2 panels and 3 collars for carts (*j sell' cum ij panell' et iij coler' pro carect'*) 17d. For sawing 600 feet 4s 6d. Sharpening and steeling of axes 8½d. Fodder [as above].   Total 33s 9½d.

Week 13   In wages*. In 4 labourers on the Work 3s 4d. In 2 other labourers there 16d. 3 stones of lard (*unci porcini*) 5s. For making 10 bands 108 dowels 2 lynches and 2 axle-plates for the carts (*x bend' cviii doulis ij lyncis ij hurter' pro carect' faciendis*) 22d. Sharpening 3½d. 13 loads of timber carried from Norton to Exeter 2s 2d. Fodder [as above].

Total 27s 6½d.

Week 14   In wages*. In 4 labourers on the Work 3s 4d. In 2 other labourers there 16d. For making 2 horse-collars (*coler'*) 4d. Sharpening 5d. 14 loads of timber carried from Norton to Exeter 2s 4d. Fodder [as above].   Total 18s.

Week 15   In wages*. In 4 labourers on the Work 3s 4d. In 3 other labourers there 2s 3d. In 3 glaziers setting glass in St Paul's tower (*iij verrator' ad ponend' vitr' in turr' sancti Pauli*) 6s. For binding 3 buckets 3d. For making 700 nails 7d. Sharpening 3d. Fodder [as above].   Total 22s 11d.

Week 16   In wages*. In 4 labourers on the Work 3s 4d. In one labourer there 8d. In 3 glaziers 6s. For shoeing horses with 9½ dozens 19d. Farriery for the horses 9d. For the stable hired at Newton 12d. For the fee of Master Thomas for this term 33s 4d. And of J. de Schyrford warden 12s 6d. For making 250 feet of glass 51s 6d. In 2 carpenters 4s 4d. For making ironwork for the great window in St Paul's tower (*In ferramenta pro magna fenestra in turr' sancti Pauli fac'*) 23s 6d. Fodder [as above].   Total £7 8s 9d.

Total of the whole quarter £30 16s 1¾d.

Purchase of oats   52 quarters 1½ bushels of oats bought for the whole term 66s 8½d.   Total 66s 8½d.

Total of both £34 2s 10¼d.

Expenses of oats   He reckons 9 quarters 1 bushel of the remainder of the preceding quarter and 51 quarters 3 bushels of previous purchase.

Total 60 quarters 4 bushels.

From this was expended in fodder of 8 horses for 16 weeks 62 quarters, to each horse as above and thus there are 1½ quarters of profit (*de advantage*). And nothing remains.

(m.4) COST OF EASTER TERM

Week 1: the feast of Easter   6 loads of timber carried from Norton to Exeter 12d. Fodder of 7 horses 3 quarters 3½ bushels. One tub bought 8d.   Total 20d.

Week 2   In wages*. In 4 labourers on the Work 3s 4d. In one labourer there 8d. Sharpening [   ]. Fodder [as above].   Total 14s 3d.

Week 3   In wages*. In 4 labourers on the Work 3s 4d. In one labourer there 8d. 6 quarters of lime 2s 6d. For binding one sieve and one bucket 3¾d. In one roofer roofing over the house of Master Thomas for 3 days 15d. Fodder [as above].   Total 18s 3¾d.

Week 4   In wages*. And 3 carpenters felling timber (*prosternent' meremium*) at Chudleigh 4s 8d. In 4 labourers on the Work 3s 4d. In one labourer there 8d. For sawing 250 feet 22d. Sharpening 1¼d. One quarter of lime 5d. Fodder [as above]. One barge-load of stones from the quarry 10s 5d.   Total 27s 10¾d.

Week 5   In wages*. And 3 other carpenters for 4 days 3s. In 4 labourers on the Work 3s 4d. One pair of cart-wheels bought at Canonsleigh (*Canonelegh*) 6s 2d. For making 800 nails 8d. 6 pairs of cart-traces 2s 6d. One quarter of charcoal (*carbon*)' 6d. 7000 roofing stones 10s 9½d. Sharpening 5d. For sawing 300 feet 2s 3d. Fodder [as above].   Total 40s 3¼d.

Week 6 In wages*. In 4 labourers on the Work 3s 4d. For sawing 300 feet 2s 3d. Fodder [as above].   Total 13s 3d.

Week 7 In wages*. In 4 labourers on the Work 3s 4d. For making 800 horse-nails 8d. For 3 saddles and 6 panniers? (*iij sellis et vj paner'*) bought 2s. For binding one tub 2d. For sharpening 1¼d. One quarter of lime 5d. For sawing 300 feet 2s 3d. Fodder [as above].   Total 17s 2¼d.

Week 8: feast of Pentecost In wages of 2 carters 2s. 550 horse-nails bought at Lopen 41s 6d. 7 dozen of cart-clouts 8s. 10000 'lathnayl' 7s 6d. 1000 'spyks' 3s. 2 cart-saddles 6d. One rope for the well (*In j cord' pro fonte*) 3d. For expenses of J. de Schyrford for 3 days with 3 boys and 4 horses 2s 6d. One glazier 2s. One brass ring (*In j anulo eneo*) 3s. In one painter (*pyctor'*) 12d. And 4 sawyers 20d. 500 gold [foils] 19s 2d. 5 lb of 'vermyloun' 4s 2d. 5 lb of 'verdegrys' 3s 4d. For putting an axle on a cart twice (*In j carect' bis axand'*) 6d. Fodder [as above].

Total £5 2s 1d.

Week 9 In wages*. And 4 labourers on the Work 3s 4d. 7 quarters of lime 2s 11d. Sharpening 2d. In 2 sawyers 2s 6d. For sharpening for the quarry 6d. For the fee of Master Thomas for this term 33s 4d. And J. de Schyrford 12s 6d. For the stable hired at Newton 12d. Farriery of the horses 9d. For shoeing horses with 8 dozens 16d. One bucket bought for the well 6d. Fodder [as above].   Total 67s 1d.

Total of the whole term £25 2s ¼d.

Purchase of oats   41 quarters 1 bushel of oats bought 56s 6d.

Total 56s 6d.

Total of both £27 18s 6¼d.

Expenses of oats He accounts for 41 quarters 1 bushel bought above. From this was expended in fodder of 7 horses for 9 weeks 30 quarters 7½ bushels, to each horse [as above]. and thus there remains 10 quarters 1½ bushels.

COST OF MIDSUMMER TERM

Week 1 In wages*. In 4 labourers on the Work 3s 4d. In 2 sawyers 2s 6d. For the burial of R. Warwest' the lord bishop (*In fossato dom R. episcopi Warwest'*)[3] 9d. For binding one tub 3d. 44 weys (*peys*) of white glass 16s. And 40 weys (*peys*) of coloured glass 30s. Sharpening 3¼d. Fodder of 7 horses [as above].   Total 62s 4¼d.

Week 2 In wages*. In 2 sawyers 2s 6d. In 5 labourers on the Work 4s 2d. One pair of cart-wheels bought 7s 6d. For 250 seams of sand 5s 6d. Fodder [as above].   Total 36s 7d.

Week 3 In wages*. And 2 sawyers 2s 6d. In one labourer 12d. In 5 other labourers 4s 2d. In 2 carters 2s. One cart-rope 12d. For making 600 nails 6d. Fodder [as above].   Total 19s 5d.

Week 4 In wages*. In 2 sawyers 2s 6d. In 2 labourers on the Work 2s. In 4 labourers there 3s 4d. 4 quarters of lime 20d. Sharpening 1d. In 2 carters 2s. Fodder [as above].   Total 16s 11d.

Week 5: 2 feasts   In wages*. In 2 sawyers 2s 1d. In 2 carters 2s. In 4 labourers on the Work 2s 10d. 5 quarters of lime 2s 1d. For making 1000 nails 10d. For putting an axle on a cart 3d. Fodder [as above].
Total 17s.

Week 6   In wages*. In 2 carters 2s. In 4 labourers on the Work 3s 4d. In one roofer with his servant (*cum suo serviente*) 2s 6d. Ironwork for the window beyond the great altar (*In ferramenta pro fenestra ultra magna altare*) 2s 6d. For 2 sawyers for 3½ days 18d. For 1000 'pynis' 1d. For one man helping to raise timber in the wood (*In j coadjutore ad levandum meremium in bosco*) 5d. Fodder [as above].
Total 26s 7d.

Week 7   In wages*. In 2 carters (*carectarerar'*) 2s. In 4 labourers on the Work 3s 4d. For sawing 450 feet at task 3s 4d. One horse-hide 16d. Fodder [as above].
Total 21s 2d.

Week 8: feasts of St Laurence and Assumption of St Mary [10 and 15 August]   In wages*. In 2 carters 2s. In 4 labourers on the Work 2s 10d. 2 great tree-trunks (*ij magnis lignis*) carried from Chudleigh to Exeter 9s. 54 elders (*alnetis*) bought near Norton (*iuxta Norton*) 12s 6d. For one horse bought at Priddy (*Pridie*) 35s. 4 quarters of lime 20d. Fodder [as above].
Total 71s 7d.

Week 9   In wages*. In 2 carters 2s. In 4 labourers on the Work 3s 4d. For sawing 150 feet 13½d. For sharpening 8¾d. For repair needed by a cart? (*In emendacione necessar' carect'*) 3d. Fodder [as above].
Total 17s 8¼d.

Week 10: 2 feasts St Bartholomew and St John [24 and 29 August]   In wages*. And 2 carters 2s. In 4 labourers on the Work 2s 10d. For repairing one panel 2d. For sawing 300 feet at task 2s 3d. Fodder [as above].
Total 15s 10d.

Week 11   In wages*. And 2 carters 2s. In 4 labourers on the Work 3s 4d. 1500 lbs of iron bought 60s 6d. 12 quarters of lime 5s. Sharpening 2d. For sawing 577 feet 4s 4d. Fodder [as above].   Total £4 3s 9d.

(m.3d) Week 12   In wages*. In 2 carters 2s. In 4 labourers on the Work 3s 4d. In the sawing of (*in serratione*) 350 feet 2s 4½d. Sharpening 3¾d. 3 quarters of lime 15d. Fodder [as above].   Total 17s 8¼d.

Week 13   In wages*. In 2 carters 2s. In 4 labourers on the Work 3s 4d. For making 600 nails 6d. In one carpenter 2s 2d. 'Vyppecord' 3d. 4 quarters of lime 20d. In the sawing of 300 feet 2s 3d. Fodder [as above].
Total 22s 5d.

Week 14   In wages*. In 2 carters 2s. In 4 labourers on the Work 3s 4d. Sharpening 3½d. 1500 gold [foils] 57s 5d. 100 lbs of white lead ('blamplum') 17s 2½d. 25 lbs of red lead ('rogeplum') 5s 2½d. For their carriage (*cariacione eiusdem*) from Winchester (*Winton'*) to Exeter 2s 6d. One lb of 'cinopele' 6s 8d. For sacks (*saccis*) for the same 3d. Paid to Bornewod' for 'tracis' made in his house at Newton 4s. Farriery for the horses for this term 9d. For the stable hired at Newton 12d. For the fee of Master Thomas 33s 4d. And of J. de Schyreford 12s 6d. For shoeing horses with 9 dozens 18d. Fodder [as above].   Total £8 2s 4½d.

Cost of hay   25 stacks bought in various places at various prices 75s 4d.
For their carriage 35s 10d viz. 70 trusses to Newton 11s 8d, 170 trusses
to Exeter 24s 2d.   Total 11s 2d.

Total of the whole quarter £35 2s 6¼d.

Purchase of oats   60 quarters 7 bushels £4 12s.   Total £4 12s.

Oats remaining   He renders account of 11 quarters 1½ bushels remaining
from the previous quarter. And of 60 quarters 7 bushels previously
bought.   Total 71 quarters ½ bushel.

From this was expended in fodder of 7 horses for 14 weeks 48 quarters 1½
bushels, to each horse [as above]. And there remains 22 quarters 7 bushels.

Total of this year within and without (*interius et exterius*)
£126 5s 5½d.

Total of all the expenses of the tabulature beyond the great
altar this year as he shows in his account £81 19s 10¾d.

Total of both £208 5s 4¼d.

And he owes £9 8s 9¼d. From this the vicar of St Erth is paid for repair
of the chancel by grace of the chapter one half mark. And thus he owes
£9 2s 1¼d.

---

* List of wages of named craftsmen is not included here, see pp. 202–3.
1 *Lacunae* supplied from the account for 1319–20.
2 The meaning of *per dictum dominum* here is not clear. The tithes in question are those of
St Erth, see pp. xii, 141, 148.
3 The reburial of Bishop Robert Warelwast (d.1161) was probably because the progress
of the building necessitated the moving of the position of his original grave.

2619   Altar account: 1320, 28 September–1321, 27 September

2 membranes, head to tail, some holes in the top of m.1, otherwise good condition. No
contemporary endorsement.

(m.1) THE ACCOUNT OF JOHN DE SCHYREFORD WARDEN OF
THE WORK OF THE CHURCH OF THE BLESSED PETER OF
EXETER CONCERNING THE TABULATURE OF THE HIGH
ALTAR OF THE SAME CHURCH FROM SUNDAY BEFORE THE
FEAST OF ST MICHAEL 1320 TO THE SAME SUNDAY IN THE
FOLLOWING YEAR.

COST OF MICHAELMAS TERM

Week 1   In wages*. In 4 carters 4s 10d. In one labourer in the quarry
11d. In 2 other labourers . . .   . . . 4 iron bars for the altar 15s 10d, that is
for iron and for making them (*pro ferro et factura*).   Total 45s 3d.

Weeks 2, 3, 4   In wages*. In 4 carters 3s 10d. In one labourer in the
quarry 11d. In 4 other labourers there 3s 4d.

Total 31s 7d [each week].

Week 5: in which are 2 feasts, SS. Simon and Jude and All Saints [28 October and 1 November]   In wages*. In 3 carters 2s 11d. In one labourer in the quarry 9d. In 4 other labourers there 2s 10d. Sharpening 1½d.   Total 27s 9½d.

Week 6   In wages*. In 2 carters 2s. In one labourer in the quarry 9d. In 4 other labourers there 2s 10d.   Total 27s ¼d.

Week 7   In wages*. In 2 carters 2s. In one labourer on the Work 9d. In 4 other labourers there 2s 10d. Sharpening 9d.   Total 27s 9¼d.

Week 8, 10, 11   In wages*. In 2 carters 2s. In one labourer in the quarry 9d. In 4 other labourers there 2s 10d.

Total 28s 8¼d [each week].

Week 9   In wages*. In 2 carters 2s. In one labourer in the quarry 9d. In 4 other labourers there 2s 10d.   Total 28s 6¼d.

Week 12   In wages*. In 2 carters 2s. In one labourer in the quarry 9d. In 4 other labourers there 2s 10d. One large barge-load of stones from Beer quarry delivered to 'La Sege' (*usque la Sege locata*) 14s.

Total 42s 8d.

Week 13: in which the feast of Christmas falls on Thursday   In wages*. In 2 carters 2s. In one labourer in the quarry 4½d. In 4 other labourers there 17d. In sharpening at the quarry for the whole term 12d.

Total 16s 4¼d.

Total of the whole term £19 16s 3½d.

COST OF CHRISTMAS TERM

The second week after Christmas   In wages*. In 2 carters 2s. In one labourer in the quarry 9d. In 4 other labourers there 2s 10d.

Total 26s 9¼d.

Week 3   In wages*. In 2 carters 2s. In one labourer in the quarry 9d. In 4 other labourers there 2s 10d. For making 2 images (*ymagnis*) 2s 6d.

Total 31s 2¼d.

Week 4   In wages*. In 2 carters 2s. In one labourer in the quarry 9d. In 4 other labourers there 2s 10d. In 2 sawyers (*serrator'*) 2s 1d.

Total 30s 9¼d.

Week 5   In wages*. In 2 carters 2s. In one labourer in the quarry 9d. In 4 other labourers there 2s 10d. Sharpening 3d.   Total 28s 11¼d.

Week 6   In wages*. In 2 carters 2s. In one labourer in the quarry 9d. In 4 other labourers there 2s 10d. 2 lbs of ochre (*hetre*) 2d.

Total 28s 10¼d.

Week 7   In wages*. In 2 carters 2s. And in one labourer in the quarry 9d. In 4 other labourers there 2s 10d. Sharpening 3½d.

Total 28s 11¾d.

Weeks 8, 11   In wages*. In 2 carters 2s. In one labourer in the quarry 9d. In 5 other labourers there 3s 6d.   Total 29s 4¾d.

Week 9   In wages*. In 2 carters 2s. In one labourer in the quarry 9d. In 5 other labourers there 3s 6½d. In sharpening 2½d.

Total 29s 7¼d.

Week 10　In wages*. In 2 carters 2s. In one labourer in the quarry 9d. In 5 other labourers there 3s 6½d. Sharpening 2d.

Total 29s 6¾d.

(m.2) Week 12: the time changes　In wages*. In 2 carters 2s. In one labourer in the quarry 11d. In 5 other labourers there 4s 2d. One lb of azure (*azur'*) bought in London by the lord [bishop?] (*empt' London' per dominum*) 3s 6d. One lb of indigo of Baghdad (*inde baudas*) 18d. 4 lbs of verdigris ('*verdegris'*) 2s 4d. 4 lbs of vermilion ('*vermilioun'*) 2s 8d. 5 lbs of white varnish (*werniz alb'*) 5s ¾d. 3 quarters (*quarteroniis*) of 'cinople' 4s 9d. For 1000 gold [foils] 38s 4d. 6 lbs of white lead ('blamppl') 18d.

Total £4 14s 5¾d.

Week 13　In wages*. In 2 carters 2s. In one labourer in the quarry 11d. In 5 other labourers there 4s 2d. One lb of white lead (blamplum') 2d.

Total 36s 2d.

Week 14　In wages*. In 2 carters 2s. In one labourer in the quarry 11d. In 5 other labourers there 4s 2d. 100 lbs of white lead and red lead ('blampplum et rogeplum') 20s 4d.　　　　Total 56s 10d.

Week 15　In wages*. In 2 carters 2s. In one labourer in the quarry 11d. In 5 other labourers there 4s 2d.　　　　Total 36s 6d.

Week 16　In wages*. In 2 carters 2s. In one labourer in the quarry 11d. In 5 other labourers there 4s 2d. Sharpening at the quarry for this term 8d.

Total 37s 7d.

Total of the whole term £27 13s 7¾d.

COST OF EASTER TERM

The second week after Easter　In wages*. In 2 carters for 2 weeks that is for the week of Easter and this week 4s. For one labourer in the quarry 11d. In 5 other labourers there 4s 2d.　　　　Total 38s 8d.

Week 3　In wages*. In 2 carters 2s. In 5 labourers in the quarry 4s 2d. In one labourer there 11d. Sharpening 7½d.　　　　Total 39s 6½d.

Week 4　In wages*. In 2 carters 2s. In one labourer in the quarry 11d. In 3 other labourers there 2s 6d.　　　　Total 29s 3d.

Week 5　In wages*. In 2 carters 2s. In one labourer in the quarry 11d. In 3 other labourers there 2s 6d. 101 lbs of white lead 17s 2d.

Total 48s 1d.

Week 6　In wages*. For one labourer in the quarry 11d. In 3 other labourers there 2s 6d. In 2 carters 2s. For 500 gold [foils] 19s 2d. 300 silver [foils] 18d. Half a lb of azure 3s. Sharpening and ironwork for the high (*maior'*) altar 18d.　　　　Total 55s 8d.

Week 7　In 2 carters 2s. In one labourer in the quarry 11d. In 4 other labourers there 3s 4d. For azure 21d.　　　　Total 33s 6d.

(m. 2d.) [No week 8]

Week 9　In wages*. In 2 carters 2s. In one labourer in the quarry 11d. In [4] other labourers there 3s 4d.　　　　Total 33s 6d.

Total of the whole quarter £13 18s 2½d.

COST OF MIDSUMMER TERM

Week 1 : the feast of St John [6 May] on Wednesday   In wages*. In 2 carters 2s. In one labourer in the quarry 11d. In 3 other labourers there 2s 6d.   Total 30s 8d.

Week 2   In wages*. In 2 carters 2s. In one labourer in the quarry 11d. In 3 other labourers there 2s 6d.   Total 30s 8d.

Week 3   In wages*. In one labour in the quarry 11d. In 3 other labourers there 2s 6d. 3 ells of linen cloth 6d for purifying colours (*iij wlnis line tele pro coloribus mundandis*). 416 seams of sand 8s 6d. 3 quarters of lime 15d. Sharpening 3½d.   Total 39s 2½d.

Week 4   In wages*. In one labourer in the quarry 11d. In 3 other labourers there 2s 6d. 20 gallons of oil for painting (*In xx lagen' olei pro pictur'*) 20s 6d.   Total 47s.

Week 5 : in which are 2 feasts, St Mary Magdalen and St James [22 and 25 July]   In wages*. In 2 labourers grinding colours (*ad molandum color'*) 2s. In one labourer in the quarry 9d. In 3 other labourers there 2s 6d. Sharpening 3½d.   Total 24s ½d.

Week 6   In wages*. In 2 labourers grinding colours 2s. And one labourer in the quarry 11d. In 3 other labourers there 2s 6d. Sharpening 3½d.
                                                             Total 24s 9½d.

Week 7   In wages*. In 2 grinders (*molator'*) 2s. In one labourer in the quarry 11d. In 3 other labourers there 2s 6d.   Total 26s 6d.

Week 8   In wages*. In 2 grinders 2s. In one labourer in the quarry 9d. In 3 other labourers there 2s 1½d. Sharpening 10d. In one grinder 12d.
                                                             Total 22s 6½d.

Week 9   In wages*. In one labourer in the quarry 11d. In 2 other labourers there 20d. In a painter? (*p . . . tor*) 12d.   Total 24s 8d.

Week 10 : two feasts, St Bartholomew and St John [24 and 29 August]   In wages*. In one labourer in the quarry 9d. In 2 other labourers there 17d. In one painter (*pyctor'*) 10d. Sharpening 4d.   Total 21s 4d.

Week 11   In wages*. In one grinder 12d. In 1 labourer in the quarry 11d. In 2 other labourers there 20d.   Total 28s 1d.

Week 12   In wages*. And one grinder 12d. In one labourer in the quarry 11d. In 2 other labourers there 20d.   Total 30s 1d.

Week 13   In wages*. And one grinder 12d. In one labourer in the quarry 11d. In 2 other labourers there 20d.   Total 30s 1d.

Week 14   In wages*. And one grinder 12d. In one labourer in the quarry 11d. In 2 other labourers there 20d.   Total 32s 1d.

Total of the whole quarter £20 11s 9d.

Total of the whole expenses through the year £81 19s 10¾d.

They are allowed on the account of the Work of this year (*qui allocantur super compotum operis istius anni*).

---

* List of wages of named craftsmen is not included here, see pp. 203–4.

2620   1321, 27 September–1322, 28 September

> 2 membranes, head to tail, good condition.
> Endorsed: *Compotus Johannis de Shireford capellani custodis operis de anno domini millesimo ccc⁰ vicesimo primo.*
> Printed: Extract in Oliver, p. 382.

(m.1) THE ACCOUNT OF JOHN DE SCHYREFORD CHAPLAIN OF THE WORK OF THE CHURCH OF THE BLESSED PETER OF EXETER CONCERNING THE COST OF THE SAME WORK FROM SUNDAY BEFORE THE FEAST OF ST MICHAEL 1321 TO THE SAME SUNDAY IN THE FOLLOWING YEAR.

RECEIPTS

The same [John] renders account of £9 2s 1¼d of arrears of the preceding account. And of £124 18s 8d from the lord bishop for the year. And of £48 from the prebend of the canons. And of £17 from the church of St Erth (*Lananduh'*). And of £6 7s 4d from the dignity of the dean. And of 64s from the dignity of the treasurer. And of £40 of the gift of the abbot of Tavistock (*Tavystok'*). And of 26s 8d from the rent of Hackworthy (*Hakeworthy*) in part payment of £10 assigned to the fabric by the executors of W. de Mollond'. And of 24s 11d from Whitsuntide offerings. And of 7s ¼d on 1 August (*gulam August'*). And of 23s 4d received from Robert de Huppehaye in final payment of 7 marks from the testament of Henry Brok'. And of 6s 8d from the testament of N. Strangg'. And of 6d from the testament of John de Raddon. And of 2d from the obit of Eustace. And of 60s from the dignity of the precentor. And of 38s from the dignity of the chancellor. And of 100s from Oliver de Esse. And of 8s 2d from rent in the town. And of 26s 9d from the red chest. And of 3s for one basin and one ewer received by the gift of dom Andrew the chaplain. And 6d from the testament of William de la Roch'. And of 6d from confessions. And of 2s from the testament of Richard the cook (*coci*) of Exeter. And of 18d from the carriage of one pipe of wine. And of 2s 8d from 4 old cart-wheels.

Total received £265 4s 7d.

EXPENSES

COST OF MICHAELMAS TERM

Week 1   In wages*. In 2 carters 2s. In 4 labourers on the Work 3s 4d. 8½ quarters of lime 3s 6½d. Sharpening 1½d. 48 lbs of pitch (*pyte*) for cement 4s. Fodder of 7 horses 3 quarters 4 bushels, to each horse for a day and night ½ bushel and 3½ bushels more for a week on account of the length of the journey from the quarry.   Total 25s 5d.

Week 2   In wages*. In 2 carters 2s. In one labourer in the quarry 11d. In one other labourer there 10d. In 4 labourers on the Work 3s 4d. Sharpening and steeling of axes 6½d. 5 quarters of lime 2s 1d. Fodder [as above].   Total 22s 9½d.

Week 3   In wages*. In 2 carters 2s. In one labourer in the quarry 11d. In one other labourer there 10d. In 3 labourers on the Work 2s 6d. For sharpening for the quarter 8d. Fodder [as above]. One barge-load of stones from the quarry to 'la Sege' 10s 6d.   Total 25s 10d.

Week 4   In wages*. In 2 carters 2s. In 2 labourers in the quarry 22d. In one other labourer there 10d. In 4 labourers on the Work 3s 4d. 2 quarters of lime 10d. For binding a bucket 3d. Fodder [as above].
                                                    Total 19s 6d.

Week 5   In wages*. In 2 carters 2s. In 2 labourers in the quarry 22d. In one labourer there 10d. In 4 labourers on the Work 3s 4d. Fodder [as above].   Total 18s 5d.

Week 6: the time changes   In wages*. In 2 carters 2s. In 2 labourers in the quarry 18½d. In one other labourer there 8½d. In 4 labourers on the Work 2s 10d. 7 quarters of lime 2s 11d. For sharpening for 2 weeks 2s 1d. Fodder [as above].   Total 20s 8d.

Week 7   In wages*. In 2 carters 2s. In 2 labourers in the quarry 18½d. In one other labourer there 8½d. In 4 labourers on the Work 2s 10d. For making 1000 nails 10d. Fodder [as above].   Total 18s 4d.

Week 8   In wages*. In 2 carters 2s. In 2 labourers in the quarry 18½d. In one other labourer there 8½d. In 4 labourers on the Work 2s 10d. Sharpening 5d. 12 quarters of lime 5s. For binding one bucket and one tub 3d. Fodder [as above].   Total 21s 6d.

Week 9   In wages*. In 2 carters 2s. In 2 labourers in the quarry 18½d. In one labourer there 8½d. In 4 labourers on the Work 2s 10d. 2 stones of mutton tallow (*cepi multon'*) bought for the carts 3s. 3 dozens of horse-shoes 3s 1d. 6½ quarters of lime 2s 8½d. Sharpening 3¾d. In one man for cleaning the quarry (*In j homine pro quarera mundand'*) 10d. Fodder [as above].
                                                    Total 25s 9¼d.

Week 10   In wages*. In 2 carters 2s. In 2 labourers in the quarry 18½d. In 2 other labourers there 17d. In 4 labourers on the Work 2s 10d. For binding one cask for oats (*In ligatione j dolei pro avena*) 5d. 2 locks? for the gallery (*ij serr' pro alur'*) 9d. Fodder [as above].   Total 17s 8½d.

Week 11   In wages*. In one roofer with his servant 2s 6d. In 2 carters 2s. In 2 labourers in the quarry 18½d. In one labourer there 8½d. In 4 labourers on the Work 2s 10d. Sharpening 4d. One horse bought 16s 1d. 6 pairs of traces for the carts 3s 4d. Fodder [as above].   Total 38s 1d.

Week 12   In wages*. In one roofer with his servant 2s 6d. In one plumber with his assistant (*coadiutore*) 2s 6d. In 2 carters 2s. In 2 labourers in the quarry 18½d. In one labourer there 8½d. In 4 labourer on the Work 2s 10d. For straw for a timber roof? (*In stramine pro coopertura merem?*) 2s 8d. Twists 3¼d. For 3000 'pynis' 3d. 2 horse-hides 2s 1d. For making 1200 horse-nails 12d. For shoeing horses with 8½ dozen 17d. Sharpening 3d. Fodder [as above].   Total 30s 5¼d.

Week 13: the feast of Christmas falls on Friday   In wages*. In one roofer and his servant 15d. In one plumber 15d. In 2 carters 2s. In 2 labourers in the quarry 9¼d. In one labourer there 4¼d. In 4 labourers on the Work 17d. For sharpening for the quarry and the Work 12d. For the stable hired at Newton 12d. Farriery for the horses 9d. For the fee of Master Thomas

33s 4d. And of J. de Schyreford 12s 6d. For rent of the mason's house 23s, viz. Easter, Midsummer and Michaelmas of the present year. One quarter of lime 5d. 2 iron bolts 2d. Fodder [as above].   Total £4 4s 7d.

Total of the whole quarter £18 9s ½d.

Purchase of oats   For 26 quarters 1 bushel 43s 6d, 20d a quarter.

Total 43s 6d.

Total of both £20 12s 6½d.

Oats remaining from the preceding quarter   He renders account of 22 quarters 7 bushels of the remainder. And of 26 quarters 1 bushel previously bought.   Total 49 quarters.

He expends this in fodder of 7 horses for thirteen weeks 49 quarters, to each horse [as above]. And nothing remains.

(m.2) COST OF CHRISTMAS TERM

Week 1: the feast [of Christmas]   In wages of 2 carters 2s. Fodder of 8 horses 3 quarters 7½ bushels.   Total 2s.

Week 2   In wages*. In 2 carters 2s. In 2 labourers in the quarry 18½d. In 2 other labourers there 17d. In 4 labourers on the Work 2s 10d. For newly binding one pair of wheels with our own iron (*de proprio ferro de novo ligand'*) 6s 6d. For making cramps 6d. Sharpening 4½d. 38 Irish boards (*bord' de Ybernia*) 10s 6d. In one carter 18d. One cart-rope and 2 pairs of traces 3s 6d. For whipcord and thread (*vppecord et filo*) 5d. Fodder [as above].   Total 39s 10d.

Week 3   In wages*. In one roofer and his servant 2s 6d. In 2 carters 2s. In 2 labourers in the quarry 18½d. In 2 other labourers there 17d. In 4 labourers on the Work 2s 10d. Sharpening 3d. For 'pinnis' 1d. 8 quarters of lime 3s 4d. Fodder [as above].   Total 20s 10d.

Week 4   In wages*. In 2 carters 2s. In 2 labourers in the quarry 1s 6½d. In 2 other labourers there 17d. In 4 labourers on the Work 2s 10d. Fodder [as above]. In 2 labourers in the quarry 17d.   Total 16s 1d.

Week 5   In wages*. In 2 carters 2s. In 2 labourers in the quarry 18½d. In 4 other labourers there 2s 10d. In 4 labourers on the Work 2s 10d. For a gratuity (*In curialitate*) to Henry Walmesford by order of the treasurer for his work about the scaffolding (*circa scaftuc'*) 6s 8d. 2 stones of tallow for the carts and other requirements 4s 6d. 4 quarters of lime 20d. 'Wyppe-cord' 6½d. In one carpenter for 2 days 6d. For fodder [as above].   Total 31s 7½d.

Week 6   In wages*. In 2 carters 2s. In 2 labourers in the quarry 18½d. In 4 other labourers there 2s 10d. In 4 labourers on the Work 2s 10d. Sharpening 11d. Fodder [as above].   Total 20s 6d.

Week 7   In wages*. In 2 carters 2s. In 2 labourers in the quarry 18½d. In 4 other labourers there 2s 10d. In 4 labourers on the Work 2s 10d. Sharpening 7¼d. 3 quarters of lime 15d. For making 1000 nails 10d. Fodder [as above].   Total 22s 3¼d.

Week 8   In wages*. In 2 carters 2s. In 2 labourers in the quarry 18½d. In 4 other labourers there 2s 10d. In 5 labourers on the Work 3s 6½d. For one horse-hide bought 18d. For sharpening for the quarry 16d. 2 quarters of lime 10d. One sieve 1d. Fodder [as above]. Total 24s 8d.

Week 9: 2 feasts, St Peter's Chair and St Mathias [22 and 24 February]
In wages*. In 2 carters 2s. In 2 labourers in the quarry 15½d. In 4 other labourers there 2s 4d. In 5 labourers on the Work 3s ¼d. In one carpenter 10d. 9 pig-skins bought for the requirements of the carts (*In ix pell' porcinis emptis pro necessar' carect'*) 4s 1½d. 4 stones of 'burll' 3s. 100 large horse-shoes 10s. Sharpening 2½d. One quarter of lime 5d. Fodder [as above].
Total 34s 7¾d.

Week 10 In wages*. In 2 carters 2s. In 2 labourers in the quarry 18½d. In 5 labourers there 3s 6½d. In 5 labourers on the Work 3s 6½d. In one carpenter 12d. 1500 lbs of iron bought 56s 3d. Sharpening 2½d. 16 quarters of lime 6s 8d. Fodder [as above]. Total £4 8s.

Week 11 In wages*. In 2 carters 2s. In 2 labourers in the quarry 18½d. In 5 other labourers there 3s 6½d. In 5 labourers on the Work 3s 6½d. In one carpenter 12d. Sharpening 2d. For binding one tub and one bucket 2d. Fodder [as above]. Total 26s 1½d.

Week 12: the time changes In wages*. And 2 carters 2s. In one labourer in the quarry 11d. In 6 other labourers there 5s. In 6 labourers on the Work 5s. For one horse-hide bought 2s. For tempering 3 stones of steel (*In iij petris aceris temperand'*) 15d. Sharpening 8½d. 20 large 'spyk' 3d. In one labourer in the quarry 8½d. Fodder [as above]. Total 39s 2d.

Week 13 In wages*. In 2 carters 2s. In one labourer in the quarry 11d. In 5 other labourers there 5s. In 7 labourers on the Work 5s 10d. 4 gallons of grease for cart-collars (*In iiij galonibus pyngedinis pro coleribus carect'*) and other requirements 3s 4d. For curing 9 hides 6d. One stone of 'burl' 8d. For making 6 collars 12d. 1600 tiles (*tegul'*) bought 8s 6d. In one plumber for 2 days 8d. Sharpening 6¼d. Fodder [as above].
Total 50s 3¼d.

Week 14 In wages*. In 2 carters 2s. In one labourer in the quarry 11d. In 6 other labourers there 5s. In 7 labourers on the Work 5s 10d. 6 pairs of traces for the carts 3s 8¼d. 3 quarters of charcoal for founding ashes (*In iij qr de carbonibus pro cineribus fundendis*) 18d. 400 'plumnayl' 10d. In one plumber 2s. 3 pairs of panniers (*In iiij pariis de paneriis*) 6d. Ironwork about the presbytery (*In ferramentis circa presbiteriam*) 3s 9d. One quarter of lime 5d. Sharpening 3d. For fodder [as above]. Total 49s 10¼d.

Week 15 In wages*. And one plumber with his assistant 3s 6d. In 2 carters 2s. In one labourer in the quarry 11d. In 6 other labourers there 5s. In 7 labourers on the Work 5s 10d. For the fee of Master Thomas for this term 33s 4d. And of J. de Schyreford warden of the Work 12s 6d. Farriery for the horses 9d. For the stable at Newton for this term 12d. For shoeing horses with 12½ dozens 2s 1d. 2 horse-hides for the requirements of the carts 2s 6d. 6 quarters of lime 2s 6d. In one roofer 3d. Sharpening 12d. Fodder [as above]. Total £4 18s 4d.

Total of the whole quarter £28 3s 10½d.

Purchase of oats   For 59 quarters 1 bushel of oats bought for £6 4s 8d.
Total £6 4s 8d.

Total of both £34 8s 6½d.

Expenses of oats   He renders account of 59 quarters 1 bushel of oats previously bought, from which were expended in fodder of 8 horses for 15 weeks above 59 quarters 1 bushel, for each horse [as above]. And thus nothing remains.

COST OF EASTER TERM

Week 1 : feast of Easter   In wages*. In one plumber 15d. In 2 carters 2s. In one labourer in the quarry 5½d. In 6 labourers there 2s 6d. In 7 labourers on the Work 2s 11d. Fodder of 8 horses 3 quarters 7½ bushels.

Total 20s 8½d.

Week 2   In wages*. In one plumber 2s. In 2 carters 2s. In one labourer in the quarry 11d. In 7 other labourers there 5s 10d. In 7 labourers on the Work 5s 10d. Sharpening 10d. Fodder [as above].   Total 42s 7d.

Week 3   In wages*. In 2 carters 2s. In one labourer in the quarry 11d. In 6 other labourers there 5s. In 7 labourers on the Work 5s 10d. One pair of cart-wheels 6s 6d. Sharpening 5d. For 'cole' for painting (*pro pyctur*') 5d. 4 quarters of lime 20d. 3 stones of steel 2s. Fodder [as above].

Total 48s 9d.

Week 4: the feasts of Holy Cross and St John [3 and 6 May]   In wages*. In 2 carters 2s. In one labourer in the quarry 9½d. In 7 other labourers there 4s 11½d. In 7 labourers on the Work 4s 11½d. One horse bought at Crediton 47s 9d. For sharpening 3½d. 8 quarters of lime 3s 4d. For fodder [as above].   Total £4 6s 2d.

Week 5   In wages*. In 2 carters 2s. In one labourer in the quarry 11d. In 7 other labourers there 5s 10d. In 7 labourers on the Work 5s 10d. 100 lbs of white lead with carriage 20s. 15000 lath-nails 13s 6d. 3 ox-hides bought for panels and other requirements of the carts 3s. For grease 12d. For turning and making the same (*In eisdem tournand' et faciend'*) 17d. 3 saddles (*sellis*) 9d. 10 gallons and 1 potel of oil for painting (*pro pyctour'*) 11s 6d. 7 large boards bought 4s 1d. 3 sieves bought 3d. 3 quarters of lime 15d. Sharpening 4d. For fodder [as above].   Total £4 15s 8¾d.

Week 6   In wages*. In 2 carters 2s. In one labourer in the quarry 11d. In 7 other labourers there 5s 10d. In 6 labourers on the Work 5s. 4 barge-loads (*bargiis*) of stones from the quarry to 'la Sege' 36s 6d. 2 horse-hides 2s 6d. 2 iron clappers (*bateris*) for bells viz. Jhesu and Marie 10s. Fodder [as above].   Total £4 8s 11d.

[1]Memorandum [added at extreme end of m.2].
John the goldsmith (*aurifaber*) received from J. de Shireford 40s by order of the treasurer. And £10 10s for gold and cloth from London (*pro aur' et pano London'*). Item 7s.

Sum total of yearly receipts? (*r' an'*) for 2? years? in question (*pro duorum* [sic] *an' rogatis*) £147 12s 9d.[1]

(m.1d) Week 7   In wages*. In 2 carters 2s. In one labourer in the quarry 11d. In 7 other labourers there 5s 10d. In 6 labourers on the Work 5s. 7 quarters 4 bushels of lime 3s 1½d. 6100 tiles 33s 6d. Sharpening 9¾d. 500 'tatnayl' 5d. Fodder [as above].   Total 77s 8¾d.

Week 8   In wages*. In 2 carters 2s. For glue (*visco*) 3½d. 400 large horse-shoes bought at Lopen 28s 6d. 300 smaller ones 21s. 11 dozen for cart-clouts 17s 8d. In expenses of J. de Schyrford with 4 men and as many horses (*tot equis*) for 4 days 3s 2d. In payment made to the lord King viz. 5d in every mark for the church of St Erth (*Launanduho*) 3s 6½d. Item 16s for the mason's house for the terms of Christmas and Easter. Fodder [as above].   Total £4 15s 2d.

Week 9   In wages*. In 2 carters 2s. In one labourer in the quarry 11d. In 7 other labourers there 5s 10d. In 7 labourers on the Work 5s 10d. Sharpening 5d. 8½ quarters of lime 3s 6½d. 1000 large spikes for the vault in St John's tower (*In jm magnis spyk' pro voutur' in turr' sancti Iohannis*) 16s 8d. 1000 smaller ones 2s 6d. One barge-load to 'la Sege' 14s 4d. Fodder [as above].   Total 74s 4½d.

Week 10   In wages*. In 2 carters 2s. In one labourer in the quarry 11d. In 7 labourers in the quarry 5s 10d. In 7 labourers on the Work 5s 10d. Sharpening 8d. 10½ quarters of lime 4s 4d. 6 ash-trees bought at Honiton (*Honeton*) for axles (*pro exil'*) of carts 6s 6d. In 3 carpenters for making the same 4s. One barge-load of stones from the quarry to 'la Sege' 11s 10d. Fodder [as above].   Total 64s 3d.

Week 11   In wages*. In 2 sawyers 2s 6d. In 2 carters 2s. In one labourer in the quarry 11d. In 7 other labourers there 5s 10d. In 7 labourers on the Work 5s 10d. 15½ quarters of lime 6s 7½d. Sharpening 10½d. One boat (*nave*) from the quarry to 'la Sege' carrying stones viz. weighing 24 tons (*dollearum*) 36s. Ironwork for one engine (*In ferramento pro j ingenio*) 18d. Ironwork for one large plane (*plana*) 7d. For the stable hired at Newton for this term 12d. For the fee of Master Thomas 33s 4d. And of J. de Schyrford 12s 6d. Farriery for the horses 9d. For shoeing horses with 9 dozens 18d. For sharpening for the quarry for the whole term 10d. For fodder [as above].   Total £6 14s 9d.

Total of the whole quarter £41 9s 1½d.

Purchase of oats   For 43 quarters 2½ bushels of oats bought for £6 5s 8d.
                                                                Total £6 5s 8d.

Total of both £47 14s 9½d.

Total of oats   43 quarters 2 bushels previously bought from which he reckons in fodder of 8 horses for 11 weeks 43 quarters 2½ bushels to each horse [as above]. And nothing remains.

COST OF MIDSUMMER TERM

Week 1   In wages*. In 2 sawyers 2s 6d. In 2 carters 2s. In one labourer in the quarry 11d. In 7 other labourers there 5s 10d. In 7 labourers on the Work 5s 10d. Sharpening 11¼d. 2 dozen alders for scaffolding (*alnetis pro scaffot'*) 4s. 5 lbs of lard (*hunci porcinis*) 6d. For curing one horse-hide 6d. 7½ quarters of lime 3s 1½d. Fodder of 8 horses 3 quarters 4 bushels.
                                                                Total 48s 5¾d.

Week 2   In wages*. In 2 sawyers 2s 6d. In 2 carters 2s. In one labourer in the quarry 11d. In 7 other labourers there 5s 10d. In 7 labourers on the Work 5s 10d. Glue 4½d. Sharpening 5¼d. For binding one bucket 1d. 3 quarters of lime 15d. Fodder [as above].   Total 41s 6¾d.

Week 3   In wages*. In 2 sawyers 2s 6d. In 2 carters 2s. In one labourer in the quarry 11d. In 7 other labourers there 5s 10d. In 7 labourers on the Work 5s 10d. For making 1100 nails 11d. 12½ quarters of lime 5s 2½d. 12000 lbs of iron 48s 8d. Sharpening 13d. Fodder [as above].
                                                                Total £4 15s 3½d.

Week 4   In wages*. In 2 sawyers 2s 6d. In 2 carters 2s. In one labourer in the quarry 11d. In 7 other labourers there 5s 10d. In 7 labourers on the Work 5s 10d. 12 quarters of lime 5s. Sharpening 12¼d. For binding a bucket 2d. 6 pairs of traces and one rope weighing 26 lbs 5s 8d. Fodder [as above].   Total 51s 3¼d.

(m.2d) Week 5   In wages*. In 2 sawyers 2s 6d. In 2 carters 2s. In one labourer in the quarry 11d. In 7 other labourers there 5s 10d. In 7 labourers on the Work 5s 10d. 'Wyppecord' 4d. 2 glue-pots (*ollis pro visco*) 2d. One lb of indigo (*hindbaud'*) 8d. 8½ quarters of lime 3s 7½d. Sharpening 3d. Fodder [as above]. 2 barge-loads of stones from the quarry to 'la Sege' 21s.   Total 69s 4½d.

Week 6   In wages*. In 2 sawyers 2s 6d. In 2 carters 2s. In one labourer in the quarry 11d. In 7 other labourers there 5s 10d. In 7 labourers on the Work 5s 10d. 6 quarters of lime 2s 6d. Sharpening 7¼d. In 2 sawyers for one day 6d. Fodder [as above].   Total 45s [?] ¼d.

Week 7   In wages*. In 2 sawyers 2s 6d. In 2 carters 2s. In one labourer in the quarry 11d. In 7 other labourers there 5s 10d. In 7 labourers on the Work 5s 10d. 14 quarters of lime 5s 10d. Sharpening 7d. For 2 loads of timber (*charg' merem'*) carried from Norton to Exeter 3s 4d. Glue 3d. Fodder [as above].   Total 51s 5d.

Week 8   In wages*. In 2 sawyers 2s 6d. In 2 carters 2s. In one labourer in the quarry 11d. In 7 other labourers there 5s 10d. In 7 labourers on the Work 5s 10d. 6 fothers 7 fotmels of lead £16 16s 8½d. For their carriage from the mine (*miner'*) to 'la Sege' 12s 6d. 126 lbs of tin 16s 5d. One rope 9d. One load (*charg'*) of timber carried from Norton to Exeter 20d. 14½ quarters of lime 6s ½d. 100 large stones carried from the quarry to the sea 3s. 226 loads of stones from Barley 9s. Fodder [as above].
                                                                Total £21 9s 6d.

Week 9   In wages*. In 2 sawyers 2s 6d. In 2 carters 2s. In one labourer in the quarry 11d. In 11 other labourers there 9s 2d. In 7 labourers on the Work 5s 10d. 31 fotmels of lead 66s 8d. Sharpening 6d. Fodder [as above].
                                                                Total 113s 11d.

Week 10   In wages*. In 2 sawyers 2s 6d. In 2 carters 2s. In one labourer in the quarry 11d. In 7 other labourers there 5s 10d. In 7 labourers on the Work 5s 10d. 17½ quarters of lime 7s 3½d. Sharpening 4¼d. Fodder [as above].   Total 49s ¾d.

Week 11   In wages*. In 2 sawyers 2s 6d. In 2 carters 2s. In one labourer in the quarry 11d. In 7 other labourers there 5s 10d. In 7 labourers on the Work 5s 10d. 12 quarters of lime 5s. For repairing one cart-panel 2d. One horse bought 10s. One rope 3s 4d. Sharpening 4½d. Fodder [as above].
                                                                Total 64s 3½d.

Week 12   In wages*. In 2 sawyers 2s 6d. In 2 carters 2s. In one labourer in the quarry 11d. In 7 other labourers there 5s 10d. In 7 labourers on the Work 5s 10d. 9 quarters of lime 3s 9d. For sharpening 5½d. In one plumber with his servant 2s 10d. One seam of white glass 10s. And 12 weys (*peyses*) of coloured glass 10s. Fodder [as above].

Total 70s 5½d.

Week 13   In wages*. In 2 sawyers 2s 6d. In 2 carters 2s. In one labourer in the quarry 11d. In 7 labourers there 5s 10d. In 7 labourers on the Work 5s 10d. For the fee of Master Thomas 33s 4d. And of John de Schyreford 12s 6d. Farriery for the horses 9d. For shoeing the horses with 10 dozens 20d. For the stable hired at Newton 12d. 4 cart-loads (*cariagiis*) of timber carried from Norton to Exeter 6s 8d. 200 loads of stones from Barley 8s. Sharpening 11d. Fodder [as above].   Total 109s 3d.

Cost of hay   For 28 stacks of hay bought at Rockbeare [corrected from Greendale] in various places 105s 11¼d. For carriage of 352 trusses 57s 8d, 2s a truss.   Total £8 3s 7¼d.

Total of the whole quarter £59 2s 6¾d.

Purchase of oats   For 45 quarters 4 bushels of oats bought £6 11s.

Total £6 11s.

Total of both £76 13s 6¾d.

Item for the rent of the mason's house for Midsummer 1322 8s. And thus the true total is £77 18¾d.

He reckons 45 quarters 4 bushels previously bought from which are expended for fodder of 8 horses for 13 weeks above-written 45 quarters 4 bushels, to each horse [as above]. And thus nothing remains.

Total of the whole expenses £179 17s 5¼d.

And he owes £85 7s 1¾d. From which he is allowed £86 4s 5d, which he expends on the account of the tabulature of the great altar as he shows in the roll of account of that same work.

And thus the total of expenses exceeds the total of receipts by 17s 3¾d, which are allowed to him in the account of the following year.

---

* List of wages of named craftsmen is not included here, see pp. 204–5.
1 ... 1 This memorandum is in a rather illegible and much abbreviated style at a point where the membrane is cut away, and the sums of money mentioned in it are not included in the total of the quarter's account.

2621   Altar account: 1321, 27 September–1322, 26 September

One membrane, good condition.
Endorsement: *Compotus de cust' tabulatur' magni altar' a dominica proxima ante festum sancti Michaelis anno domini m⁰ccc⁰xxj usque eandem dominicam anno revoluto.*

(m.1) THE ACCOUNT OF JOHN DE SCHYREFORD CHAPLAIN WARDEN OF THE WORK OF THE CHURCH OF THE BLESSED PETER OF EXETER CONCERNING THE COST OF THE TABU-LATURE OF THE HIGH ALTAR OF THE SAME CHURCH FROM THE SUNDAY BEFORE THE FEAST OF ST MICHAEL 1321 TO THE SAME SUNDAY IN THE NEXT YEAR.

COST OF MICHAELMAS TERM

Week 1   In wages*. In wages of one labourer in the quarry 11d. In one other labourer there 10d.   Total 27s 1d.

Weeks 2, 3, 4   In wages*.   Total 25s 4d [each week].

Week 5   In wages*. 100 lbs of white lead (*blamplum*) 20s.
                                                             Total 45s 4d.

Week 6   In wages*. 1500 gold [foils] (*m. et di. aur'*) £6 8s 4d. 2 lbs of azure (*azura*) 20s 6d. 600 silver [foils] 3s. One quarter of 'cinople' 3s 6d. 16 cramps for the altar 16d.   Total £8 14s 5d.

Week 7   In wages*. 12 dishes bought for colours (*discis pro coloribus emptis*) 3d.   Total 20s 1d.

Week 8   In wages*.   Total 19s 10d.

Week 9   In wages*.   Total 18s.

Weeks 10, 11, 12   In wages*.   Total 18s 10d [each week].

Week 13   In wages*.   Total 9s 5d.

Total of the whole quarter £22 6s 8d.

COST OF CHRISTMAS TERM

The first week after the feast of Christmas   In wages*.
                                                             Total 16s 4d.

Week 2   In wages*. For making two images (*In ij imaginibus faciendis*) 2s 4d. One lb of 'cinopel' 3s 1d.   Total 19s 6d.

Week 3   In wages*. For making 3 images 4s 8d.   Total 18s 1d.

Week 4   In wages*. For making 7 images 8s 3d.   Total 22s 3d.

Week 5   In wages*. For making 3 images (*ymag'*) 3s 6d. One lock for the door behind the high altar (*In j serur' pro hostio retro maior' altar'*) 2s.
                                                             Total 19s 7d.

Week 6   In wages*. For making 4 images 4s 6d.   Total 18s 7d.

Week 7   In wages*. For making 3 images 3s 6d. Sharpening for the Work 5d.   Total 19s 8d.

Week 8: 2 feasts   In wages*. For making 2 images 2s 4d.
                                                             Total 15s 7d.

Week 9   In wages*. For making 2 images 2s 4d.   Total 19s 9d.

Week 10   In wages*. For making 4 images 4s 8d.
                                                             Total 20s 2½d.

Week 11: the time changes   In wages*. For making 5 images 5s 10d. 10 lbs of vermilion (*verm'*) 5s 3d.   Total 29s 10d.

Week 12   In wages*. For making 6 images 7s.   Total 25s 9d.

Week 13   In wages*. For making 4 images 4s 8d. In sharpening 3d.
                                                             Total 26s 11d.

Week 14   In wages*. For making 2 images 2s 4d.   Total 24s 4d.

Total of the whole quarter £14 16s 4½d.

(m.1d) COST OF EASTER TERM

Week 1   In wages*. In sharpening for the quarry for the whole term 8d.
Total 10s 8d.

Week 2   In wages*. In making one image 14d. In wages of Peter the painter (*pictor'*) for 1½ weeks 3s.   Total 24s 2d.

Week 3   In wages*. 600 foils of gold (*foliis auri*) 23s 6d.
Total 43s 6d.

Week 4: 2 feasts, Holy Cross and St John [3 and 6 May]   In wages*. For metal foils for the lily (*In foliis de metallo pro lilia*) 2s 2½d.
Total 19s ½d.

Weeks 5, 6, 7   In wages*.   Total 20s 2d [each week].

Week 9   In wages*. 3000 foils of gold with carriage 113s. For 2000 silver foils 11s.   Total £7 4s 2d.

Week 10   In wages*.   Total 20s 4d.

Week 11   In wages*. For writing 550 letters (*In v^c di. literis scribentis*) 11d. Glue 4d. 3 gallons of oil 3s.   Total 25s 11d.

Total of the whole quarter £17 8s 3½d.

COST OF MIDSUMMER TERM

Week 1   In wages*. 21 pieces of fabric bought in London (*In xxj pecia de carde¹ empta London'*) 108s 6d, for their carriage 2s.
Total £6 11s 10d.

Week 2   In wages*. One marble stone for grinding colours (*In j petra marmorea pro color' moland'*) 18d.   Total 22s 10d.

Week 3   In wages*.   Total 19s 1d.

Week 4   In wages*.   Total 21s 4d.

Week 5   In wages*.   Total 21s 8d.

Week 6   In wages*. 3200 gold [foils] £5 18s 4d. For 5 lbs of vermilion (*wermillon*) 5s. For their carriage 18d.   Total £7 7s 6d.

Week 7   In wages*.   Total 22s 8d.

Week 8   In wages*. 3000 gold foils 105s 6d. Sharpening 8d. For making a key? (*In clavis faciend'*) 6d.   Total £6 16s 10d.

Week 9   In wages*.   Total 25s 2d.

Week 10   In wages*.   Total 20s 2d.

Weeks 11, 12   In wages*.   Total 19s 8d [each week].

Week 13   In wages*.   Total 23s 8d.

Total of the whole quarter £31 13s 1d.

Total of the whole expenses £86 4s 5d.

This is allowed to him in the account of the Work of the present year (*qui sibi allocantur in comp' operis anni present'*).

---

* List of wages of named craftsmen is not included here, see pp. 205–6.
¹ The nature and purpose of the fabric called *carda* is not known.

2622   1323, 2 October–1324, 30 September

2 membranes, head to tail, good condition.
Endorsement: *Compotus J. de Shyreford custodis operis beati Petri Exon' de anno domini millesimo ccc⁰vicesimo quarto.*
Printed: Extract in Oliver, p. 382.

(m.1) THE ACCOUNT OF JOHN DE SCHYREFORDE CHAPLAIN WARDEN OF THE WORK OF THE CHURCH OF THE BLESSED PETER OF EXETER FROM SUNDAY AFTER THE FEAST OF ST MICHAEL 1323 UNTIL THE SAME SUNDAY IN THE FOLLOW-ING YEAR.

Receipts

The same [John] renders account of £33 10s of arrears of the preceding account. And of £124 18s 8d from the lord bishop for the year. And of £48 from the prebend of the canons. And of £17 from the church of St Erth in Cornwall. And of £6 7s 4d from the dignity of the dean. And of 60s from the dignity of the precentor. And of 64s from the dignity of the treasurer. And of [   ]¹ from the dignity of the chancellor. And of 8s 2d from rent in the town for the year. And of 26s 8d from the rent of Hackworthy (*Hakeworth'*) for the third year in part payment of £10 assigned to the said Work from the testament of W. de Mollande by one instalment (*per j statuta*). And of 12s 7d from the red chest (*de rubea archa*) opened on the feast of St Peter-*ad-vincula* [1 August]. And of 28s ½d from Whitsuntide offerings. And of 6s 5½d from offerings on 1 August (*ad gul' August'*). And of 40s from the burial (*fossat'*) of James Reven. And of 12d from dom Richard Pestor of Fenton (*Fenhampton*). And 10s from one old cart-wheel sold. And 2d from the obit of Eustace. And of 7s from tree-bark² (*corticibus*) sold at Langford (*Langhford*). And of 20s from the testament of dom John de Cnowille in part payment of 40s on the feast (*in festo*) of the said John for the Work of the Blessed Peter of Exeter aforesaid. And of 6d from the testament of William Attehope of the parish of Clyst Hydon. And of 20s from the testament of dom William de Traci rector of the church of Morthoe (*Mortehoe*).

Total of all the receipts £244 11s 5d.

Expenses

COST OF MICHAELMAS TERM

Week 1   In wages*. In 3 labourers on the Work 2s 6d. 2 locks for 2 doors of the great altar (*In ij serrur' pro ij host' magn' altar'*) 4s. Sharpening 4½d. 3 quarters of lime 15d.   Total 29s 6½d.

Week 2   In wages*. In 3 labourers on the Work 2s 6d. For making iron-work for the engines (*ingeniis*) 18d. Sharpening 2d. 55 lbs of white lead (*blamplum*) with carriage 11s 3d.   Total 36s 10½d.

Week 3   In wages*. In 3 labourers on the Work 2s 6d. Sharpening 1d. 3 quarters of lime 15d. 1½ lbs of black colouring? (*arnam[ent]a*)³ 7s 4d.

600 foils of silver 3s. 4 lbs of 'verdegrys' 3s 8d. 5 timber beams bought outside the gate (*In v lygnis merem' extra portam emptis*) 31s 3d.

Total 71s 6d.

Week 4   In wages*. In 3 labourers on the Work 2s 6d. 3 loads of plaster (*de plastro*) 9d.   Total 26s 5d.

Week 5: the feast of All Saints [1 November] and the time changes   In wages*. In 3 labourers on the Work 21¾d. In 2 sawyers for 4 days 21d. 30 lbs of white lead 5s 9d. For writing 250 letters around the bishop's throne (*In ij c et di. literis scribendis circa sedem episcopi*) 5d.

Total 26s 4d.

Week 6   In wages*. In 2 sawyers 2s 1d. In 3 labourers on the Work 2s 1½d, 8½d each. Sharpening 4d.   Total 34s 2½d.

Week 7   In wages*. In 2 sawyers 2s 1d. In 3 labourers on the Work 2s 1½d. Ironwork for the summit of the vault in St John's tower (*In ferrament' pro summitate voutur' in turri sancti Iohannis*) 5s 3d.

Total 38s.

Week 8: 2 feasts, the Dedication of the Church and St Katherine [21 and 25 November]   In wages*. In 2 sawyers 21d. In 3 labourers 21¾d. Candles for the painter (*In candel' pro pictor'*) 5½d.   Total 28s 1d.

Week 9   In wages*. In 3 labourers on the Work 2s 1½d. 11 gallons of oil for the painter 10s 2d. For one rope weighing 14 lbs 14d.

Total 35s 10½d.

Week 10   In wages*. In 3 labourers on the Work 2s 1½d. Ironwork about (*circa*) the bishop's throne 15s 2d. 100 large spikes 12d.

Total 40s 8½d.

Week 11   In wages*. In 3 labourers on the Work 2s 1½d. For additional (*ad huc*) ironwork about the bishop's throne 3s 7d. Sharpening 7d.

Total 28s 8½d.

Week 12   In wages*. In 3 labourers on the Work 2s 10d. 100 lbs of iron bought 4s. For the fee of Master Thomas for this term 33s 4d. And of John of Schyreford warden of the Work 12s 6d.   Total 75s 1d.

Total of the whole quarter £33 16d.

COST OF CHRISTMAS TERM

Week 1: after the feast of Circumcision [1 January]   In wages*. In 3 labourers on the Work 2s 1½d. For making one saw? (*In j serr' faciend'*) 3d. For binding 2 tubs and one vat (*cuva*) 6d.   Total 24s 11½d.

Week 2   In wages*. In 3 labourers on the Work 2s 1½d. For sharpening for 2 weeks 7½d. 5 quarters 4 bushels of lime 2s 3½d.

Total 28s 9½d.

Week 3   In wages*. In 3 labourers on the Work 2s 1½d. Sharpening 10d. For binding 2 vats 10d.   Total 24s 6½d.

Week 4   In wages*. In 3 labourers on the Work 2s 1½d. For one roofer with his servant 2s. 3000 'spyk' and 8000 'lathenayl' in all 12s 11d. One iron knob? behind the high altar (*In j boteo ferreo retro summum altar'*) 4d.

For 2 keys (*clavibus*) to the 2 doors (*hostia*) of the quire 4d. One lock and 2 keys for the belfry (*In j seria et ij clavibus ad clocher'*) 8d.

Total 42s 1½d.

Week 5   In wages*. In 3 labourers on the Work 2s 1½d. 100 loads of stones from Barley 4s. 2 quarters of lime 10d. Sharpening 3d.

Total 32s 7½d.

Week 6   In wages*. In 2 sawyers 2s 1d. In 3 labourers on the Work 2s 1½d. 300 loads of stones from Barley 12s. In 2 masons (*lathom'*)[4] 3s for one week. Sharpening 3d. 3 bowls (*gatis*) 3d.   Total 48s 5½d.

(m.2) Week 7   In wages*. In 2 sawyers 2s 1d. In 3 labourers on the Work 2s 1½d. 100 foils of gold 4s. One half lb of 'verdegrist' 7d. Poplar wood bought at Lustleigh (*copelis meremii emptis apud Lusteleghe*) 63s 4d. In one plasterer for 4 days 8d. Sharpening 12d.   Total 102s 10½d.

Week 8: 2 feasts, St Peter's Chair and St Mathias [22 and 24 February] In wages*. In 3 labourers on the Work 21¾d. One lock with many intricate parts (*cum multis ingeniis*) for the door by the wall (*pro hostico iuxta murum*) in 'La Polpitte' 3s. In one plasterer (*plastrator'*) for 2 days 4d.

Total 25s 1¾d.

Week 9   In wages*. In 3 labourers on the Work 2s 1½d. Sharpening 7d.

Total 26s 5½d.

Week 10   In wages*. In 3 labourers on the Work 2s 1½d. For binding one bucket 1d. Sharpening 6½d. 2 barrows bought 14d.

Total 27s 8d.

Week 11   In wages*. In 3 labourers on the Work 2s 6d. In one labourer there 9d. In one other labourer there 8d. For binding one vat 2d. In one roofer with his servant for 2 days 10d. 325 seams of sand 5s 5d. Sharpening 8d. 22 poplar boards (*In xxij bord' de pypeler*) 2s 3d.   Total 41s 5d.

Week 12   In wages*. In 4 labourers on the Work 3s 4d. In 2 other labourers there 18d. In 2 other labourers there 16d. 400 seams of sand 6s 8d. 500 loads of stones from Barley 20s. 3 fotmels of lead bought 6s 6d. Sharpening 11d. For size (*cole*) 7½d. 12 quarters of lime 5s.

Total 79s 10½d.

Week 13   In wages*. In 4 masons (*lathom'*) 7s 4d. In 5 labourers on the Work 4s 2d. In 2 sawyers 2s 6d. In 7 other labourers 5s 3d. 500 seams of sand 8s 4d. 500 loads of stones from Barley 20s. Sharpening 9½d. 28 quarters of lime 11s 8d.   Total £4 14s ½d.

Week 14   In wages*. 2 carpenters 4s. And 4 masons (*lathom'*) 7s 4d. In 2 sawyers 2s 6d. In 7 labourers on the Work 5s 10d. In 7 other labourers there 5s 3d. 550 loads of stones from Barley 22s. 550 seams of sand 9s 2d. Sharpening 8d. 20 quarters of lime 8s 4d. 500 laths 2s 3d.

Total 100s 6d.

Week 15   In wages*. 2 carpenters 4s. And 4 masons (*lathom'*) 7s 4d. And 2 sawyers 2s 6d. In 8 labourers on the Work 6s 8d. In 9 other labourers there 6s 9d. 10 little hinges for the interclose (*pro interclauso*) 10s. For the fee of Master Thomas 33s 4d. And of J. de Schyreforde 12s 6d. For payment made to the stewards for the rent of the house in which Master Thomas lives for the terms of Christmas and Easter 16s. And for the tithes of the church of St Erth granted to our lord king for St Martin's term 5s 8d.

Sharpening 7½d. 1500 lbs of iron bought 76s 8d. 500 loads of stones from Barley 20s. 500 seams of sand 8s 2d. 20 quarters of lime 8s 4d. 3 fotmels of lead 6s 8d. Total £12 18s 4½d.

Total of the whole term £47 17s 10¼d.

COST OF EASTER TERM

Week 1: in the feast of Easter   1000 lbs of iron bought 38s with carriage. 600 laths 2s 8½d. In 4 labourers for 3 days 20d. 200 loads of stones from Barley 8s. 30 quarters of lime 12s 6d. 200 seams of sand 3s 4d. 4½ fotmels of lead 9s 4d. Total 75s 6½d.

Week 2   In wages*. And 2 sawyers 2s 6d. And 3 masons (*lathom'*) 5s 6d. In 4 labourers on the Work 3s 4d. In 5 other labourers there 3s 9d. Sharpening 8½d. For binding one vat and 2 buckets 5d. 200 stones from Barley 8s. 550 seams of sand 9s 2d. 6 quarters of lime 2s 6d.

Total 71s 2½d.

Week 3: 2 feasts   In wages*. And 2 sawyers 2s 1d. In 4 labourers on the Work 2s 10d. In 3 other labourers on the Work 22½d. For payment made for cleaning the quarry (*In solucione facta per quarrera mundanda*) 13s 4d. 12 quarters of lime 5s. 4 horses bought at Crediton (*Cryditone*) 74s 8d. 2 horse-hides for the requirements of the carts 2s 4d. 6 pig-skins for the same 3s 2d. 2 gallons of grease for curing the said skins 2s. For making and re-pairing panels, collars, halters and other requirements 18d. One sieve for mortar 2d. For sharpening and 4 rings and 2 cart-pins (*pynnis pro carect'*) 19d. Fodder of 4 horses from Wednesday before the feast of the Invention of the Holy Cross for 4 days 1 quarter, each horse taking for a day and night ½ bushel. Total £7 2s 2½d.

Week 4   In wages*. In 2 carvers (*ymaginator'*) 3s 5d. In one labourer in the quarry 11d. In the other labourer there 10d. In 3 other labourers there 2s 3d. In 4 labourers on the Work 3s 4d. In one other labourer there 9d. 8 quarters of lime 3s 4d. 350 seams of sand 5s 10d. Sharpening 8d. 2000 'lathenayl' 20d. Fodder of 4 horses 1 quarter 6 bushels as above.

Total 62s 10d.

Week 5   In wages*. In 2 carters 2s. In one labourer in the quarry 11d. In one other labourer there 10d. In 3 other labourers there 2s 3d. In 3 labourers on the Work 2s 6d. 2000 'lathenayl' 22d. 100 horse-shoes bought 10s ½d. One horse-hide for the carts 18d. 24 lbs of grease and for requirements 2s. Cart-rope 18d. 'Wyppecord' 2d. 8½ quarters of lime 3s 6½d. Sharpening 11d. One horse bought 10s. 27 seams of sand bought 2s 8d. 130 loads of stones from Barley 6s 1d. In one labourer for 3 days 3d. Fodder of 8 horses 2 quarters 1½ bushels. Total £4 8s 10d.

Week 6   In wages*. In 2 carters 23d. In 2 sawyers for 2 days 7½d. In one labourer in the quarry 11d. In one other labourer there 10d. In 3 other labourers there 2s 3d. In 4 labourers on the Work 3s 4d. One horse bought 25s 2d. 6 pairs of traces and one cart-rope weighing 40 lbs 3s. 25 seams of sand 5d. For mending 2 buckets 2d. Sharpening 5d. In one labourer for 3 days 3d. 216 loads of stones from Barley 8s 8d. For cleaning Beer quarry 18s 8d. Fodder of 6 horses 2 quarters 5 bushels.

Total 116s 2½d.

Week 7   In wages*. In 2 carters 23d. In 2 sawyers 2s 6d. In one labourer in the quarry 11d. In one other labourer there 10d. In 3 other labourers there 2s 3d. In 4 labourers on the Work 3s 4d. For payment made to Walter French for timber at Lustleigh 13s 8d, that is for 2 'coples'. 5 pig-skins for the carts 6d. Cart-collars (*coler'*) 2s 6d. Iron hinges hooks and bolts for the doors of 'la polpytte' 10s. For repair of one bell 6d. Ironwork 4d. Sharpening 4d. 550 loads of stones from Barley 22s. For binding a wagon (*In plaustro colligend'*) 6d. Fodder [as above].
Total 100s 11d.

Week 8   In wages of 6 masons (*lathom'*) for 3 days 4s 2d. And 4 labourers on the Work 20d. 148 loads of stones from Barley 5s 11d. 3½ quarters of lime 17½d. 6 large trees bought at Langford 42s. For 400 horse-shoes at Lopen 37s. 6 dozens of 'tack' for the carts 8s. One cart-binding (*ligatur' pro carect'*) 10s. For expenses of J. de Schyreford at Lopen fair with 3 boys and 4 horses for 3 days 2s. In 2 carters 22d. 60 feet of 'crest' 20d. Fodder [as above].
Total 115s 9½d.

Week 9   In wages*. In 3 carpenters 4s. In 2 carpenters 4s 4d. In 4 sawyers 5s. In one labourer in the quarry 11d. In one other labourer there 10d. In 3 other labourers there 2s 3d. In 4 labourers on the Work 3s 4d. In 3 other labourers there 2s 3d. One pair of cart-wheels bought at Taunton (*Taundene*) 7s 6d. 8500 'lathenayle' 7s 6¼d. 700 'spyk' 12½d. In 2 carters 23d. 350 loads of stones from Barley 14s. 4 fothers and 4 fotmels of lead bought at Dartmouth (*Derthmue*) £4 4s in all (*in toto*). Fodder [as above].
Total £14 14s 4¾d.

Week 10   In wages*. 2 carpenters 4s 4d. In 2 sawyers 2s 6d. In one labourer in the quarry 11d. In one other labourer there 10d. In 3 other labourers there 2s 3d. In 4 labourers on the Work 3s 4d. In payment made to the stewards for the house of Master Thomas for this term 8s. Sharpening 12d. For the fee of Master Thomas for this term 33s 4d. And of J. de Schyreford warden 12s 6d. 500 loads of stones from Barley 20s. For sharpening for the quarry for this term 12d. For shoeing horses with 6½ dozens of our own iron 13d. Farriery for the horses 9d. Fodder [as above]. And in 2 carters 23d.
Total £6 9s 5d.

Total of the whole quarter £59 7s 6¼d.

(m.1d) Purchase of oats   He reckons 18 quarters ½ bushel bought for 25s 8d, 17d a quarter.
Total 25s 8d.

Total of both £60 13s 2¼d.

Expenses of oats   He renders account of 18 quarters ½ bushel of oats previously bought from which are expended for fodder of 4 horses from Wednesday before the feast of the Invention of the Holy Cross for 1 week and 4 days 2 quarters 6 bushels to each horse [as above]. And in fodder of 5 horses for one week 2 quarters 1½ bushels as above. And in fodder of 6 horses for 5 weeks 13 quarters 1 bushel [as above].

COST OF MIDSUMMER TERM

Week 1   In wages*. In 2 sawyers 2s 6d. In 2 carters 23d. In one labourer in the quarry 11d. In one other labourer there 10d. In 3 other labourers there 2s 3d. In 4 labourers on the Work 3s 4d. 16 fotmels of lead bought 33s 6d. 2 lbs of wax for cement 14d. Sharpening 10d. 16 cart-loads (*carreagiis*) of timber from Langford (*Langheford*) to Exeter 32s 6d. And 7s 4d for cleaning the quarry 'de la wode'. One horse-hide 2s 4d. Fodder of 6 horses [as above]. Total £6 4s 9d.

Week 2   In wages*. And 2 carpenters [4s 4d]. . . . And 2 carpenters [4s]. And 2 sawyers 2s 6d. In 2 labourers in the quarry 22d. In 4 other labourers there 3s 4d. In 5 other labourers there 3s 9d. In 4 labourers on the Work 3s 4d. In one other labourer there 9d. 6 cart-loads (*carrectar'*) carrying timber from Langford (*Langheford*) to Exeter 12s. For cleaning the quarry 'de la wode' 6s 8d. Sharpening 6½d. For newly binding one vat 4d. In 2 carters 23d. For payment made to the stewards for the tithes of the church of St Erth granted to the lord King for the last term of the second year 5s 8d. For making a tie and nails for the bell called Walt[er] (*In ligatur' faciend' et clavibus pro campana vocatur Walt'*) 6d. Fodder [as above]. Total £4 9s 1½d.

Week 3   In wages*. . . . 2 carpenters [4s 4d] . . . 2 carpenters [4s]. And 2 labourers in the quarry 22d. In 4 other labourers there 3s 4d. In 5 other labourers there 3s 9d. In 5 labourers on the Work 3s 4d. In one labourer there 3d. 14 quarters of lime 5s 5d. For carriage of 5 cart-loads of timber from Lustleigh to Exeter 13s 8d. For the repair of the bell called Marie and sharpening ('baterie') 21d. In one roofer (*coopercor'*) and his servant 2s 6d. In 2 carters 23d. Fodder [as above]. Total £4 5s 5d.

Week 4   In wages*. . . . 2 carpenters [4s 4d] . . . 2 carpenters [4s]. In 2 labourers in the quarry 22d. In 4 other labourers there 3s 4d. In 5 other labourers there 3s 9d. In 4 labourers on the Work 3s 4d. In 3 other labourers there 2s 3d. For repair of 2 bells 2s 6d. For the carriage of 2 cart-loads of timber from Lustleigh to Exeter 5s 8d. Sharpening 5d. 5 quarters of lime 2s 1d. For one roofer with his servant 2s 6d. For carving 4 heads for the vault of the cloister (*In v capet' talliand' pro voutur' claustr'*) 5s. In 2 carters 23d. 12 weys (*peys*) of coloured glass 8s. 8 weys (*peys*) of white glass 2s 8d. For newly binding one cart 6s 8d. Timber bought for the stable at Newton 12d. One rope weighing 40 lbs 2s 6d. For payment made to the carver from London for carving images (*In solucione facta ymaginator' de Londonia pro imaginibus talliandis*) by order of the treasurer 39s. 'Vyppe-cord' 6d. Fodder [as above]. Total £6 17s 7d.

Week 5   In wages*. 2 carpenters [4s 4d]. . . . 2 carpenters 4s. In 2 carters 23d. In 2 labourers in the quarry 22d. In 4 other labourers there 3s 4d. In 5 other labourers there 3s 9d. In 9 labourers on the Work 7s 6d. In one plumber with his servant 2s 8d. For carriage of 2 cart-loads of timber from Lustleigh to Exeter 6s 8d. Sharpening with mending of sieves 13d. 7 quarters of lime 2s 11d. In one man cleaning the gallery (*pro alur' mundand'*) 6d. Fodder [as above]. Total 73s 10d.

Week 6   In wages*. . . . 2 carpenters [4s]. And 2 carters 23d. In 2 labourers in the quarry 22d. In 4 labourers in the quarry 3s 4d. In 5 other labourers there 3s 9d. In 9 labourers on the Work 7s 6d. In one plumber with his servant 2s 8d. 2 cart-loads of timber carried from Lustleigh to Exeter 6s 8d. For carrying 200 large stones from the quarry to the sea 6s. For making 600 nails 6d. Sharpening 7d. Fodder [as above]. Total 72s 1d.

Week 7   In wages*. In 2 carters 23d. In 2 labourers in the quarry 22d. In 4 other labourers there 3s 4d. In 5 other labourers there 3s 9d. In 4 labourers on the Work 3s 4d. Sharpening 13d. 28 quarters of lime 11s 8d. Fodder [as above]. For mending and putting an axle on a cart 4d.

Total 61s 9d.

Week 8   In wages*. In one plumber with his servant 2s 8d. In 2 carters 23d. In 2 labourers in the quarry 22d. In 4 other labourers there 3s 4d. In 5 other labourers there 3s 9d. In 6 labourers on the Work 5s. 4 stones of steel (*acerris*) bought 2s 9d. 2 cart-saddles 6d. Rope for the well (*In cord' pro font'*) 3d. For sharpening and making nails 2s. 8½ quarters of lime 3s 6½d. Fodder [as above].   Total 64s 2½d.

The cost of hay   He reckons in 29 stacks of hay bought at Duryard (*Durehard*) Rockbeare and Greendale for £7 6s 4d. For carriage viz. 72 trusses carried from Duryard to Exeter 6s, 1d each truss. And 80 trusses carried from Greendale to Newton 13s 4d, 2d a truss. And 180 trusses carried from Rockbeare and Greendale to Exeter 30s 8d, 2d a truss. Item for 3 stacks bought at Greendale 15s 8d. For carrying them to Exeter viz. in 32 trusses 5s 4d.   Total £10 17s 4d.

Week 9   In wages*. . . . 2 carpenters 4s 4d. And one plumber with his servant 2s 8d. In 2 carters 23d. In 2 labourers in the quarry 22d. In 4 other labourers there 3s 4d. In 5 other labourers there 3s 9d. In 6 labourers on the Work 5s. 3 cart-loads of timber carried from Lustleigh to Exeter 10s. 14 quarters of lime 5s 10d. For making 200 'spykys' 12d. For tempering 40 lbs of steel 20d. Sharpening 6d. And 2 sawyers 2s 6d. Fodder [as above].   Total £4 7s 2d.

Week 10   In wages*. . . . 2 carpenters 4s 4d. And one plumber with his servant 2s 8d. In 2 sawyers 2s 6d. In 2 carters 23d. In 2 labourers in the quarry 22d. In 4 other labourers there 3s 4d. In 5 other labourers there 3s 9d. In 6 labourers on the Work 5s. For mending the ironwork and making nails for the bell called Jesus 2s. Sharpening and ironwork for a certain engine (*pro quodam ingenio*) 15d. 3 cart-loads of timber carried from Lustleigh to Exeter 10s. 10 quarters of lime 4s 2d. 2 fothers of lead bought £4 19s 3d. Fodder [as above].   Total £9 4s 10d.

Week 11   In wages*. 2 carpenters 4s 4d. In one plumber with his servant 2s 8d. In 2 sawyers 2s 6d. In 2 carters 23d. In 2 labourers in the quarry 22d. In 4 other labourers there 3s 4d. In 3 other labourers there 2s 3d. In 6 labourers on the Work 5s. 10 quarters of lime 4s 2d. Ironwork and one scraper (*strigil'*) bought 13d. For making 700 horse-nails 7d. One sieve bought 1d. For carving 3 heads for the vault of the cloister (*In iij capitibus talliand' pro voutur' claustr'*) 3s. For fodder [as above].

Total 73s 7d.

Week 12   In wages*. 2 carpenters 4s 4d. In 2 sawyers 2s 6d. In 2 carters 23d. In 2 labourers in the quarry 22d. In 4 other labourers there 3s 4d. In 4 other labourers there 3s. In 6 labourers on the Work 5s. For binding 2 buckets 3d. 11 quarters of lime 4s 7d. Sharpening and steeling of axes 18d. 120 lbs of tin for solder 13s 4d, with carriage. Fodder [as above].

Total £4 2s 5d.

Week 13   In wages*. And 2 carpenters 4s 4d. In 2 carters 23d. In 2 labourers in the quarry 22d. In 4 other labourers there 3s 4d. In 4 other labourers there 3s. In 4 labourers on the Work 3s 4d. 2500 tiles bought 20s. Item for the hire of a boat carrying 15 tons from Salcombe quarry to 'le Sege' (*Item in j nave locat' de quarrera de Saltcombe usque le Sege portant' pond' xv doleas*) 22s 6d. One lb of lard (*unct' porcinis*) and 2 lbs of mutton tallow (*cepi multon'*) 3s 4d. 7 quarters of lime 2s 11d. Sharpening 6d. Fodder [as above]. Total 102s 8d.

(m.2d) Week 14   In wages*. 2 carpenters 4s 4d. In 2 carters 23d. In 2 labourers in the quarry 22d. In 4 other labourers there 3s 4d. In 4 other labourers there 3s. In 4 labourers on the Work 3s 4d. For carrying 4 cart-loads of timber from Lustleigh to Exeter 10s. For the hire of 2 boats carrying 32 tons from Salcombe quarry 48s. Sharpening and steeling of axes 13d. For carrying 200 'petrys' from the quarry to the sea 6s. For sharpening for the quarry for the whole term 2s. For the fee of Master Thomas for this term 33s 4d. And of J. de Schyreford warden 12s 6d. Farriery for the horses 9d. For the stable hired at Newton 9d. For shoeing horses with 10 dozens 20d. Fodder [as above]. Total £8 11s 6d.

Cost of images and marble (*Custus ymag' et marrimor'*)   For 45 images. For 11 panels with a Judgment? and one image in a corner (*xj panel' cum Jud' et j imag' in angulo*) for 'la pollepytte' £7 17s 6d. [Cancelled: And to William Canoun of Corfe 100s for 2 letters of obligation in error for the greater marble columns (*Will' Canoun c.s pro ij litteras obligator' in herres pro maioribus colupmnis marmor'*) in the church of the Blessed Peter in Exeter. And the said William receives 12d for every foot. And the said letters are hanging from the principal roll]. Total £7 17s 6d.

Total of the whole quarter £89 5s 9d.

Purchase of oats   The same reckons 29 quarters of oats 43s 6d. And for 7 quarters 7 bushels of oats 8s 7d. Total 52s 1d.

Total of both £91 17s 10d.

Expenses of oats   The same renders account of 36 quarters 7 bushels previously bought from which are expended in fodder of 6 horses for 14 weeks above-written 36 quarters 7 bushels, to each horse [as above] and 1 bushel more in the total and nothing remains.

Expenses of houses in Kalendarhay (*Calenderehaye*)

Week 1   In wages of 2 masons (*lathomorum*) 3s. And 4 others 4s. 250 loads of stones from Barley 10s. 8½ quarters of lime 3s 6½d. Total 20s 6½d.

Week 2   In wages of Sewane Adam the carpenter 2s 9½d. 2 masons 2s 6d. And 8 masons 6s 8d. And 5 labourers 2s 11d. 200 loads of stones from Barley 8s. Total 22s 10½d.

Week 3   In wages of 3 carpenters 5s. And 2 masons 3s. And 11 masons 12s. And 10 labourers there 7s 1d. 500 loads of stones from Barley 20s. 56 quarters of lime 23s 4d. Total 72s 2d.

Week 4   In wages of 3 carpenters 5s. And 2 masons 3s 6d. And 8 other masons 8s. And 10 labourers there 7s 1d. 550 loads of stones from Barley 22s. 226 seams of sand 3s 9d. 30 quarters 4 bushels of lime 12s 8½d. In 2 sawyers 2s 1d. Total 67s 1½d.

Week 5 In wages of 3 carpenters 6s 6d. And 7 masons 12s 10d. And 3 other masons 4s 6d. In 4 labourers 3s 4d. In 5 other labourers there 3s 9d. In 2 sawyers 2s 6d. 25½ quarters of lime 10s 7½d. 300 loads of stones from Barley 12s. 5000 'latthenayl' 11s 5d.   Total 67s 5½d.

Week 6 In wages of one carpenter 2s 2d. And 3 masons 7s 4d. And 8 labourers 6s. In 2 sawyers 2s 6d. 500 laths 2s 3d.   Total 20s 3d.

Week 7 In wages of one carpenter 2s 2d. In labourers there 20d.

                                    Total 3s 10d.

Week 8 In wages of Sewane 2s 2d. 500 'lath' 2s 3d.

                                    Total 3s 5d.

Week 9 In wages of Sewane 2s 2d. For roofing the said houses complete (*in toto*) 14s. 19000 'pynnys' 17d. For 2000 laths 9s. 60 feet of cresting (*crestr'*) 20d.   Total 28s 3d.

Item 10400 tiling stones (*petr' tegul'*) 16s 6d. 100 'spykys' 9d.

                                    Total 17s 3d.

Total of the totals £16 14d.

Total of the whole expenses £239 11s 4½d.

And thus in his reckoning (*computans*) he owes 100s ½d.

[Cancelled: Memorandum that of the said arrears in reckoning he has released to William Canoun 100s for marble which will be allowed him in the following year (*de predictis arr' computans liberavit Willelmo Canun pro marmor' c.s qui sibi allocabuntur in anno sequenti*)].

---

*   List of wages of named craftsmen is not included here, see pp. 207–8.
1   MS leaves blank.
2   The sale of bark, which was used in tanning, makes it likely that oak-trees were among the timber supplied from Langford, since this was the most suitable bark for the process.
3   *arnamentum* is almost certainly a colouring matter. MLW suggests the word as an alternative form of *atramentum*, black ink.
4   This is the first time in these accounts that the term *lathomus* rather than *cementarius*, is used for 'mason'.

2623   1324, 30 September–1325, 29 September

    4 membranes, head to tail, good condition (The heading of the roll is repeated on a docket sewn to the head of it).
    Endorsement: . . . *irford pro beati Petri Exon' de anno domini xxv.*
    Printed: Extract in Oliver p. 382.

(m.1) THE ACCOUNT OF JOHN DE SCHYREFORD WARDEN OF THE WORK OF THE CHURCH OF THE BLESSED PETER OF EXETER FROM SUNDAY AFTER THE FEAST OF ST MICHAEL 1324 TO SUNDAY THE FEAST OF ST MICHAEL IN THE FOLLOWING YEAR

RECEIPTS

The same John renders account of 100s ½d of arrears of the preceding account. And of £124 18s 8d of the gift of the lord bishop for the year. And of £48 of the prebend on the canons. And of £17 from the church of St Erth. And of £6 7s 4d from the dignity of the lord dean. And of 60s from the dignity of the precentor. And of 64s from the dignity of the treasurer. And of 38s from the dignity of the chancellor. And of 38s from the dignity of the chancellor in 1323. And of 19s received from Master Henry de Stoford for half of the dignity of the chancellorship for 1322. And of 19s received from Baldwin Gyffard for the other half of the same year. And of 8s 2d received from rent in the town. And of 26s 8d from the rent of Hackworthy (*Hakeworthe*) in part payment of £10 assigned to the said Work from the testament of W. de Mollond' viz. for the fourth year. And of 8½d from the red chest. And of 33s 9¼d from Whitsuntide offerings. And of 5s 9½d on 1 August (*ad gulam Augusti*). And of 2s from the testament of J. de Yollestone of the parish of Buckfastleigh (*Leynbuc'*) by one tally. And of 6d from the testament of Jordan de Assewat'. And of 2s 4d from the testament of Margery Marescal of Broadhembury (*Brodehembiri*). And of £4 6s 8d received from the archdeacon of Barnstaple from perquisites (*de arch' Barnastopolee viz. de perquisit'*) by one account. And of £8 2½d from the archdeacon of Totnes (*Totton'*) by 2 accounts (*per ij ac'*). And of £4 6s 3d from the archdeacon of Exeter by one account. And of £6 9s 2d from the archdeacon of Cornwall by 2 accounts. And of 38s 4d from the peculiar jurisdiction (*de peculiar' iuredicion'*) by 2 accounts. And of 6d from the church of Stoke Canon. And of 21d from St Marychurch (*Seynte Marchurche*). And of 2s from Sidbury (*Sydebyry*). And of 11d from Topsham (*Thopysham*). And of 26s 5¼d for tree barks (*corticibus*) sold at Langford (*Langhford*). And of 7d from Woodbury (*Wodebyry*). And of £4 received from the stewards of the exchequer from the prebends of Master W. Gyffard and J. Cnowile owed after their deaths assigned to the said Work by the assignment of the lord prior of Plympton. And of 4s received from the testament of dom John lately rector of St Martin in the city of Exeter. And of 20s received from the testament of dom John Moris. And of 9s from the testament of Master John de Milletone. And of 6s 8d received for one stone moved over the tomb (*j lapido amoto super tumbam*) of William de Gathepath. And of 2d from the obit of Eustace.

Total of all the receipts £249 13s 8¾d.

EXPENSES

(m.2) COST OF MICHAELMAS TERM

Week 1   In wages*. 2 carpenters 4s 4d. In 2 carters 23d. In 2 labourers in the quarry 22d. In 4 other labourers there 3s 4d. In 4 other labourers there 3s. In 4 labourers on the Work 3s 4d. 6 cart-loads (*carrectar'*) of timber carried from Lustleigh (*Losteleghe*) to Exeter 20s. 4½ quarters of lime 22½d. Sharpening 4½d. For making 72 horse-shoes from our own iron 2s. Fodder of 6 horses 2 quarters 5 bushels.   Total 79s 8d.

Week 2   In wages*. 2 carpenters 4s 4d. In 2 carters 23d. In 2 labourers in the quarry 22d. In 4 other labourers there 3s 4d. In 4 other labourers there 3s. In 4 labourers on the Work 3s 4d. Sharpening 9d. One horse-hide 16d. 2 quarters of lime 10d. For carrying 24 cart-loads of stones from 'La Sege' to Exeter 18s. Fodder [as above].   Total 76s 4d.

Week 3   In wages*. 2 carpenters 4s 4d. In 2 carters 23d. In 2 labourers in the quarry 22d. In 4 other labourers there 3s 4d. In 4 other labourers there 3s. In 4 labourers on the Work 3s 4d. In one roofer with his servant for 3 days 15d. For making a barrow 4d. One quarter of lime 5d. Sharpening and steeling of axes 18d. Straw bought for covering over hay (*pro coopertur' feni*) 12½d. In one man repairing the road near (*iuxta*) Clyst 2d. For carrying 8 cart-loads of stones from 'la Sege' to Exeter 5s 4d. For making 26 iron rods (*virg' ferreis*) for the interclose (*interclausum*) 21s 8d. Fodder of [as above].   Total £4 3s 11½d.

Week 4   In wages*. 2 carpenters 4s 4d. In 2 carters 23d. In 2 labourers in the quarry 22d. In 4 other labourers there 3s 4d. In 4 other labourers there 3s. In 4 labourers on the Work there 3s 4d. In one roofer with his servant 2s. 23 feet of stones bought at Silverton (*Silferton*) for gutters of the cloister (*pro guteras claustri*) 6s 9d. One cart-wheel bought 6s 8d. For sharpening and steeling of axes 8d. Fodder [as above].

                    Total 70s 4d.

Week 5: 2 feasts, All Saints and All Souls [1 and 2 November] and the time changes   In wages*. 2 carpenters, 18¼d each. And 2 carters 23d. In 2 labourers in the quarry 16d. In 4 other labourers there 2s 4d, 7½d each. In 4 other labourers there 2s 3d. In 5 labourers on the Work 2s 11¼d, 7¼d each. 24 lbs of white lead (*blauncplum*) 4s 6d. 4 quarters of lime 20d. Twists bought 3d. Sharpening and steeling of axes 8½d. 'Wyppecord' 2¼d. 4 fothers and 10 fotmels of lead bought £10 10s. Fodder [as above].   Total £12 18s 7¾d.

Week 6   In wages*. 2 carpenters 22d each. In 2 carters 23d. In one plumber 22d. In 2 labourers in the quarry 18d. In 4 other labourers there 2s 10d, 8½d each. In 4 other labourers there 2s 8d, 8d each. In 4 labourers on the Work 2s 10d. 1000 'spyk' bought 3s. For hire of one barge carrying stones weighing 8 tons from Beer quarry to 'la Sege' (*In j bargea locata de quarera de Bere usque la Sege portant' pond' viij dolearum petrarum*) 12s. Sharpening and steeling of axes 12d. Sharpening for Beer quarry 8¼d. 5 quarters of lime 2s 1d. For carrying 200 stones from the quarry to the sea 6s. For carrying 50 stones from Beer quarry to the sea 2s. Fodder [as above].   Total 76s 1¼d.

Week 7   In wages*. 2 carpenters 3s 8d. In 2 carters 23d. In 2 labourers in the quarry 18d. In 3 other labourers there 2s 1½d. In 3 labourers on the Work 2s 1½d. For making hooks hinges locks and other ironwork for the interclose (*interclausis*) near 'la Pulpytte' 3s 8d. Sharpening 8d. For carrying 53 large stones from Beer quarry to the sea 4s 4d. For fodder [as above].   Total 43s 9d.

Week 8   In wages*. 2 carpenters 3s 8d. In 2 glaziers 20d. In 2 carters 23d. In 2 labourers in the quarry 18d. In 3 other labourers there 2s 1½d. In 3 labourers on the Work 2s 1½d. Sharpening 9d. For binding 2 cart-wheels 3s, viz. with our own binding. 2000 tiles for 'la Pulpytte' 16s. Fodder [as above].   Total 56s 6d.

Week 9   In wages*. 2 carpenters 3s 8d. In 2 carters 23d. In 2 labourers in the quarry 18d. In 3 other labourers there 2s 1½d. In 4 labourers on the Work 2s 10d. Sharpening 4d. 6 pairs (*paria*) of traces and one rope bought 3s 7d. Fodder [as above].   Total 42s 10½d.

Week 10   In wages*. 2 carpenters 3s 8d. In 2 sawyers 2s 1d. In 2 carters 23d. In 2 labourers in the quarry 18d. In 3 other labourers there 2s 1½d. In 3 labourers on the Work 2s 1½d. 32 weys (*peys*) of white glass 12s 4d. 18 weys of coloured [glass] 13s 6d. 2 stones of mutton tallow for the carts 3s 2d. 3 stones of 'burlis' for cart-collars (*coloribus*) 2s 3d. For making 3 collars and one panel for the carts and the purchase of one pig-skin for the same 16d. Sharpening 3d. One rope called 'lod rop' and 'wyppecord' 2s 2d. For fodder [as above].   Total 72s 2d.

Week 11   In wages*. 2 carpenters 3s 8d. In 2 carters 23d. In one roofer and his servant for 1½ days 7d. In 2 labourers in the quarry 18d. In 3 other labourers there 2s 1½d. In 3 labourers on the Work 2s 1½d. Sharpening 13d. 6 lbs of wax for cement 3s 6d. And 4 labourers in the quarry 2s 10d. For making ironwork carrying the great Cross (*In factura ferrament' portant' magnam crucem*) 12s 4d. Item 12 images in the 2 furthest panels in 'la Polpitte' (*pro xij ymag' in ij ultimis panellis in la Polpitte*) 42s. Fodder [as above].   Total 100s 9d.

Week 12   In wages*. 2 carpenters 3s 8d. In 2 carters 23d. In 2 labourers in the quarry 18d. In 3 other labourers there 2s 1½d. In 3 labourers on the Work 2s 1½d. In 2 labourers in Beer quarry 17d. For sharpening 15d. For making 1200 nails 12d. For a barge carrying 12 tons of stones from Beer quarry to 'la Sege' 18s. For the fee of Master Thomas for this term 33s 4d. And of J. de Schyreford warden of the Work 12s 6d. For the stable hired at Newton for this term 12d. Farriery for the horses 9d. For shoeing horses with 8½ dozens 17d. For cutting 9 small images near (*iuxta*) 'la Pulpitte' 15s. 26 boards bought at Teignmouth (*Teygnemue*) 4s. For sharpening for the quarry for the whole term 18d. 14 cart-loads of stones from Beer quarry to Blackdown (*la Blake Doune*) 23s 4d. Fodder [as above].

Total £7 11s 3d.

Total of the whole quarter £55 12s 4d.

Purchase of oats   He reckons 31 quarters 4 bushels of oats bought 39s 3d.

Total 39s 3d.

Total of both £57 11s 7d.

Expenses of oats   He renders account of 31 quarters 4 bushels of oats previously bought from which are expended in fodder of 6 horses for the 12 weeks above 31 quarters 4 bushels, to each horse taking for a day and a night half a bushel. And nothing remains.

COST OF CHRISTMAS TERM

Week 1: in which Christmas falls on Tuesday   In wages of 2 carters 23d. Fodder of 6 horses 2 quarters 5 bushels.   Total 23d.

Week 2   In wages*. 2 carpenters 3s 8d. In 2 sawyers for one day 5d. In 2 carters 23d. In 2 labourers in the quarry 18d. In 3 other labourers there 2s 1½d. In 2 labourers on the Work 17d. Sharpening 3d. Fodder [as above].   Total 35s ½d.

(m.3) Week 3   In wages*. 2 carpenters 3s 8d. In 2 sawyers 2s 1d. In 2 carters 23d. In 2 labourers in the quarry 18d. In 3 other labourers there 2s 1½d. In 2 labourers on the Work 17d. Sharpening 4d. In 3 other labourers for cleaning the quarry (*pro quarera mundanda*) 2s 1d. Fodder [as above]. Total 39s 1½d.

Week 4   In wages*. 2 carpenters 3s 8d. In 2 carters 23d. In one labourer in the quarry 18d. In 6 other labourers there 4s 3d. In 2 labourers on the Work 17d. Sharpening 4d. Fodder [as above]. Total 38s 11d.

Week 5   In wages*. 2 carpenters 3s 8d. In one glazier (*verrator'*) 20d. In 2 carters 23d. In 2 labourers in the quarry 18d. In 6 other labourers there 4s 3d. In 2 labourers on the Work 17d. Fodder [as above].
Total 40s 3d.

Week 6   In wages*. 2 carpenters 3s 8d. In 2 carters 23d. In 2 labourers in the quarry 18d. In 6 other labourers there 4s 3d. In 2 labourers on the Work 17d. 2 ropes for binding carts 18d. 2 stones of 'burl' 18d. Fodder [as above]. Total 46s 7d.

Week 7   In wages*. 2 carpenters 3s 8d. In 2 carters 23d. In 2 labourers on the Work 17d. Sharpening 12d. In one labourer in the quarry 9d. In 6 other labourers there 4s 3d. Fodder [as above]. Total 40s 6d.

Week 8   In wages*. 2 carpenters 3s 8d. And 2 sawyers 2s 1d. In 2 carters 23d. In one labourer in the quarry 9d. In 6 other labourers there 4s 3d. In 2 labourers on the Work 17d. For one tree-trunk (*lingno*) bought outside the gate (*extra port'*) 3s. Sharpening and for mending of barrows 6d. Fodder [as above]. Total 43s 2½d.

Week 9   In wages*. 2 carpenters 3s 8d. In 2 sawyers 2s 1d. In 2 carters 23d. In one labourer in the quarry 9d. In 6 other labourers there 4s 3d. In 2 labourers on the Work 17d. Sharpening 16d. 2 stones of 'burl' 16d. For making 1300 horse-nails and 'tacknayl' 13d. Fodder [as above].
Total 43s 5½d.

Week 10   In wages*. 2 carpenters 3s 8d. In 2 sawyers 2s 1d. In 2 carters 23d. In one labourer in the quarry 9d. In 6 others there 4s 3d. In 2 labourers on the Work 17d. For assistance (*ausilio*) hired for timber at Topsham (*Thopysham*) for landing it from the boat (*ad terram ponend' de batill'*) 2s. Sharpening 2d. 20 lbs of lard for the carts 2s 6d. One lb of mutton tallow 20d. For a boat hired with the said wood by the lord bishop from London to the port of Topsham (*In j nave locat' cum predicto meremio per dominum episcopum de London' usque ad portum de Thopysham*) viz. for freight (*haulo*) 100s. Fodder [as above]. Total £7 7s 8½d.

Week 11   In wages*. 2 carpenters 3s 8d. In 2 sawyers 2s 1d. In 2 carters 23d. In one labourer in the quarry 9d. In 6 other labourers there 4s 3d. In 2 labourers on the Work 17d. 200 lbs of iron bought 8s 3d. For making 40 horse-shoes 3s. For making 1000 nails 10d. Sharpening and steeling of axes 9d. Fodder [as above]. Total 52s 6¼d.

Week 12: the time changes   In wages*. 2 carpenters 4s 4d. In 2 sawyers 2s 6d. For 2 carters 23d. In one labourer in the quarry 11d. In 6 other labourers there 5s. In 2 labourers on the Work 20d. Sharpening 7d. For making a saw (*serra*) 8d. Fodder [as above]. Total 47s 10d.

Week 13   In wages*. 2 carpenters 4s 4d. In 4 sawyers in the wood (*in bosco*) 6s. In 2 carters 23d. In one labourer in the quarry 11d. In 6 other labourers there 5s. In 2 labourers on the Work 20d. In 6 men hired for 3 days at Topsham for carrying timber from the sea to land (*ad portand'* *merem' de mare usque ad terram*) 12d. For one horse hired to carry carpenters' tools from Exeter to Norton for 2 trips (*In j equo locato ad portand' utensilia carpentar' de Exon' usque Norton per ij vices*) 6d. For carrying 5 cart-loads of timber from Topsham to Exeter 4s 2d. One barge-load of stones from Salcombe quarry to 'la Sege' 9s. Sharpening 6¼d. Fodder [as above].

Total 65s 3¼d.

Week 14   In wages*. 2 carpenters 4s 4d. In 4 sawyers in Norton wood 6s. In 2 carters 23d. In one labourer in the quarry 11d. In 6 other labourers there 5s. In 2 labourers on the Work 20d. For carrying 12 cart-loads of timber from Topsham to Exeter 10s. For carrying a barge-load of stones from Salcombe to Exeter 9s. Sharpening 3d. Fodder [as above].

Total 67s 2d.

Week 15   In wages*. 2 carpenters 4s 4d. In 2 sawyers 2s 6d. In 2 carters 23d. In one labourer in the quarry 11d. In 6 other labourers there 5s. For 2 labourers on the Work 20d. For sharpening for the quarry for this term 10d. For the fee of Master Thomas for this term 33s 4d. And of J. de Schereford warden of the Work 12s 6d. For the stable hired at Newton 12d. For carrying 15 loads of timber from Norton to Exeter 2s 2d. Farriery for the horses 9d. For shoeing the horses with 12 dozens of our own iron 18d. For sharpening for the Work 12d. For carrying 9 cart-loads of timber from Topsham to Exeter 7s 6d. For a boat hired for 23 ton-tight of stones from Beer quarry to 'la Sege' (*In j nave petrarum de quarera de Bere usque la Sege locat' pro taut' pond' xxiij dolearum*) 36s. Item one barge-load of stones from Salcombe quarry to 'la Sege' 9s. Fodder [as above].

Total £7 12s 2d.

Total of the whole quarter except oats £43 20¼d.

Purchase of oats   He reckons 59 quarters 5 bushels of oats bought for 77s 2d.

Total 77s 2d.

Total of both £46 18s 10¼d.

Expenses of oats   He renders account of 59 quarters 5 bushels previously bought from which are expended for fodder of 6 horses for 15 weeks above 39 quarters 3 bushels, to each horse [as above]. And 20 quarters 2 bushels remain.

COST OF EASTER TERM

Week 1 after Easter   In wages*. 2 carpenters 4s 4d. In 2 sawyers 2s 6d. In 2 carters 23d. In one labourer in the quarry 11d. In 6 other labourers there 5s. In 2 labourers on the Work 20d. For carrying 18 cart-loads (*carectar'*) of timber from Topsham to Exeter 15s 2d. For carrying 3 cart-loads of timber from Norton to Exeter 5s. For carrying 2 loads of wood from Norton to Exeter 3½d. Fodder of 6 horses for 2 weeks viz. for Easter week and the above week 5 quarters 2 bushels.

Total 67s ½d.

(m.2d) Week 2   In wages*. 2 carpenters 4s 4d. In 2 carters 23d. In one labourer in the quarry 11d. In 6 other labourers there 5s. In 2 labourers on the Work 20d. Sharpening 3d. For assistance in raising timber at Norton before sawing (*ante secacion'*) 10d. 3 barge-loads of stones from Salcombe to 'la Sege' 30s. Fodder of 5 horses 2 quarters 5 bushels.

Total 75s 2d.

Week 3: 2 feasts, SS Philip and James and Holy Cross [1 and 3 May] In wages*. 2 carpenters 3s 8d. In 2 carters 23d. In one labourer in the quarry 9d. In 6 other labourers there 4s 3d. In 2 labourers on the Work 17d. For carrying 7 cart-loads from Norton to Exeter 11s 8d. For carrying 23 cart-loads of marble stones (*petrarum de marmor'*) from 'La Sege' to Exeter 15s 11d, 8d a cart-load. Sharpening 2d. One horse bought 22s viz. a cart-horse. Fodder of 7 horses 3 quarters ½ bushel.

Total £4 6s 6d.

Week 4   In wages*. 4 carpenters 8s 8d. And 3 carpenters 6s 3d. And 2 carpenters 2s 6d. In 8 sawyers 12s. In 2 carters 23d. In one labourer in the quarry 11d. In 6 other labourers there 5s. In 2 labourers on the Work 20d. 3 barge-loads of stones from Salcombe quarry to 'la Sege' 27s. For carrying 300 stones from Salcombe quarry to the sea 9s. 6 pairs of traces weighing 40 lbs 2s 8d. 1000 lbs of iron bought 40s. Fodder [as above].

Total £7 9s 6d.

Week 5   In wages*. 4 carpenters 8s 8d. And 3 carpenters 6s 3d. And 2 carpenters 2s 6d. And 8 sawyers 12s. In 2 carters 23d. In one labourer in the quarry 11d. In 6 other labourers there 5s. In 2 labourers on the Work 20d. 2 empty casks for making buckets (*pro boket' fac'*) and other requirements 14d. 48 large trees bought at Langford (*Langheford*) £11 15s. Sharpening 4d. For carrying 2 cart-loads of timber from Norton to Exeter 3s 4d. Fodder [as above].   Total £15 10s 8d.

Week 6   In wages*. 4 carpenters 8s 8d. And 3 carpenters 6s 3d. And 2 carpenters 2s 6d. And 8 sawyers 12s. And 2 carters 23d. In one labourer in the quarry 11d. In 6 other labourers there 5s. In 2 labourers on the Work 20d. For making 1000 nails 10d. For hauling (*trahend'*) 100 large stones from the quarry to the sea 3s. Ironwork nails hinges hooks and other requirements for St John's tower 32s 8d. 4 barge-loads of stones from Salcombe quarry to 'la Sege' 36s. For carrying 14 cart-loads of stones from 'la Sege' to Exeter 9s 4d. Sharpening 12d. Fodder [as above].

Total £7 13s 8d.

Week 7: the feast of Pentecost   In wages of 2 carters 23d. 400 horse-shoes bought at Lopen 24s 10d. Item 7½ dozen of cart-tacks (*tackis pro carect'*) bought there 7s 9d. 1000 nails 15d. In a tiler (*tegulator'*) tiling for 2 days around 2 doors in the choir (*circa ij hostiis in cor'*) 6d. Item 4000 tiles bought 32s. 2 cart-loads (*cariag'*) of timber carried from Norton to Exeter 3s 4d. Item in expenses of J. de Schyreford for 3½ days at Lopen 2s 6d, with 4 horses. Fodder [as above].   Total 74s 1d.

Week 8   In wages*. 3 carpenters 6s 6d. And one carpenter 2s 1d. In 2 carters 23d. In 6 sawyers 9s. In one labourer in the quarry 11d. In 6 other labourers there 5s. In 4 labourers on the Work 3s 4d. For making 2 tubs and 9 buckets and binding 2 vats 2s 2d. For binding 3 buckets with iron 16d. Sharpening 4d. Fodder [as above].   Total 64s 3d.

Week 9   In wages*. 3 carpenters 6s 6d. And one carpenter 2s 1d. And 2 carpenters 3s. In 6 sawyers 9s. In 2 carters 23d. In one labourer in the quarry 11d. In 6 other labourers there 5s. In 5 labourers on the Work 4s 2d. 12 quarters of lime 5s. Sharpening 3d. Fodder [as above].

Total 70s 1d.

Week 10   In wages*. In 4 sawyers 6s. In 2 carters 23d. In one labourer in the quarry 11d. In 6 other labourers there 5s. In 5 labourers on the Work 4s 2d. 10 quarters of lime 4s 2d. For sharpening for 2 quarries for the whole term 2s 1d. 10 boards for centerings (*cinternis*) 14d. For one stone of 'burel' 8d. For repair of a cart 18d. Sharpening and steeling of axes 10d. For hauling 200 large stones to the sea 6s. For the stable hired at Newton 12d. For the fee of Master Thomas for this term 33s 4d. And of J. de Schyreford 12s 6d. Farriery for the horses 9d. For shoeing horses with 8 dozens of our own iron 16d. For 10000 lath-nails 8s 4d. Fodder [as above].
Total £6 19d.

Total of the whole quarter except oats £58 12s 6½d [altered from £59 10s 1½d].

Purchase of oats   He reckons in 12 quarters 1 bushel of oats bought for 26s 3d.
Total 26s 3d.

Total of both £59 18s 9½d [altered from £60 16s 4½d].

Expenses of oats   He renders account of 12 quarters and one bushel of oats previously bought and of 20 quarters 2 bushels remaining from the preceding quarter from which are expended in fodder of 6 horses for 3 weeks above 7 quarters 7 bushels. And in fodder of 7 horses for 7 weeks above-written 24 quarters 4 bushels, to each horse [as above]. And thus nothing remains.

COST OF MIDSUMMER TERM

Week 1: in which are 2 feasts, St John and Apostles Peter and Paul [24 and 29 June]   In wages*. 2 carpenters, to each 22d. In 2 carters 23d. In one labourer in the quarry 9d. In 6 other labourers there 4s 3d, 8½d each. In 5 labourers on the Work 3s 6½d. 8½d each. In one plumber 22d. Sharpening 6d. 6½ quarters of lime 2s 8½d. One rope for binding a cart 13d. In one carpenter for 2 days 6d. Fodder [as above].
Total 46s 6d.

(m.3d) Week 2   In wages*. 2 carpenters 4s 4d. In 2 carters 23d. In one labourer in the quarry 11d. In 6 other labourers there 5s. In 5 labourers on the Work 4s 2d. 3 barge-loads of stones from the quarry to 'la Sege' 27s. 6 quarters of lime 2s 6d. For mending a bucket 2d. One gallon (*galone*) of grease for the requirements of the carts 10d. For mending cart-collars 8d. Sharpening and 2 axes 2s 2d. Fodder [as above].
Total £4 23d.

Week 3   In wages*. In 2 carters 23d. In one labourer in the quarry 11d. In 6 other labourers there 5s. In 5 labourers on the Work 4s 2d. For carrying 124 cart-loads of timber from Langford to Exeter £12 8s, viz. 2s a cart. Item for carrying 10 cart-loads of stones from 'La Seghe' to Exeter 6s 8d. One barge-load of stones from Salcombe to 'la Seghe' 9s. Sharpening 8d. 7½ quarters of lime 3s 1½d. Fodder [as above].
Total £15 9s 4½d.

Week 4   In wages*. In 2 carters 23d. In one labourer in the quarry 11d. In 6 other labourers there 5s. In 6 labourers on the Work 5s. One rope bought 18d. 5½ quarters of lime 2s 3½d. Sharpening 11d. Fodder [as above].
Total 42s 10½d.

Week 5: in which are 2 feasts viz. Magdalene and St James the Apostle [22 and 25 July] In wages*. In 2 carters 23d. In one labourer in the quarry 9d. In 6 other labourers there 4s 3d. In 6 labourers on the Work 4s 3d. 12½ quarters of lime 5s 2½d. Sharpening 6½d. Fodder [as above].
Total 38s 5½d.

Week 6 In wages*. In 2 carters 23d. In one labourer in the quarry 11d. In 6 other labourers there 5s. In 6 labourers on the Work 5s. 5 stones of steel bought 3s 9d. Iron binding for a cart with nails for the same 9s. Sharpening 4d. Fodder [as above].   Total 60s 2d.

Week 7 In wages*. 3 carpenters 6s 6d. In 2 sawyers 3s. In 2 carters 23d. In one labourer in the quarry 11d. In 5 other labourers there 4s 2d. In 5 labourers on the Work 4s 2d. Sharpening 4d. For binding one bucket 2d. 8 quarters of lime 3s 4d. Fodder [as above].   Total 52s 4d.

Week 8 In wages*. 3 carpenters 6s 6d. In 2 sawyers 3s. In 2 carters 23d. In one labourer in the quarry 11d. In 5 other labourers there 4s 2d. In 5 labourers on the Work 4s 2d. 5 quarters of lime 2s 1d. Sharpening 6¾d. One horse-hide bought for the requirements of the carts 18d. Fodder [as above].   Total 52s 8¾d.

Week 9 In wages*. 4 'carpunters' 6s 6d. In 2 sawyers 3s. In 2 carters 23d. In one labourer in the quarry 11d. In 5 other labourers there 4s 2d. In 5 labourers on the Work 4s 2d. 6 quarters of lime 2s 6d. Fodder [as above].
Total 51s.

Week 10 In wages*. 3 carpenters 6s 6d. In 2 sawyers 3s. In 2 carters 23d. In one labourer in the quarry 11d. In 5 other labourers there 4s 2d. In 5 labourers on the Work 4s 2d. 7 quarters of lime 2s 11d. Sharpening 6¾d. Fodder [as above].   Total 51s 11¾d.

Week 11 In wages*. 2 carpenters 4s 4d. In 2 sawyers 3s. In 2 carters 23d. In one labourer in the quarry 11d. In 5 other labourers there 4s 2d. In 5 labourers on the Work 4s 2d. Sharpening 6d. 2 cart-wheels bought at Taunton (*Taundene*) 7s 6d. For binding them 3s. In one carpenter for 3 days in mending a cart 12d. Fodder [as above].   Total 58s 4d.

Week 12 In wages*. 2 carpenters 4s 4d. In 2 carters 23d. In one labourer in the quarry 11d. In 5 other labourers there 4s 2d. In 5 labourers on the Work 4s 2d. 7 quarters of lime 2s 11d. For binding one vat and 3 buckets 5d. Sharpening 7d. For repair of carts 6d. Fodder [as above].
Total 47s 9d.

Cost of hay He reckons 28 stacks of hay bought in various places £7 4s 9d. For carrying them to Exeter and Newton 35s 4d, viz. 212 trusses, 2d a truss.
Total £9 1d.

Week 13 In wages*. In 2 carters 23d. In one labourer in the quarry 11d. In 5 other labourers there 4s 2d. In 4 labourers on the Work 3s 4d. 7½ quarters of lime 3s 1½d. For carrying 11 cart-loads (*cariagiis*) of marble stones from 'la Sege' to Exeter 7s 4d. For hire of one boat from Topsham to Torre abbey, hired for taking 2 tree-trunks to 'la Sege' (*In locatione j batell' de Thopisham usque ad abbathiam de Torre locat' pro ij lignis ducendis usque la Sege*) 3s. For carrying the same to Exeter 8d. Sharpening 7¼d. For making and writing 750 briefs (*brevettis*) for this year 12s 6d. And 800 briefs (*brevet'*) for the coming year (*pro anno futuro*) 18s. Fodder [as above].
Total £4 12¾d.

[Cancelled: He reckons in payment made to William Canoun of Corfe for 29½ feet of marble columns and marble in the church of the Blessed Peter of Exeter £17 8s viz. 12s a foot. Total £17 8s].

The cost of marble is cancelled (*vacat*) here because it is entered at the foot of the account.

Week 14   In wages*. In 2 carters 23d. In one labourer in the quarry 11d. In 5 other labourers there 4s 2d. In 4 labourers on the Work 3s 4d. For sharpening for the quarry for the whole term 2s 2d. For the fee of Master Thomas for this term 33s 4d. And of J. de Schireford 12s 6d. For the stable hired at Newton 12d. For one plumber 2s 2d. Farriery for the horses 9d. For shoeing horses with 8 dozens 16d. Sharpening 8¼d. (m.4d) 5½ quarters of lime 6s 3½d. Fodder [as above]. Total £4 12s ¾d.

Total of the whole quarter except oats £72 6s 6½d.
[altered from £79 14s 6½d].

Purchase of oats   He reckons in 24 quarters 4 bushels of oats bought for 53s 1d and 9 quarters 1½ bushels for 15s 3d. And in 9 quarters 1½ bushels for 10s 9d. Total 79s 1d.

Total of both £66 5s 7½d [altered from £83 13s 7½d].

Expenses of oats   He renders account of 42 quarters 7 bushels of oats previously bought from which are expended in fodder of 7 horses for 14 weeks above 42 quarters 7 bushels, to each horse half a bushel for a day and a night. And nothing remains.

The silver table (*Tabula argentea*)   He reckons [cancelled: 118s] in final payment made to Master John the goldsmith for the work of the silver table whence he has (*unde habet*) 118s . . .

Default of rent   And 1d in default of rent of a certain tenement in 'Comestrete' because no-one lives there nor can be destrained.

Total of the whole expenses £236 12s 11¼d.

And in his reckoning he owes £13 9½d. And memorandum that the said arrears and other goods are in the hands of William Canun for marble received from him and to be received £17 8s, as appears by obligations and tallies which are with the accountant. And the said sum is allowed in the following year and is cancelled here because it is in the end of the account for the following year (*de predictis arreragiis et aliis bonis computantis sunt in manibus Willelmi Canun pro marmore ab eodem recepto et recipiendo prout patet per obligacionis et tall' qui sunt penes computantem. Et dicta summa allocabitur in anno sequenti cancellatur hic quia est in fine computi anni sequentis*).

---

* List of wages of named craftsmen is not included here, see pp. 208–10.

2624   1325, 29 September–1326, 28 September

4 membranes, head to tail, fairly sound condition but some small holes throughout; m.1 defective and repaired with paper.
Endorsed: *Compotus Johannis de Schireford custodis operis de anno domini etc xxvjto*
Printed: Extract in Oliver, p. 382.

(m.1) THE ACCOUNT OF JOHN DE SCHYREFORDE WARDEN OF THE WORK OF THE CHURCH OF THE BLESSED PETER OF EXETER FROM SUNDAY ON THE FEAST OF ST MICHAEL 1325 TO THE SUNDAY BEFORE THE FEAST OF ST MICHAEL 1326

RECEIPTS

The same John renders account of £13 9½d of arrears of the preceding account. And of £285 13s 4d received of the total of 1000 marks of the gift of the venerable father the lord W[alter] to the said Work. And of £48 from the prebend of the canons. And of £17 from [the church of] St Erth . . . And of £6 7s 4d from the dignity of the dean. And of 60s from the dignity of the precentor. And of 64s from the dignity of the treasurer. And of 2[6]s 8d from [the rent of Ha]ckworthy for the fifth year. And of 11s 8¾d from the red chest. And of 21s 9d from [Whitsuntide] offerings (. . . *obventionibus*). And of 6s 1d on 1 August (*ad gulam Augusti*). And of 2d from the obit of Eustace. And of £4 3s 7½d from the archdeacon of Barnstaple. And of 104s 1½d from the archdeacon of Exeter. And of £7 11s 4¾d from the archdeacon of Cornwall. And of £6 18s 2¼d from the archdeacon of Totnes. And of 36s 11¼d from the peculiar jurisdiction. And of 10¾d received from Ashburton (*Aspertone*). And of 5d from Stoke Canon. And of 17d from Staverton (*Stavertone*). And of 6s 8d from the testament of Peter rector of Huxham (*Hokysham*). And of 6s 8d from the testament of Amicia de Cobeham. And of 6d from Adam de Lomchurche. And of 7d from the precentor for 2 carpenters on one Saturday (*per j diem Sabbat'*). And of 10d from the testament of Robert Kemewordi. And of 3d from the testament of John Hutecote. And of 12d from the testament of Jordan Wynkelegh. And of 12d from the testament of N. de Kentelysbeare. And of the testament of Adam de Servintone 6s 8d.

Total of all the receipts £408 19s 3¼d.

EXPENSES

(m.2) COST OF MICHAELMAS TERM

Week 1   In wages*. In 2 carters 23d. In one labourer in the quarry 11d. In 5 other labourers there 4s 2d. In 5 labourers on the Work 4s 2d. In one roofer with his servant 2s 6d. 7½ quarters of lime 3s 1½d. Fodder of 7 horses 3 quarters ½ bushel.   Total 42s 3½d.

Week 2   In wages*. In 2 carters 23d. In one labourer in the quarry 11d. In 5 other labourers there 4s 2d. In 5 labourers on the Work 4s 2d. In one roofer with his servant 2s 6d. For making a certain engine 2s. Sharpening 8d. 7 quarters of lime 2s 11d. Fodder [as above].

Total 44s 9d.

Week 3   In wages*. 2 carpenters 4s 4d. In 2 carters 23d. In one labourer in the quarry 11d. In 5 other labourers there 4s 2d. In 5 labourers on the Work 4s 2d. For 24 iron rods for the enclosure by 'la Pulpytte' (*In xxiiij virg' ferr' pro clausur' iuxta la Pulpytte*) 20s. 14 quarters of lime 5s 10d. Sharpening 6d. In one plasterer (*Plastrator'*) 12d. Fodder [as above].

Total 70s 8d.

Week 4   In wages*. 2 carpenters 4s 4d. In 2 carters 23d. In one labourer in the quarry 11d. In 5 other labourers there 4s 2d. In 5 labourers on the Work 4s 2d. In one plasterer 14d. 300 loads of stones from Barley 12s. 10 quarters of lime 4s 2d. Fodder [as above].   Total 58s 8d.

Week 5: 2 feasts, All Saints and All Souls [1 and 2 November].   In wages*. 2 carpenters 22d each. In 2 carters 23d. In one labourer in the quarry 9d. In 6 other labourers there 4s 3d, 8½d each. In 5 labourers on the Work 3s 6½d, 8½d each. 9½ quarters of lime 3s 11½d. One pair of cart-wheels bought at Taunton 7s. Sharpening 8d. For fodder [as above].
                                                   Total 47s 9½d.

Week 6: the time changes   In wages*. 2 carpenters 3s 8d. In 2 sawyers 2s 6d. In 2 carters 23d. In one labourer in the quarry 9d. In 6 other labourers there 4s 3d. In 5 labourers on the Work 3s 6½d. 10 quarters of lime 4s 2d. For mending carts 9d. For timber carried from Sidbury wood for the quarry (*In meremio car' de bosco de Sydebyry pro quarera*) 10d. Sharpening 7d. Fodder [as above].   Total 44s 8d.

Week 7   In wages*. 2 carpenters 3s 8d. In one plasterer 14d. In 2 carters 23d. In one labourer in the quarry 9d. In 6 other labourers there 4s 3d. In 4 labourers on the Work 2s 10d. 5 quarters of lime 2s 1d. 2 stones of mutton tallow and one stone of lard for the carts and other engines (*et aliis ingeniis*) 6s. Sharpening 1d. For newly making one cart-binding from our own iron 7s. Fodder [as above].   Total 51s 5½d.

Week 8   In wages*. 2 carpenters 3s 8d. And one carpenter 15d. And one plasterer 12d. In 2 carters 23d. For one labourer in the quarry 9d. In 7 other labourers there 5s 1d. For 4 labourers on the Work 2s 10d. 6 quarters of lime (*carc'*) 2s 6d. 100 lbs of pitch bought for cement 5s 10d. Sharpening 4d. For mending and binding 2 buckets 2d. For 2 sawyers 2s 6d. Fodder [as above].   Total 49s 2½d.

Week 9: in which are 2 feasts, St Katherine and St Andrew the Apostle [25 and 30 November]   In wages*. 2 carpenters 18½d each. And one carpenter 15d. In 2 sawyers 2s 1d. In 2 carters 23d. In one labourer in the quarry 7½d. In 7 other labourers there 4s 2¾d, 7¼d each. In 4 labourers on the Work 2s 5d, 7¼d each. Sharpening 3d. 3½ quarters of lime 17½d. Fodder [as above].   Total 36s 3¼d.

Week 10   In wages*. 2 carpenters 3s 8d. In 2 sawyers 2s 6d. In 2 carters 23d. In one labourer in the quarry 9d. In 4 other labourers there 2s 10d. In 4 labourers on the Work 2s 10d. 6 pairs of cart-traces weighing 40 lbs 2s 6d. 'Wyppecord' 3d. 3 quarters of lime 15d. Sharpening 4d. For making ironwork for 2 barrows 10d. For tiles: 9650 tiles 77s 3d. For making 2000 nails 20d. For fodder [as above].   Total £6 3½d.

Week 11   In wages*. 2 carpenters 3s 8d. In 2 carters 23d. In one labourer in the quarry 9d. In 6 other labourers there 4s 3d. In 2 labourers on the Work 17d. One cart-horse bought 20s. Sharpening and steeling of axes 8½d. For 2 locks and hooks and hinges for 2 doors of the interclose (*pro ij hostiis interclaus'*) 6s 1d. 150 large 'spykis' 13d. Fodder [as above].
                                                   Total 61s 7d.

Week 12   In wages*. 2 carpenters 3s 8d. In 2 carters 23d. In one labourer in the quarry 9d. In 6 other labourers there 4s 3d. In 2 labourers on the Work 17d. For the fee of Master Thomas for this term 33s 4d. And of J.

de Schyreford warden of the Work 12s 6d. For the stable hired at Newton
12d. Farriery for the horses 9d. For a barge hired [for carrying] stones
from the quarry to 'la Sege' 9s. Cart-collars and other requirements for
mending carts 12d. For shoeing horses with 8 dozens 16d. For sharpening
for the quarry for the whole term 2s 2d. Fodder [as above].

Total £4 14s 9½d.

Week 13: in which Christmas falls on Wednesday In wages*. And 2
carpenters for 2 days 14d. And 2 carters 23d. For making ironwork for
the bell called Walter 2s 2d. 26 cart-dowels (*doules pro carect'*) bought 4d.
For 6 pairs of cart-traces 2s 6d. For repair of one hand-cart (*In emendacione
j carre*) 4d Fodder [as above].   Total 9s 1d.

Total of the whole quarter except oats £36 11s 10¼d.

Purchase of oats   He reckons 53 quarters 7½ bushels for 69s 11½d.

Total 69s 11½d.

Total of both £40 21¾d.

(m.3) Expenses of oats   He renders account of 53 quarters 7½ bushels
previously bought from which are expended in fodder of 7 horses for 13
weeks above 39 quarters 6½ bushels, to each horse etc. And 14 quarters 1
bushel remain.

COST OF CHRISTMAS TERM

Week 1: after the feast of Christmas   In wages*. And 2 carpenters for the
whole week 3s 8d. In 2 sawyers for 3 days 12d. In 2 carters 23d. In 3
labourers on the Work 2s 1½d. Fodder [as above].

Total 18s 9½d.

Week 2   In wages*. 2 carpenters 3s 8d. In 2 carters 23d. In one labourer
in the quarry 9d. In 7 other labourers there 4s 11½d. In 2 labourers on the
Work 17d. Sharpening 8d. Fodder [as above].   Total 38s 9d.

Week 3   In wages*. 2 carpenters 3s 8d. In 2 carters 23d. In one labourer
in the quarry 9d. In 7 other labourers there 4s 11½d. In 2 labourers on the
Work 17d. 400 lbs of iron bought 13s. Fodder [as above].

Total 51s 1d.

Week 4   In wages*. 2 carpenters 3s 8d. In 2 carters 23d. In one labourer
in the quarry 9d. In 7 other labourers there 4s 11½d. In 2 labourers on the
Work 17d. Sharpening 4d. Fodder [as above].   Total 38s 5d.

Week 5   In wages*. 2 carpenters 3s 8d. In 2 carters 23d. In one labourer
in the quarry 9d. In 7 other labourers there 4s 11½d. In 2 labourers on the
Work 17d. For making one hammer (*martello*) and 18 iron wedges (*weggis*)
for the quarry 4s 1½d. Sharpening 6d. One stone of 'burell' 8d. 3 stones of
steel 2s. Fodder [as above].   Total 45s 4½d.

Week 6   In wages*. 2 carpenters 3s 8d. And in one roofer with his servant roofing over 'le tracour' 2s 1d. In one mason (*lathemo*) for 5 days
12½d. In 2 carters 23d. In one labourer in the quarry 9d. In 7 other
labourers there 4s 11½d. In 2 labourers on the Work 17d. Sharpening and
steeling of axes 10d. 11500 tiling stones (*de petris tegul'*) bought for roofing
13s 5d. For their carriage 4s 3¾d. Fodder [as above].

Total 59s 9½d.

Week 7   In wages*. 2 carpenters 3s 8d. In one roofer with his servant 2s 1d. In 2 carters 23d. In one labourer in the quarry 9d. In 7 other labourers there 4s 11¼d. In 3 labourers on the Work 2s 1½d. For sharpening 6d. 3 cart-loads (*cariag'*) of stones carried from 'la Sege' to Exeter 2s. For one barge-load of stones 10s. Fodder [as above].

Total 55s ¼d.

Week 8   In wages*. 2 carpenters 3s 8d. In 2 carters 23d. In one labourer in the quarry 9d. In 7 other labourers there 4s 11¼d. In 3 labourers on the Work 2s 1¼d. For making one bucket 4d. For putting an axle on a cart 3d. 15 large poplars (*pupeleris*) bought for scaffolds (*scaffoth'*) 11s 6¼d. 100 alders bought 13s 6d. One stone of mutton tallow for the carts 2s. 16 lbs of tin (*stagno*) 2s. Sharpening and 100 large 'pyk' 18d. For one labourer for 4 days 4d. Fodder [as above].

Total 73s 8¾d.

Week 9   In wages*. 2 carpenters 3s 8d. In 2 carters 23d. In one labourer in the quarry 9d. In 7 other labourers there 4s 11½d. In 3 labourers on the Work 2s 1½d. For one carpenter for 2 days 6d. 100 'spyk' 4d. For digging out 12 large stones (*In xij magnis petris fodiendum*) in Beer quarry 4s. One pair of cart-wheels 6s 2d. One barge-load of stones from the quarry to 'la Sege' 8s. Item 5s released to W. Felstede by order of the stewards for courtesy (*pro curialitate*). Sharpening 3d. For making one bucket 4d. In one man hired for one day 3d. Fodder [as above].

Total 63s 6¾d.

Week 10   In wages*. One carpenter 22d. In 2 carters 23d. In one labourer in the quarry 9d. In 7 other labourers there 4s 11½d. In 2 labourers on the Work 22d. Sharpening 9d. Fodder [as above].

Total 37s 4¼d.

Week 11: the time changes   In wages*. One carpenter 2s 2d. In 2 labourers in the quarry 22d. In 8 other labourers there 6s 8d. In 2 labourers on the Work 20d. In 2 sawyers 3s. In 2 carters 23d. Sharpening 4d. 6 quarters of lime 2s 6d. For carrying 150 stones from Salcombe quarry to the sea 3s. Fodder [as above].

Total 53s 8d.

Week 12   In wages*. 2 carpenters 4s 4d. In 2 sawyers 3s. In 2 carters 23d. In 2 labourers in the quarry 22d. In 8 other labourers there 6s 8d. In 2 labourers on the Work 20d. 29 boards bought for making formes (*formis*) 4s 6¼d. For making 2000 nails 20d. For sharpening for the quarry 17d. For the fee of Master Thomas for this term 33s 4d. And of J. de Schyreforde 12s 6d. For the stable hired at Newton 12d. Farriery for the horses 9d. For putting an axle on a cart 3d. Item 11s paid to a tiler (*tegulator'*) for laying (*ponend'*) 11000 tiles in St John's tower. And of 4s for 4 locks 4 hinges and hooks for 'la Pulpitte'. Item for mending one panel for a cart 2d. For shoeing the horses with 8½ dozens 17d. One barge-load of stones from the quarry to 'la Sege' 12s. 3 quarters of lime 15d. Sharpening 8d. 13 loads of alders carried from Clyst to Exeter 2s 2d. 5 cart-loads of alders carried to Exeter from Clyst 6s. Fodder [as above].

Total £7 4s 1½d.

Total of the whole quarter except oats £33 19s 8d.

Purchase of oats   He reckons 22 quarters 5 bushels bought for 27s 3d.

Total of oats 27s 3d.

Total of both £35 6s 11d.

Expenses of oats   He renders account of 14 quarters 1 bushel of oats remaining from the preceding quarter. And of 22 quarters 5 bushels previously bought from which are expended in fodder of 7 horses for 12 weeks above 36 quarters 6 bushels, to each horse [as above]. And nothing remains.

(m.2d) COST OF EASTER TERM

Week 1 in the feast of Easter   In wages of 2 carters 23d. And of 4 labourers for 3 days 20d. 2 cart-loads of alders carried from Clyst to Exeter 2s 2d. 3 loads of alders carried from the same to Exeter 6d. Buckets and bowls (*gatis*) bought 15d. One large barge-load of stones from the quarry to 'La Sege' 20s. For fodder [as above].   Total 27s 6d.

Week 2   In wages*. And 2 carpenters 3s. And 2 sawyers 4s. In 2 carters 23d. In one labourer in the quarry 11d. In 7 other labourers there 5s 10d. In 4 labourers on the Work 3s 4d. Sharpening and steeling of axes 23d. Hooks and hinges bought 10d. For fodder [as above].   Total 58s 1d.

Week 3   In wages*. And 2 carpenters 3s. In 2 sawyers 3s. In 2 carters 23d. In one labourer in the quarry 11d. In 10 other labourers there 8s 4d. In 3 labourers on the Work 2s 6d. In 2 plasterers plastering in the church (*In ij plastr' in ecclesia plastrand'*) 2s. Sharpening and steeling of axes 9d. For 2 small boats (*farcostes*) carrying 40 tons (*ponder' xl dolearum*) from the quarry to 'la Sege' 53s 4d. For one man hired for 1½ days carrying stones in the church 2d. For fodder [as above].   Total 113s 3d.

Week 4   In wages*. 2 carpenters 4s 4d. In 2 sawyers 3s. In one carpenter 2s. In 2 carters 23d. In one labourer in the quarry 11d. In 10 other labourers there 8s 4d. In 5 labourers on the Work 4s 2d. Paid (*Soluto*) to Gilbert Wetene for 232 loads of clay for making plaster in the church (*glyr' pro plaustr' faciend' in ecclesia*) 4s 8d. For newly making a bucket 4d. For binding 2 buckets with iron 16d. 3 locks in the church for doors in the cloister (*pro host' in claustr'*[1]) 12d. An ox-hide bought with 3 pig-skins for the requirements of the carts 4s 3d. 2 gallons of grease for the same 20d. For carriage of the same 7d. Sharpening 8½d. Fodder [as above].
                Total 76s 7½d.

Week 5   In wages*. And one carpenter 2s 2d. And one carpenter 21d. In 2 sawyers 3s. In 2 carters 23d. In one labourer in the quarry 15d. In 2 other labourers there 22d. In 10 other labourer there 8s 4d. In 6 labourers on the Work 5s. Sharpening 8½d. For binding 2 tubs and one bucket 3d. In 4 labourers in Beer quarry 3s 4d. For 1000 laths for a great [amount] of plaster (*In m latthis pro magno plaustro*[2]) 6s 8d. For carrying 200 stones from the quarry to the sea 6s. For making one cart-panel and 2 cart-collars 8d. One stone of burl' 8d. 100 loads of clay (*gliris*) 2s. Fodder [as above].   Total £4 2s 10½d.

Week 6: in which are 2 feasts, Ascension and Holy Cross [3 May]   In wages*. In 2 sawyers 2s 6d. In 2 carters 23d. In 2 labourers in the quarry 18d. In 10 other labourers there 7s 1d. In 6 labourers on the Work 4s 3d. 9 pairs of traces 3s 6d. For carrying 200 stones from the quarry to the sea 6s. Sharpening 3d. 1000 'bordnayl' 3s. 10000 'lathnayl' 7s 8d. 24 'tacks' for carts 3s. Fodder [as above].   Total 68s 9½d.

Week 7   In wages*. In 2 sawyers 3s. In 2 carters 23d. In 2 labourers in the quarry 22d. In 10 other labourers there 8s 4d. In 6 labourers in Beer quarry 5s. In 6 labourers on the Work 5s. 3 cart-saddles and 3 panels with all their equipment (*cum toto apparatu earumdem*) 3s 5d. 6 baskets (*paners*) bought 6d. 500 lbs of iron bought 17s 8d. One boat-load (*nave*) of stones from Beer quarry to 'la Sege' 26s 8d. For carrying 23 cart-loads of stones from Beer and Salcombe from 'la Sege' to Exeter 15s 4d. 17 cart-loads of marble (*marmor*') from 'la Sege' to Exeter 12s 4d. One cart-horse bought 13s 4d. Fodder [as above].   Total £7 10s 11d.

Week 8: the feast of Pentecost   In wages of 2 carters 23d. And 6 labourers on the Work for 3 days 2s 6d. 350 horse-shoes bought at Lopen 29s 2d. 6 dozens of iron 'tack' for the carts 6s. 1500 'spyk' 5s. 2 ropes 4d. 16 cart-loads and 7 loads of stones carried from 'La Sege' to Exeter 11s 3d. In expenses of J. de Schyrforde at Lopen fair 2s. 600 lbs of iron bought 24s 6d. For sharpening 8¾d. Fodder [as above].   Total £4 3s 4¾d.

Week 9   In wages*. In 2 sawyers 3s. In 2 carters 23d. In 2 labourers in the quarry 22d. In 9 other labourers there 7s 6d. In 3 labourers in Beer quarry 2s 6d. In 6 labourers on the Work 5s. Sharpening 6½d. For binding 2 vats (*cuvis*) 6d. For carrying 4 cart-loads from 'la Sege' to Exeter 2s 8d. One horse-hide bought 12d. 6 alders 12d. Fodder [as above].

                    Total 61s 10½d.

Week 10   In wages*. In 2 carters 23d. In 2 labourers in the quarry 22d. In 8 other labourers there 6s 8d. In 4 labourers in Beer quarry 3s 4d. In 4 labourers on the Work 3s 4d. Fodder [as above].   Total 49s 6d.

Week 11   In wages*. In 2 carters 23d. In 2 labourers in the quarry 22d. In 8 other labourers there 6s 8d. In 4 labourers in Beer quarry 3s 4d. In 5 labourers on the Work 4s 2d. For putting axles on 2 carts 6d. For sharpening and steeling of axes for 2 weeks 16½d. For binding one vat and 2 buckets 4½d. For making 2400 nails 2s. Item 3 barge-loads of stones from Beer and Salcombe quarries 24s 8d. For carriage (*In cariacione*) of 12 cart-loads and 3 loads (*summis*) of stones from 'la Sege' to Exeter 13s 8½d. For loading (*carkiand*') one barge of stones 16d. For carriage of 26 large stones from the quarry to the sea 15d. For repair of one cart-collar 2d. 7 lbs of lard bought for the engines (*In vij li uncti porcini emptis pro ingeniis*) 8d. Fodder [as above].   Total £4 16s 1½d.

Week 12   In wages*. In 2 carters 23d. In 3 labourers in the quarry 2s 9d. In 8 other labourers there 6s 8d. In 3 labourers on the Work 2s 6d. In 2 other labourers there 18d. Sharpening 4d. 2 cart-rails (*scalis*) bought 18d. Straw for roofing over the timber (*In stramine pro coopertur' meremie*) 18d. Item for carrying 10 cart-loads of stones from 'la Sege' to Exeter and also 1½ loads 6s 9½d. Fodder [as above].   Total 59s 10½d.

Week 13   In wages*. In 2 carters 23d. In one labourer in the quarry 11d. In 8 other labourers there 6s 8d. In 3 labourers on the Work 2s 6d. In 3 other labourers there 2s 3d. 3 pick-axes (*pycoseys*) 6 hinges with 3 locks for 3 altars 2s. For steel (*in aceto*) for one horse 1½d. For shoeing horses with 7 dozens 14d. For the stable hired at Newton 12d. For the fee of Master Thomas for this term 33s 4d. And of J. de Schyreforde 12s 6d. For sharpening 3d. 3 barge-loads of stones from Beer to 'la Sege' 23s 4d. For carrying the same stones to Exeter 6s 8d. Farriery for the horses 9d. For fodder [as above]. Total £6 9s 9½d.

Total of the whole quarter £52 18s 7¼d.

Purchase of oats   The same reckons 39 quarters 6½ bushels of oats bought for 46s 7d. Total 46s 7d.

Total of both £55 5s 2¼d.

Expenses of oats   The same renders account of 39 quarters 6½ bushels of oats previously bought from which are expended in fodder of 7 horses for 13 weeks above 39 quarters 6½ bushels viz. to each horse [as above]. And nothing remains.

COST OF MIDSUMMER TERM

Week 1   In wages*. In 2 sawyers 2s 6d. In 2 carters 23d. In one labourer in the quarry 11d. In 11 other labourers there 9s 2d. In 3 labourers on the Work 2s 6d. In 3 other labourers there 2s 3d. For sharpening for the quarry for the whole term 2s 5d. For sharpening for the Work 6d. For making one large hammer and 11 iron wedges 3s 1d. 950 lbs of iron bought 33s 7d. 12000 'lathnayl' 10s. 200 sheaves (*manipulis*)[3] of straw with carriage 3s. 8 poplar boards for centerings (*bordis de pypeler pro cinteris*) 8d. One cart-load of stones from Salcombe quarry to Blackdown 18d. Fodder of 7 horses [as above]. Total 110s 7d.

Week 2   In wages*. In 2 sawyers 3s. In 2 carters 23d. In one labourer in the quarry 11d. In 11 other labourers there 9s 2d. In 3 labourers on the Work 2s 6d. In 3 other labourers there 2s 3d. Sharpening and steeling of tools 11d. 5½ quarters of lime 2s 3½d. 5200 lbs of iron bought in Exeter £9 2s 6d. 8 cart-loads and one load of marble (*marmor*') 5s 1d. 12½ cart-loads of stones carried from 'la Sege' to Exeter 8s 6d. One sack for the horses' fodder (*In j sacco pro brebend' equorum*) 7d. 14 cart-loads of stones from Salcombe quarry to Blackdown 21s. For one plumber for 4 days 15d. For 83 alders bought 34s 7d. 24 cart-loads of alders carried from 'la Sege' to Exeter 16s 8d. Fodder [as above]. Total £16 7s 6½d.

Week 3   In wages*. In 2 sawyers 3s. In 2 carters 23d. In 2 labourers in the quarry 22d. In 11 other labourers there 9s 2d. In 6 labourers on the Work 5s. In 4 other labourers there 3s. In repair of carts 22d. 10½ quarters of lime 4s 7d. For making a saw (*serra*) 12d. Sharpening and steeling of axes 15½d. 19 cart-loads of stones carried from the quarry to Blackdown 29s 3d. Fodder [as above]. Total 103s ½d.

Week 4   In wages*. In 2 carters 23d. In 2 labourers in the quarry 22d. In 11 other labourers there 9s 2d. In 6 labourers on the Work 5s. In 4 other labourers there 3s. 8½ quarters of lime 3s 6½d. Sharpening 8¼d. 8 cart-loads of stones from Salcombe quarry to Blackdown 12s. One brass wheel for a certain engine (*In j eneo pro quoddam ingenio*) 4s 3d. An iron binding for the same engine 12d. For making 6 iron wedges (*weggis*) 9d. Fodder [as above]. Total £4 3s 11d.

Week 5: in which are 2 feasts, St Mary Magdalene and St James [22 and 25 July]   In wages*. In 2 carters 23d. In 3 labourers in the quarry 2s 4½d. In 11 other labourers there 8s. In 7 other labourers on the Work 4s 11½d. In 4 other labourers there 2s 10d. 11½ quarters of lime 4s 9½d.

For curing one horse-hide 6d. Sharpening and steeling of tools 14d. In one carpenter 18½d. 10 cart-loads of stones from the quarry to Blackdown 15s. 2 barge-loads of stones from the quarry to 'la Sege' 20s. Fodder [as above].

Total 100s 8d.

Week 6   In wages*. And 2 carters 23d. In 2 labourers in the quarry 22d. In 11 other labourers there 9s 2d. In 7 labourers on the Work 5s 10d. In 4 other labourers there 3s. 9 quarters of lime 3s 9d. One cart bought 2s 1d. 24 lbs of steel (*acer'*) 12d. In one carpenter 22d. Sharpening 6½d. Fodder [as above].

Total 73s 8½d.

Week 7   In wages*. In one carpenter 22d. In 2 carters 23d. In one labourer in the quarry 11d. In 9 other labourers there 7s 6d. In 6 labourers on the Work 5s. In 3 other labourers there 2s 3d. Fodder [as above].

Total 62s 2d.

Week 8   In wages*. And one carpenter 22d. In 2 carters 23d. In 2 labourers in the quarry 22d. In 10 other labourers there 8s 4d. In 7 labourers on the Work 5s 10d. In 4 other labourers there 3s. 17½ quarters of lime 7s 3½d. Sharpening for 2 weeks 2s. For binding vats and buckets 4½d. For one glazier (*verrator'*) for 2 weeks 4s. Fodder [as above].

Total 79s 2d.

Week 9   In wages*. And one carpenter 22d. In 2 carters 23d. In 2 labourers in the quarry 22d. In 10 other labourers there 8s 4d. In 7 labourers on the Work 5s 10d. In 2 other labourers there 2s 3d. 132 feet of 'ogives' bought 14s 10½d. 150 stones bought at Beer weighing 52 tons 43s 4d. For carrying 4 cart-loads of marble from 'la Sege' to Exeter 2s 8d. 11 cart-loads of stones from Salcombe quarry to Blackdown 16s 6d. For sharpening and steeling of axes 22d. 7 quarters of lime 2s 11d. For one glazier 2s. For putting an axle on a cart 3d. Fodder [as above].

Total £7 8s 7½d.

Cost of lead and timber   28 fothers of lead less 1½ feet £67 18d. And 8 fothers 4 fotmels £19 12s. For carrying the said lead by sea to 'La Sege' 48s 10d. And carrying it from the church of Sutton to the sea and from a [store-] house at Dartmouth to the sea[4] (*Et de ecclesia de Sottone ad mare portand' et de domo de Dertemue ad mare portand'*) 12s 9½d. And carrying it from 'la Sege' to Exeter 24s 4d. And for timber bought by the lord [bishop] in London (*per dominum emptum apud Londone*) £13 6s 1d. And the whole by tally against Master T.

Total £104 5s 6½d.

(m.4d) Week 10   In wages*. And one carpenter 22d. In 2 labourers in the quarry 22d. In 11 other labourers there 9s 2d. In 7 labourers on the Work 5s 10d. In 3 other labourers there 2s 3d. 12 quarters of lime 5s. In one roofer roofing over the cloister 2s 1d. For 2 carters 23d. Size (*cole*) bought for the Cross 5d. For making 600 lbs of ironwork for the windows 18s 6d. One horse bought 26s 8d. For binding one cart 6s. Fodder [as above].

Total £6 10s.

Week 11   In wages*. And one carpenter 22d. In 2 carters 23d. In 2 labourers in the quarry 22d. In 7 labourers on the Work 5s 10d. In 3 other labourers there 2s 3d. 6½ quarters of lime 2s 8½d. Sharpening and steeling of axes 17½d. For making 'pynnis' and other requirements for a certain engine 16d. 11000 tiles bought £4 8s. In 15 labourers in the quarry 12s 6d. 100 loads of stones bought 3s. Fodder [as above].

Total £8 14s 3d.

Week 12　In wages*. And one carpenter 22d. In 2 carters 23d. In 2 labourers in the quarry 22d. In 15 other labourers there 12s 6d. In 7 labourers on the Work 5s 10d. In 3 other labourers there 2s 3d. In 2 sawyers 3s. 300 lbs of tin 37s. For 2950 'gadd' of steel bought for 44s 3d. Sharpening 8¼d. Size (*cole*) 7d. 9 quarters of lime 3s 9d. Fodder [as above].

Total £8 5s 2¼d.

Cost of hay　He reckons in 35 stacks bought in various places £16 18s 1½d. And for carriage of the same from Newton to Exeter 40s 6d viz. 178 trusses, 3d for each of 130 trusses and 2d for each of 48 trusses.

Total £18 18s 7½d.

Week 13　In wages*. In a sawyer 3s. In 2 carters 23d. In 3 labourers in the quarry 2s 9d. In 15 other labourers there 12s 6d. In 7 labourers on the Work 5s 10d. In 3 other labourers there 2s 3d. For one roofer over the cloister with his servant 2s 6d. One large rope called a 'hautour' and one other rope called 'lod rop' weighing 17 stones 19s 10d. 12 quarters of lime 5s. For carrying 18 cart-loads of stones from Salcombe quarry to Blackdown 27s 8d. Fodder [as above].　Total £6 10s 1d.

Week 14　In wages*. In 2 carters 23d. In 3 labourers in the quarry 2s 9d. In 15 other labourers there 12s 6d. In 7 labourers on the Work 5s 10d. In 3 other labourers there 2s 3d. For one rope called 'lodrop' 4s. For the fee of Master Thomas 33s 4d. And of J. de Schyreford 12s 6d. For the stable at Newton 12d. 'Vyppecord' 6d. For shoeing the horses with 8 dozens 16d. Farriery for the horses 9d. Sharpening for 2 weeks 18½d. 13 quarters of lime 5s 5d. For sharpening for 2 quarries for the whole term 4s 3d. For carrying 11 cart-loads of stones from Salcombe quarry to Blackdown 16s 6d. One cart-load of stones from Beer quarry to Blackdown 2s.

Colours for the great Cross　One lb of azure 9s. 6 lbs of 'tenabr' and 6 lbs of 'verdegrys' 10s 4d. 1000 gold foils 36s 8d. 1000 silver foils 5s. 3 lbs of white varnish (*de albo vernic*') 2s. For carriage of the said colours 12d. For one horse bought 29s 6d. Fodder [as above].

Total £12 8s 2¼d.

Total of the whole quarter except oats and lead £115 15s 9¼d.

Purchase of oats　He reckons in 42 quarters 7 bushels bought for 55s 1d.

Total 55s 1d.

Total of both with lead £222 16s 4¾d.

Expenses of oats　He renders account of 42 quarters 7 bushels previously bought from which are expended in fodder of 7 horses for 14 weeks above 42 quarters 7 bushels, to each horse [as above]. And nothing remains.

External expenses (*Expens' forinsec*')　232 loads of fire-wood (*busce*) carried from Langford to Exeter 38s 8d. Item in default of rent of a certain house in 'Combestrete' 1d. Item to nuncios of the lord pope (*nunciis domini pape*) 4¼d for the church of St Erth viz. one farthing in the pound (*de libr. q.*). Item for writing 800 briefs (*brevibus*) for making collections for the fabric 20s.　Total 59s 1¼d.

Total of the whole quarter £225 15s 6d.

Total of the totals of the whole expenses £356 9s 5d.

And he owes £52 9s 10d. Memorandum that of the said arrears £45 6d remain in the hands of William Canun for marble received and to be received from him, as is shown by tally under the seal of the said William which remains with the accountant and will be allowed in the following year.

---

* List of wages of named craftsmen is not included here, see pp. 210–11.
1 MS reads *plaustr'*.
2 The meaning of *magno plaustro* is uncertain.
3 *manipul'* is a small measure, literally 'handful'.
4 The storage and transporting of the lead in this section is not clearly explained by the entries. This large quantity of lead seems to have been divided between two quite different places, a church at Sutton [Plymouth] and a store-house at Dartmouth. From both of these locations it was taken to the sea, and thence by water to 'La Sege' and from there overland to Exeter, though the cost for carrying it by water to 'La Sege' is entered in first.

Surnames are presented as they appear in the accounts, without any attempt to extend or indicate suspensions, which are often random; significant alternative spellings are given if they appear in the same quarter of the year. Forenames are left suspended, followed by a point, as they appear, except some very common short names which are given in modern English form e.g. Adam, John, Hugh, Peter. Work performed at task by named persons included in the text is not included here. The occasional explicit indications given in the accounts that less than a full week of work has been completed, have been omitted on grounds of saving space, since they can be deduced from the figures and are not in any case consistently supplied. To deduce daily rates, these tables must be used in conjunction with the text itself, where marginalia indicating summer and winter hours, feast days kept as holidays etc. are given after the week heading if they appear at all.

Craft or trade descriptions are given after the names if they appear with the name in any weekly entry of a particular quarter.

2602 1299–1300

MICHAELMAS WEEK:	1	2	3	4	5	6	7	8	9	10	11	12	13	14	15
Ric. de la Streme mason	2/3	2/3	2/3	2/3	2/3	1/10½	1/10½	1/10½	1/10½	1/10½	1/10½	1/10½	–		
John de la More, Ric. de Hegham, Walt. de Hampton, John de Corfe, Will. de Mandevile, masons	2/2	2/2	2/2	2/2	2/2	1/9¾	1/9¾	1/9¾	1/9¾	1/9¾	1/9¾	1/9¾	–		
Peter de Bridiport	2/0	2/0	2/0	2/0	2/0	1/8	1/8	1/8	1/8	–	–	–	–		
Adam Reymund	2/0	2/0	2/0	2/0	2/0	1/8	1/8	1/8	1/8	1/8	1/8	1/8	–		
Thom. de Filton mason	1/10	1/10	1/10	1/10	1/10	1/6½	1/6½	1/6½	1/6½	–	–	–	–		
John de Worth/Lolleworth mason	1/10	1/10	1/10	1/10	1/10	1/6½	1/6½	1/6½	1/6½	1/6½	1/6½	1/6½	–		
Walt. de Lovepitte mason	1/10	1/10	1/10	1/10	1/10	1/6½	1/6½	1/6½	1/6½	–	–	–	–		
Nich. Mantel mason	1/10	1/10	1/10	1/10	1/10	1/8	1/8	1/8	1/8	1/8	1/8	1/8	–		
John de Cristechurche mason	1/10	1/10	1/10	1/10	1/10	1/6½	1/6½	1/6½	1/6½	–	–	–	–		
Thom. Giles mason	1/6½	1/6½	1/6½	1/6½	1/6½	1/6½	–	–	–	–	–	–	–		
Ric. de Teingemewe/Tengham mason	1/9	1/9	1/9	1/9	1/9	1/5½	1/5½	1/5½	–	–	–	–	–		
Will. Aston mason, Phil. de Cornubia mason	1/9	1/9	1/9	1/9	1/9	1/5½	1/5½	1/5½	1/5½	–	–	–	–		
Golofre quarryman	7/0	7/0	7/0	7/0	–	7/0	7/0	–	7/0	7/0	–	7/0	–		
Will. de Pontingdon	–	2/0	2/0	2/0	2/0	1/8	1/8	1/8	–	–	1/8	1/8	–		
Rob. Wyroc	–	1/10	1/10	1/10	1/10	1/6½	–	–	–	–	–	–	–		
John de Forde	–	–	1/10	1/10	1/10	–	–	–	–	–	–	–	–		
Will. de Merton	–	–	–	2/2	2/2	1/9¾	1/9¾	1/9¾	1/9¾	1/9¾	1/9¾	1/9¾	0/11		
R. de Abbodesbiri, T. de Merton	–	–	–	2/2	2/2	1/9¾	1/9¾	1/9¾	1/9¾	1/9¾	1/9¾	1/9¾	–		
Hugh de Prato	–	–	–	–	–	1/3	–	1/3	–	–	–	–	–		
Master John	–	–	–	–	–	–	–	–	–	–	–	2/0	1/0		
CHRISTMAS															
John de la More, Ric. de Hegham	–	1/9¾	1/9¾	1/9¾	1/9¾	1/9¾	1/9¾	1/5¾	1/10	1/10	2/2	2/2	2/2	2/2	
Golofre quarryman	–	7/0	7/0	–	7/0	–	7/0	7/0	7/0	7/0	–	7/0	–	7/0	

[1299–1300 cont.] WEEK:	1	2	3	4	5	6	7	8	9	10	11	12	13	14	15
Ric. de la Streme	–	–	1/10½	1/10½	1/10½	1/10½	1/10½	1/6¾	1/10½	1/10½	2/3	2/3	2/3	2/3	
Rad. de Abbedesbiri	–	–	1/9¾	1/9¾	1/9¾	1/9¾	1/9¾	1/5¼	1/10	1/10	2/2	2/2	2/2	2/2	
Will. Mandevile	–	–	1/2½	1/9¾	1/9¾	1/9¾	1/9¾	1/5¼	1/10	1/10	2/2	2/2	2/2	2/2	
W. de Pontingdon	–	–	1/1½	1/8	1/8	1/8	1/8	1/4¾	1/8	1/8	2/0	2/0	2/0	2/0	
John de la Forde	–	–	0/6	1/6½	1/6½	1/6½	1/6½	1/3½	1/6½	1/10	1/10	1/10	1/10	1/10	
Nich. Mantel mason	–	–	1/8	1/8	1/8	1/8	1/8	1/4¾	–	–	–	–	2/0	2/0	
John de Lolleworth	–	–	–	–	1/6½	1/6½	1/6½	1/3½	–	–	–	–	–	–	
Adam Reymund	–	–	–	–	–	1/8	1/8	1/4½	–	–	2/0	2/0	2/0	2/0	
Will. de Merton	–	–	–	–	–	–	1/9¾	1/5¼	–	1/10½	–	–	–	–	
Thom. de Merton	–	–	–	–	–	–	1/9¾	1/5¼	–	–	–	–	2/2	2/2	
Phil. de Cornubia	–	–	–	–	–	–	1/5½	1/5½	1/5	1/5	1/9	1/9	1/9	1/9	
John de Cherde	–	–	–	–	–	–	–	–	1/5	1/5	1/9	1/9	1/9	1/9	
Hugh de Prato	–	–	–	–	–	–	–	–	1/3	1/3	1/6	1/6	1/6	1/6	
John de Cruce	–	–	–	–	–	–	–	–	–	1/6½	1/10	1/10	1/10	1/10	
Will. de Meriet carpenter	–	–	–	–	–	–	–	–	–	–	2/3	2/3	2/3	2/3	
Adam de Chuddeleghe carpenter	–	–	–	–	–	–	–	–	–	–	2/1	2/1	2/1	2/1	
Will. de Herford	–	–	–	–	–	–	–	–	–	–	2/0	2/0	2/0	2/0	
Will. de Holdham/Hodleham	–	–	–	–	–	–	–	–	–	–	1/10	1/10	1/10	1/10	
Rob. Penng	–	–	–	–	–	–	–	–	–	–	1/7	1/8	1/8	1/8	
Mich. le Daubere	–	–	–	–	–	–	–	–	–	–	–	2/0	2/0	2/0	
Master Walter carpenter	–	–	–	–	–	–	–	–	–	–	–	2/3	2/3	2/3	
EASTER															
Ric. de Streme, Will. de Meriet	–	2/3	2/3	1/10½	2/3	2/3	2/3	–	2/3	2/3	2/3				
John de la More, Ric. de Hegham	–	2/2	2/2	1/9¾	2/2	2/2	2/2	–	–	2/2	2/2				
Rad. de Abbedesbiri	–	2/2	2/2	1/9¾	2/2	2/2	2/2	–	2/2	2/2	2/2				
Will. de Puntingdon	–	2/0	2/0	1/8	2/0	2/0	–	–	–	–	–				
Adam Reymund	–	2/0	2/0	1/8	2/0	2/0	2/0	–	–	2/0	2/0				
John de Forde	–	1/10	1/10	1/6½	1/10	1/10	1/10	–	–	1/10	1/10				
John de Cruce	–	1/10	1/10	1/6½	1/10	1/10	1/10	–	–	–	–				
Phil. de Cornubia, John de Cherde	–	1/9	1/9	1/4½	1/9	1/9	1/9	–	–	–	–				
Hugh de Prato	–	1/6	1/6	1/3	1/6	1/6	1/6	–	–	–	–				
Mich. le Dauber	–	2/0	–	1/8	–	2/0	2/0	–	2/0	–	–				
Golofre quarryman	–	7/0	7/0	7/0	7/0	–	7/0	–	7/0	7/0	–				
Master Walter carpenter	–	2/3	2/3	1/10½	2/3	2/3	2/3	–	–	2/3	2/3				
Adam de Chuddelegh	–	2/1	2/1	1/9	2/1	2/1	2/1	–	2/1	2/1	2/1				
Will. de Herford/Hereford	–	2/0	2/0	1/8	2/0	2/0	2/0	–	2/0	2/0	2/0				
Will. de Holdham/Holdeham	–	1/10	1/10	1/6½	1/10	1/10	1/10	–	1/10	1/10	1/10				
Rob. Penng	–	1/8	1/8	1/4¾	1/8	1/8	1/8	–	1/8	–	1/8				
Galfr./Giffard de Cruce	–	–	–	1/3	1/6	1/6	1/6	–	1/6	–	1/6				

[1299–1300 cont.] WEEK:	1	2	3	4	5	6	7	8	9	10	11	12	13	14	15
Walt. de Hampton	–	–	–	–	2/2	2/2	2/2	–	–	–	–				
John de Lolleworth	–	–	–	–	1/10	1/10	1/10	–	–	–	–				
Will. de Merton	–	–	–	–	–	2/2	2/2	–	–	–	–				
John de Cristchurch	–	–	–	–	–	–	1/10	–	–	–	–				
Galfrid. Unfrai/Unfrei, Nich. Alain	–	–	–	–	–	–	1/9	–	1/9	–	–				
Hen. Odin, Rad. Pope	–	–	–	–	–	–	1/6	–	1/6	–	–				
Giles de Fercombe/Ferncombe	–	–	–	–	–	–	1/8	–	1/8	–	–				
Adam de Pederton	–	–	–	–	–	–	–	–	–	2/0	2/0				
Thom. de Molton	–	–	–	–	–	–	–	–	–	–	2/0				
MIDSUMMER															
Ric. de la Streme	2/3	2/3	2/3	2/3	2/3	2/3	2/3	2/3	2/3	2/3	2/3	2/3	2/3		
Will. de Meriet	2/3	2/3	2/3	2/3	2/3	2/3	2/3	–	–	–	–	–	2/3		
John de la More, Ric. de Hegham, Rad. de Abbedesbiri	2/2	2/2	2/2	2/2	2/2	2/2	2/2	2/2	2/2	2/2	2/2	2/2	2/2		
Adam de Pederton, W. de Herford	2/0	2/0	2/0	2/0	2/0	2/0	2/0	2/0	2/0	2/0	2/0	2/0	2/0		
Golofre	7/0	7/0	–	7/0	7/0	7/0	7/0	7/0	7/0	7/0	7/0	–	7/0		
Master Walt. carpenter	2/3	2/3	2/3	2/3	2/3	2/3	2/3	2/3	2/3	2/3	2/3	2/3	2/3		
Adam de Chuddelegh	2/1	2/1	2/1	2/1	2/1	2/1	2/1	2/1	2/1	2/1	2/1	2/1	2/1		
John de Forde	1/10	1/10	1/10	1/10	1/10	1/10	1/10	1/10	–	–	–	–	–		
Thom. de Molton	2/0	2/0	2/0	2/0	2/0	2/0	2/0	2/0	2/0	–	–	–	–		
Will. de Holdleham	1/10	1/10	1/10	1/10	1/10	1/10	1/10	1/10	1/10	1/10	1/10	1/10	1/10		
Rob. Penng	1/8	1/8	1/8	1/8	1/8	1/8	1/8	1/8	1/8	1/8	1/8	1/8	1/8		
Giffard de Cruce	1/6	1/6	1/6	1/6	1/6	1/6	1/6	1/6	–	–	–	–	–		
Phil. de Cornubia, John de Meriet	–	–	–	1/10	1/9	1/9	–	–	–	–	–	–	–		
Adam Reymund	–	–	–	–	2/0	2/0	2/0	2/0	2/0	2/0	2/0	2/0	2/0		
John de Lolleworth	–	–	–	–	1/10	1/10	1/10	1/10	1/10	–	–	–	–		
Will. de Pontingdon	–	–	–	–	–	2/0	2/0	2/0	2/0	–	–	–	–		
Will. Turgis/Torgis	–	–	–	–	–	–	2/0	2/0	2/0	2/0	2/0	2/0	2/0		
Walt. de Hampton	–	–	–	–	–	–	–	2/2	2/2	2/2	2/2	2/2	2/2		

2603 1301–2

MICHAELMAS	1	2	3	4	5	6	7	8	9	10	11	12
Ric. de la Streme, Rob. de Forde	2/3	2/3	2/3	2/3	1/10½	1/10½	1/10½	1/10½	1/10½	1/10½	1/10½	1/10½
Will de Monte Acuto	2/3	2/3	2/3	–	–	–	–	–	–	–	–	–
Hen. de Monte Acuto	–	–	–	–	1/9¾	1/9¾	1/9¾	1/9¾	1/9¾	1/9¾	–	–
John de la More	2/2	2/2	2/2	2/2	–	–	–	–	–	–	–	–
Ric. de Hegham, Rad. de Abbedesbiri, Walt. de Hampton	2/2	2/2	2/2	2/2	1/9¾	1/9¾	1/9¾	1/9¾	1/9¾	1/9¾	1/9¾	1/9¾

[1301–2 cont.] WEEK:	1	2	3	4	5	6	7	8	9	10	11	12	13	14	15
Adam Reymund, Walt. de Stoke	2/0	2/0	2/0	2/0	1/8	1/8	1/8	1/8	1/8	1/8	1/8	1/8			
Mich. le Dauber	2/0	2/0	2/0	2/0	–	–	–	–	–	–	–	1/8			
John de Lolleworthy, John de Christchurche, Will. le King, John Havel	1/10	1/10	1/10	1/10	1/6½	1/6½	1/6½	1/6½	1/6½	1/6½	–	–			
Rob. Wirok, John de Forde	1/10	1/10	1/10	1/10	1/6½	1/6½	1/6½	1/6½	1/6½	1/6½	1/6½	–			
Thom. de Brompton	1/10	1/10	–	1/10	–	–	–	–	–	–	–	–			
Master Walt. carpenter	2/3	2/3	2/3	2/3	–	1/10½	1/10½	1/10½	1/10½	1/10½	–	–			
Rob. de Byredone carpenter	2/0	2/0	2/0	2/0	1/8	1/8	1/8	–	–	–	–	–			
Will. de Holdham	–	1/10	1/10	–	–	–	–	–	–	–	–	–			
R. Penng	–	–	–	1/10	–	–	–	–	–	–	–	–			
J. de Cruce	–	–	–	–	1/6½	1/6½	1/6½	1/6½	1/6½	1/6½	1/6½	–			
G. de Somerton, J. de Cherde	–	–	–	–	–	1/4	1/4	1/4	1/4	1/4	–	–			
Golofre quarryman	7/0	7/0	7/0	7/0	7/0	7/0	7/0	7/0	7/0	7/0	7/0	7/0			
Thom. de Hampton	–	–	1/10	–	–	–	–	–	–	–	–	–			
CHRISTMAS WEEK:	**3**	**4**	**5**	**6**	**7**	**8**	**9**	**10**	**11**	**12**	**13**	**14**	**15**	**16**	**17**
Ric. de la Streme, R. de Forde	1/10½	1/10½	1/10½	1/10½	1/10½	1/10½	1/6¾	1/10½	1/10½	2/3	2/3	2/3	2/3	2/3	2/3
Ric. de Hegham	1/9¾	1/9¾	1/9¾	1/9¾	1/9¾	1/9¾	1/6¼	1/10¾	1/10¾	–	–	–	–	–	–
Rad. de Abbedesbiri	1/9¾	1/9¾	1/9¾	1/9¾	1/9¾	1/9¾	1/6¼	1/10¾	1/10¾	2/2	2/2	2/2	2/2	2/2	2/2
Adam Reymund, Rob. Payn	1/8	1/8	1/8	1/8	1/8	1/8	1/4¾	1/8	1/8	2/0	2/0	2/0	2/0	2/0	2/0
John de Forde	1/6½	1/6½	1/6½	1/6½	1/6½	1/6½	1/3½	1/6½	1/6½	1/10	1/10	1/10	1/10	1/10	1/10
Will. de Monteacuto	–	2/1	2/1	2/1	2/1	–	–	–	–	–	–	–	–	–	–
J. de Christchurche	–	1/6½	1/6½	1/6½	1/6½	1/6½	–	–	1/6½	1/10	1/10	1/10	1/10	1/10	1/10
Hen. de Monteacuto	–	1/9¾	1/9¾	1/9¾	1/9¾	1/9¾	1/6¼	1/10¾	1/10¾	2/2	2/2	2/2	2/2	2/2	2/2
Walt. de Hampton	–	0/10	–	1/6½	1/6½	1/6½	–	1/6½	1/6½	1/10	1/10	1/10	1/10	1/10	1/10
J. de Lolleworth	–	–	–	1/6½	1/6½	1/6½	1/3½	1/6½	1/6½	1/10	1/10	1/10	1/10	1/10	1/10
Mich. le Daubeur	–	–	–	1/8	1/8	1/8	1/4¾	1/8	–	–	–	2/0	2/0	2/0	2/0
W. carpenter	–	–	–	–	1/10½	–	–	–	–	–	–	–	–	2/3	2/3
Will. de Meriet	–	–	–	–	–	1/10½	1/6¾	1/10½	1/10½	–	2/3	2/3	2/3	2/3	2/3
Hugh de la Wyle	–	–	–	–	–	–	1/6¼	1/10¾	1/10¾	2/2	2/2	2/2	2/2	2/2	2/2
J. de Hampton	–	–	–	–	–	–	1/3½	–	–	–	–	–	–	–	–
R. Wyrok	–	–	–	–	–	–	1/3½	1/6½	1/6½	1/10	1/10	1/10	1/10	1/10	1/10
J. le Sauser	–	–	–	–	–	–	–	1/10¾	1/10¾	2/2	2/2	2/2	2/2	2/2	2/2
J. de Cruce	–	–	–	–	–	–	–	–	1/6½	1/10	1/10	1/10	1/10	1/10	1/10
Ric. de Teingemue	–	–	–	–	–	–	–	–	–	–	1/6	1/6	–	–	–
John Luve, Will. de Ermington, Ph. de Cornubia	–	–	–	–	–	–	–	–	–	–	–	1/6	1/6	1/6	1/6
Rog. de Kilmington	–	–	–	–	–	–	–	–	–	–	–	–	1/6	1/6	1/6
Hugh de Prato, Rob. le Clerk	–	–	–	–	–	–	–	–	–	–	–	–	1/6	1/6	1/4
Golofre	–	7/0	7/0	7/0	–	7/0	7/0	7/0	7/0	–	7/0	7/0	7/0	7/0	7/0

[1301–2 cont.]

EASTER

WEEK:	2	3	4	5	6	7	8	9
Ric. de la Streme, R. de Forde, Will. de Meriet	1/10½	2/3	2/3	2/3	2/3	2/3	–	2/3
Rad. de Abbedesbiri, Hen. de Monteacuto, J. Sauser	1/9¾	2/2	2/2	2/2	2/2	2/2	–	2/2
Hugh de la Wile	1/9¾	2/2	2/2	2/2	2/2	2/2	–	–
J. de Corfe	1/9¾	2/2	–	–	–	–	–	2/2
Ad. Reymund, Rob. Payn, Mich. le Daubeur	1/8	2/0	2/0	2/0	2/0	2/0	–	2/0
J. de Ford, J. de Lolleworth	1/6½	1/10	1/10	1/10	–	–	–	–
Walt. de Hampton, Rob. Wyrok	1/6½	1/10	1/10	–	1/4	1/10	–	–
J. de Christchurche	1/6½	1/10	–	–	–	–	–	1/10
J. de Cruce	–	–	1/10	–	–	–	–	1/10
John Luve, Phil. de Cornubia, Rog. de Kilmington	1/3	1/6	–	–	–	–	–	–
Hugh de Prato, Rob. le Clerk	1/1½	1/4	–	–	–	–	–	–
Walt. carpenter	1/8½	2/3	2/3	2/3	2/3	–	–	1/10
Will. King, Symon de Kent	–	–	–	–	–	–	–	–
Golofre	7/0	7/0	7/0	7/0	7/0	7/0	–	–

MIDSUMMER

WEEK:	1	2	3	4	5	6	7	8	9	10	11	12	13	14	15
R. de la Streme, R. de Forde	1	2/3	2/3	2/3	2/3	2/3	2/3	2/3	2/3	2/3	2/3	2/3	–	–	–
Rad. de Abbedesbiri	2/3	2/3	2/3	2/3	2/3	2/3	2/3	2/3	–	–	–	–	–	–	–
H. de Monteacuto, John de Corf	2/2	2/2	2/2	2/2	2/2	2/2	2/2	2/2	–	–	–	–	–	–	–
J. Sauser	2/2	2/2	–	–	–	–	–	–	–	–	–	–	–	–	–
Adam Reymund	2/0	2/0	–	–	–	–	–	–	–	–	–	–	–	–	–
R. Payn	2/0	2/0	2/0	2/0	2/0	2/0	2/0	–	–	–	–	–	–	–	–
M. le Daubeur	2/0	2/0	2/0	2/0	2/0	2/0	2/0	–	–	–	–	–	–	–	–
W. de Hampton, Symon de Kent	1/10	1/10	1/10	1/10	–	–	–	–	–	–	–	–	–	–	–
R. Wirok, J. de Cruce	1/10	1/10	1/10	–	–	–	–	–	–	–	–	–	–	–	–
W. King	1/6	1/6	–	–	–	–	–	–	–	–	–	–	–	–	–
W. de Ermington	1/6	1/6	1/6	–	–	–	–	–	–	–	–	–	–	–	–
J. de Forde	1/6	1/6	1/10	–	–	–	–	–	–	–	–	–	–	–	–
John Luve, Rog. de Kilmington	–	1/6	–	–	–	–	–	–	–	–	–	–	–	–	–
Hugh de Yalim/Yalem	1/6	1/6	–	–	–	–	–	–	–	–	–	–	–	–	–
Mich. Coppe/Chope	–	1/8	1/8	–	–	–	–	–	–	–	–	–	–	–	–
Golofre	7/0	–	–	–	7/0	–	7/0	–	–	–	–	–	–	–	–
Master W. carpenter	–	2/3	2/3	2/3	2/3	2/3	2/3	2/3	2/3	2/3	2/3	2/3	–	2/3	–
Adam de Chuddeleghe	–	2/1	2/1	2/1	2/1	–	3/1	2/1	2/1	2/1	2/1	2/1	–	1/0½	–
Will. de Holdham	–	–	–	–	–	–	–	–	–	–	–	1/10	–	–	–

2604 1302–3

MICHAELMAS WEEK:	1	2	3	4	5	6	7	8	9	10	11	12	13	14	15
Ric. de la Streme, R. de Forde	–	–	2/3	2/3	1/10½	1/10½	1/10½	1/10½	1/10½	1/10½	1/10½	1/10½			
J. le Sauser	–	–	2/2	2/2	1/9¾	1/9¾	1/9¾	1/9¾	1/9¾	–	–	–			
Adam Reymund	–	–	2/0	–	0/8	1/8	1/8	1/8	1/8	1/8	1/8	1/8			
Rad. de Abbedesbiri	–	–	–	–	1/9¾	1/9¾	1/9¾	1/9¾	1/9¾	–	–	–			
Adam de Chuddelegh	2/1	2/1	2/1	2/1	–	–	–	–	–	–	–	–			
Walt. de Corf	–	–	–	–	–	1/6½	1/6½	1/6½	1/6½	1/6½	1/6½	1/6½			
Hugh de Sidmewe, Will. de Ermington/Hermington	–	–	–	–	1/3	1/3	1/3	1/3	1/3	–	–	–			
Will. le King	–	–	–	–	–	0/9¼	1/6½	1/6½	1/6½	1/6½	–	–			
Will. le Luve	–	–	–	–	–	–	–	0/10½	–	–	–	–			
Will. de Meriet	–	–	–	–	–	–	–	–	1/10½	1/10½	1/10½	1/10½			
John de Odington	–	–	–	–	–	–	–	–	1/8	–	–	–			
John de Forde	–	–	–	–	–	–	–	–	–	1/6½	1/6½	1/6½			
John de Cruce	–	–	–	–	–	–	–	–	–	–	1/6½	1/6½			
Master Walt. carpenter	2/3	–	–	–	–	–	–	–	–	–	–	1/10½			
Golofre quarryman	–	7/0	–	7/0	–	–	7/0	–	–	–	7/0	–			
CHRISTMAS															
Rob. de Forde	–	–	–	–	–	1/10½	1/10½	1/10½	1/10½	1/10½	1/10½	–			
Will. le King	–	–	–	–	–	1/6½	1/6½	1/6½	1/6½	1/6½	1/6½	–			
Phil. de Cornubia	–	–	–	–	–	–	1/3	1/3	1/3	1/3	–	–			
Golofre	–	–	–	–	–	–	7/0	–	–	7/0	–	–			
Will. Turgis carpenter	–	–	–	–	–	–	–	1/8	1/8	–	–	–			
Walter carpenter	–	–	–	–	–	–	–	–	1/10½	1/10½	1/10½	–			
Will. de Her[ford]	–	–	–	–	–	–	–	–	–	–	1/8	–			
EASTER															
Walter carpenter	–	2/3	2/3	1/10½	2/3	–	2/3	–	–	2/3	2/3	–			
Will. de Herford/Hereford	–	2/0	2/0	1/8	2/0	2/0	2/0	–	2/0	2/0	2/0	–			
Will. de Monte Acuto	–	2/6	2/6	2/0	2/6	2/6	2/6	–	2/6	2/6	–	–			
R. de Forde	–	–	2/3	–	–	–	–	–	–	–	–	–			
Golofre quarryman	–	–	–	7/0	–	–	–	–	–	–	–	–			
MIDSUMMER															
Will. de Hereford	1/8	2/0	2/0	2/0	2/0	–	2/0	2/0	2/0	2/0	–	–			
Will. de Monte Acuto	–	2/6	2/6	2/6	–	–	–	2/6	2/6	2/6	2/6	–			
Walter carpenter	–	–	2/3	2/3	–	–	–	–	2/3	–	–	–			
Walter le Tourner	–	–	3/0	–	–	–	–	–	–	–	–	–			
John de Cruce	–	–	–	0/11	–	–	–	–	1/3	1/3	–	–			

2605 1303–4

MICHAELMAS

No wage lists

WEEK:	1	2	3	4	5	6	7	8	9	10	11	12	13	14	15
CHRISTMAS															
Rob. de Forde	1/10½	1/10½	1/10½	1/10½	–	–	–	1/10½	2/3	2/3	1/10½				
Adam de Chuddelegh	1/8	1/8	1/8	1/8	1/8	1/8	1/8	1/8	2/0	–	–				
Ric. de la Streme, Will. Meriet	–	1/10½	1/10½	1/10½	1/10½	1/10½	1/10½	1/10½	2/3	2/3	1/10½				
Will. de Hereford	–	1/8	1/8	1/8	1/8	1/8	1/8	1/8	2/0	2/0	1/8				
Adam Reymund	–	–	1/9¾	1/9¾	–	–	–	1/9¾	–	–	–				
Rad. de Abbedesbiri	–	–	–	–	–	–	–	1/9¾	2/2	2/2	1/9¾				
Will. de Stoke, Hen. Kyrie	–	–	–	–	–	–	–	–	2/0	2/0	1/8				
Rob. Wyrok	–	–	–	–	–	–	–	–	–	1/10	1/6½				
Ric. de Tengemue	–	–	–	–	–	–	–	–	–	1/8	1/4¾				
Golofre quarryman	7/0	–	7/0	–	7/0	7/0	–	7/0	10/0	10/0	10/0				
EASTER															
R. de la Streme, R. de Forde, W. de Meriet	–	2/3	2/3	2/3	2/3	1/10½	2/3	–	2/3	2/3	2/3	2/3			
Adam Reymund, Rob. de Yartecombe, Hen. de Parco	–	2/2	2/2	2/2	2/2	1/9¾	2/2	–	2/2	2/2	2/2	2/2			
Hen. Kyrie	–	2/0	2/0	2/0	2/0	1/8	2/0	–	2/0	2/0	2/0	2/0			
R. Wyrok/Wirok	–	1/10	1/10	1/10	1/10	1/6½	1/10	–	1/10	1/10	1/10	1/10			
J. de Lolleworthi	–	1/10	1/10	1/10	–	–	1/10	–	1/10	1/10	1/10	1/10			
J. de Totton	–	1/10	1/10	1/10	1/10	1/6½	1/10	–	1/10	1/10	1/10	1/10			
Ric. de Teingemue	–	1/8	1/8	1/8	1/8	1/4¾	1/8	–	1/8	1/8	1/8	1/8			
W. de Stoke, Nich. de Parco	–	–	2/0	2/0	2/0	1/8	2/0	–	2/0	2/0	2/0	2/0			
Rad. de Abbedesbiri	–	–	–	–	–	1/9¾	2/2	–	2/2	2/2	2/2	2/2			
Hugh de Taunton	–	–	–	–	–	1/8	–	–	2/0	2/0	2/0	2/0			
Walt. de Lovepitte	–	–	–	–	–	1/8	2/0	–	2/0	2/0	2/0	2/0			
Will. Cope	–	–	–	–	–	1/8	2/0	–	2/0	–	–	–			
W. de Holdeham carpenter	–	–	–	–	–	1/6½	–	–	–	–	–	–			
H. de Totton	–	–	–	–	–	–	2/0	–	–	–	–	–			
W. de Pontington	–	–	–	–	–	–	2/0	–	2/0	–	–	–			
Nic. Mantel	–	–	–	–	–	–	–	–	2/0	2/0	2/0	2/0			
Adam de Taunton	–	–	–	–	–	–	–	–	1/10	1/10	1/10	1/10			
Nic. de Stoke	–	–	–	–	–	–	–	–	–	–	–	2/0			
Golofre	–	10/0	10/0	17/0	10/0	10/0	10/0	–	10/0	10/0	10/0	10/0			
MIDSUMMER															
Rob. de Forde	2/3	2/3	2/3	2/3	1/10½	2/3	2/3	1/10½	2/3	1/10½	2/3	2/3	2/3	2/3	
Ric. de la Streme	2/3	2/3	2/3	2/3	1/10½	2/3	2/3	1/10½	2/3	–	2/3	2/3	2/3	2/3	

[1303–4 cont.] WEEK:	1	2	3	4	5	6	7	8	9	10	11	12	13	14	15
Will. de Meriet	2/3	2/3	2/3	2/3	1/10½	2/3	2/3	1/10½	–	–	2/3	2/3	2/3	2/3	
Rob. de Yartecombe	2/2	2/2	2/2	2/2	1/9¾	2/2	2/2	–	–	–	–	–	–	–	
Ad. Reymund, Rad. de Abbedesbiri, Nic. Mantel	2/2	2/2	2/2	2/2	1/9¾	2/2	2/2	1/9¾	2/2	1/11¼	2/2	2/2	2/2	2/2	
Hen. de Parco	2/2	2/2	2/2	2/2	1/9¾	2/2	2/2	1/9¾	2/2	–	2/2	2/2	2/2	2/2	
Hen. Kyrie	2/0	2/0	2/0	2/0	–	–	–	–	–	–	–	–	–	–	
Walt. de Stoke, Nic. de Parco	2/0	2/0	2/0	2/0	1/8	2/0	2/0	1/8	2/0	1/8	2/0	2/0	2/0	2/0	
Hugh de Taunton	2/0	2/0	2/0	2/0	1/8	2/0	2/0	–	–	–	–	–	–	–	
W. de Lovepitt	2/0	2/0	2/0	2/0	1/8	2/0	2/0	1/8	2/0	1/8	2/0	2/0	2/0	2/0	
Adam de Taunton	2/2	2/0	2/0	2/0	1/8	2/0	2/0	–	–	1/8	2/0	2/0	2/0	2/0	
Rob. Wyrok	1/10	1/10	1/10	1/10	1/6½	1/10	1/10	1/6½	1/10	1/6½	1/10	1/10	1/10	1/10	
John de Totton	1/10	1/10	1/10	–	1/8	2/0	2/0	1/8	2/0	1/8	2/0	2/0	2/0	2/0	
John de Lolleworthi	1/10	1/10	1/10	–	–	1/10	1/10	1/6½	1/10	1/6½	1/10	1/10	1/10	1/10	
John de Telesford	1/10	1/10	1/10	1/10	1/6½	1/10	1/10	1/6½	1/10	1/6½	1/10	1/10	1/10	1/10	
Ric. de Teingemue	1/8	1/8	1/8	–	1/4¾	1/8	1/8	1/4¾	1/8	1/5	1/8	1/8	1/8	1/8	
Rob. de Mochelni	1/8	1/8	1/8	–	–	1/8	1/8	1/4¾	1/8	1/5	1/8	–	–	–	
Will. de Keynesham	–	2/0	2/0	–	–	–	–	–	–	–	–	–	–	–	
G. de Taunton	–	2/0	2/0	2/0	1/8	2/0	2/0	1/8	2/0	–	2/0	2/0	–	–	
J. Havel	–	2/0	2/0	2/0	1/8	2/0	2/0	1/8	2/0	–	2/0	2/0	2/0	2/0	
Galf. le Mey	–	–	2/0	2/0	1/8	2/0	2/0	1/8	2/0	–	2/0	2/0	2/0	2/0	
J. de Taunton	–	–	–	2/0	–	–	–	–	–	–	–	–	–	–	
Walt. de Corf, Rad. de Corf	–	–	–	–	1/6½	1/10	1/10	1/6½	–	–	–	1/10	1/10	1/10	
Will. de Hereford carpenter	–	–	–	–	1/8	2/0	2/0	1/8	2/0	1/8	2/0	2/0	2/0	2/0	
John de Coscombe	–	–	–	–	–	2/2	2/2	1/9¾	2/2	1/11¼	2/2	2/2	2/2	2/2	
Will. de Holdham	–	–	–	–	0/11	1/10	1/10	1/6½	1/10	1/6½	1/10	1/10	1/10	1/10	
J. de Forde	–	–	–	–	–	–	–	–	–	1/5	–	1/10	1/10	1/10	
J. de Hoddingham/Oddingham	–	–	–	–	–	–	–	–	–	–	–	–	2/0	2/0	
Golofre	10/0	10/0	10/0	20/0	10/0	10/0	10/0	7/0	7/0	7/0	7/0	7/0	7/0	7/0	

2606/7 1306–7

MICHAELMAS

	1	2	3	4	5	6	7	8	9	10	11
Rob. de Forde, Ric. de la Streme	2/3	2/3	2/3	2/3	1/6¾	1/10½	1/10½	1/6¾	1/10½	1/10½	1/10½
Rad. de Abbedesbiri, Ad. Raymund, Rob. de Merwe, Rob. de Schute, Thom. de Merton	2/2	2/2	2/2	2/2	1/6¼	1/9¾	1/9¾	1/6¼	1/9¾	1/9¾	1/9¾
John de Schorham	2/1	2/1	2/1	2/1	–	–	–	–	–	–	–
Walt. de Corf, Ad. le Jay	2/0	2/0	2/0	2/0	1/4¾	1/8	1/8	1/4¾	1/8	1/8	1/8
John de Lolleworthi	1/11	1/11	1/11	1/11	–	–	–	–	–	–	–
Rob. Wirok	1/10	1/10	–	–	–	–	–	–	–	–	–

[1306–7 cont.] WEEK:	1	2	3	4	5	6	7	8	9	10	11	12	13	14	15
Ric. de Tengemue, John le Luve, Hugh de Morton	1/8	–	–	–	–	–	–	–	–	–	–				
John de Cherde	1/6	–	–	–	–	–	–	–	–	–	–				
Will. de Taunton, John de Bradenstoke, Walt. de Stafford	1/0	1/0	1/0	1/0	0/10	0/10	0/10	0/10	0/10	0/10	0/10				
Walter carpenter	2/3	2/3	–	–	–	1/10½	1/10½	0/3½	–	1/10½	–				
W. de Holdham	–	–	–	–	–	1/6½	1/6½	1/3½	–	–	–				
Golofre quarryman	7/0	7/0	7/0	7/0	7/0	7/0	–	7/0	7/0	7/0	–				
CHRISTMAS															
R. de Forde, Ric. de Streme	–	–	1/10½	1/10½	1/10½	1/10½	1/10½	1/10½	1/6¾	1/10½	1/10½	2/3	2/3		
Rad. de Abbedesbiri, Adam Reymund, Rob. de Schute, Thom. de Merton	–	–	1/9¾	1/9¾	1/9¾	1/9¾	1/9¾	1/9¾	1/6¼	1/9¾	1/9¾	2/2	1/9¾		
Walt. de Corfe, W. de Lovepitte	–	–	1/8	1/8	1/8	1/8	1/8	1/4¾	1/4¾	1/8	1/8	2/0	1/8		
W. de Taunton, W. de Stafford, J. de Bradenstoke	–	–	0/10	0/10	0/10	0/10	0/10	0/10	0/10	1/0	1/0	1/0	0/10		
Golofre	–	7/0	–	7/0	7/0	–	7/0	7/0	–	7/0	7/0	–	7/0		
EASTER															
R. de Forde	–	2/3	2/3	–	–	–	–	–	–	–	–	–	–		
R. de la Streme	–	2/3	2/3	2/3	2/3	2/3	2/3	–	2/3	2/3	2/3	2/3	2/3		
Adam Reymund, R. de Abbedesbiri, T. de Merton	–	2/2	2/2	2/2	2/2	1/5½	2/2	–	2/2	2/2	2/2	2/2	2/2		
Rob. de Schute	–	2/2	2/2	2/2	2/2	1/5½	2/2	–	–	?	?	–	–		
Hen. de Monte Acuto	–	2/2	2/2	2/2	2/2	1/5½	2/2	–	2/2	2/2	2/2	–	–		
Walt. de Corf	–	2/0	2/0	2/0	2/0	1/4	2/0	–	2/0	2/0	2/0	2/0	–		
Walt. de Lovepitt	–	2/0	2/0	2/0	2/0	1/4	2/0	–	2/0	2/0	2/0	2/0	2/0		
John de Lolleworthi	–	2/0	2/0	–	2/0	2/0	2/0	–	?	–	–	2/0	–		
Adam le Jay	–	2/0	2/0	2/0	2/0	1/4	2/0	–	?	–	2/0	–	–		
Will. de Taunton	–	1/0	1/0	1/0	1/0	0/8	1/0	–	1/0	?	1/0	–	–		
J. de Bradenstoke, Walt. de Stafford	–	1/0	1/0	1/0	1/0	0/8	1/0	–	1/0	?	1/0	1/0	1/0		
Master Walter carpenter	–	2/3	–	–	–	–	–	–	–	–	2/3	2/3	2/3		
Will. de Chuddelegh	–	–	1/10	–	–	–	–	–	–	?	2/3	2/3	2/3		
J. de Cherde	–	–	–	–	1/6	1/0	1/6	–	1/6	–	1/6	1/6	1/6		
J. de Cruce	–	–	–	–	–	1/2	1/10	–	1/10	–	–	–	–		
Will. de Tengemue	–	–	–	–	–	–	–	–	–	?	1/6	1/6	1/6		
Will. Cropping	–	–	–	–	–	–	–	–	–	1/9	1/9	1/9	1/9		
Thom. de Schute	–	–	–	–	–	–	–	–	2/2	?	2/2	2/2	2/2		
Will. de Holdham	–	–	–	–	–	–	–	–	–	–	1/10	–	–		
Will. de Hembiri	–	–	–	–	–	–	–	–	–	–	1/10	1/10	1/10		
Rad. Popa, Gerv. de Chuddelegh	–	–	–	–	–	–	–	–	–	–	1/6	1/6	1/6		

[1306–7 cont.] WEEK:	1	2	3	4	5	6	7	8	9	10	11	12	13	14	15
Walt. Rowa carpenter	—	—	—	—	—	—	—	—	—	—	1/1	1/1	1/1	1/1	
Peter Flori	—	—	—	—	—	—	—	—	—	—	—	2/2	2/2	2/2	
Adam de Chuddelegh	—	—	—	—	—	—	—	—	—	—	—	—	2/1	2/1	
Rob. de Taunton	—	—	—	—	—	—	—	—	—	—	—	—	1/10	—	
Ric. Forester, Steph. sawyer	—	—	—	—	—	—	—	—	—	—	—	—	1/8	—	
Adam de Pruston	—	—	—	—	—	—	—	—	—	—	—	—	0/8	—	
Ric. de Chuddelegh	—	—	—	—	—	—	—	—	—	—	—	7/0	0/6	—	
Golofre	7/0	—	7/0	7/0	7/0	7/0	7/0	7/0	—	—	7/0	7/0	—	—	
MIDSUMMER															
Ric. de la Streme	2/3	2/3	2/3	2/3	2/3	2/3	2/3	—	—	—	2/3	2/3	2/3	2/3	
Rad. de Abbedesbiri, Adam Reymund, Th. de Schute, Th. de Merton	2/2	2/2	2/2	2/2	2/2	2/2	2/2	2/2	2/2	2/2	2/2	2/2	2/2	2/2	
W. de Lovepitte	2/0	2/0	2/0	2/0	2/0	2/0	2/0	2/0	2/0	2/0	2/0	2/0	2/0	2/0	
W. de Corf	2/0	2/0	2/0	2/0	—	—	—	—	—	—	—	—	—	—	
J. de Cherde, W. de Tengemue	1/6	1/6	1/6	1/6	1/6	1/6	1/6	1/6	1/6	1/6	—	—	—	—	
W. de Taunton, J. de Bradenstoke, Walt. de Stafford	1/0	1/0	1/0	1/0	1/0	1/0	1/0	1/0	1/0	1/0	1/0	1/0	1/0	1/0	
Master W. carpenter	2/3	2/3	1/3	2/3	2/3	2/3	—	—	—	—	—	—	—	—	
Will. de Hembiri carpenter	1/10	1/10	—	1/10	1/10	1/10	1/10	1/10	1/10	—	—	—	—	—	
Cropping	1/9	1/9	2/0	2/0	—	—	—	—	—	—	—	—	—	—	
J. de Lolleworthi	—	2/0	1/10	—	—	2/0	2/0	2/0	—	1/10	—	—	—	—	
J. de Cruce	—	—	0/9	—	—	—	—	—	—	—	—	—	—	—	
Gervas. carpenter	—	—	1/2	—	—	—	—	—	—	—	—	—	—	—	
Rob. Penng	—	—	—	1/9	1/9	1/9	—	—	—	—	—	—	—	—	
Peter and Phil. de Somersete	—	—	—	1/8	1/8	—	—	1/8	1/8	1/8	1/8	—	—	—	
Rob. de Somersete	—	—	—	1/8	—	—	—	—	—	—	—	—	—	—	
J. de Forde	—	—	—	—	1/10	—	1/10	—	—	—	—	—	—	—	
R. de Pokington, Peter de Cornub	—	—	—	—	1/8	2/2	2/2	2/2	2/2	2/0	—	—	—	—	
Hen. de Monte Acuto	—	—	—	—	—	2/0	2/0	2/0	—	1/8	—	—	—	—	
Adam le Jay/Gay	—	—	—	—	—	—	1/8	1/8	1/8	1/8	2/2	2/2	2/2	2/2	
Nic. Copa, Ph. de Cornub	—	—	—	—	—	—	—	1/8	1/8	1/8	1/8	—	—	—	
John Selman	—	—	—	—	—	—	—	—	—	1/10	1/10	—	—	—	
N. de Insula	—	—	—	—	—	—	—	—	—	—	—	—	—	—	
N. de Wyxt	—	—	—	—	—	—	—	—	—	—	—	—	—	—	
Rob. de Forde	—	—	—	—	—	—	—	—	—	—	—	—	2/3	2/3	
Rob. Cropping carpenter	—	—	—	—	—	—	—	—	—	—	—	—	1/9	1/9	
Ric. Copa	—	—	—	—	—	1/6	1/6	1/6	1/6	1/6	—	—	—	—	
Golofre	7/0	7/0	7/0	7/0	7/0	7/0	7/0	7/0	—	7/0	7/0	7/0	7/0	—	

2608 1308–9

MICHAELMAS WEEK:	**1**	**2**	**3**	**4**	**5**	**6**	**7**	**8**	**9**	**10**	**11**	**12**	**13**	**14**	**15**
Rob. de Forde/Vorde, Ric. de la Streme	2/3	2/3	2/3	2/3	1/6¾	1/10½	–	–	1/6¾	1/10½	1/10½	1/10½			
Rad. de Abbedesbiri, Ad. Reymund, Rob. de Schute, Thom. de Merton	2/2	2/2	2/2	2/2	1/6¾	1/9¾	1/9¾	1/9¾	1/6¾	1/9¾	1/9¾	1/9¾			
Hen. de Monte Acuto	2/2	2/2	2/2	2/2	–	1/9¾	1/9¾	1/9¾	1/6¾	1/9¾	1/9¾	1/9¾			
Walt. de Lovepitte, Ad. le Gay, Walt. de Somersete, Nic. Mantel	2/0	2/0	2/0	2/0	1/4¾	1/8	1/8	1/8	1/4¾	1/8	1/8	1/8			
J. de Lolleworthi	2/0	2/0	2/0	2/0	?	–	1/8	1/8	1/4¾	1/8	1/8	1/8			
Will. de Puntingdon	2/0	2/0	2/0	2/0	–	1/8	–	–	–	–	–	–			
J. de Forde/Vorde, H. de Morton, J. de Stoke, Gilb. de Exon	1/10	1/10	1/10	1/10	–	–	–	–	–	–	–	–			
R. Wyrok	1/10	1/10	1/10	1/10	1/3½	1/6½	–	–	–	–	–	–			
John Selman	1/9	1/9	1/9	1/9	–	–	–	–	–	–	–	–			
John de Cumba	1/9	1/9	1/9	1/9	1/3½	–	–	–	–	–	–	–			
Walt. Luve, Rog. de Welles, Will. de Taunton, Walt. de Stafford	1/3	1/3	1/3	1/3	–	–	–	–	–	–	–	–			
J. de Bradenstoke	1/3	1/3	1/3	1/3	?	1/0½	1/0½	1/0½	1/0½	1/0½	1/0½	1/0½			
Rad. de Wileton	1/0	–	1/0	1/0	–	–	–	–	–	–	–	–			
Master Walt. carpenter	2/3	2/3	2/3	2/3	1/6¾	–	1/10½	1/10½	1/10½	1/10½	1/10½	1/10½			
Adam de Chuddelegh	2/1	2/1	2/1	2/1	1/5¾	–	1/9	1/9	1/5½	1/9	1/9	1/9			
Ric. le Forester	?	1/10	1/10	1/10	1/3	1/6½	1/6½	1/6½	1/3½	1/6½	1/6½	1/6½			
Rob. Croppe/Cropping	1/9	1/9	1/9	1/9	–	1/5½	1/5½	1/5½	1/3	1/5½	1/5½	1/5½			
Hen. de Torre	1/9	–	–	–	–	–	–	–	–	–	–	–			
Will. de Meriet	–	–	2/3	2/3	1/6¾	1/10½	1/10½	1/10½	1/6¾	1/10½	1/10½	1/10½			
J. de Honeton	–	–	1/6	1/6	–	–	–	–	–	–	–	–			
P. Flori	–	–	–	–	–	–	1/9¾	1/9¾	1/6¼	1/9¾	1/9¾	1/9¾			
[W.] de Hembiri	–	–	–	–	–	–	–	1/6½	–	–	–	–			
W. de Holdham/Holdleham	–	–	–	–	–	–	–	1/6½	1/3½	1/6½	1/6½	1/6½			
W. de Hereford	–	–	–	–	–	–	–	?	1/4½	1/8	1/8	1/8			
Will. de Osterton	–	–	–	–	–	–	–	?	1/4¾	–	1/8	1/8			
Golofre	7/0	7/0	7/0	7/0	–	7/0	7/0	7/0	7/0	7/0	7/0	7/0			
CHRISTMAS															
Master Walt. carpenter	0/7½	–	–	1/3	0/3¾	–	–	–	–	–	–	2/3	2/3	0/4	
W. de Herford carpenter	0/6½	1/1¼	–	–	–	–	–	–	–	–	–	–	–	–	
Rad. de Abbedesbiri	–	–	1/9¾	1/9¾	1/9¾	1/9¾	1/9¾	1/9¾	1/9¾	1/9¾	1/9¾	2/2	2/2	1/9¾	
R. de Forde, R. de la Streme, W. de Meriet	–	–	–	1/10½	1/10½	1/10½	1/10½	1/10½	1/10½	1/10½	1/10½	2/3	2/3	1/10½	

[1308–9 cont.] WEEK:	1	2	3	4	5	6	7	8	9	10	11	12	13	14	15
Ad. Reymund, R. de Schute, Th. de Merton, Ric. Croc	–	–	–	1/9¾	1/9¾	1/9¾	1/9¾	1/9¾	1/9¾	1/9¾	1/9¾	2/2	2/2	1/9¾	
Walt. de Lovepitt	–	–	–	1/8	1/8	–	–	–	1/8	1/8	1/8	2/0	2/0	1/8	
Walt. de Somersett	–	–	–	1/8	1/8	1/8	1/8	1/8	–	–	–	–	2/0	–	
J. de Lolliworth	–	–	–	1/8	1/8	–	–	–	1/8	1/8	1/8	2/0	2/0	1/8	
J. de Bradenstoke	–	–	–	1/0½	1/0½	1/0½	1/0½	1/0½	1/0½	1/0½	1/0½	1/4	1/4	1/1½	
Pet. Flori	–	–	–	–	–	1/9¾	1/9¾	1/9¾	1/9¾	1/9¾	1/9¾	2/2	2/2	1/9¾	
Rob. de Westone	–	–	–	–	–	–	–	–	1/10½	1/10½	–	–	–	–	
Hugh Yle	–	–	–	–	–	–	–	–	–	1/9¾	–	–	–	–	
Ric. Crok	–	–	–	–	–	–	–	–	–	–	1/9¾	–	–	–	
J. Luve	–	–	–	–	–	–	–	–	–	1/8	1/8	2/1	2/1	–	
Ad. le Gay	–	–	–	–	–	–	–	–	–	1/8	1/8	2/0	2/0	1/8	
J. de Forde	–	–	–	–	–	–	–	–	–	1/6	1/1¾	1/10	1/10	1/6½	
Walt. de Somerton	–	–	–	–	–	–	–	–	1/8	1/8	1/8	2/0	–	1/8	
Hugh de Morton, Will. de Wodebiri	–	–	–	–	–	–	–	–	–	–	1/1¾	1/10	1/10	1/6½	
Hen. de la [Bi]rche	–	–	–	–	–	–	–	–	–	–	1/4¾	–	–	–	
Ric. le Forester carpenter	–	–	–	–	–	–	–	–	–	–	1/6½	1/10	1/10	–	
Rob. de Taunton	–	–	–	–	–	–	–	–	–	–	–	2/0	2/0	–	
Walt. de Axeminstre	–	–	–	–	–	–	–	–	–	–	–	–	1/8	1/4¾	
Gilb. Axeminstre	–	–	–	–	–	–	–	–	–	–	–	–	1/10	1/6½	
Golofre	–	–	7/0	7/0	7/0	7/0	7/0	7/0	7/0	–	7/0	7/0	–	–	
EASTER															
R. de Forde, R. de la Streme	–	2/3	2/3	2/3	1/10½	1/10½	2/3	–	2/3	2/3	2/3	2/3			
W. de Meriet	–	2/3	–	–	–	–	–	–	–	–	–	–			
Rad. de Abbedesbiri, Ad. Reymund, Th. de Merton, Pet. Flori, Ric. Crok, J. de Corf	–	2/2	2/2	2/2	1/9¾	1/9¾	2/2	–	2/2	2/2	2/2	2/2			
Rob. de Schute	–	2/2	2/2	2/2	1/9¾	1/9¾	2/2	–	–	–	–	–			
J. Luve	–	2/1	–	–	–	–	–	–	–	–	–	–			
Walt. de Somersete	–	2/0	2/0	2/0	1/8	1/8	2/0	–	–	2/0	–	2/0			
Walt. de Luvepit	–	2/0	2/0	2/0	1/8	1/8	2/0	–	2/0	2/0	2/0	2/0			
J. de Lolleworth, Warin de Compton, Rob. de Chinnok	–	2/0	–	–	–	–	–	–	–	–	–	–			
Ad. le Gay	–	2/0	2/0	2/0	1/8	1/8	2/0	–	2/0	2/0	2/0	2/0			
J. de Forde, Hugh de Morton	–	1/10	1/10	1/10	1/7½	1/6½	1/10	–	1/10	1/10	1/10	1/10			
Will. de Wodebiri	–	1/10	1/10	1/10	1/7½	1/6½	1/10	–	1/10	–	–	–			
Pet. de Athelingenie, J. de Bradenstoke	–	1/6	1/6	1/6	1/3	1/3	1/6	–	1/6	1/6	1/6	1/6			
Stephen le Gay	–	–	–	–	–	–	–	–	–	–	1/6	1/6			

[1308–9 cont.] WEEK:	1	2	3	4	5	6	7	8	9	10	11	12	13	14	15
Master W. carpenter	–	–	–	–	–	1/10½	2/3	–	2/3	2/3	2/3	2/3			
J. de Coscombe	–	–	–	–	–	–	–	–	2/2	2/2	2/2	2/2			
Walt. de Somerton	–	–	–	–	–	–	–	–	2/0	–	2/0	–			
Golofre	–	7/0	7/0	7/0	7/0	7/0	7/0	–	7/0	7/0	7/0	7/0			
MIDSUMMER															
Rob. de la Forde, Ric. de la Streme	2/3	2/3	2/3	2/3	1/10½	2/3	2/3	2/3	2/3	2/3	2/3	2/3	2/3	2/3	
R. de Abbedesbiri, Ad. Reymund, J. de Coscomb, Th. de Merton, Ric. Crok, J. de Corf	2/2	2/2	2/2	2/2	1/9¾	2/2	2/2	2/2	2/2	2/2	2/2	2/2	2/2	2/2	
P. Flori	2/2	–	–	–	–	–	–	–	–	–	–	–	–	–	
Walt. de Somersete	2/0	2/0	2/0	2/0	2/0	2/0	2/0	2/0	2/0	2/0	2/0	–	–	–	
Walt. de Lovepit	2/0	2/0	–	–	–	–	–	–	–	–	–	–	–	–	
Adam le Gay	2/0	–	2/0	2/0	1/8	2/0	2/0	–	–	2/0	2/0	2/0	2/0	2/0	
J. de Forde	1/10	1/10	–	–	–	–	–	–	–	–	–	1/10	1/10	1/10	
Hugh de Morton	1/10	–	–	–	–	–	1/10	1/10	1/10	1/10	1/10	1/10	1/10	1/10	
P. de Athelenye	1/6	–	–	–	–	–	–	–	–	–	–	–	–	–	
J. de Bradenstoke	1/6	1/6	1/6	1/3	1/6	1/6	1/6	1/6	1/6	1/6	1/6	1/6	1/6	1/6	
Steph. Gay	1/6	1/6	–	–	–	–	–	–	–	1/6	1/6	1/6	1/6	1/6	
Master W. carpenter	–	–	0/4½	–	–	–	–	–	1/1½	–	–	–	–	–	
Hen. de Poghehille	–	–	–	–	–	–	–	2/0	2/0	2/0	2/0	–	–	–	
Rob. Wyroc	–	–	–	–	–	–	–	1/10	1/10	1/10	1/10	–	–	–	
J. de Kingesbrigge	–	–	–	–	–	–	–	1/10	1/10	1/10	1/10	1/10	1/10	–	
Hen. de la Birchen	–	–	–	–	–	–	–	1/10	1/10	1/10	1/8	1/8	1/8	–	
Th. de Kilmington	–	–	–	–	–	–	–	1/9	1/9	1/9	1/9	1/9	1/9	1/9	
J. de Cherde, Rob. de Carswille	–	–	–	–	–	–	–	–	–	–	1/8	1/8	1/8	–	
Golofre	7/0	7/0	–	7/0	7/0	7/0	7/0	7/0	7/0	–	7/0	7/0	–	7/0	

2609 1309–10

No full wage-lists, see p. 212

2610 1310–11

MICHAELMAS	1	2	3	4	5	6	7	8	9	10	11	12	13
Rob. de Forde, Ric. de la Streme, J. de St Donato, Thom. de Gloucestr masons	2/3	2/3	2/3	2/3	2/3	1/10½	1/10½	1/10½	1/10½	1/10½	1/10½	1/10½	0/11¼
Rad. de Abbedesbiri, Ad. Reymund, Ric. Croc, Will. de Mochelni	2/2	2/2	2/2	2/2	2/2	1/9¾	1/9¾	1/9¾	1/9¾	1/9¾	1/9¾	1/9¾	0/10¾

[1310–11 cont.] WEEK:	1	2	3	4	5	6	7	8	9	10	11	12	13	14	15
J. de Corf, Hugh de Yle	2/2	2/2	2/2	2/2	2/2	1/9¾	1/9¾	1/9¾	1/9¾	1/9¾	1/9¾	1/9¾	–		
Galf. de Taunton, P. Chamund	2/1	2/1	2/1	2/1	2/1	1/9	1/9	1/9	1/9	1/9	1/9	1/9	–		
Adam Gay	2/1	2/1	2/1	2/1	2/1	1/9	1/9	1/9	1/9	1/9	1/9	1/9	0/10½		
Walter de Corf	2/0	2/0	0/8	–	–	–	1/8	1/8	1/8	1/8	1/8	1/8	–		
Walt. de Lovepitt, Reg. de Barnstaple	2/0	2/0	2/0	2/0	2/0	1/8	1/8	1/8	1/8	1/8	1/8	1/8	–		
Rob. de Kerdif	2/0	2/0	0/8	–	–	–	–	–	–	–	–	–	–		
J. de Sancto Fogano	–	2/0	0/8	–	–	–	–	–	–	–	–	–	–		
Galf. de Sancto Fogano, Galf. de Axeminstre	2/0	–	–	–	–	–	–	–	–	–	–	–	–		
J. de Parco	2/0	2/0	2/0	2/0	2/0	1/8	1/8	1/8	1/8	1/8	1/8	1/8	0/10		
Rob. Paves/Panes	2/0	2/0	2/0	2/0	2/0	–	–	–	–	–	–	–	–		
J. Luve	1/10	1/10	1/10	1/10	1/10	1/6½	1/6½	1/6½	1/6½	1/6½	1/6½	1/6½	0/9¼		
Will de Wistham/Wixtham	1/9	1/9	1/9	1/9	1/9	1/6	–	–	–	–	–	–	–		
J. de Bradenstoke, Steph. Gay, Will. de Taunton	1/8	1/8	1/8	1/8	1/8	1/6	1/6	1/6	1/6	1/6	1/6	1/6	0/9		
Rob. le Yunge	1/2	1/2	1/2	1/2	1/2	1/0	1/0	1/0	1/0	1/0	1/0	–	–		
Th. de Pederton, J. de Gardino	1/0	1/0	1/0	1/0	1/0	0/10	0/10	0/10	0/10	0/10	0/10	0/10	0/5		
Master Walt. carpenter	2/3	2/3	2/3	2/3	2/3	1/10½	1/10½	1/10½	1/10½	1/10½	1/10½	1/10½	–		
Will. de Saram	2/2	2/2	2/2	2/2	2/2	1/9¾	1/9¾	1/9¾	1/9¾	1/9¾	1/9¾	1/9¾	–		
Rob. Wyroc	–	–	–	1/10	1/10	1/6½	1/6½	1/6½	1/6½	1/6½	–	–	–		
J. de Merton	–	–	–	–	–	1/8	1/8	1/8	1/8	1/8	1/8	1/8	0/10		
James mason	–	–	–	–	–	1/6	1/6	1/6	1/6	–	–	–	–		
J. le Yunge	–	–	–	–	–	–	–	–	–	–	–	1/0	–		
Will. de Holdham	–	–	–	–	–	–	–	–	–	–	–	1/8	–		
Gilb. de Axeminstre	–	2/0	2/0	2/0	1/8	1/8	1/8	1/8	1/8	1/8	1/8	1/8	0/10		
CHRISTMAS															
Rad. de Abbedesbiri	–	1/9¾	1/9¾	1/9¾	1/9¾	1/9¾	1/9¾	1/9¾	1/6½	1/9¾	1/9¾	2/2	2/2	2/2	2/2
R. de Forde, R. de la Streme, J. de Sancto Donato	–	–	1/10½	1/10½	1/10½	1/10½	1/10½	1/10½	1/7	1/10½	1/10½	2/3	2/3	2/3	2/3
Th. de Gloucestre	–	–	1/10½	1/10½	1/10½	1/10½	1/10½	1/10½	–	–	–	–	–	–	–
Ad. Reymund, Ric. Croc, Will. de Mochelni, Hen. de Monte Acuto	–	–	1/9¾	1/9¾	1/9¾	1/9¾	1/9¾	1/9¾	1/6½	1/9¾	1/9¾	2/2	2/2	2/2	2/2
Peter Chamund	–	1/9	1/9	1/9	1/9	1/9	1/6	1/9	1/6	1/9	–	2/1	–	–	–
Walt. de Taunton	–	–	1/8	1/8	–	–	–	–	–	–	–	–	–	–	–
Walt. de Corf	–	–	1/8	1/8	1/8	1/8	1/8	1/8	1/4½	1/8	1/8	2/0	2/0	–	–
J. de Parco	–	–	1/8	1/8	1/8	1/8	1/8	1/8	1/4½	1/8	1/8	–	–	–	2/0
G. de Axeminstre	–	–	1/8	1/8	1/8	1/8	1/8	1/8	–	–	1/8	2/0	–	2/0	2/0
J. de Morton/Merton	–	–	1/8	1/8	1/8	1/8	1/8	1/8	1/4½	1/8	1/8	2/0	2/0	2/0	–
J. Luve	–	–	1/6½	1/6½	1/6½	1/6½	1/6½	1/6½	1/3½	1/6½	1/6½	1/10	–	–	–

[1310–11 cont.] WEEK:	1	2	3	4	5	6	7	8	9	10	11	12	13	14	15
Hen. de Polslo	–	–	1/6½	1/6½	1/6½	1/6½	1/6½	–	–	–	1/6½	1/10	–	–	–
J. de Bradenstok	–	–	1/6	1/6	1/6	1/6	1/6	1/6	1/3	1/6	1/6	1/9	1/9	1/9	1/9
J. de Gardino, Th. de Pederton	–	–	0/10	0/10	0/10	0/10	0/10	0/10	0/10	0/10	0/10	1/0	1/0	1/0	1/0
Will. de Wixtham	–	–	–	1/6	1/6	1/6	1/6	1/6	1/3	1/6	1/6	1/9	1/9	1/9	1/9
Walt. de Lovepit	–	–	–	–	1/8	1/8	1/8	1/8	1/4¾	1/8	1/8	2/0	2/0	2/0	2/0
Master W. carpenter	–	–	–	1/10½	–	–	–	–	–	1/10½	1/10½	2/3	2/3	2/3	2/3
W. de Saram	–	–	–	1/9¾	–	–	1/9¾	1/9¾	1/6½	1/9¾	1/9¾	2/1	2/2	2/2	2/2
J. Kylue	–	–	–	–	1/6½	1/6½	–	1/6½	1/3½	1/6½	1/6½	1/10	1/10	1/10	1/10
J. le Yunge	–	–	–	1/0	1/0	1/0	1/0	1/0	–	–	–	–	–	–	–
Walt. de Herford carpenter	–	–	–	–	–	1/9¾	–	–	–	–	–	–	–	–	–
W. de Bacabre	–	–	–	–	–	–	1/4	1/4	1/2	1/4	1/4	1/6	1/6	1/6	1/6
Will. Ataslade	–	–	–	–	–	–	–	–	1/3½	1/6½	1/8	2/0	–	2/0	2/0
R. Wyroc	–	–	–	–	–	–	–	–	1/5½	1/6	1/6	1/9	1/9	1/9	1/9
Hen. de Bruges	–	–	–	–	–	–	–	–	1/6	1/5½	–	–	–	–	–
R. le Yunge	–	–	–	–	–	–	–	–	0/10	1/0	1/0	1/2	1/2	1/2	1/2
J. le Fotur/Botur	–	–	–	–	–	–	–	–	–	1/8	1/8	2/0	–	–	2/0
Hen. de la Birche	–	–	–	–	–	–	–	–	–	1/6	–	–	–	–	–
Rob. de Bruges	–	–	–	–	–	–	–	–	–	1/5	1/5	–	–	–	–
J. de Sancto Fogano	–	–	–	–	–	–	–	–	–	–	–	1/10½	–	–	–
Reg. de Barnstaple	–	–	–	–	–	–	–	–	–	–	–	1/8	–	–	–
Rob. Paves	–	–	–	–	–	–	–	–	–	–	1/9	2/1	–	–	2/1
J. de Stoke	–	–	–	–	–	–	–	–	–	–	–	–	–	2/0	–
EASTER															
Rob. de Forde, Ric. de la Streme, John de Sancto Donato	–	2/3	2/3	1/10½	2/3	2/3	2/3	–	2/3	2/3	2/3				
R. Abbedesbiri, A. Reymund, R. Croc	–	2/2	2/2	1/9¾	2/2	2/2	2/2	–	2/2	2/2	2/2				
Symon de Cerne	–	2/2	–	–	–	–	–	–	–	–	–				
Walt. de Lovepit, Will. Ataslade, J. de Stoke, J. de Parco	–	2/0	2/0	1/8	2/0	2/0	2/0	–	2/0	2/0	2/0				
Rob. Paves	–	2/1	2/1	–	–	–	–	–	–	–	–				
Galf. de Taunton	–	2/1	2/1	1/9	2/1	2/1	2/1	–	2/1	2/1	2/1				
J. Kylve	–	1/10	–	–	–	–	–	–	–	–	–				
J. de Bradenstoke	–	1/9	1/9	1/6	1/9	1/9	1/9	–	1/9	1/9	1/9				
Will. de Wistham, Rob. Wyroc	–	1/9	–	–	–	–	–	–	–	–	–				
Will. de Bacabre	–	1/6	1/6	1/4	1/6	1/6	1/6	–	1/6	1/6	1/6				
Rob. le Younge	–	1/2	1/2	1/0	1/2	1/2	1/2	–	1/2	1/2	1/2				
Th. de Pederton, J. de Gardino	–	1/0	1/0	0/10	1/0	1/0	1/0	–	1/0	1/0	1/0				
Master Walter carpenter	–	2/3	2/3	0/9	–	–	–	–	–	0/9	2/3				
Will. de Saram	–	2/2	2/2	–	–	–	–	–	–	–	–				
W. de Corf	–	–	2/0	1/8	2/0	2/0	2/0	–	2/0	2/0	2/0				

[1310–11 cont.] WEEK:	1	2	3	4	5	6	7	8	9	10	11	12	13	14	15
G. de Axminstre	—	—	2/0	1/8	2/0	2/0	2/0	—	2/0	—	—	—	—	—	
Reg. de Barnstaple	—	—	2/0	1/6½	1/10	1/10	1/10	—	1/10	1/10	1/10	—	—	—	
J. Luve, Thom. Wylet/Wilet	—	—	1/10	1/6½	—	—	—	—	—	—	1/9	—	—	—	
Will. Kilve	—	—	1/10	1/6	—	—	—	—	—	—	—	—	—	—	
Will. de Taunton	—	—	1/9	1/10½	1/9	1/9	1/9	—	1/9	1/9	—	—	—	—	
Dygon de Crane	—	—	—	1/6	2/3	2/3	2/3	—	2/3	—	—	—	—	—	
Will. de Welles	—	—	—	—	1/9	1/9	1/9	—	1/9	—	—	—	—	—	
Thom. de Forde /Ataforde	—	—	—	—	—	1/9	1/9	—	1/8	1/8	—	—	—	—	
Will. Atabirche	—	—	—	—	—	1/8	1/8	—	1/8	1/8	—	—	—	—	
J. de Freysford /Freyford	—	—	—	—	—	—	—	—	2/1	2/1	2/1	—	—	—	
Peter Chamund	—	—	—	—	—	—	—	—	1/10	2/1	1/10	—	—	—	
J. Luci	—	—	—	—	—	—	—	—	1/9	1/8	1/9	—	—	—	
Walt. de Stafford	—	—	—	—	—	—	—	—	1/10	1/10	—	—	—	—	
Michael and his boy	—	—	—	—	—	—	—	—	1/9	4/4	—	—	—	—	
MIDSUMMER															
Rob. de Forde, Ric. de la Streme, John de Sancto Donato	2/3	2/3	2/3	2/3	2/3	2/3	2/3	2/3	2/3	2/3	2/3	2/3	2/3	2/3	
Rad. de Abbedesbiri, Ad. Reymund, Ric. Croc	2/2	2/2	2/2	2/2	2/2	2/2	2/2	2/2	2/0	2/2	2/2	2/2	2/2	2/2	
Galf. de Taunton	2/1	2/1	2/1	—	—	2/1	2/1	2/1	2/0	2/1	2/0	2/0	2/0	2/0	
Peter Chamund	2/0	2/0	2/0	2/0	2/0	2/0	2/0	2/0	2/0	2/0	2/0	2/0	2/0	2/0	
Walt. de Corf	2/0	2/0	2/0	2/0	2/0	2/0	2/0	2/0	2/0	2/0	2/0	2/0	2/0	2/0	
Walt. de Lovepit, J. de Stoke, Will. Ataslade, J. de Parco, J. de Freysford	2/0	2/0	2/0	2/0	2/0	2/0	2/0	2/0	2/0	2/0	2/0	2/0	2/0	2/0	
J. Luve, Th. Wylet	1/10	1/9	1/10	1/10	1/10	—	—	1/10	1/10	1/10	1/10	—	1/10	1/10	
Will. Atabirche/de la Birche	1/9	1/9	1/9	1/9	1/9	1/9	1/9	1/9	1/9	1/9	1/9	1/9	1/9	1/9	
J. de Bradenstoke, W. de Stafford, Will. de Taunton	1/9	1/9	1/9	1/9	1/9	1/9	1/9	1/9	1/9	1/9	—	1/9	1/9	1/9	
Will. de Bacalre	1/6	1/6	1/6	1/6	—	—	—	—	—	1/9	—	1/0	1/0	1/0	
Rob. le Younge	1/0	—	—	1/2	—	1/0	1/0	1/0	1/0	—	1/0	0/9	1/0	1/0	
Th. de Pederton, J. de Gardino	2/3	—	—	2/3	2/3	2/3	2/3	—	1/1½	—	—	—	—	—	
Master Walt. carpenter	2/3	2/3	1/1½	2/0	—	—	—	—	—	—	—	—	—	—	
Hen. Bosse	—	—	—	—	—	—	—	1/9	1/9	1/9	—	1/0	—	—	
Rob. Wyroc	—	—	—	—	—	—	—	1/9	1/0	1/9	—	—	—	—	
Th. de Forde	—	—	—	—	—	—	—	—	2/1	2/1	—	2/1	2/1	2/1	
Adam le Gay	—	—	—	—	—	—	—	—	1/10	1/10	—	1/10	1/10	1/10	
J. Luci	—	—	—	—	—	—	—	—	1/9	1/9	—	1/9	1/9	1/9	
Will. de Brompton	—	—	—	—	—	—	—	—	—	1/10	—	—	—	—	
Galf. de Beredon	—	—	—	—	—	—	—	—	—	—	—	—	—	—	

[1310–11 cont.] WEEK:	1	2	3	4	5	6	7	8	9	10	11	12	13	14	15
J. de Lolleworthi	–	–	–	–	–	–	–	–	–	–	2/0	2/0	2/0	2/0	
Reg. de Brompton, Reg. de Barnstaple	–	–	–	–	–	–	–	–	–	–	2/0	–	–	–	
J. de Brompton	–	–	–	–	–	–	–	–	–	–	1/9	1/9	–	1/9	
Mich. le Daubour with his boy	–	–	–	–	4/4	4/4	4/4	–	–	–	–	–	–	–	
Rad. de Beredon	–	–	–	–	–	–	–	–	–	–	1/10	1/10	1/10	1/10	
2611 1312–13															
MICHAELMAS															
R. de Ford, Ric. de la Streme	2/3	2/6	2/3	2/3	1/10½	?	?	?	1/10½	1/10½	1/10½	?			
Ric. de Malmesbiri mason	2/3	2/6	2/3	2/3	1/10½	–	–	?	–	–	–	–			
Rad. de Abbedesbiri, Hen. de Witein	2/2	2/2	2/2	2/2	1/9¾	1/9¾	1/9¾	1/9¾	1/9¾	1/9¾	1/9¾	1/9¾			
Ad. Gay, Galf. de Axem, Peter Chamund, Ph. de Sotton	2/1	2/1	2/1	2/1	1/9	?	1/9	1/5¾	1/9	1/9	1/9	1/9			
Will. de Mochelni, Ric. Croc	2/2	2/2	2/2	2/2	1/9¾	–	1/9¾	1/9¾	1/9¾	1/9¾	1/9¾	1/9¾			
Walt. de Louepit, Will. Frik	2/0	2/0	2/0	2/0	1/8	?	1/8	?	1/8	1/8	1/8	1/8			
John de Lolleworth, J. de Stoke	2/0	2/0	2/0	2/0	–	–	1/8	–	–	–	–	–			
H. de Merton/Morton	2/0	2/0	2/0	2/0	–	–	–	–	–	–	–	–			
John de Forde	2/0	2/0	2/0	2/0	–	–	–	–	–	–	–	?			
John de Merton/Morton	2/0	2/0	2/0	2/0	–	–	1/8	1/4¾	1/8	1/8	–	–			
Ric. de Horsi	2/0	2/0	2/0	2/0	–	–	1/8	1/4¾	1/8	1/8	1/8	1/8			
Thom. Reymund	1/11	1/11	1/11	1/11	1/7¾	–	1/7¾	1/4	–	–	–	–			
J. de Cerne	1/11	1/11	1/11	1/11	–	?	1/7¾	1/4	1/7¾	–	1/9¾	–			
Rob. de Stoke	1/10	1/10	1/10	1/10	–	?	–	1/3¼	1/6½	1/6½	1/2½	1/6½			
Thom. Wylet	1/10	1/10	1/10	1/10	1/6½	–	–	–	–	–	–	–			
Will. de Taunton	1/10	1/10	1/10	1/10	1/8	–	–	1/3¼	1/6½	1/6½	1/2½	1/6½			
Stephen Gay	1/10	1/10	1/10	1/10	1/8	–	1/6½	1/3¼	1/6½	1/6½	1/2½	1/6½			
Hen. de Sotton	1/8	1/8	1/8	1/8	–	–	–	–	–	–	–	–			
J. Fabel	1/6	1/6	1/6	1/6	–	–	–	–	–	–	–	–			
J. de Gardino	1/0	1/0	1/0	1/0	0/10	–	0/10	0/10	0/10	0/10	0/10	0/10			
Ric. de Welles	–	–	–	–	–	?	1/8	1/4¾	1/8	1/8	1/8	1/8			
Hen. de la Birche	–	–	–	–	–	–	–	–	–	–	1/8	1/8			
Ric. de Stoke	–	–	–	–	–	–	1/6½	1/4¾	–	–	–	–			
Mich. le Dauber	–	–	–	–	–	–	2/0	–	–	–	–	–			
Ric. de Brompton	–	–	–	–	–	–	–	1/4¾	1/8	1/8	1/8	1/8			
Master Walt. carpenter	–	–	–	–	–	–	–	–	1/10½	1/10½	1/10½	–			
Will. de Monte Acuto	–	1/8	?	–	–	–	–	–	–	–	–	–			
Hen. de Criditon	–	–	–	–	–	–	–	–	1/10½	1/10½	–	–			
Will. Haileman	–	–	–	–	–	–	–	–	1/9¾	–	–	–			

[1312–13 cont.] WEEK:	1	2	3	4	5	6	7	8	9	10	11	12	13	14	15
Walt. de Horsi, Will. de Stoke	–	–	–	–	1/6½	–	–	–	–	–	–	–			
CHRISTMAS WEEK:	3	4	5	6	7	8	9	10	11	12	13	14	15	16	
Rob. de Forde, Ric. de la Streme	1/10½	1/10½	1/10½	1/10½	1/10½	1/10½	1/6¾	1/10½	1/10½	2/3	2/3	2/3	2/3	2/3	
Rad. de Abbedesbiri, Ric. Croc, Hen. de Witein	1/9¾	1/9¾	1/9¾	1/9¾	1/9¾	1/9¾	1/6¼	1/9¾	1/9¾	2/2	2/2	2/2	2/2	2/2	
G. de Axem	1/9	1/9	1/9	1/9	1/9	1/9	1/6	1/9	1/9	2/1	2/1	2/1	2/1	2/1	
Pet. Chamund	1/9	1/9	1/9	1/9	1/9	1/9	1/6	1/9	1/9	2/2	2/2	2/2	2/2	2/2	
Walt. de Lovepit	1/8	1/8	1/8	1/8	1/8	1/8	1/4¾	1/8	1/8	–	–	–	–	–	
W. Frik, Hen. de la Birche	1/8	1/8	1/8	1/8	1/8	1/8	1/4¾	1/8	1/8	2/0	2/0	2/0	2/0	2/0	
Hugh de Morton	1/8	–	–	–	–	–	–	–	–	–	–	–	–	–	
Will. de Taunton	1/6½	1/6½	1/6½	1/6½	1/6½	1/6½	1/3¼	1/6½	1/6½	1/10	1/10	1/10	1/10	1/10	
J. de Gardino	0/10	0/10	0/10	0/10	0/10	0/10	0/10	0/10	0/10	–	–	–	–	–	
W. de Mochelni	–	1/9¾	1/9¾	1/9¾	1/9¾	1/9¾	1/6¼	1/9¾	1/9¾	2/2	2/2	2/2	2/2	2/2	
Ad. Gay	–	1/9	1/9	1/9	–	–	–	–	–	–	–	–	–	–	
Ric. de Horsi, J. Lolleworth	–	1/8	1/8	1/8	1/8	1/8	1/4¾	1/8	1/8	2/0	2/0	2/0	2/0	2/0	
Ric. de Stoke	–	1/6½	1/6½	1/6½	1/9	1/9	1/6	1/9	1/9	2/1	2/1	2/1	2/1	2/1	
Rob. de Stoke	–	–	–	–	1/6½	1/6½	1/3¼	1/6½	1/6½	1/10	1/10	1/10	1/10	1/10	
R. de Beredon	–	–	–	–	–	–	1/3¼	1/6½	–	–	–	–	–	–	
Rob. de Pederton	–	–	–	–	–	–	–	–	1/6½	–	–	–	–	–	
J. le Parkere/de Parco	–	–	–	–	–	–	–	–	–	2/0	2/0	2/0	2/0	–	
Ric. de Pederton	–	–	–	–	–	–	–	–	–	1/10	1/10	1/10	1/10	1/10	
Thom. de Pederton	–	–	–	–	–	–	–	–	–	1/10	1/8	1/8	1/8	1/8	
Thom. de Meryet	–	–	–	–	–	–	–	–	–	1/8	–	–	–	–	
Ric. de Merton	–	–	–	–	–	–	–	–	–	–	1/10	1/10	1/10	1/10	
Ric. Dygon	–	–	–	–	–	–	–	–	–	–	–	–	–	2/3	
Master Walt. carpenter	–	–	–	1/4	1/10½	1/10½	–	1/10½	–	2/3	2/3	2/3	2/3	2/3	
Ad. de Chuddelee	–	–	–	–	–	–	–	–	–	2/2	2/2	2/2	2/2	2/2	
Crop Penung	–	–	–	–	–	–	–	–	–	–	2/0	–	1/10	–	
Robert de Galmeton	–	–	–	–	–	–	–	–	–	–	–	–	2/2	2/2	
J. Schire	–	–	–	–	–	–	–	–	–	–	–	–	1/6	–	
EASTER WEEK:	1	2	3	4	5	6	7	8	9	10					
R. de Ford, R. de la Streme	–	2/3	1/10½	2/3	2/3	2/3	2/3	–	2/3	2/3					
R. Digon stone cutter	–	2/3	2/9	2/9	2/3	2/3	2/3	–	2/3	2/3					
Rad. de Abbedesbiri, Ric. Croc, W. de Mochelni, P. Chamund	–	2/2	1/9¾	2/2	2/2	2/2	2/2	–	2/2	2/2					
G. de Axem	–	2/1	1/9	2/1	2/1	2/1	2/1	–	2/1	2/1					
Will. Fric, J. de Lolleworth, Th. Wylet, Thom. Reymund, J. de Freiford, Hugh de Morton	–	2/0	1/8	2/0	2/0	2/0	2/0	–	2/0	2/0					

WEEK:	1	2	3	4	5	6	7	8	9	10	11	12	13	14	15
[1312–13 cont.]															
J. de Forde	—	2/0	1/8	—	2/0	2/0	2/0	—	2/0	2/0					
John le Bailiff, W. de Taunton	—	1/11	1/7½	—	1/11	1/11	1/11	—	1/9	1/9					
Thom. de Pederton	—	1/8	1/5½	1/8	1/8	1/8	1/8	—	1/8	1/8					
J. de Weston	—	—	2/2	2/2	2/2	2/2	2/2	—	2/2	2/2					
R. de Beredon, W. de Wicroft	—	—	2/0	2/0	2/0	2/0	2/0	—	2/0	2/0					
J. Fabel	—	—	1/9	1/9	1/9	1/9	1/9	—	1/9	1/9					
Master Walt. carpenter	—	2/3	1/10½	2/3	2/3	2/3	2/3	—	2/3	—					
Adam de Chuddelee	—	2/2	1/9¾	2/2	2/2	2/3	—	—	2/2	—					
W. de Holdeham	—	—	—	—	2/0	2/0	—	—	2/2	—					
J. de Stouton	—	—	—	—	—	—	2/0	—	2/1	2/1					
J. de Fonte	—	—	—	—	—	—	2/1	—	1/8	1/8					
J. de Sauser	—	—	—	—	—	—	—	—	—	2/2					
R. de Galmeton	2/0	—	—	—	—	—	—	—	—	—					
Crop Penung	—	1/8	—	—	—	—	—	—	—	—					
MIDSUMMER															
R. de Forde, R. de la Streme, R. Dygon	2/3	2/3	2/3	2/3	2/3	2/3	2/3	2/3	2/3	2/3	2/3	2/3	2/3	2/3	
R. de Abbedesbiri, R. Croc, P. Chamund	2/2	2/2	2/2	2/2	2/2	2/2	2/2	2/2	2/2	2/2	2/2	2/2	2/2	2/2	
Will. de Mochelni	2/2	2/2	2/2	2/2	2/2	2/2	2/2	2/2	2/2	2/2	2/2	—	—	—	
J. de Weston	2/1	2/1	2/1	2/1	2/1	2/1	2/1	2/1	2/1	2/1	2/1	—	2/1	2/1	
Gilb. de Axem	2/0	2/0	2/0	2/0	2/0	2/0	2/0	2/0	2/0	2/0	2/0	—	2/0	2/0	
W. Fric, T. Wilet, J. de Forde	2/0	2/0	2/0	2/0	2/0	2/0	2/0	2/0	2/0	2/0	—	—	—	—	
Hugh Morton	1/10	—	2/0	—	—	—	—	—	—	—	—	—	—	—	
W. de Taunton	2/0	2/0	2/0	—	—	—	—	—	—	—	—	—	—	—	
W. de Wircroft, J. de Lolleworth	—	—	—	—	2/0	2/0	2/0	—	—	—	—	2/0	2/0	2/0	
J. de Merton	—	—	—	1/10	1/10	1/10	1/10	1/10	1/8	—	1/8	1/10	1/8	1/8	
Thom. de Pederton, Rob. Kech	1/8	?	1/8	1/8	1/8	1/8	1/8	1/8	1/8	1/8	—	—	1/10	—	
J. de Meret	—	1/10	—	—	—	—	—	—	—	—	—	—	—	—	
W. de Holdeham	—	—	—	—	—	—	—	—	2/0	2/0	2/0	2/0	2/0	2/0	
J. Sauser	2/1	2/1	2/1	—	—	—	—	—	—	—	—	—	—	—	
J. de Stouton	2/2	2/0	2/0	2/0	—	—	—	—	—	—	—	—	—	—	
Th. Reymund	2/1	2/1	2/1	—	—	—	—	—	—	—	—	—	—	—	
J. de Freyford, R. de Beredon	2/0	2/0	—	—	—	—	—	—	—	—	—	—	—	—	
J. le Bailiff	2/0	1/10	—	—	—	—	—	—	—	—	—	—	—	—	
J. Fabel	1/10	1/10	—	—	—	—	—	—	—	—	—	—	—	—	
Master Walt. carpenter	—	—	—	—	—	—	—	—	2/3	2/3	2/3	2/0	2/0	2/0	
Benedict Scrogeyn carpenter	—	—	—	—	—	—	—	—	2/0	2/0	2/0	1/10	1/10	2/0	
Crop Penung	—	—	—	—	—	—	—	—	1/9	1/9	1/9	1/9	1/9	—	
Ric. de Brigges /Bruges /Burges	—	—	—	—	—	—	—	—	1/9	2/3	2/3	2/3	2/3	—	
Will. de Membiri	—	—	—	—	—	—	2/3	2/3	—	—	—	—	—	—	

2612 1316–17

MICHAELMAS WEEK:	1	2	3	4	5	6	7	8	9	10	11	12	13	14	15
Ric. de la Streme, Rob. de Ford masons	2/3	2/3	2/3	2/3	2/3	1/6¾	1/10½	1/10½	1/10½	1/10½	1/10½	1/10½	1/6¼		
Rad. de Abbedesbiri, P. Chamund, John de Parco/de la More Parco	2/2	2/2	2/2	2/2	2/2	1/6¼	1/9¾	1/9¾	1/9¾	1/9¾	1/9¾	1/9¾	1/6¼		
John de Gardino, J. Bailly	2/0	2/0	2/0	2/0	2/0	1/4¾	1/8	1/8	1/8	1/8	1/8	1/8	1/4¾		
J. de Wyxt	2/0	2/0	2/0	2/0	2/0	1/4¾	1/8	1/8	–	–	–	–	–		
John Luve/Luva	0/6	0/6	0/6	0/6	0/6	0/4	0/5	0/5	0/5	0/5	0/5	0/5	0/4		
Will. de Membiri carpenter	2/3	2/3	2/3	2/3	2/3	1/6¾	1/10½	1/10½	–	1/10½	–	–	–		
W. Lacy carpenter	2/0	2/0	2/0	2/0	2/0	1/4¾	1/8	–	–	–	1/8	1/8	–		
Tho. Wite carpenter	1/8	2/0	2/0	1/0	–	–	–	–	–	–	–	–	–		
John Prodom carpenter	1/7	–	1/7	1/7	1/7	1/1½	1/4	1/4	–	1/4	1/4	1/4	1/1½		
Benedict	–	–	2/0	2/0	2/0	–	1/8	–	–	–	–	–	–		
J. de Colyton	–	–	1/8	–	–	–	–	–	–	–	–	–	–		
J. de Hatheheie/Yatheheye	–	–	1/6	1/6	1/6	1/0½	1/3	1/3	–	1/4	–	–	–		
Sim. de Oggeburghe/Coggeburghe	–	–	1/6	1/6	1/6	1/0½	1/3	1/3	–	–	–	–	–		
Hamund mason	–	–	–	–	–	1/4½	–	–	–	–	–	–	–		
W. de la Slade, J. Grace masons	–	–	–	–	–	–	1/8	1/8	–	–	–	–	–		
Rob. de Galmeton carpenter	–	–	–	–	–	–	–	1/10	–	–	–	–	–		
Thom. Weylands carpenter	–	–	–	–	–	–	–	1/6½	–	–	–	–	–		
J. de Hagenedon carpenter	–	–	–	–	–	–	–	–	–	1/4	–	–	–		
CHRISTMAS															
R. de la Streme, R. de Forde	–	1/10½	1/10½	1/10½	1/10½	1/10½	1/10½	1/10½	1/6¾	1/10½	1/10½	2/3	2/3	2/3	
R. de Abbedesbiri, J. de Parco	–	1/9¾	1/9¾	1/9¾	1/9¾	1/9¾	1/9¾	1/9¾	1/6¾	1/9¾	1/9¾	2/2	2/2	2/2	
J. de Gardino	–	1/8	1/8	1/8	–	–	–	–	–	1/8	1/8	2/0	2/0	2/0	
J. Bailly/Baillif	–	1/8	1/8	1/8	–	–	–	–	–	–	–	–	–	–	
Pet. Chamund	–	–	1/9¾	1/9¾	1/9¾	1/9¾	1/9¾	1/9¾	1/6¾	1/9¾	1/9¾	2/2	2/2	2/2	
J. Luve	–	–	0/5	0/5	0/5	0/5	0/5	0/5	0/4	0/5	0/5	0/6	0/6	0/6	
Ric. Foghel/Fogel	–	–	–	0/11¼	1/10½	1/10½	1/10½	1/10½	1/6¾	1/10½	1/10½	2/3	2/3	2/3	
W. de Membiri carpenter	–	–	–	–	–	–	–	1/10½	1/6¾	1/10½	1/10½	2/3	–	–	
Will. Laci carpenter	–	–	–	–	–	–	–	1/8	1/4¾	1/8	1/8	2/1	–	–	
J. Grace	–	–	–	–	–	–	–	–	–	1/8	1/8	2/0	2/0	2/0	
Th. Wite carpenter	–	–	–	–	–	–	–	–	–	1/8	1/8	–	1/4	–	
John Prodome	–	–	–	–	–	–	–	–	–	1/4½	1/4½	1/7	1/0	–	
J. de Camera	–	–	–	–	–	–	–	–	–	–	1/8	2/0	2/0	2/0	
Walt. Freynsche	–	–	–	–	–	–	–	–	–	–	–	2/1	–	–	
Warun. de Axem	–	–	–	–	–	–	–	–	–	–	–	1/4	0/10	–	
Symon de Oggeburghe	–	–	–	–	–	–	–	–	–	–	–	0/2	–	–	
R. de Galmeton carpenter	–	–	–	–	–	–	–	–	–	–	1/10	2/2	–	–	

[1316–17 cont.]

WEEK:	1	2	3	4	5	6	7	8	9	10	11	12	13	14	15
EASTER															
R. de la Streme, R. de Forde	1/1½	2/3	2/3	2/3	1/10½	2/3	2/3	—	2/3	2/3	2/3	2/3	—	—	—
R. Foghel	1/1½	2/3	2/3	?	—	—	—	—	—	—	—	—	—	—	—
Peter Chamound, R. Abbedesbiri	1/1	2/2	2/2	2/2	1/9¾	2/2	2/2	—	2/2	2/2	2/2	2/2	—	—	—
J. Gardino	1/0	2/0	2/0	2/0	1/8	2/0	2/0	—	2/0	2/0	2/0	2/0	—	—	—
J. Grace	1/0	2/0	2/0	2/0	—	2/0	2/0	—	2/0	2/0	—	—	—	—	—
J. Lewe/Leue	0/3	0/6	0/6	0/6	0/6	0/6	?	—	0/6	0/6	0/6	0/6	—	—	—
R. Croc, J. de Parco	—	2/2	2/2	2/2	1/9¾	2/2	2/0	—	2/2	2/2	2/2	2/2	—	—	—
W. Slade	—	2/0	2/0	2/0	?	2/0	—	—	2/0	2/0	2/2	2/2	—	—	—
J. Chaumberlayn	—	—	2/0	?	—	—	—	—	2/2	2/2	—	—	—	—	—
J. de Forde	—	—	—	—	2/0	2/0	2/0	—	2/0	2/0	—	—	—	—	—
Will. de Stokelond	—	—	—	—	1/8	1/8	1/8	1/8	1/8	1/8	1/8	1/8	—	—	—
R. de Galmeton	—	0/9	—	—	—	—	—	—	—	—	1/9½	0/4½	—	—	—
Ad. de Chuddelegh carpenter	—	—	—	—	—	—	2/0	—	—	—	—	—	—	—	—
MIDSUMMER															
R. de la Streme, R. de Forde	2/3	2/3	2/3	2/3	2/3	2/3	2/3	2/3	2/3	2/3	2/3	2/3	2/3	—	—
R. Abbedesbiri, Peter Chamound, R. Croc, J. de Parco	2/2	2/2	2/2	2/2	2/2	2/2	2/2	2/2	2/2	2/2	2/2	2/2	2/2	—	—
J. de Gardino	2/0	2/0	2/0	2/0	2/0	2/0	2/0	2/0	2/0	2/0	2/0	2/0	—	—	—
W. de Stoke mason	1/8	1/8	1/8	1/8	1/8	1/8	1/8	1/8	1/8	1/8	1/8	1/8	1/8	—	—
J. Walauns/Walanz	1/6	1/6	—	—	—	—	—	—	—	—	—	—	—	—	—
J. Love/Leve	0/6	0/6	0/6	0/6	0/6	0/6	0/6	0/6	0/6	0/6	0/6	0/6	0/6	—	—
J. de Forde mason	2/0	2/0	2/0	2/0	2/0	2/0	2/0	2/0	2/0	2/0	2/0	2/0	2/0	—	—
W. de Slade mason	2/0	2/0	2/0	2/0	2/0	1/0	2/0	2/0	2/0	2/0	2/0	—	—	—	—
J. Chamberlayn mason	—	—	—	—	—	—	—	—	—	—	—	—	—	—	—
J. Pestouri mason	—	—	1/8	1/8	1/8	1/8	1/8	1/8	1/8	1/8	1/8	—	1/8	—	—
Ric. de Wyzt	—	—	—	—	—	—	—	—	—	—	1/8	—	—	—	—
J. de Stoke	—	—	—	—	2/2	—	—	—	—	—	—	—	—	—	—
Rob. Galmeton carpenter	2/2	—	1/1	2/2	2/3	2/2	—	—	2/2	—	—	—	1/8	—	—
Will de Membiri	—	—	—	0/8	2/2	—	—	—	—	—	—	—	—	—	—
Walter Frensch	—	—	—	0/7	1/9	—	—	—	—	—	—	—	—	—	—
Edeward	—	—	—	0/6½	1/7	—	—	—	—	—	—	—	—	—	—
Symon	—	—	—	—	2/0	2/0	—	—	—	—	—	—	—	—	—
W. Laci	—	—	—	—	—	0/3½	—	—	—	—	—	—	—	—	—
J. Prodomme	—	—	—	—	—	—	—	—	—	—	—	—	—	—	—

2612A ALTAR 1316–17

WEEK:	**1**	**2**	**3**	**4**	**5**	**6**	**7**	**8**	**9**	**10**	**11**	**12**	**13**	**14**	**15**
John de Baunebiri	2/9	2/9	2/9	2/9	2/9	2/9	2/9	2/9	2/9	2/9	2/9	2/9	2/9	2/9	2/9
Rob. Payne	–	2/9	2/9	2/9	2/9	2/9	2/9	2/9	2/9	2/9	2/9	2/9	2/9	2/9	2/9
Adam son of John Baunebiri	0/9	0/9	0/9	0/9	0/9	0/9	0/9	0/9	0/9	0/9	0/9	0/9	0/7	0/7	0/7
Robert Ataboxe	–	–	–	–	–	–	–	1/2	2/4	2/4	2/4	2/4	2/6	2/6	2/6
WEEK:	**16**	**17**	**18**	**19**	**20**	**21**	**22**	**23**	**24**	**25**	**26**	**27**	**28**	**29**	**30**
J. de Baunebiri, Rob. Payne	2/9	2/9	2/9	2/9	1/11	2/4	2/4	2/4	2/4	2/4	2/4	2/4	2/4	1/11	2/4
Adam de Baunebiri	0/7	0/7	0/7	0/7	0/7	0/7	0/5	0/6	0/6	0/6	0/6	0/6	0/6	0/5	0/6
Rob. Ataboxe	2/6	2/6	2/6	2/6	2/6	2/6	1/9	2/1	2/1	2/1	2/1	2/1	2/1	1/9	2/1
Hugh de Dorsete, Peter de Dene	2/3	2/3	2/3	2/3	2/3	2/3	1/7	1/10½	1/10½	1/10½	1/10½	1/10½	1/10½	1/7	1/10½
John de la Chaumbre/de Camera	–	–	–	–	–	–	–	–	–	1/8	1/8	1/8	1/8	1/4¾	1/8
R. de Galmeton carpenter	–	–	–	–	–	–	–	–	–	–	–	–	–	0/11	–
WEEK:	**31**	**32**	**33**	**34**	**35**	**36**	**37**	**38**	**39**	**40**	**41**	**42**	**43**	**44**	**45**
John de Baunebiri	2/4	2/4	2/4	2/4	2/4	2/4	1/11	2/4	2/4	2/9	2/9	2/9	1/4½	2/9	2/9
Rob. Payne	2/4	2/4	2/4	2/4	2/4	2/4	1/11	2/4	2/4	–	2/9	2/9	–	–	–
Adam de Baunebiri	0/6	0/6	0/6	0/6	0/6	0/6	0/5	0/6	0/6	0/7	0/7	0/7	0/3½	0/7	0/7
Rob. Ataboxe	2/1	2/1	2/1	2/1	2/1	2/1	1/9	2/1	2/1	2/6	2/6	2/6	1/3	2/6	2/6
Hugh de Dorsete	1/10½	1/10½	1/10½	1/10½	1/10½	1/10½	1/7	1/10½	1/10½	2/3	2/3	2/3	–	–	–
Peter de Dene	1/10½	1/10½	1/10½	1/10½	1/10½	1/10½	1/7	1/10½	1/10½	2/3	2/3	2/3	1/1½	2/3	2/3
John de la Chaumbre	1/8	1/8	1/8	1/8	1/8	1/8	1/4¾	1/8	–	–	–	–	–	–	–
Th. Atteboxe	–	–	1/10½	1/10½	1/10½	1/10½	1/7	1/10½	1/10½	2/3	2/3	2/3	1/1½	2/3	2/3
Ph. (Walt.?) de Wirale	–	0/9	–	–	1/6	1/6	1/3	1/6	1/6	1/9	1/9	1/9	0/10½	1/9	1/9
Elias de Nyweton	–	–	–	–	–	–	–	–	–	–	–	–	–	1/6	2/3
J. de Eston	–	–	–	–	–	–	–	–	–	–	–	–	–	2/3	2/3
WEEK:	**46**	**47**	**48**	**49**	**50**	**51**	**52**	**53**	**54**	**55**	**56**	**57**	**58**	**59**	**60**
J. de Baunebiri	2/9	2/3½	2/9	2/9	2/9	2/9	2/9	2/9	2/9	2/9	2/9	2/9	2/9	2/9	2/9
R. Attaboxe	2/6	2/1	2/6	2/6	2/6	2/6	2/6	2/6	2/6	2/6	2/6	2/6	2/6	2/6	2/6
Adam de Baunebiri	0/7	0/3	0/7	0/7	0/7	0/7	0/7	0/7	0/7	0/7	0/7	0/7	0/7	0/7	0/7
Ph. de Wirale	1/5½	1/9	1/9	1/9	1/9	1/9	1/9	1/9	1/9	1/9	1/9	1/9	1/9	1/9	1/9
Peter de Dene, Th. Ataboxe, E. de Nyweton, J. de Eston	2/3	1/10½	2/3	2/3	2/3	2/3	2/3	2/3	2/3	2/3	2/3	2/3	2/3	2/3	2/3
J. de Gardino, Rob. Copa mason	–	–	–	–	–	2/0	–	–	–	–	–	–	–	–	–
J. Grace	–	–	–	–	–	–	2/0	1/6	2/0	2/0	2/0	2/0	2/0	2/0	2/0
Walt. Daunteshere	–	–	–	–	–	–	1/8	1/8	1/8	1/8	1/8	–	–	–	–
Symon Snele/Snelle	–	–	–	–	–	–	1/1	1/1	1/1	1/1	1/1	1/1	1/1	1/1	1/1
WEEK:	**61**	**62**	**63**	**64**	**65**	**66**									
J. de Baunebiri	2/9	2/9	–	–	–	–									
R. Ataboxe	2/6	2/6	2/6	2/6	2/6	2/6									
Peter de Dene, Th. Ataboxe, J. de Easton, Elias de Nyweton	2/3	2/3	2/3	2/3	2/3	2/3									

[ALTAR 1316–17 cont.] WEEK:	61	62	63	64	65	66
Adam de Baunebiri	0/7	0/7	–	–	–	–
Ph. de Wirale/Wyrrale	1/9	1/9	1/9	1/9	1/9	1/9
J. Grace	2/0	–	–	–	–	–
Symon Snele/Snelle	1/1	1/1	1/1	1/1	1/1	1/1
J. de Hornton	–	1/8	1/8	1/8	1/8	1/8

2613 1317–18

No full wage-lists, see p. 212

2614 1318–19

MICHAELMAS WEEK:	1	2	3	4	5	6	7	8	9	10	11	12	13	14	15
R. de Forde, J. Baret	2/3	2/3	2/3	2/3	1/6¾	1/10½	1/10½	1/6¾	1/10½	1/10½	1/10½	1/10½			
R. Abbed	2/2	2/2	2/2	2/2	1/6¼	1/9¾	1/9¾	1/9¾	1/9¾	1/9¾	1/9¾	1/9¾			
R. Croc	2/2	2/2	–	–	–	–	–	–	–	–	–	–			
J. de Parco	2/2	2/2	2/2	2/2	1/6¼	1/9¾	1/9¾	1/6¼	1/8	1/8	1/8	1/8			
J. Chamberleyn	2/0	2/0	2/0	2/0	1/4½	1/8	1/8	1/4½	1/8	1/8	1/8	1/8			
R. Priour	2/0	2/0	–	–	–	–	–	–	–	–	–	–			
R. Waleys	1/10	1/10	1/10	1/10	1/3¼	1/6½	1/6½	1/3¼	1/6½	1/6½	1/6½	1/6½			
J. plasterer	1/10	1/10	–	–	–	–	–	–	–	–	–	–			
J. Leva	0/6	0/6	0/6	0/6	0/4	0/6	0/6	0/5	0/6	0/6	0/6	0/6			
R. Galmeton, Nich. Frensch	2/2	2/2	2/2	2/2	1/6¼	1/10	1/10	1/6½	1/10	1/10	1/10	1/10			
Walt. Frensch	2/2	–	–	–	–	–	–	–	–	–	–	–			
Adam Baunebiri	–	1/0	1/0	1/0	0/8½	0/10	0/10	0/8½	0/10	0/10	0/10	0/10			
Peter de Dene	–	–	–	–	–	1/10½	1/10½	1/6¾	1/10½	1/10½	–	1/10½			
J. de Eston, Eli. de Nyweton	–	–	–	–	–	1/10½	1/10½	1/6¾	1/10½	1/10½	1/10½	1/10½			
Symon	–	–	–	–	–	1/1½	1/1½	1/1½	1/1½	–	1/1½	1/1½			
J. Daubour	–	–	–	–	–	–	–	–	–	–	–	1/6½			
CHRISTMAS															
R. de Forde, J. Baret, J. de Eston, E. de Nyweton	–	1/6¾	1/10½	1/10½	1/10½	1/10½	1/10½	1/10½	1/6¾	1/10½	1/10½	2/3	2/3	2/3	2/3
R. Abbedesbiri, J. de Parco	–	1/6¼	1/9¾	1/9¾	1/9¾	1/9¾	1/9¾	1/9¾	1/6¼	1/9¾	1/9¾	2/2	2/2	2/2	2/2
J. Chamberleyn	–	1/4½	1/8	1/8	1/8	1/8	1/8	1/8	1/4½	1/8	1/8	2/0	2/0	2/0	2/0
R. Waleys	–	1/3¼	1/6½	1/6½	1/6½	1/6½	1/6½	1/6½	1/3	1/6½	1/6½	1/10	1/10	1/10	1/10
Ad. Baunebiri	–	0/8½	0/10	0/10	0/10	0/10	–	0/10	0/8½	–	–	–	–	–	–
Symon	–	0/11¼	1/1½	1/1½	1/1½	2/3	1/1½	1/1½	0/11½	1/1½	1/1½	1/5	1/5	1/5	1/5
J. Leva	–	–	–	0/6	0/6	0/6	0/6	0/6	0/5	0/6	0/6	0/8	0/8	0/7	0/8
W. Frensch	–	–	–	1/10	1/10	–	–	–	–	–	1/10	2/2	2/2	2/2	2/2
R. Galmeton	–	–	–	0/11	1/10	1/10	1/10	1/10	1/6½	1/10	1/10	2/2	2/2	2/2	1/1
G. de la Batayle/de Bello	–	–	–	–	1/8	1/8	1/8	1/8	1/4½	1/8	1/8	2/0	2/0	2/0	2/0
Peter de Dene	–	–	–	–	–	1/10½	1/10½	1/10½	1/6¾	1/10½	1/10½	2/3	2/3	2/3	2/3

[1318–19 cont.]

WEEK:	1	2	3	4	5	6	7	8	9	10	11	12	13	14	15
Hugh de Dorsete	—	—	—	—	—	—	1/10½	1/10½	—	1/10½	1/10½	2/3	2/3	2/3	2/3
W. Laci	—	—	—	—	—	—	—	—	—	—	1/10	—	—	—	—
EASTER															
R. de Forde, J. Baret, Peter Dene,	—	2/3	2/3	1/10½	2/3	2/3	2/3	—	2/3	2/3	2/3	—	—	—	—
J. Eston, Elias, Hugh de Dorsete	—	2/2	2/2	1/9¾	2/2	2/2	2/2	—	2/2	2/2	2/2	—	—	—	—
R. Abbed, J. de Parco	—	2/0	2/0	1/6½	2/0	2/0	2/0	—	2/0	2/0	2/0	—	—	—	—
J. Chamberleyn, G. de Bello	—	1/10	1/10	1/1½	1/10	1/10	1/10	—	1/10	1/10	1/10	—	—	—	—
R. Waleys	—	1/5	1/5	1/1	1/5	1/5	1/5	—	1/5	1/5	1/5	—	—	—	—
Symon	—	0/8	0/8	0/7	0/8	0/8	0/8	—	—	—	—	—	—	—	—
J. Leva	—	1/1	1/4	1/1	—	1/4	1/4	—	—	—	—	—	—	—	—
Adam Baunebiri	—	1/1	1/10	1/1	—	—	—	—	—	—	—	—	—	—	—
R. Galmeton	—	—	—	—	2/2	—	—	—	—	—	2/2	—	—	—	—
W. Frensch, N. Frensch	—	—	1/10	—	2/2	—	—	—	—	—	—	—	—	—	—
MIDSUMMER															
R. de Forde	2/3	2/3	2/3	2/2	2/3	2/3	2/3	2/3	2/3	2/3	2/3	2/3	2/3	2/3	—
J. Baret	2/3	2/3	2/3	2/2	2/3	2/3	2/3	2/3	—	—	—	—	—	—	—
Peter de Dene	2/3	2/3	2/3	2/2	2/3	2/3	2/3	2/3	—	—	—	—	—	—	—
J. de Eston, Elias, Hugh	2/3	2/3	2/3	2/2	2/3	2/3	2/3	2/2	—	—	—	—	—	—	—
R. Abbed	2/2	2/2	2/2	2/0	2/2	2/2	2/2	2/0	—	—	—	—	—	—	—
J. de Parco	2/0	2/0	2/0	2/0	2/0	2/0	2/0	2/0	2/0	2/0	2/0	2/0	2/0	2/0	—
J. Chamberleyn	2/0	2/0	2/0	2/0	2/0	2/0	2/0	—	—	—	—	—	—	—	—
W. de Bello	2/0	2/0	2/0	2/0	2/0	2/0	2/0	2/0	2/0	2/0	2/0	2/0	2/0	2/0	—
R. Waleys	1/10	1/10	1/10	1/5	—	—	—	—	—	—	—	—	—	—	—
Simon	1/5	1/5	1/5	1/5	—	—	—	—	—	—	—	—	—	—	—
R. Galmeton	2/2	2/2	—	2/2	2/2	—	—	—	—	—	—	—	—	—	—
N. Frensch	2/2	2/2	—	2/2	—	—	—	—	—	—	—	—	—	—	—

2615 ALTAR 1318–19

[MICHAELMAS]

WEEK:	1	2	3	4	5	6	7	8	9	10	11	12
R. de Attaboxe	2/6	2/6	2/6	2/6	1/9	2/1	—	2/1	2/1	2/1	2/1	2/1
Peter Dene	2/3	2/3	2/3	2/3	1/6¾	—	—	—	—	—	—	—
J. de Eston	2/3	2/3	—	—	1/6¾	—	2/1	—	—	—	—	—
T. Attaboxe	2/3	2/3	—	—	—	—	2/1	—	—	—	—	—
Elias de Neweton	2/3	2/3	2/3	2/3	1/6¾	—	—	—	—	—	—	—
Ph. de Wyppale	1/10	1/10	—	—	0/11	—	—	—	—	—	—	—
Symon Snelle	1/4	1/4	1/4	1/4	1/9	2/1	—	2/1	2/1	2/1	2/1	2/1
J. de Sar	2/4	2/4	2/4	2/4	1/9	2/1	—	2/1	2/1	2/1	2/1	2/1
T. de Sar	1/8	1/8	1/8	1/8	1/3	1/5	1/5	1/5	1/5	1/5	1/5	1/5

[ALTAR 1318-19 cont.]

WEEK:	1	2	3	4	5	6	7	8	9	10	11	12	13	14	15
[CHRISTMAS]															
R. Boxe	–	1/9	2/1	2/1	2/1	2/1	2/1	2/1	1/9	2/1	2/1	–	–	–	–
J. Sar	–	1/9	2/1	2/1	2/1	2/1	2/1	2/1	–	2/1	2/1	2/4	2/4	–	–
T. Sar	–	1/3	1/5	1/5	1/5	1/5	1/5	1/5	1/2½	1/5	1/5	1/8	1/8	1/8	1/8
[EASTER]															
J. Sar	2/4	2/4	2/1	2/0	2/0	2/0	–	2/0	2/6	2/6					
T. Sar	1/8	1/8	1/5	2/0	2/0	2/0	–	2/0	1/4	1/4					
R. Attebroxe	2/6	2/6	2/1	2/6	2/6	2/6	–	2/6	2/6	2/6					
Adam Baunebiri	–	–	–	1/4	–	–	–	1/4	–	–					
J. Baunebiri	–	–	–	–	2/6	2/6	–	–	2/6	2/6					
J. Leva	–	–	–	–	–	–	–	0/8	0/8	0/8					
[MIDSUMMER]															
R. Atteboxe	2/6	2/6	2/6	2/6	2/6	2/6	2/6	2/6	2/6	2/6	2/6	2/6	2/6	2/6	
Ad. Baunebiri	1/4	1/4	1/4	1/4	–	–	–	–	–	–					
J. Leva	0/8	0/8	0/8	0/8	0/8	0/8	0/8	0/8	0/8	0/8	0/8	0/8	0/8	0/8	
J. de Sar					2/6	–									
J. Baret					2/3	2/3	2/3	2/3	2/3	2/3	2/3	2/3	2/3	2/3	
T. de Sar, J. Chamberleyn					2/0	2/0	2/0	2/0	2/0	2/0					
R. Waleys						1/10	1/10	1/10	1/10	1/10					
his associate (*socio*)						1/10	1/10	1/10	1/10	1/10					
R. mason (*lathem*)							1/6	1/6		2/0				1/6	
Simon							2/0	2/0	2/0	2/0	1/6	1/6	1/6	1/6	
R. Galmeton							1/6	2/2	1/5	2/2	2/2	2/2	2/2	2/2	
R. Abbod							2/2	2/2	2/2	2/2	2/2	2/2	2/2	2/2	
N. Frensch							2/2	2/2	2/2	2/2	2/2	2/2	2/2	2/2	
Eli., J. Eston, Hugh										2/3	2/3½	2/3	2/3	2/3	
J. Parco										2/2	2/2	2/2	2/2	2/2	
R. Silferton															
Phil. [de Wyppale]										2/0	2/0	2/0	2/0	2/0	
Peter Dene													2/3	2/3	

2616   1319-20

MICHAELMAS

	1	2	3	4	5	6	7	8	9	10	11	12
R. de Forde	2/3	2/3	2/3	2/3	1/10½	1/10½	1/10½	1/10½	1/10½	1/10½	1/10½	1/10½
J. de Parco	2/2	2/2	2/2	2/2	1/10	1/10	1/10	1/10	1/10	1/10	1/10	1/10
T. de Bello	2/0	2/0	2/0	–	–	–	–	–	–	–	–	–
N. Frensch	–	–	–	2/2	–	1/10	1/10	1/8	1/8	1/8	1/10	1/10
J. Chaumberleyn	–	–	–	2/0	1/6	1/8	1/8	1/8	1/8	1/8	1/8	1/8
Simon Snel	–	–	–	1/6	1/6	1/3	1/3	1/3	1/3	1/3	1/3	1/3

[1319–20 cont.] WEEK:	1	2	3	4	5	6	7	8	9	10	11	12	13	14	15
W. Frensch	–	–	–	–	–	–	1/10	–	–	–	–	–			
R. Galmeton, R. de Abbod	–	–	–	–	–	–	–	1/10	1/10	1/10	1/10	1/10			
CHRISTMAS															
R. de Forde	–	1/10½	1/10½	1/10½	1/10½	1/10½	1/10½	1/10½	1/10½	1/10½	1/10½	2/3	2/3	1/10½	
R. de Abbod/Abbodesburi	–	1/10	1/10	1/10	1/10	1/10	–	–	–	–	–	–	–	–	
J. de Parco	–	1/10	1/10	1/10	1/10	1/10	1/10	1/10	1/10	1/10	1/10	2/2	2/2	1/10	
R. de Galmeton, N. Frensch	–	1/10	1/10	1/10	1/10	1/10	–	1/10	1/10	–	–	2/2	2/2	1/10	
Simon Snel	–	1/3	1/3	1/3	1/3	1/3	1/3	1/3	1/3	1/3	1/3	1/6	1/8	1/4	
EASTER															
R. de Ford	1/1½	2/3	2/3	2/3	1/10½	1/10½	2/3	–	2/3	2/3	2/3	2/3			
J. de Parco	1/1	2/2	2/2	2/2	1/10	1/10	2/2	–	2/2	2/2	2/2	2/2			
S. Snel	0/10	1/8	1/8	1/8	1/4¾	1/4¾	1/8	–	1/8	1/8	1/10	1/10			
R. Galmeton	–	0/8	–	2/2	1/10	1/10	2/2	–	–	–	2/2	–			
N. Frensch	–	0/8	–	–	–	1/10	2/2	–	–	–	2/2	–			
R. Waleys	–	–	1/10	1/10	1/6½	1/6½	1/10	–	1/10	1/10	1/10	1/10			
Will. Chamberleyn	–	–	1/10	1/10	1/6½	1/6½	1/10	–	1/10	1/10	1/8	–			
MIDSUMMER															
R. de Ford, J. de Parco	2/3	2/3	2/3	2/3	1/10½	2/3	2/3	2/3	2/3	2/3	2/3	2/3	2/3	2/3	
R. Galmeton	2/2	2/2	2/2	1/9½	1/10	2/2	2/2	2/2	2/2	2/2	2/2	2/2	2/2	–	
N. Frensch	2/2	2/2	2/2	1/9½	1/10	2/2	2/2	2/2	2/2	2/2	2/2	2/2	–	–	
R. Waleys	1/10	1/10	–	–	–	–	–	–	–	–	–	–	–	–	
S. Snel/Sneula/Snella	1/10	1/10	1/10	1/10	1/6½	1/10	1/10	1/10	1/10	1/10	1/10	1/10	1/10	1/10	
R. Priour	–	–	–	2/0	1/8	2/0	2/0	2/0	2/0	2/0	2/0	2/0	2/0	2/0	
W. Coppa/Copa	–	–	–	–	1/8	2/0	2/0	2/0	2/0	2/0	2/0	2/0	2/0	2/0	
Steph. de Wilton/Wyllton mason	–	–	–	–	1/5	1/8	1/8	1/8	1/8	1/8	1/8	1/8	1/8	1/8	
J. Chamberleyn	–	–	–	–	–	–	2/0	2/0	2/0	2/0	2/0	2/0	2/0	2/0	
J. Copa mason	–	–	–	–	–	1/8	1/8	1/8	1/8	1/8	1/8	1/8	1/8	1/8	
W. Frensch	–	–	–	–	–	–	–	3/2	–	–	–	2/2	–	–	
J. Millehole	–	–	–	–	–	–	–	–	–	–	–	–	1/6	1/6	

2617 ALTAR 1319–20

	1	2	3	4	5	6	7	8	9	10	11	12
MICHAELMAS												
R. Boxe	2/6	2/6	2/6	2/6	2/1	2/1	2/1	2/1	2/1	2/1	2/1	2/1
Peter de Dene, J. de Eston, Hugh de Dorsete, J. Barat, Elias	2/3	2/3	2/3	2/3	1/10½	1/10½	1/10½	1/10½	1/10½	1/10½	1/10½	1/10½
R. Abbod	2/2	2/3	2/2	2/2	1/10	1/10	1/10	–	–	–	–	–
R. Galmeton	2/2	2/3	2/2	2/2	1/10	–	–	–	–	–	–	–
N. Frensch	2/2	2/3	2/2	–	–	–	–	–	–	–	–	–

[ALTAR 1319–20 cont.] WEEK:

Name	1	2	3	4	5	6	7	8	9	10	11	12	13	14	15
T. de Sar	2/0	2/0	2/0	2/0	1/8	1/8	1/8	1/8	1/8	1/8	1/8	1/8	—		
J. Chamberleyn	2/0	2/0	2/0	—	—	—	—	—	—	—	—	—	—		
Ph. [de Wyppale]	2/0	2/0	2/0	2/0											
Simon Snelle	1/6	1/6	1/6												
J. Leva	0/8	0/8	0/8	0/8	0/8	0/8	0/8	0/8	0/8	0/8					
J. de Sar	—	2/6	2/6	2/6	2/1	2/1	2/1	2/1	2/1	2/1	2/1	2/1	2/1		
J. de Bosco	—	2/0	—												
Thom. de Bello	—														
CHRISTMAS															
J. de Sar	2/1	2/1	2/1	2/1	2/1	2/1	2/1	2/1	—	2/1	—	2/6	2/1		
P. Dene, J. de Eston, J. Barat	1/10½	1/10½	1/8	1/10½	1/10½	1/10½	1/10½	1/10½	1/10½	1/10½	2/3	2/3	1/10½		
T. Sar, T. de Bello	1/8	1/8	1/8	1/8	1/8	1/8	1/8	1/8	1/8	1/8	2/0	2/0	1/8		
J. Chamberleyn	1/8	1/8	1/8	1/8	1/8	1/8	1/8	1/8	1/8	1/8	1/0	1/0	1/8		
R. Leve	0/8	0/8	0/8	0/8	0/8	0/8	0/8	0/8	0/8	0/8	2/6	2/6	0/8		
Hugh, Elias	—	2/1	2/1	—	2/1	2/1	2/1	2/1	2/1	2/1	2/6	2/6	2/1		
Philip	—	1/8	1/8	—	1/10½	1/10½	1/10½	1/10½	1/10½	1/10½	2/3	2/3	1/10½		
R. Abbodesbiri	—	—	—	—	—	1/10	1/10	1/10	1/10	1/10	2/2	2/2	1/10		
R. Galmeton, N. Frensch	—	—	—	—	—	1/10	—	—	—	—	—	—	—		
Ric. Croc, J. Nepperyde / Nerpedon	—	—	—	—	—	—	—	—	—	—	—	—	—		
EASTER															
R. Payne	1/3	2/6	2/6	2/6	—	2/1	2/6	2/6	2/6	2/6	2/6	—			
J. de Sar	1/3	—	2/6	2/6	2/1	2/1	2/2	2/2	—	2/2	2/6	—			
P. Dene, Elias, J. de Eston, Hugh, J. Baret	1/1½	2/3	2/3	2/3	1/10½	1/10½	2/3	2/3	2/3	2/3	2/3	—			
R. Abbodesbiri, R. Croc, J. Neperude	1/1	2/2	2/2	2/2	1/10½	1/10½	2/2	2/2	2/2	2/2	2/2	2/2			
T. de Sar	1/0	2/0	2/0	2/0	1/8	1/8	2/2	2/0	2/0	2/0	2/0	2/0			
T. de Bello	1/0	2/0	2/0	2/0	1/8	1/8	2/0	2/0	2/0	2/0	2/0	2/0			
J. Chamberleyn	1/0	2/0	2/0	2/0	1/8	1/8	2/0	2/0	2/0	—	—	—			
J. Leve	0/6	1/0	1/0	1/0	0/10	0/10	2/0	2/0	—	2/0	1/0	—			
MIDSUMMER															
R. Payn	2/6	2/6	2/6	—	—	2/3	—	—	—	2/6	2/6	2/6	2/6	—	
P. de Dene, J. de Eston, Hugh, J. Barat	2/3	2/3	2/3	2/3	1/10½	2/3	2/3	2/3	2/3	2/3	2/3	2/3	2/3	2/3	
Elias	2/3	2/3	2/3	2/3	1/10½	2/3	2/3	2/3	2/3	2/3	2/3	2/3	2/3	—	
R. Abbedesbiri, R. Croc. J. Nepperud	2/2	2/2	2/2	2/2	1/10	2/2	2/2	2/2	2/2	2/2	2/2	2/2	2/2	2/2	

[ALTAR 1319–20 cont.] WEEK:	1	2	3	4	5	6	7	8	9	10	11	12	13	14	15
T. Sar	2/0	2/0	2/0	–	1/8	2/0	2/0	2/0	2/0	2/0	2/0	2/0	2/0	2/0	
R. Priour	2/0	2/0	–	–	–	–	–	–	–	–	–	–	–	–	
J. Leve	1/0	1/0	1/0	1/0	0/10	1/0	1/0	1/0	1/0	1/0	1/0	1/0	1/0	1/0	
J. Sar	–	–	–	–	2/1	2/6	2/6	2/6	2/6	2/6	2/6	2/6	2/6	2/6	
2618 1320–1															
MICHAELMAS															
R. de Ford	2/3	2/3	2/3	2/3	1/10½	1/10½	1/10½	1/10½	1/10½	1/10½	1/10½	1/10½	0/11¼		
J. de Parco	2/2	2/2	2/2	2/2	1/10	1/10	2/2	2/2	1/10	1/10	1/10	1/10	0/11		
R. Galmeton	2/2	2/2	2/2	2/2	1/10	1/10	2/2	2/2	1/10	1/10	1/10	1/10	–		
W. Frensch	2/2	2/2	2/2	–	–	1/10	–	–	1/10	1/10	1/3	–	–		
N. Frensch	2/2	–	2/2	2/2	1/10	1/10	2/2	2/2	1/10	1/10	1/10	1/10	–		
W. Copa	2/0	2/0	2/0	2/0	–	–	–	–	–	–	–	–	–		
R. Priour, J. Chamberleyn	2/0	2/0	2/0	2/0	1/8	1/8	1/8	1/8	1/8	1/8	1/8	1/8	1/8		
R. Chuddelegh	1/8	–	–	–	–	–	–	–	–	–	–	–	–		
R. Copa	1/10	–	1/10	1/10	–	1/6½	–	–	–	–	–	–	–		
S. Snella	1/10	1/10	1/10	1/10	–	1/6½	1/6½	1/6½	1/6½	1/6½	1/6½	1/6½	0/9¼		
J. Copa, S. Wilton	1/8	1/8	1/8	1/8	–	–	–	–	–	–	–	–	–		
W. Loges	–	–	–	–	1/8	1/8	1/8	–	–	1/8	–	–	–		
H. Chuddelegh	–	–	–	–	1/8	1/8	1/8	1/8	1/8	1/8	1/8	1/8	–		

CHRISTMAS WEEK:	2	3	4	5	6	7	8	9	10	11	12	13	14	15	16
R. de Ford	1/10½	1/10½	1/10½	1/10½	1/10½	1/10½	1/10½	1/10½	1/10½	1/10½	2/3	2/3	2/3	2/3	2/3
J. de Parco	1/10	1/10	1/10½	1/10½	1/10	1/10	1/10	1/10	1/10	1/10	2/2	2/2	2/2	2/2	2/2
R. Galmeton, N. Frensch	1/10	1/10	1/10½	1/10½	1/10	1/10	1/10	1/10	1/10	1/10	2/2	–	–	–	–
R. Priour, J. Chamberleyn	1/8	1/8	1/8	1/8	1/8	1/8	1/8	1/8	1/8	1/8	2/0	2/0	2/0	2/0	2/0
H. Chuddelegh	1/8	1/8	1/8	1/8	1/8	1/8	1/8	1/8	1/8	1/8	2/0	–	–	–	–
Simon Snella	1/6½	1/6½	1/6½	1/6½	1/6½	1/6½	1/6½	1/6½	1/6½	1/6½	1/10	1/10	1/10	1/10	1/10
William glazier	1/8	–	–	–	–	–	–	–	–	–	–	–	–	–	–
Adam glazier	0/7	–	–	–	–	–	–	–	–	–	–	–	–	–	–
W. Frensche	–	1/10	1/10½	1/10½	1/10	1/10	1/10	1/10	1/10	1/10	2/2	–	–	–	–
W. Loges	–	0/5	1/8	1/8	1/8	1/8	1/8	1/8	1/8	1/8	–	–	–	–	–
N. painter	–	–	–	–	–	1/2	1/2	1/2	1/2	1/2	1/6	1/6	–	–	–
J. mason (*lathom*)	–	–	–	–	–	–	–	–	–	–	–	1/8	–	–	–
EASTER															
R. de Forde	2/3	2/3	2/3	2/3	2/3	2/3	–	2/3							
J. de Parco	2/2	2/2	2/2	2/2	2/2	2/2	–	2/2							
R. Priour	2/0	2/0	–	2/0	–	–	–	2/0							
J. Chamberleyn	2/0	2/0	2/0	–	2/0	2/0	–	–							
Simon	1/10	1/10	–	–	1/10	1/10	0/7	1/10							

[1320–1 cont.] WEEK:	1	2	3	4	5	6	7	8	9	10	11	12	13	14	15
R. Galmeton	–	–	–	–	1/5	–	–	0/9	–						
N. Frensch, W. Frensch	–	–	–	–	1/5	–	–	–	–						
Walter Roke	–	–	–	–	–	–	–	0/7	–						
Finamour	–	–	–	–	–	–	–	0/3	–						
MIDSUMMER															
R. Ford	2/3	2/3	2/3	2/3	1/10½	2/3	2/3	1/10½	2/3	1/10½	2/3	2/3	2/3	2/3	
J. Parco	2/2	2/2	2/2	2/2	1/10	2/2	2/2	1/10	2/2	1/10	2/2	2/2	2/2	2/2	
J. Chamberleyn	2/0	2/0	2/0	–	1/8	2/0	2/0	1/8	2/0	1/8	2/0	2/0	2/0	2/0	
Simon	1/10	1/10	1/10	0/11	1/6½	1/10	1/10	1/6	1/10	1/6½	–	–	1/10	1/10	
R. Galmeton	–	2/2	–	–	–	2/2	1/0	–	–	–	–	–	–	2/2	
N. Frensch, W. Frensch, T. Roke	–	2/2	–	–	–	–	–	–	–	–	–	–	–	–	
H. Chuddelegh	–	–	–	–	–	2/0	–	–	–	–	–	–	–	–	
J. Roke	–	–	–	–	–	1/10	–	–	–	–	–	–	–	2/0	
W. mason	–	–	–	–	–	–	2/0	1/8	2/0	1/8	2/0	2/0	2/0	2/0	

2619 ALTAR 1320–1

MICHAELMAS	1	2	3	4	5	6	7	8	9	10	11	12	13
R. Payn, J. Sar	2/6	2/6	2/6	2/6	2/1	2/1	2/1	2/1	2/1	2/1	2/1	2/1	1/0½
Peter Dene, J. de Eston, Hugh, J. Baret	2/3	2/3	2/3	2/3	1/10½	1/10½	1/10½	1/10½	1/10½	1/10½	1/10½	1/10½	0/11¼
R. Abbod, R. Croc	2/2	2/2	2/2	2/2	1/9¾	1/9¾	1/9¾	1/9¾	1/9¾	1/9¾	1/9¾	1/9¾	0/11¼
T. Sar	2/0	2/0	2/0	2/0	1/8	1/8	1/8	1/8	1/8	1/8	1/8	1/8	0/10
J. Leva	1/0	1/0	1/0	1/0	0/10	1/0	1/0	1/0	1/0	1/0	1/0	1/0	0/6
J. Nepperid	–	2/2	2/2	2/2	1/9¾	1/9¾	1/9¾	1/9¾	1/9¾	1/9¾	1/9¾	1/9¾	0/11¼
Alexander	–	–	–	–	1/8	1/8	1/8	1/8	1/8	1/8	1/8	1/8	0/10
N. painter (for an image)	–	–	–	–	–	–	–	1/8	–	–	–	–	–
Adam Baunebiri	–	–	–	–	–	–	–	–	1/6	1/8	1/8	1/8	0/10

CHRISTMAS WEEK:	2	3	4	5	6	7	8	9	10	11	12	13	14	15	16
R. Payn, J. Sar	2/1	2/1	2/1	2/1	2/1	2/1	2/1	2/1	2/1	2/1	2/6	2/6	2/6	2/6	2/6
P. Dene, J. Eston, Hugh	1/10½	1/10½	1/10½	1/10½	1/10½	1/10½	1/10½	1/10½	1/10½	1/10½	2/3	2/3	2/3	2/3	2/3
R. Abbod, R. Croc, J. Nepperid	1/9¾	1/9¾	1/9¾	1/9¾	1/9¾	1/9¾	1/9¾	1/9¾	1/9¾	1/9¾	2/2	2/2	2/2	2/2	2/2
T. Sar, Alexander, A. Baunebiri	1/8	1/8	1/8	1/8	1/8	1/8	1/8	1/8	1/8	1/8	2/0	2/0	2/0	2/0	2/0
J. Leva	1/0	1/0	1/0	1/0	1/0	1/0	1/0	1/0	1/0	1/0	1/3	1/3	1/3	1/3	1/3
J. Baret	–	1/10½	1/10½	1/10½	1/10½	1/10½	1/10½	1/10½	1/10½	1/10½	2/3	2/3	2/3	2/3	2/3
N. painter	–	–	–	–	–	–	–	–	–	–	–	–	1/6	1/6	1/6
EASTER															
R. Payne, J. Sar	2/6	2/6	2/6	2/6	2/6	2/6	–	2/6							
Peter Dene, J. Eston, J. Baret	2/3	2/3	2/3	2/3	2/3	2/3	–	2/3							
Hugh	–	2/3	2/3	2/3	2/3	2/3	–	–							

[ALTAR 1320–1 cont.] WEEK:	1	2	3	4	5	6	7	8	9	10	11	12	13	14	15
R. Abbod, Alexander	–	2/2	2/2	2/2	2/2	2/2	2/2	–	2/2						
R. Croc, J. Nepperid	–	2/2	2/2	–	–	–	–	–	–						
T. Sar	–	2/0	2/0	–	–	–	2/0	–	2/0						
Adam Baunebiri	–	2/0	2/0	2/0	2/0	2/0	–	–	2/0						
N. painter	–	1/8	1/8	–	1/8	1/8	1/8	–	1/8						
J. Leva	–	1/3	1/3	1/3	1/3	1/3	1/3	–	1/3						
Elias	–	–	2/3	2/3	2/3	2/3	2/3	–	2/3						
MIDSUMMER															
R. Payn, J. Sar	2/6	2/6	2/6	2/6	2/1	2/6	2/6	2/1	2/6	2/1	2/6	2/6	2/6	2/6	
P. Dene, J. Eston, Elias, J. Baret	2/3	2/3	2/3	2/3	1/10½	2/3	2/3	1/10½	2/3	1/10½	2/3	2/3	2/3	2/3	
R. Abbod	2/2	2/2	2/2	2/2	1/10	2/2	2/2	1/10	2/2	1/10	2/2	2/2	2/2	2/2	
Alexander	2/2	2/2	2/2	–	–	–	–	–	–	1/10	2/2	2/2	2/2	2/2	
T. Sar	2/0	2/0	2/0	2/0	1/8	–	2/0	1/8	2/0	1/8	2/0	2/0	2/0	2/0	
Adam Baunebiri	2/0	2/0	2/0	2/0	1/8	–	–	–	–	–	–	2/0	2/0	2/0	
J. Leva	1/3	1/3	1/3	1/3	0/11	1/3	1/3	1/0	1/3	1/0	1/3	1/3	1/3	1/3	
N. painter	1/8	1/8	1/8	1/8	?	1/8	1/8	1/8	1/8	–	1/8	1/8	1/8	1/8	
R. painter	–	–	–	–	–	–	–	–	–	–	1/3	1/3	1/3	1/3	
R. Priour	–	–	–	–	–	–	–	–	–	–	–	–	–	2/0	
2620 1321–2															
MICHAELMAS															
R. Ford	2/3	2/3	2/3	2/3	2/3	1/10½	1/10½	1/10½	1/10½	1/10½	1/10½	1/10½	1/10½		
J. de Parco, R. de Abbod	2/2	2/2	2/2	2/2	2/2	1/10	1/10	1/10	1/10	1/10	1/10	1/10	0/11		
J. Chamber	2/0	2/0	–	2/0	2/0	1/8	1/8	1/8	1/8	1/8	1/8	1/8	0/10		
Simon	1/10	1/10	1/10	1/10	1/10	1/6½	1/6½	1/6½	1/6½	1/6½	1/6½	1/6½	0/9¼		
W. Rok carpenter	–	0/8	–	–	–	–	1/8	–	–	–	–	–	–		
W. mason	2/0	2/0	–	–	–	–	–	–	–	–	–	–	–		
CHRISTMAS															
R. Ford	–	1/10½	–	–	–	–	–	–	–	–	–	–	–	–	–
J. Parco, R. Abbod	–	1/10	1/10	1/10	1/10	1/10	1/10	1/10	1/6½	1/10	1/10	2/2	2/2	2/2	2/2
J. Chamber	–	1/8	1/8	1/8	1/8	1/8	1/8	1/8	1/4½	1/8	1/8	2/0	2/0	2/0	2/0
Simon	–	1/6½	1/6½	1/6½	1/6½	1/6½	1/6½	–	–	–	–	–	–	–	2/0
William	–	–	–	–	1/8	1/8	1/8	1/8	1/4¾	1/8	1/8	2/0	2/0	2/0	2/0
N. Frensch	–	–	–	–	–	1/10	1/10	1/10	1/6½	1/10	1/10	2/2	2/2	2/2	2/2
R. Galmeton	–	–	–	–	–	–	–	1/10	–	0/11	1/10	2/2	2/2	2/2	2/2
R. Croc	–	–	–	–	–	–	–	–	–	1/10	1/10	2/2	2/2	2/2	2/2
Warin	–	–	–	–	–	–	–	–	–	1/8	1/8	2/0	2/0	2/0	2/0

	1	2	3	4	5	6	7	8	9	10	11	12	13	14	15
WEEK:															
[1321–2 cont.]															
J. Sidewine /Sydewine	–	–	–	–	–	–	–	–	–	–	–	–	2/2	2/2	2/2
J. Volham /Woldeham, J. Bensted –													1/2	1/2	1/2
W. Roke													–	–	1/10
EASTER															
R. Croc, J. Parco, R. Abbod, R. Galmeton, N. Frensch		2/2	2/2	1/10	2/2	2/2	2/2	–	2/2	2/2	2/2				
J. Sydewine	1/1	2/2	2/2	1/10	–	2/2	2/2	1/1	2/2	2/2	2/0				
W. Chamber, J. Chamber, Warin 1/0	1/0	2/0	2/0	–	2/0	2/0	2/0	–	2/0	2/0	2/0				
W. Roke /Roky	0/11	–	–	1/8	1/10	1/10	1/10	–	–	–	–				
J. Woldeham	0/7	1/2	1/0	1/2	1/2	1/2	1/2	–	1/2	1/2	1/2				
J. Bensted	0/7	2/0	2/0	1/8	2/0	2/0	2/0	–	–	–	2/2				
Simon	–	1/10	1/10	1/7	2/0	–	2/0	1/1	2/2	2/2	–				
J. Roke	–	–	–	1/10	–	–	–	0/10	–	–	–				
W. Felstede	–	–	–	1/10	–	–	–	–	–	–	–				
Benedict															
MIDSUMMER															
R. Croc, J. Parco, A. Abbod, R. Galmeton, N. Frensch, J. Sidewin, W. Felstede	2/2	2/2	2/2	2/2	2/2	2/2	2/2	2/2	2/2	2/2	2/2	2/0	2/2		
W., J. Chamber, Warin	2/0	2/0	2/0	2/0	2/0	2/0	2/0	2/0	2/0	2/0	2/0	2/0	2/0		
J. Bensted	1/2	1/2	1/2	1/2	2/0	2/0	2/0	2/0	2/0	2/0	2/0	1/2	1/0		
Will. Woldeham															
J. Woldeham															
Rob. [Copa]	–	–	–	–	–	–	–	2/0	2/0	2/0	2/0	2/0	2/0		
W. Copa	–	–	–	–	–	–	–	2/0	2/0	2/0	2/0	–	–		
Simon	–	–	–	–	–	–	–	–	–	2/2	–	2/0	2/0		
Hen. Drayton	–	–	–	–	–	–	–	–	–	–	–	–	1/0		
2621 ALTAR 1321–2															
MICHAELMAS															
R. Payn, J. Sar	2/6	2/6	2/6	2/6	2/6	2/1	2/1	2/1	2/1	2/1	2/1	2/1	1/0½		
Peter Dene, J. Eston, Elias, J. Baret	2/3	2/3	2/3	2/3	2/3	–	1/10½	1/10½	1/10½	1/10½	1/10½	1/10½	0/11¼		
Alexander	2/2	2/2	2/2	2/2	2/2	–	1/10	1/10	1/10	1/10	1/10	1/10	0/11		
T. Sar	2/0	2/0	2/0	2/0	2/0	1/8	1/8	1/8	1/8	1/8	1/8	1/8	0/10		
Adam Baunebiri	1/8	1/8	1/8	1/8	1/8	1/6	1/8	1/8	1/8	1/8	1/8	1/8	0/10		
N. painter	1/3	1/3	1/3	1/3	1/3	1/0½	1/2	1/2	1/2	1/2	1/2	1/2	0/10		
J. Leva	1/3	1/3	1/3	1/3	1/3	1/0½	1/0	1/0	1/0	1/0	1/0	1/2	0/10		
R. painter	1/3	1/3	1/3	1/3	1/3	1/0½	1/0	1/0	1/0	1/0	1/0½	1/2	0/7		

[ALTAR 1321–2 cont.] WEEK:	1	2	3	4	5	6	7	8	9	10	11	12	13	14	15
J. grinder (*molator*)	1/0	1/0	1/0	1/0	1/0	0/10	0/10	0/10	–	–	–	–	–	–	
Will. painter	–	–	–	–	–	–	–	–	–	0/10	0/10	0/5	–	–	
CHRISTMAS															
R. Payn	2/1	2/1	2/1	2/1	2/1	2/1	2/1	1/9	2/1	2/1	2/6	2/6	2/6	2/6	
J. Sar	2/1	–	–	–	–	–	–	–	–	–	–	–	–	–	
Peter Dene, J. Eston, Elias	1/10½	1/10½	1/10½	1/10½	1/10½	1/10½	1/10½	1/7	1/10½	1/10½	2/3	2/3	2/3	2/3	
J. Baret	1/10½	1/10½	1/10½	1/10½	1/10½	1/10½	1/10½	1/7	1/10½	–	–	–	–	–	
Alexander	1/10	–	–	–	–	–	–	–	–	–	–	–	–	–	
Ad. Baunebiri	1/8	1/8	1/8	1/8	1/8	1/8	1/8	1/4¾	1/8	1/8	2/0	2/0	2/0	2/0	
J. Leva	1/2	1/2	1/2	1/2	1/2	1/2	1/2	0/11¾	1/2	1/2	1/6	1/6	1/6	1/6	
N. painter	–	1/8	1/8	1/8	1/8	1/8	1/8	1/4¾	1/8	1/8	2/0	2/0	2/0	2/0	
R. Priour	–	–	–	–	–	–	1/8	1/4¾	1/8	1/8	2/0	2/0	2/0	2/0	
Ric. Eston	–	–	–	–	–	–	–	–	1/8	1/8	2/0	2/0	2/0	2/0	
Benedict painter	–	–	–	–	–	–	–	–	–	–	–	–	1/0	1/0	
EASTER															
R. Payn	1/3	2/6	2/6	2/1	2/6	2/6	2/6	–	2/6	2/6	2/6				
Peter Dene, J. Eston, Elias, Alexander	1/1½	2/3	2/3	1/10½	2/3	2/3	2/3	–	2/3	2/3	2/3				
R. Eston, R. Priour, N. painter	1/0	2/0	2/0	1/8	2/0	2/0	2/0	–	2/0	2/0	2/0				
J. Leva	0/9	1/6	1/6	1/3	1/6	1/6	1/6	–	1/6	1/6	1/6				
Benedict	0/6	1/0	1/0	1/0	1/2	1/2	1/2	–	1/2	1/4	1/4				
R. painter	–	–	–	–	–	–	–	–	–	–	1/4				
MIDSUMMER															
R. Payn	2/6	2/6	2/6	2/6	2/6	2/6	2/6	2/6	2/6	2/6	2/6	2/6	2/6		
P. Dene, J. Eston	2/3	2/3	2/3	2/3	2/3	2/3	2/3	2/3	2/3	2/3	2/3	2/3	2/3		
Elias	2/3	2/3	–	2/3	2/3	–	–	–	–	–	–	–	–		
Alexander	2/3	2/3	2/3	2/3	2/3	2/3	2/3	2/3	2/3	–	–	–	–		
R. Eston, R. Priour, W. painter	2/0	2/0	2/0	2/0	2/0	2/0	2/0	2/0	2/0	2/0	2/0	2/0	2/0		
J. Leva	1/6	1/6	1/6	1/6	1/6	1/6	1/6	1/6	1/6	1/6	1/6	1/6	1/6		
Benedict painter	1/4	1/4	1/4	1/4	1/4	1/4	1/4	1/4	1/4	1/4	1/4	1/4	1/4		
Richard painter	1/0	1/0	1/0	1/0	1/0	1/0	1/0	1/0	1/0	0/6	–	–	–		
Will. painter	–	–	–	–	1/4	1/4	1/4	1/4	1/4	1/4	1/4	1/4	1/4		
J. Ford	–	–	–	–	–	2/3	–	–	–	–	–	–	–		
Will. Jore/Yore	–	–	–	–	–	–	2/3	2/6	2/6	2/6	2/6	2/6	2/6		
Will. More	–	–	–	–	–	–	–	2/3	2/3	–	–	–	–		
Symon painter	–	–	–	–	–	–	–	–	–	–	–	–	2/0		
Thomas painter	–	–	–	–	–	–	–	–	–	–	–	–	2/0		

2622 1323–4

MICHAELMAS WEEK:	**1**	**2**	**3**	**4**	**5**	**6**	**7**	**8**	**9**	**10**	**11**	**12**	**13**	**14**	**15**
P. Dene, Elias	2/3	2/3	2/3	2/3	1/7¼	1/10½	1/10½	1/7¼	1/10½	1/10½	1/10½	1/10½			
W. Felstede	2/3	2/3	2/3	–	–	–	1/10½	1/8	2/0	2/0	2/0	2/0			
R. Croc, J. Parco, J. Baret	2/2	2/2	2/2	2/2	1/6½	1/10	1/10	1/6½	1/10	1/10	1/10	1/10			
R. Pryor, N. painter	2/0	2/0	2/0	2/0	1/4¾	1/8	1/8	1/4¾	1/8	1/8	1/8	1/8			
J. Leva	1/6	1/6	1/6	1/6	1/3	1/6	1/6	1/3	1/6	1/6	1/6	1/6			
T. Botiler/Boteler	1/4	1/4	1/4	1/4	0/11½	1/1½	1/4	1/1½	1/4	1/4	1/4	1/4			
Benedict	1/4	1/4	1/4	1/4	0/11½	1/1½	0/10	0/8½	0/10	0/10	0/10	0/10			
Nicholas	–	–	1/0	1/0	0/8½	0/10	0/10	0/8½	0/10	0/10	0/10	0/10			
J. Rok	–	–	–	2/0	1/4¾	1/8	1/8	1/4¾	–	–	–	–			
Rand. Roke	–	–	–	1/0	0/8½	0/10	0/10	0/8½	–	–	–	–			
Hen. de Cruditone, Walt. de Cruditone	–	–	–	–	–	–	1/10½	1/6½	–	–	–	–			
Ad. Baunelyry, Sewane/Sewele carpenter	–	–	–	–	–	–	1/8	1/4¾	1/8	1/8	1/8	1/8			
CHRISTMAS															
W. Felstede	2/0	2/0	2/0	2/0	2/0	2/0	2/0	1/8	2/0	2/0	2/4	2/4	2/4	2/4	2/4
Peter Dene, Elias	1/10½	1/10½	1/10½	1/10½	1/10½	1/10½	1/10½	1/7¼	1/10½	1/10½	2/3	2/3	2/3	2/3	2/3
J. Parco, R. Croc, J. Baret	1/10	1/10	1/10	1/10	1/10	1/10	1/10	1/6½	1/10	1/10	2/2	2/2	2/2	2/2	2/2
R. Priour	1/8	1/8	1/8	1/8	1/8	1/8	1/8	1/4¾	1/8	1/8	2/0	2/0	2/0	2/0	2/0
N. painter	1/8	1/8	–	1/8	1/8	1/8	1/8	–	–	–	–	–	–	–	–
Sewane/Sewaune/Sewale	1/8	1/8	1/8	1/8	1/8	1/8	1/8	–	–	–	–	–	–	–	–
J. Leva/Luva	1/6	1/6	1/6	1/6	1/6	1/6	1/6	1/3	1/6	1/6	1/10	1/10	1/10	1/10	1/10
T. Botiler	1/4	1/4	1/4	1/4	1/4	1/4	1/4	1/1½	1/4	1/4	1/6	1/6	1/6	1/6	1/6
J. Bensted	1/4	1/4	–	1/4	1/4	1/4	1/4	1/1½	1/4	1/4	1/6	1/6	1/6	1/6	1/6
Benedict	0/10	0/10	0/10	0/10	0/10	0/10	1/0	0/8½	0/10	0/10	1/0	1/0	1/0	–	–
N.	0/10	0/10	0/10	0/10	0/10	0/10	1/0	0/8½	0/10	0/10	1/0	1/0	1/0	1/2	1/2
A. Baunebiri	–	1/8	1/8	1/8	1/8	1/8	1/8	1/4¾	1/8	1/8	2/0	2/0	2/0	2/0	2/0
J. More	–	–	–	–	1/8	1/8	1/8	1/4¾	1/8	1/8	2/0	2/0	2/0	2/0	2/0
J. Orchard/Horchard	–	–	–	–	–	1/8	1/8	1/4¾	1/8	1/8	2/0	2/0	2/0	2/0	2/0
Adam carpenter	–	–	–	–	–	1/8	1/8	–	–	–	–	–	–	–	–
Gal. Bromtone, W. Byrche	–	–	–	–	–	–	–	–	–	–	–	2/0	2/0	2/0	2/0
Nic. Chynnot	–	–	–	–	–	–	–	–	–	–	–	1/10	1/10	1/10	1/10
EASTER															
W. Felstede	–	2/4	2/0	2/4	2/4	2/4	2/4	–	2/4	2/4					
P. Dene, Elyas	–	2/3	1/10½	2/3	2/3	2/3	2/3	–	2/3	2/3					
J. Parco, R. Crok, J. Baret	–	2/2	1/10	2/2	2/2	2/2	2/2	–	2/2	2/2					
J. More, R. Pryor, A. Baunebyri, J. Orchard	–	2/0	1/8	2/0	2/0	2/0	2/0	–	2/0	2/0					

WEEK:	1	2	3	4	5	6	7	8	9	10	11	12	13	14	15
[1323–4 cont.]															
J. Brydiport, R. carpenter	–	2/0	1/8	–	–	–	–	–	–	–	–	–	–	–	–
G. Branton	–	2/0	1/8	2/0	2/0	2/0	2/0	–	2/0	2/0	–	–	–	–	–
W. Byrych	–	2/0	1/7	1/10	1/10	1/10	1/10	–	–	–	–	–	–	–	–
J. Leva/Luva	–	1/10	1/3	1/6	1/6	1/6	1/6	–	1/6	–	–	–	–	–	–
Thom. Botiler	–	1/6	1/3	1/6	1/6	1/6	1/6	–	1/6	1/6	–	–	–	–	–
J. Benstede	–	1/6	1/0	1/2	1/2	1/2	1/2	–	1/2	1/6	–	–	–	–	–
N.	–	1/2	–	–	–	–	–	–	–	1/2	–	–	–	–	–
J. carpenter, Sewane	–	1/10	–	–	–	–	–	–	–	–	–	–	–	–	–
J. Raumnysbyry/Reminisbyry	–	–	1/8	2/1	2/1	2/1	2/1	–	2/1	2/1	–	–	–	–	–
R. Abbedesbyry	–	–	–	2/1	2/1	2/1	2/0	–	2/1	2/1	–	–	–	–	–
R. Hopere	–	–	–	2/0	2/0	2/0	2/0	–	2/0	2/0	–	–	–	–	–
J. Nepperid, W. Lowepytte	–	–	–	–	–	–	–	–	2/0	2/0	–	–	–	–	–
MIDSUMMER															
Peter Dene, Elias	2/3	2/3	2/3	2/3	2/3	2/3	2/3	2/3	2/3	2/3	2/3	2/3	2/3	2/3	–
J. Parco, R. Croke, J. Baret	2/2	2/2	2/2	2/2	2/2	2/2	2/2	2/2	2/2	2/2	2/2	2/2	2/2	2/2	–
J. Reminisbyry, R. Abbodesbyry	2/1	2/1	2/1	2/1	2/1	2/1	2/1	2/1	2/1	2/1	2/1	2/1	2/1	2/1	–
R. Pryor, J. Mor, J. Orchard, J. Neperude, W. Lowepytte, W. Byrych	2/0	2/0	2/1	–	–	–	–	–	–	–	–	–	–	–	–
W. Loges	2/0	2/0	–	–	–	–	2/0	2/0	2/0	2/0	2/0	2/0	2/0	2/0	–
T. Botiler, J. Benstede	1/6	1/6	1/6	1/6	1/6	1/6	1/6	1/6	1/6	1/6	1/6	1/6	1/6	1/6	–
R. Hopere	2/0	2/0	–	–	–	–	–	–	2/0	2/0	2/0	2/0	2/0	2/0	–
Nicholas	1/2	1/2	1/2	1/2	1/2	1/2	1/2	1/2	1/2	1/2	1/2	1/2	1/2	1/2	–
W. Felstede	–	2/4	2/4	2/4	2/4	2/4	2/4	2/4	2/4	2/4	2/4	2/4	2/4	2/4	–
Symon Snella	–	2/0	2/0	2/0	2/0	2/0	2/0	2/0	2/0	2/0	2/0	2/0	2/0	2/0	–
N. painter	–	–	–	–	–	–	2/0	–	–	–	–	–	–	–	–
J. Legh	–	–	–	–	–	–	–	1/2	1/2	1/2	1/2	1/2	–	–	–
Sewane	–	–	–	–	–	–	–	2/2	–	–	–	–	–	–	–
J. Logys/Loges	–	–	–	–	–	–	–	–	2/0	2/0	2/0	2/0	–	–	–
Ric. Chuddelegh	–	–	–	–	–	–	–	–	–	–	–	–	–	–	–
H. Chuddeleghe	–	–	–	–	–	–	–	–	–	–	2/2	2/0	–	2/0	–
2623 1324–5															
MICHAELMAS															
W. Felstede	2/4	2/4	2/4	2/4	2/0	2/0	2/0	2/0	2/0	2/0	2/0	2/0	–	–	–
Peter Dene, Elias	2/3	2/3	2/3	2/3	1/7¼	1/10½	1/10½	1/10½	1/10½	1/10½	1/10½	1/10½	–	–	–
J. Parco, R. Crok, J. Bareth	2/2	2/3	2/2	2/3	1/6¼	1/10	1/10	1/10	1/10	1/10	1/10	1/10	–	–	–
J. Reminysbyry, R. Abbodisbyry	2/1	2/1	2/2	2/1	1/5¾	1/9	1/9	1/9	1/9	1/9	1/9	1/9	–	–	–

[1324–5 cont.] WEEK:	1	2	3	4	5	6	7	8	9	10	11	12	13	14	15
R. Prior, J. Orchard	2/0	2/0	2/0	2/0	1/4¾	1/8	1/8	1/8	1/8	1/8	1/8	1/8			
J. Mor, J. Nepperude, W. Lowepitte	2/0	2/0	2/0	2/0	1/4¾	1/8	–	–	–	–	–	–			
W. Byrych	2/0	2/0	–	2/0	1/4¾	1/8	–	–	1/8	–	–	–			
S. Snella	2/0	2/0	2/0	2/0	1/4¾	1/8	–	–	–	–	1/8	1/8			
H. Chuddelegh	2/0	2/0	2/0	2/0	1/4¾	1/8	1/8	1/8	–	–	–	–			
Th. Botiler, J. Bensted	1/6	1/6	1/6	1/6	1/3¼	1/6	1/6	1/6	1/6	1/6	1/6	1/6			
N.	1/2	1/2	–	–	1/0	1/0	1/0	1/0	1/0	1/0	1/0	1/0			
W. glazier	–	–	–	–	–	–	–	–	1/8	1/8	1/8	1/8			
W. tiler	–	–	–	–	–	–	–	–	1/6	–	–	–			
CHRISTMAS															
W. Felstede	–	2/0	2/0	2/0	2/0	2/0	2/0	2/0	2/0	2/0	2/0	2/4	2/4	2/4	2/4
Peter Dene, Elias	–	1/10½	1/10½	1/10½	1/10½	1/10½	1/10½	1/10½	1/10½	1/10½	1/10½	2/3	2/3	2/3	2/3
J. Parco, R. Crok	–	1/10	1/10	1/10	1/10	1/10	1/10	1/10	1/10	1/10	1/10	2/2	2/2	2/2	2/2
J. Bareth	–	1/10	1/10	1/10	1/10	1/10	1/10	1/10	1/10	1/10	1/10	2/2	2/2	–	2/2
J. Reminisbiri, R. Abbodisbiri	–	1/9	1/9	1/9	1/9	1/9	1/9	1/9	1/9	1/9	1/9	2/1	2/1	2/1	2/1
R. Prior, J. Orchard	–	1/8	1/8	1/8	1/8	1/8	1/8	1/8	1/8	1/8	1/8	2/0	2/0	2/0	2/0
Tho. Botiler, J. Bensted	–	1/6	1/6	1/6	1/6	1/6	1/6	1/6	1/6	1/6	1/6	1/8	1/8	1/8	1/8
N.	–	1/0	1/0	1/0	1/0	1/0	1/0	1/0	1/0	1/0	1/0	1/2	1/2	1/2	1/2
Simon Snella	–	1/8	–	–	–	1/8	1/8	1/8	1/8	1/8	1/8	2/0	2/0	2/0	2/0
J. Henslegh/Stenlegh/Stumlegh	–	–	1/10½	1/10½	1/10½	1/10½	1/10½	–	–	–	–	–	–	–	–
Ric. sculptor (*imaginator*)	–	–	–	1/10½	1/10½	1/10½	–	–	–	–	–	–	–	–	–
W. glazier	–	–	–	–	–	1/8	–	–	–	1/8	–	–	–	–	–
J. Ford	–	–	–	–	–	1/8	–	–	–	–	–	–	–	–	–
R. Cotes	–	–	–	–	–	–	–	1/10½	1/10½	1/10½	1/10½	2/3	2/3	2/3	2/3
EASTER															
W. Felsted	2/4	2/4	2/4	2/4	2/4	2/4	–	2/4	2/4	–					
P. Dene, Elias	2/3	2/3	1/6½	2/3	2/3	2/3	–	2/3	2/3	2/3					
R. Cotes	2/3	2/3	1/6½	2/3	2/3	2/3	–	–	2/3	2/3					
J. Parco, R. Crok, J. Bareth	2/2	2/2	1/10	2/2	2/2	2/2	–	2/2	2/2	2/2					
J. Remmisbiri, R. Abbodesbiri	2/1	2/1	1/9	2/1	2/1	2/1	–	2/1	2/1	2/1					
R. Prior, J. Orchard, S. Snella	2/0	2/0	1/8	2/0	2/0	2/0	–	2/0	2/0	2/0					
Th. Botiler, J. Bensted	1/8	1/8	1/5	1/8	1/8	1/8	–	1/8	1/8	1/8					
N.	1/2	1/2	1/0	1/2	1/2	1/2	–	1/2	1/2	1/2					
J. Mor carpenter	–	–	–	1/8	1/8	1/8	–	1/8	–	–					
W. Byrych	–	–	–	–	–	–	–	2/0	2/0	2/0					

[1324–5 cont.]

MIDSUMMER WEEK:	1	2	3	4	5	6	7	8	9	10	11	12	13	14	15
W. Felsted	2/4	2/4	–	–	–	2/4	2/4	2/4	2/4	2/4	2/4	2/4	–	–	
Peter Dene, Elyas	1/10½	2/3	2/3	2/3	1/10½	2/3	2/3	2/3	2/3	2/3	2/3	2/3	2/3	2/3	
R. Cotes	1/10½	2/3	2/3	–	–	–	–	–	–	–	–	–	–	–	
J. Parco, R. Croke, J. Bareth	1/10	2/2	2/2	2/2	1/10	2/2	2/2	2/2	2/2	2/2	2/2	2/2	2/3	2/3	
J. Remmisbyry	1/9	2/1	2/1	2/1	1/9	–	–	–	–	–	–	–	–	–	
R. Abbodesbiri	1/9	2/1	2/1	2/1	1/9	2/0	2/0	2/0	2/0	2/0	2/0	2/0	2/0	2/0	
R. Prior, J. Orchard, W. Birich	1/8	2/0	2/0	2/0	1/8	2/0	2/0	2/0	2/0	2/0	2/0	2/0	2/0	2/0	
Thos. Botiler, J. Bensted	1/4¾	1/8	1/8	1/8	1/4¾	1/8	1/8	1/8	1/8	1/8	1/8	1/8	1/8	1/8	
N.	1/0	1/2	1/2	1/2	1/0	1/2	1/2	1/2	1/2	1/2	1/2	1/2	1/2	1/2	
S. Snella	–	2/0	2/0	–	–	–	–	–	–	–	–	–	–	–	
R. de London/Londone	–	–	–	–	–	2/0	2/0	2/0	2/0	2/0	2/0	2/0	2/0	2/0	

2624 1325–6

MICHAELMAS	1	2	3	4	5	6	7	8	9	10	11	12	13	14	15
Peter Dene, Elyas	2/3	2/3	2/3	2/3	1/10½	1/10½	1/10½	1/10½	1/6¾	1/10½	1/10½	1/10½	–		
J. Parco, R. Croke, J. Bareth	2/2	2/2	2/2	2/2	1/10	1/10	1/10	1/10	1/6½	1/10	1/10	1/10	–		
R. London, R. Prior, J. Orchard, W. Byrych	2/0	2/0	2/0	2/0	1/8	1/8	1/8	1/8	1/4¾	1/8	1/8	1/8	–		
R. Abbodesbiri	2/0	2/0	2/0	–	–	–	–	–	–	–	–	–	–		
J. Bensted, Tho. Botiler	1/8	1/8	1/8	1/8	1/4¾	1/4¾	1/4¾	1/4¾	1/4¾	1/4¾	1/4¾	1/4¾	–		
N.	1/2	1/2	1/2	1/2	1/0	1/0	1/0	1/0	0/10	1/0	1/0	1/0	–		
W. Felsted	–	–	2/4	2/4	2/4	2/0	2/0	2/0	2/0	2/0	2/0	2/0	0/8		
CHRISTMAS															
W. Felsted	2/0	2/0	2/0	2/0	2/0	2/0	2/0	2/0	–	–	–	–			
Peter Dene, J. Parco	1/10½	1/10½	1/10½	1/10½	1/10½	1/10½	1/10½	1/10½	1/10½	1/10½	2/3	2/3			
Elyas	0/11¼	1/10½	1/10½	1/10½	1/10½	1/10½	1/10½	1/10½	1/10½	1/10½	2/3	2/3			
R. Croke, J. Bareth	0/11¼	1/10	1/10	1/10	1/10	1/10	1/10	1/10	1/10	1/10	2/2	2/2			
R. Priour	0/10	1/8	1/8	1/8	1/8	1/8	1/8	1/8	1/8	1/8	2/1	2/1			
J. Bensted	0/8½	1/4¾	1/4¾	1/4¾	1/4¾	1/4¾	1/4¾	1/4¾	–	1/4¾	1/9	1/9			
W. Purreburgh/Porburgh	–	1/10	1/10	1/10	1/10	1/10	1/10	–	–	–	–	–			
W. Wycrofte	–	1/10	1/10	1/10	1/10	1/10	1/10	1/10	1/10	1/10	2/2	2/2			
J. Bordene, J. Orchard	–	1/8	1/8	1/8	1/8	1/8	1/8	1/8	1/8	1/8	2/0	2/0			
R. Londone	–	1/8	1/8	1/8	1/8	1/8	1/8	1/8	1/8	1/8	2/1	2/1			
Thos. Botiler	–	1/4¾	1/4¾	1/4¾	1/4¾	1/4¾	1/4¾	1/4¾	1/4¾	–	–	–			
N.	–	1/0	1/0	1/0	1/0	1/0	1/0	1/0	1/0	1/0	1/3	1/3			
J. Fater (?smith)	–	–	–	–	–	–	1/8	1/8	1/8	1/8	2/0	2/0			
R. Galmeton	–	–	–	–	–	–	–	2/0	–	–	–	–			
Edw. Kynghe	–	–	–	–	–	–	–	1/8	1/8	1/8	2/0	2/0			
J. Wyoth/Vioth	–	–	–	–	–	–	–	–	1/10	1/10	2/2	2/2			

[1325–6 cont.]

EASTER

WEEK:	1	2	3	4	5	6	7	8	9	10	11	12	13	14	15
Peter Dene, J. de Parco	—	2/3	2/3	2/3	2/3	1/10½	2/3	—	2/3	2/3	2/3	2/3	2/3	2/3	
Elyas	—	2/3	2/3	2/3	2/3	1/10½	2/3	—	2/3	2/3	—	2/3	2/3	2/2	
R. Crok, J. Bareth, W. Wycroft	—	2/2	2/2	2/2	2/2	1/10	2/2	—	2/2	2/2	2/2	2/2	2/2	2/2	
N. Frensch	—	2/1	2/1	2/1	2/1	1/9	2/1	—	2/1	2/1	2/1	2/1	2/1	2/1	
R. Prior, R. Londone	—	—	—	—	—	—	—	—	—	—	—	—	—	—	
J. Bordene, J. Orchard, J. smith, Rand. Beridone, J. Baylif	—	2/0	2/0	2/0	2/0	1/8	2/0	—	2/0	2/0	2/0	2/0	2/0	2/0	
Peter Porbit/Pourbyk	—	2/0	2/0	2/0	2/0	2/0	2/0	—	2/0	2/0	2/0	2/0	2/0	2/0	
E. Kyngh	—	2/0	2/0	2/0	—	—	—	—	—	—	—	—	—	—	
H. Chuddeleghe	—	1/9	1/9	1/9	1/9	1/5½	1/9	—	1/9	1/9	1/9	1/9	1/9	1/9	
J. Bensted	—	—	—	—	—	1/8	—	—	—	—	—	—	—	—	
S. Snella	—	—	2/0	2/0	2/0	1/10	—	—	—	—	—	—	—	—	
W. Morelode	—	—	—	—	—	1/10½	—	—	—	—	—	—	—	—	
N.	—	—	—	—	—	—	—	—	—	—	—	—	—	—	
Ric. Baunewylle	—	—	—	—	—	—	—	—	—	—	—	—	—	—	

MIDSUMMER

WEEK:	1	2	3	4	5	6	7	8	9	10	11	12	13	14	15
Peter Dene, Elyas, J. Parco	2/3	2/3	2/3	2/3	1/10½	2/3	2/3	2/3	2/3	2/3	2/3	2/3	2/3	2/3	
R. Crok, J. Bareth, W. Wycrofte	2/2	2/2	2/2	2/2	1/9¾	2/2	2/2	2/2	2/2	2/2	2/2	2/2	2/2	2/2	
R. Prior, R. London	2/1	2/1	2/1	2/1	1/9	2/1	2/1	2/1	2/1	2/1	2/1	2/1	2/1	2/1	
J. Bordene, J. Orchard, J. smith, J. Baillyf, P. Pourbyk, R. Baunevile, R. Beridone	—	2/0	2/0	2/0	1/8	2/0	2/0	2/0	2/0	2/0	2/0	2/0	2/0	2/0	
N. Frensche	2/0	—	2/0	2/0	1/9¾	2/0	2/0	2/0	2/0	2/0	2/0	2/0	2/0	2/0	
J. Bensted	2/2	1/9	1/9	1/9	1/6¼	1/9	1/9	1/9	1/9	1/9	1/9	1/9	1/9	1/9	
N.	1/3	1/3	1/3	1/3	1/0½	1/3	1/3	1/3	1/3	1/3	1/3	1/3	1/3	1/3	
R. Galmetone	—	—	—	—	1/9¾	—	2/2	2/2	2/2	2/2	2/0	—	—	—	
R. Martyn/Martin	—	—	—	—	1/8	—	2/0	2/0	—	—	—	—	—	—	
W. Tauntone	—	—	—	—	—	—	—	2/0	2/0	—	—	—	—	2/0	
W. Byrych	—	—	—	—	—	—	—	—	2/0	2/6	2/0	2/0	2/0	2/0	
Rob. Tengemue	—	—	—	—	—	—	—	—	1/6	1/6	—	—	—	1/6	
N. painter	—	—	—	—	—	—	—	—	2/3	2/3	2/3	2/3	2/3	2/3	
W. glazier	—	—	—	—	—	—	—	—	2/0	2/0	2/0	—	2/0	—	
Adam carpenter	—	—	—	—	—	—	—	—	—	—	1 4½	—	—	—	
J. Hylle	—	—	—	—	—	—	—	—	2/0	—	2/0	2/0	2/0	2/0	
Will. Heddesdone	—	—	—	—	—	—	—	—	1/6	—	2/0	0/11	—	—	
J. Grigori	—	—	—	—	—	—	—	—	—	—	—	—	—	—	

APPENDIX : DEFECTIVE WAGES LISTS

Two of the accounts are so much damaged that only some of the names and no significant amounts of wages can be deciphered. The number of weeks in which the named men have been found to have worked are given in brackets.

2609 1309–10
Only the 3 last weeks of Christmas, the first 5 weeks of Easter and the last 2 weeks of Midsummer terms have survived: J. de Upperton (5), Th. Reymund (3), J. de Hembiri (3), Robert le Yunge (8), Golofre (7), Master Walter carpenter (6), Rad. de Abbedesbiri (7), Th. de Merton (7), Ric. Croc (7), J. de Coscombe (6), Hugh de Morton (3), J. de Bristollia (2), Rob. Wyroc (6), J. Broun (3), J. de Bradenstoke (7), Greg. de Aun (3), J. de la Bocher (2), Adam Reymund (6), Robert Paves/Panes (3), J. de Forde (2), W. de Wistham (7), Thom. de Kilmington (6), J. de Northampton (3), Hugh de Dorsete (5), J. de Cos[combe] (1), J. de Corfe (7), Peter Chamund (4), Thom. de Brompton (1), J. de Luci (1), N. de Chinnoc (5), Thom. de Forde (5), J. de Lecthe (1), R. de Forde (6), H. de Monte Acuto (2), Walt. de Corfe (2), Walt. de Love (1), Walt. de Lovepit (1), J. de Luve (1), J. de Gardino (1), Thom. de Pederton (1), W. de Sar (3).

2613 1317–18
No part of the roll is missing, but the right-hand half is washed away and stained by galls.

MICHAELMAS: R. de Wyzt (9), Will. de Stoke (6), R. de Galmeton (2), W. Frensche (3), R. Abbod (9), P. Chamund (3), W. Slade (1), J. Luve/ Love/Leva (7), R. de la Streme (1), R. de Forde (11), R. Croc (9), J. de Parco (7).

CHRISTMAS: R. de Wyzt (12), R. de Galmeton (6), R. de Forde (13), R. Croc (15), J. de Parco (14), W. Frensche (7), R. Abbod (14), Peter Chamund (2), J. Luve (5), Geoffrey carpenter (1), Richard mason (2).

EASTER: R. de Galmeton (7), R. de Forde (8), R. Croc (8), J. de Parco (8), W. Frensche (7), R. Abbod (7), J. Baret (5), J. Chamberleyn (4), Henry de Monte Acuto (4), J. de Ford (4), R. Waleys (1).

MIDSUMMER: R. de Galmeton (5), R. Croc (9), J. de Parco (8), W. Frensche (5), R. Abbod (5), J. de Leva (8), J. Baret (3), J. Chamberleyn (9), Henry de Monte Acuto (2), J. de Forde (7), R. Waleys (2), R. Priour (7).